ENTERED MAY 0 2 2007

STUDIES IN AFRICAN AMERICAN HISTORY AND CULTURE

Edited by
Graham Hodges
Colgate University

A ROUTLEDGE SERIES

Studies in African American History and Culture
Graham Hodges, *General Editor*

Troubling Beginnings
Trans(per)forming African American History and Identity
Maurice E. Stevens

The Social Teachings of the Progressive National Baptist Convention, Inc., Since 1961
A Critical Analysis of the Least, the Lost, and the Left-out
Albert A. Avant, Jr.

Giving a Voice to the Voiceless
Four Pioneering Black Women Journalists
Jinx Coleman Broussard

Constructing Belonging
Class, Race, and Harlem's Professional Workers
Sabiyha Prince

Contesting the Terrain of the Ivory Tower
Spiritual Leadership of African-American Women in the Academy
Rochelle Garner

Post-Soul Black Cinema
Discontinuities, Innovations, and Breakpoints, 1970–1995
William R. Grant, IV

The Mysterious Voodoo Queen, Marie Laveaux
A Study of Powerful Female Leadership in Nineteenth-Century New Orleans
Ina Johanna Fandrich

Race and Masculinity in Contemporary American Prison Narratives
Auli Ek

Swinging the Vernacular
Jazz and African American Modernist Literature
Michael Borshuk

Boys, Boyz, Bois
An Ethics of Black Masculinity in Film and Popular Media
Keith M. Harris

Movement Matters
American Antiapartheid Activism and the Rise of Multicultural Politics
David L. Hostetter

Slavery, Southern Culture, and Education in Little Dixie, Missouri, 1820–1860
Jeffrey C. Stone

Courting Communities
Black Female Nationalism and "Syncre-Nationalism" in the Nineteenth-Century North
Kathy L. Glass

The Selling of Civil Rights
The Student Nonviolent Coordinating Committee and the Use of Public Relations
Vanessa Murphree

Black Liberation in the Midwest
The Struggle in St. Louis, Missouri, 1964–1970
Kenneth S. Jolly

When to Stop the Cheering?
The Black Press, the Black Community, and the Integration of Professional Baseball
Brian Carroll

WHEN TO STOP THE CHEERING?
The Black Press, the Black Community, and the Integration of Professional Baseball

Brian Carroll

Routledge
New York & London

Routledge
Taylor & Francis Group
270 Madison Avenue
New York, NY 10016

Routledge
Taylor & Francis Group
2 Park Square
Milton Park, Abingdon
Oxon OX14 4RN

© 2007 by Taylor & Francis Group, LLC
Routledge is an imprint of Taylor & Francis Group, an Informa business

Printed in the United States of America on acid-free paper
10 9 8 7 6 5 4 3 2 1

International Standard Book Number-10: 0-415-97938-2 (Hardcover)
International Standard Book Number-13: 978-0-415-97938-2 (Hardcover)

No part of this book may be reprinted, reproduced, transmitted, or utilized in any form by any electronic, mechanical, or other means, now known or hereafter invented, including photocopying, microfilming, and recording, or in any information storage or retrieval system, without written permission from the publishers.

Trademark Notice: Product or corporate names may be trademarks or registered trademarks, and are used only for identification and explanation without intent to infringe.

Library of Congress Cataloging-in-Publication Data

Carroll, Brian, 1965-
    When to stop the cheering? : the black press, the black community, and the integration of professional baseball / Brian Carroll.
        p. cm. -- (Studies in African American history and culture)
    Includes bibliographical references and index.
    ISBN 0-415-97938-2 (alk. paper)
    1. Negro leagues--History. 2. African American baseball players--History. 3. Baseball--United States--History. 4. African American press--History. 5. African American newspapers--History. 6. United States--Race relations--History. I. Title.

GV863.A1C373 2006
796.357'6408996073--dc22
                                          2006024489

Visit the Taylor & Francis Web site at
http://www.taylorandfrancis.com

and the Routledge Web site at
http://www.routledge-ny.com

This book is dedicated to the memory of Mom, who embraced every race, every ethnicity, every people, believing us all to be God's runny-nosed children. Her spirit was a kind of metaphysical glue that held this project together. It is also dedicated to the memory of Pops, for sparking a love of learning, then fanning the flames at the nightly dinner table. For Papa, no question was too big or strange, and every answer came with a story he willingly and wisely told.

Contents

Foreword by Larry Lester — ix

Acknowledgments — xiii

About the Author — xv

List of Figures — xvii

Introduction — 1

Chapter One
The Origins of Black Baseball — 7

Chapter Two
"We Are The Ship. . . . All Else The Sea" — 25

Chapter Three
From Fraternity to Fracture — 47

Chapter Four
Transitions — 69

Chapter Five
Interventionism — 89

Chapter Six
Preparing the Way — 125

Chapter Seven
The Promised Land   141

Chapter Eight
Staying Away in Crowds   159

Chapter Nine
Sunset   175

Epilogue   187

Notes   195

Bibliography   249

Index   263

Foreword

Long before the Civil Rights movement, before *Brown vs. Topeka Board of Education*, before the Harlem Renaissance, before Reconstruction, before the Civil War between the states, newspapers provided black people with a voice. The black press was the redeeming document of black America. This press educated an audience about social concerns and racist attitudes while fighting against incredible odds merely to survive. This press hoped to maintain an African American identity by revealing astonishing facts about minority life.

This press's call to action came on March 16, 1827, in the same year that slavery was abolished in New York. Two Yankees, Rev. Samuel Cornish and John Brown Russwurm, published a black newspaper in an un-liberated America. In accordance with the racial attitudes and political climate of the period, it was called *Freedom's Journal*, and it began a tradition in newspapers of focusing on the lives of African Americans in their churches and colleges, in the military and society, and of course in sports, with a focus on their struggles merely for recognition. These newspapers were, as one documentary described them, "Soldiers Without Swords."

Soon after, in 1847, Frederick Douglass started a paper called the *North Star*, appropriately named after the beacon of freedom for those who traveled the Underground Railroad. Douglass surmised that the mission of his paper was "to attack slavery in all its forms and aspects; advocate Universal Emancipation; the moral and intellectual improvement of colored people; and to hasten the day of freedom to our three million enslaved fellow countrymen."

Nine score since the first black publication, Brian Carroll explores the impact, importance, and overall necessity of a black voice in the sports community. Just as the editorial in the first edition of *Freedom's Journal* stated, "We wish to plead our own cause. Too long have others spoken for us. Too long has the public been deceived by misrepresentation in things which concern us dearly," Carroll shows how the black press represented blacks in their own words and images in its task to break down racial barriers in sports and beyond.

Often the white press promoted the white athlete and his exploits, ignoring his equally talented black counterpart in similar sporting pursuits. Thus the bias in the white daily newspapers created a need for a vehicle of expression, articulation, and reporting on other professional sports, especially the national pastime—baseball. You will find in this scholarship, black sportswriters insisting that the black ballplayer was the equal of the white ballplayer.

Along with sports, it was not uncommon for the white press to ignore the charity events, births, funerals, and weddings of African Americans. Thus the need for a black newspaper was born to cover black sports and the community's social news. Carroll documents how the black press fulfilled its mission, and how it used involvement in and coverage of baseball to do it. As the number one team sport in the country, baseball became a galvanizing influence in the inner city. It was the common ground for a variety of discussions in barbershops, beauty salons, shoeshine parlors, pool halls, soul food restaurants, and nightclubs.

In Carroll's work you will find references to the *Atlanta Daily World*, in 1932 the first successful black daily. Earlier, in 1909, P. Bernard Young, Sr., started the *Norfolk Journal & Guide*, and in publishing it avoided the sensationalism and "yellow journalism" prominent in many newspapers at the time. Lacking the constitutional liberties of northern newspapers, Young's *Journal & Guide* was respected as a quality newspaper that emphasized accuracy.

In regard to baseball, the *Pittsburgh Courier* and the *Chicago Defender* arguably carried the most detailed information. The *Defender*, which billed itself as "The World's Greatest Weekly," focused on games and players from the Midwest, while the *Courier* tended to emphasize players and games played along the Eastern seaboard. During World War I, the *Defender* advocated the "The Great Migration" or field-to-factory movement that relocated many baseball players from the South into northern cities from roughly 1915 to 1925.

The most widely circulated black newspaper, the *Courier* was especially visible during World War II with its "Double V" campaign that sought victory abroad and victory at home. The paper demanded a stop to lynching, segregation, and the disfranchisement of black soldiers. This campaign became the launch pad for the de-segregation of baseball, with themes such as, "They can stop bullets on the battlefield, but not baseballs on the baseball field." Demanding full citizenship rights in freedom's fight was a challenge accepted by many black papers of the period.

Other noteworthy papers with great coverage of Negro league baseball included *Indianapolis Freeman*, *Philadelphia Tribune*, Baltimore *Afro-American*, Kansas City *Call*, *New York Age*, and the New York *Amsterdam News*, located in Harlem, which became the mouthpiece for one of the largest African American communities in the country. This paper featured some of America's most prominent African American personalities as columnists: W.E.B. Du Bois, Adam Clayton Powell, Jr., and Roy Wilkins. In Carroll's work you will also read about editorials written by players, managers and owners like the majestic Andrew "Rube" Foster, C.I. Taylor, and Cum Posey.

Carroll presents the Mount Rushmore of black writers from the socially retarded period of institutional racism that shaped American minds during the 1920s, 1930s, and 1940s. Introducing us to Hall of Fame writer Sam Lacy of the Baltimore *Afro-American*, the dean of sportswriters, whose longevity in the field is unsurpassed. Discovering Frank "Fay" Young, of the *Chicago Defender*, the first full-time black sportswriter. Learning about the creative stylist Dr. W. Rollo Wilson (a.k.a. Franklin Penn) of the *Pittsburgh Courier* and the *Philadelphia Tribune*, a pharmacist by trade who was called by one writer the Red Smith of his day. And meeting Wendell Smith of the *Pittsburgh Courier*, the instigator and promoter of racial parity on the baseball diamond and a man rightfully honored in the Writers' Wing of the National Baseball Hall of Fame. Smith covered the equality field like grass seed.

Additionally, Carroll introduces you to the multi-talented Dan "Back Door Stuff" Burley, who wrote for the *Defender*, *Amsterdam News*, *Jet* and *Ebony* magazines, and Chester "Sez Ches" Washington of the *Courier*, the *Defender*, and later with the Los Angeles *Wave* and the *Sentinel*, whose articles were almost always upbeat, regardless of the hardships or attitudes of the day. So many writers and so many agendas! They are all here, so read, discover, and learn how the black press became the lever with which the doors to major league baseball were pried open to blacks, providing a start of equal opportunity in many walks of life across America.

> Larry Lester
> Co-founder of the Negro Leagues Museum in Kansas City, and author of several books on the Negro leagues, including, *Baseball's First Colored World Series: The 1924 Meeting of the Hilldale Giants and Kansas City Monarchs*

Acknowledgments

The largest measure of gratitude I give of course to my family—my bride, Hisayo, and our daughters, Hannah, Sarah, and Mary Arden—for joining in the journey and sharing in its swamps, valleys, jungle paths, and mountain views. We did this together in true partnership. I also thank Dad for his encouragement throughout the process, for taking me to games and away from the microforms, and for feigning interest in bygone baseball players.

I am humbled by and indebted to my dissertation committee for their involvement in the early stages. Tribute of the most special kind is reserved for the memory of Margaret Blanchard. "Ma Blanch" patiently shaped whatever I submitted into something much finer. She did this by overcoming obstacles that would have stopped mere mortals in their tracks. Her thumbprints can be found especially throughout the endnotes, for which we shared an uncommon enthusiasm. Any mistake or oversight in this document, of course, is wholly my own.

Chuck Stone ensured that I did not patronize, and he provided an eyewitness and visceral connection to many of the events and people described in this work. Harry Amana grounded my history and understanding of the black press and pointed out a number of valuable resources. Don Shaw asked the big-picture questions and demanded an explanation of how and why their answers matter. The Colonel's recommendations on the architecture of this project were invaluable. Chris Lamb at the College of Charleston provided essential expertise on the Negro leagues and the sportswriters who covered them. He identified critical lines of inquiry, spotted gaps in the research, and provided invaluable source material, some of which I probably need to return. His love for baseball and his appreciation for the sport's role in some of the great social dramas are wonderfully contagious.

Much is owed to Larry Lester of Kansas City, whose knowledge of the black press, the black struggle, and of the Negro leagues is vast and valuable, matched only by his willingness to share that knowledge. William Simons of the State University of New York at Oneonta expertly edited two articles that became chapters in this volume; Pat Washburn at Ohio University deftly edited another. The staff at the A. Bartlett Giamatti Research Center at the National Baseball Hall of Fame, under the direction of Tim Wiles, regularly goes the extra step that separates merely answering a question and providing insight. Wyonella Smith of Chicago was very gracious with her time and with her memories of her husband, Wendell Smith, and of Jackie Robinson.

I wish to also thank Deb Aikat at the University of North Carolina at Chapel Hill for liberally and unselfishly sharing his time, resources, advice, energy, experience, and, perhaps most of all, laserjet printer. I could not have made the hard turns and steep banks without regular and frequent pit stops in his office. I especially thank him for having faith in me to do things I had never done before, especially since failure in those situations would have carried for him both a personal and professional price.

Bob Frank at Berry College provided unflagging support and the freedom a project like this requires, while Berry as an institution made it financially possible to devote a summer to revisions and editing, a subsidy for which I am deeply appreciative. Robin Hubier proved a superhero with logistics, which of course was no surprise to anyone who knows her. Also on a logistical level, this project depended on the interlibrary loan services at UNC and at Berry College, and in particular on Ariel Davis at UNC, who kept the reels of old newspapers coming and going, and Xiaojing Zu at Berry. The staff of Davis Library's microfilms department, too, especially Katherine Thornton, provided great service and a friendly face.

Finally, I thank Davis at the Rat for feeding the hungry and providing a great good place for editing; Ben Holtzman at Routledge, who believed in the value of this project from Day One; Diane Land for reading so many of these words so many times; and Ross McDuffie, who fielded a lot of ground balls without error.

About the Author

Brian Carroll is an assistant professor of journalism in the department of communication at Berry College in Mount Berry, Georgia. He earned his Ph.D. from the School of Journalism and Mass Communication at the University of North Carolina at Chapel Hill in June 2003. He also holds an M.A. in political science from the University of North Carolina at Greensboro and a B.A. in journalism, also from UNC Chapel Hill. He lives in Rome, Georgia.

List of Figures

Figure 1.	Cartoon depicting Rube Foster and C. I. Taylor fighting over the World Colored Championship."	111
Figure 2.	The Black Sox scandal in 1919 gave the Negro leagues reason to celebrate "crooked" baseball's color bar.	112
Figure 3.	"Sanity Slicker" advertisement.	113
Figure 4.	Rube Foster.	114
Figure 5.	Paseo Street YMCA.	115
Figure 6.	The Blue Room restaurant.	115
Figure 7.	Rickwood Field.	116
Figure 8.	For white Birmingham Barons games in the 1950s, blacks had to sit in this right-field section of Rickwood Field.	116
Figure 9.	*Pittsburgh Courrier* sports editor, Wendell Smith.	117
Figure 10.	Sam Lacy, Dan Bankhead, and Wendell Smith wait for a flight in Daytona Beach.	118
Figure 11.	Satchel Paige.	119

Figure 12.	Jackie Robinson.	120
Figure 13.	Black teams had to resort to barnstorming to survive	121
Figure 14.	Dr. J.B. Martin, longest-serving Negro league president	122
Figure 15.	White Sox advertisement.	123

Introduction

Kansas City's 18th Street and Vine section serves as a sort of counterpoint to Cooperstown, New York, the mythical home of the national pastime. At that intersection sits what was Kansas City's "colored" YMCA, now decrepit but once a nexus of black community life on The Paseo. Inside the Y the Negro National was born, the first enduring Negro professional baseball league. More than 85 years since that founding in February 1920, the building is neither venerated nor visited, even though the Negro League Baseball Museum is just two blocks away. Waves of nostalgia don't sweep aficionados in like the tides, as they do in Cooperstown. No one even mows the grass. Judging by the blighted building's brick façade, most of the attention the old Y gets these days is of the destructive kind. Graffiti profanes its exterior, which is punctuated with plywood substituting for glass where windows once welcomed light. The Paseo Y's neglect and dilapidation in many ways represents the segregated sport's complex relationship to its past, and it is this past that this book explores.

The 18th-and-Vine street scene was so vastly different in 1920. Peeking into the lobby of the Streets Hotel, just a block from the Paseo Y, one would have seen well-dressed men in derby hats smoking big cigars and bantering in the lingo of baseball. The Streets hosted Negro baseball's luminaries and black newspapermen who gathered in the "Paris of the Plains" to launch the first viable all-black baseball federation, the Negro National League. In uniting newspapermen and businessmen, the meetings forged a partnership that sought to use baseball to force the issue of integration, an objective that would not be accomplished until Jackie Robinson took the field as a member of the Brooklyn Dodgers more than a quarter-century later.

In the first half of the twentieth century, during the "bleak decades of racial exclusion," baseball joined banking, insurance, gambling, and printing in the pantheon of important African American business enterprises.[1]

Culturally, the sport provided one of the more important summertime distractions for black communities throughout the country. Games often were as much social events as athletic contests, particularly on Sundays, when churches would be sure to let out early so fans could get to the ballpark.[2] Ticket buyers wore their newest and finest to Sunday doubleheaders to see a style of play that rivaled anything major league baseball had to offer. Historian Neil Lanctot described opening games at Philadelphia's Hilldale Park in 1920 as being marked by "band concerts and flag raising exercises" and attracting "beautifully gowned ladies and Philadelphia's 'professional men,' the elite of black society."[3]

Over and above providing diversion, black baseball became a rallying point for the communities that supported it, engendering pride and showcasing and symbolizing black achievement. The sport created, in the words of Jules Tygiel, "a sphere of style and excitement that overlapped with the worlds of black business, politics, religion, and entertainment."[4] Prior to Robinson's breakthrough in Brooklyn, baseball brought more blacks together on a regular basis than any other endeavor.[5]

On opening day in 1938, for example, the Kansas City Monarchs and their rivals, the Chicago American Giants, were greeted in Kansas City by a parade of 500 decorated cars, two marching bands, local law enforcement, and the renowned Monarch Booster Club, which included in its membership black business, church, and fraternal organization leaders.[6] Tickets to Monarchs games could be purchased at, among other establishments, the Monarch Billiard Parlor, Stark's Newspaper Stand, the Panama Taxi Stand, and McCampbell's and Hueston's Drug stores. Pictures of Monarch players, advertisements for games, and footage of the opening day ceremonies were offered as part of the daily fare at the city's Elbon and Lincoln movie theaters.[7]

Baseball's leaders were the black communities' business leaders. As an entrepreneur, "Race man," and advocate for his people, Andrew "Rube" Foster, principal founder of the Negro National League, was also a prominent Chicago businessman who dealt with discrimination by creating a vibrant, job-producing black institution.[8] His success and the nobility of his aims were celebrated on his death, when 3,000 mourners attended funeral services for him in December 1930. Foster's body lay in state, like a president or prime minister, for three days.[9]

The drama of baseball's re-integration offers an opportunity to examine the ways in which the issues of race, segregation, and civil rights were covered by the black press, as well as how they were not covered, and compare them to coverage in the white mainstream press. Specifically, this book attempts to document the close, often conflicted relationship between the black press and black baseball beginning with the Negro National League in 1920 and finishing with the dissolution of the last league of substance, the Negro American, which faded from existence in the 1950s. Explored is the multidimensional relationship newspapers had with baseball, including their treatment of and relationships with baseball officials, team owners, players, and fans. Over time, these relationships changed, resulting in shifts in coverage that can be described as moving from brotherhood to paternalism, then from paternalism to nostalgic tribute and even regret.

The nostalgia evidenced in the writings of the black sportswriters of the mid-1950s and later point to a process and a problem central to American culture, particularly in the racially charged 1950s and 1960s. To preserve the flower—in this case the Negro leagues—would have been to limit the opportunities of blacks and to perpetuate disenfranchisement and subordination. Achieving larger societal goals of integration and equal opportunity and access, however, came with the pain of watching the flower die on the vine, a pain not unlike that caused by the sacrifice of other once-vibrant black institutions, such as those in education and entertainment. This book seeks to chart, describe, and analyze this deliberate but wrenching sacrifice of Negro league baseball for those larger societal goals, a sacrifice that represents in many ways W. E. B. Du Bois's notions of a double-consciousness, or the idea that blacks have to reconcile the desire for assimilation with the equal desire to preserve their distinctive African heritage and culture. This attempt at reconciliation produces what Du Bois called the "double life" that every American Negro of the twentieth century experienced.[10]

The black press of the 1920s through 1950s served many roles in American society. Called a "fighting press," black newspapers campaigned for the integration of society, for equal access and opportunity, and for full participation in the democratic experiment. The black press also served as the black community's voice and, by its expression, as a preservative of that community's identity, or what one veteran of the black press called "negritude."[11] The newspapers imbued African Americans with a sense of purpose and destiny, functioning as an "instrument of social change, enterprise, artistic self-esteem, and racial solidarity," wrote a historian of the black press.[12] In fulfilling these roles the newspapers contributed to the development of a national black consciousness.[13]

Baseball coverage provides a convenient lens through which to examine these roles and their facets. In the arena of sport, all of the black press's purposes and its plans to carry out those purposes are on microcosmic display. The Negro leagues populated an all-black professional baseball world that was a vital thread in the tapestry of northern, urban black life during the period under study.

Specifically, this book seeks to explore and analyze the very conflicted, multidimensional relationship the press had with the Negro leagues, including its officials, team owners, players, and fans. When black papers such as the *Pittsburgh Courier, Chicago Defender, Afro-American,* New York *Amsterdam News,* and *Indianapolis Ledger,* the same newspapers that helped found the Negro leagues, began filling their sports pages with news of Jackie Robinson and his Brooklyn Dodgers beginning in 1947, little room or resource remained to spend on Negro league teams. The once-strong ties of brotherhood in the fight for equality and full access broke apart as the black newspapers neared their goal. The stance of the black papers towards the leagues became paternalistic and highly critical, and it remained highly critical through the 1940s. Only after the Negro leagues had largely faded in the 1950s did newspapermen show signs of nostalgia and, in a few instances, hints of regret, a posture that was perhaps the result of integration's toll on the importance of the black press itself.

These transitions, from brotherhood to paternalism to grandfatherly nostalgic tribute, are examined, as are the costs of integration. American society claims allegiance to the ideals of integration and equal access, but often it fails to make an accounting of the social and economic costs to the black community of fulfilling these ideals. When viewed as a whole, the coverage dramatizes how one-sided integration has been for the most part. In the case of baseball, it benefited the white-owned major league teams at the expense of the black-owned, black-run Negro leagues. The expectation that blacks had to move into the mainstream was not challenged; the cost to the black community in terms of its own cultural institutions was not calculated or even considered.

The black community's sacrifices meant a loss of control. When organized as the Negro leagues, black baseball controlled its own destiny and made its own rules. As members of an integrated baseball scene, black ball players had to play by someone else's rules and always as a minority. This aspect of integrated baseball has changed little, in fact. Major league baseball did not hire a black field manager until 1975, when the Cleveland Indians tapped former playing great Frank Robinson. The Chicago Cubs, as just one example, did not hire its first black skipper (Don Baylor) until 1999. The Negro National boasted seven black owners, which is exactly seven more than the number of blacks who have owned major league teams.

There remain in contemporary baseball fewer opportunities for blacks off the field than there were at any point on the Negro leagues' topsy-turvy timeline, and the thoroughly segregated state of baseball for such a long period is a significant reason why. Segregation allowed for and even required institutional, economic, and political forces that had their stake almost exclusively in the black community. Paired with white interests in preserving and pursuing this thoroughly separate development, assimilation and integration were structurally impossible.

A few disclaimers might aid the reader. First, the term *Negro league* is used in this book to refer to primarily but not exclusively to three federations of black teams—the Negro National League, the Negro American League, and the Eastern Colored League. These were the "big leagues" of black baseball, qualitatively and administratively different from the many semi-pro and amateur Negro leagues, such as the Negro Southern League and the Texas Oklahoma Louisiana League, among others. This scope also for the most part excludes the hundreds of independent and barnstorming black baseball teams, even though virtually all black teams, including Negro league teams of the first rank, extensively barnstormed in order to survive.[14]

Second, the term "integration" admittedly is problematic. For the sake of simplicity, in this paper it refers to a team or institution opening itself for membership by blacks. Obviously, true integration as a social ideal is a complex process, or what cultural critic Gerald Early has described as a "tangled loom." One player obviously does not "integrate" a team, and one player cannot change the norms, policies, and practices of an institution.[15]

Finally, it is acknowledged that in writing history and in interpreting the past, an historian has to choose which facts seem most worthy of note and which, however important, can be omitted from the narrative. These choices inevitably include some measure of personal taste and, therefore, reflect to some degree the biases and experiences of the historian. The result can be a truth, or some truths, but not necessarily *the* truth, which perhaps no one can truly know. Two historians of the first rank can and often do arrive at very different explanations for the same event or pattern because, unlike physics or mathematics, history is in part the product of accidents and chance events, an unpredictable sequence of antecedent states and contingencies. Any change in the sequence would have affected all that followed. Resisted, therefore, are explanations of causality; emphasized are descriptions and documented events, people, transactions, and decisions. The truth we may never know, in other words, but history we will always have.

Chapter One
The Origins of Black Baseball

Baseball's history is America's history, and this fusion is no small part of the sport's revered status as the "national pastime," however mythic that status has become. Black baseball's history, typically treated as little more than a footnote in the sport's larger narrative, can and perhaps should be considered as a chronicle of race relations in America, of "the strange career of Jim Crow," as C. Vann Woodward put it.[1] This shadowy history's timeline begins when federal troops were withdrawn from the South, which in 1877 was home to approximately 90 percent of America's blacks. The exodus marked the end of Reconstruction and of the brief, post-war status of blacks as wards of the government. Systematic disenfranchisement resulted throughout the South, pushing black community life to the margins of society.

It was in these margins that professional black baseball was born, a product of a racial ostracism that produced separate and unequal schools, churches, housing, jobs, and entertainments. Economic development and urbanization facilitated separation and segregation, as did an eagerness on the part of many Americans to sweep the "Race problem" under the carpet of American life. But segregation's logic was predicated on notions of white sovereignty and superiority, a logic that athletes such as Joe Louis, Jesse Owens, Satchel Paige, and Jackie Robinson rendered patently ridiculous.

Another product of blacks' minority political and social status—the black press—partnered with baseball to challenge the illogicality of racism. Black newspapers joined with black baseball to promote the sport even before the founding of the first Negro league of substance, the Negro National League in 1920. For decades this alternative press's writers helped arrange games and schedules, adjudicate disputes, and, of course, drum up fan support. The histories of the black press and black baseball are inextricably intertwined, sharing as they do so many of the same key figures. The collaboration dates back at least to the League of Colored Base Ball Players, a short-lived federation begun in 1887.[2] This early league originated with Walter S. Brown, a correspondent covering Pittsburgh for the *Cleveland Gazette,* a prominent black weekly in the late 1800s, making Brown one of the first to see a business opportunity in segregated baseball.[3]

Like white Americans, blacks in the United States have enjoyed baseball and its precursors during leisure time since before the Civil War. There is a record of all-black cricket clubs and town ball teams organizing as early as the 1850s.[4] By the end of the Civil War, baseball had become popular among blacks in urban areas like New York and Philadelphia, as is evidenced by the proliferation of amateur and semi-professional teams in those cities. These early clubs were as much social clubs as athletic teams. There is record of Philadelphia's Excelsiors, a leading all-black amateur club after the Civil War, playing a Long Island, New York, team in an amateur baseball championship of sorts in October 1867.[5]

In the mid-1860s baseball was considered by some to be "the leading feature of the out-door sports of the United States," a popularity propelled by the sport's excitement and "wholesomeness," as well as by "the relatively low cost incurred to equip and field a team."[6] An early historian of America's recreations wrote in 1866 that baseball had "no debasing attributes and being worthy of the presence of the good and refined, it has everywhere been countenanced and encouraged by our best citizens; and, of the thousands who gather at important matches, we have always noted with sincere gratification that the ladies constituted an honored proportion."[7]

According to Sol White, perhaps black baseball's first true historian, the first professional black baseball team played for the Argyle Hotel in Babylon, Long Island, in July 1885, or sixteen years after the formation of the first white professional team, the Cincinnati Red Stockings.[8] The Argyle was a 350-room, whites-only resort built in 1882 that opened toward the end of the Northeast's big resort era; it was never more than one-third full, and it shuttered for good in 1897. The resort's ball team, organized by hotel employee Frank Thompson, played mostly white teams from elsewhere in greater New York to entertain the Argyle's guests. The players were paid both to play and, during the off-season, to work at the resort, mostly as hotel waiters.[9]

According to one of baseball's first historians, Albert G. Spalding, the first white professional baseball team was the Red Stockings of Cincinnati, which salaried all its players first in 1869. The Red Stockings went on "the first tour of a professional ball club in any direction" in 1869, winning all of their games on the tour and going 56–1 for the season.[10] "The meteoric career of the Cincinnati Red Stockings," Spalding wrote, "had wrought a very great change in public sentiment, and in the minds of players as well, regarding professionalism." The public was forced to recognize that "professionalism had come to stay,"[11] he wrote. The National Association of Professional Base Ball Players—subsequently the National League—formed in New York on March 4, 1871, uniting professional teams in Boston, Brooklyn, New York, Philadelphia, Chicago, and Cleveland.

The Argyle team entertained the hotel's white, mostly affluent guests, who were led to believe with two deceptions that the players were Cuban rather than black. In 1885, Thompson changed the team name to Cuban Giants, while on the field the players began speaking a kind of gibberish designed to sound like Spanish, a charade aided by the fact that a few of the players had actually played in Cuba. (Throughout the history of the black leagues, players frequently traveled to play in Cuba, Mexico, Puerto Rico, and countries in Latin America, none of which had an ideology of white supremacy and, therefore, laws or norms producing any kind of strict segregation. In fact, by 1855, all slaves in Latin America were free except for those in Cuba and Brazil.)

In addition to introducing overtly entertaining elements, the Cuban Giants pioneered many other business and promotional tactics that later would become common in black baseball, including year-round play. Thompson and the team's manager, S. K. Govern, booked winter games in St. Augustine, Florida, at the Hotel Ponce de Leon, and throughout the Caribbean. A native of the Virgin Islands, Govern no doubt knew that baseball even by 1885 had become popular throughout the region.[12] The Cuban Giants also introduced the idea of black teams playing all-white major league all-star teams. After winning forty consecutive games, the hotel team lost to the St. Louis Browns 9–3 in May 1886 during a stop in Trenton, New Jersey.

If "Cuban" in the new team name was part subterfuge, "Giants" was pure tribute. The white New York Giants were hugely popular and, more importantly, the club's manager in the early 1900s, John McGraw, was considered a friend to the race for attempting to include black players on his teams.[13] Because so many black teams used "Giants" in their names, it also became shorthand for black baseball and, therefore, a convenient, low-cost marketing technique in an era without broadcast media. According to Negro leagues historian Larry Lester, if fans saw "Giants" on an announcement, they would know it likely was a black team.[14]

The athletic and financial successes of the Cuban Giants fueled a boom in black baseball in New York, a boom that paralleled the proliferation of black newspapers in the city and the concentration of free blacks in urban areas. As the Cuban Giants' popularity and following increased, the team's business plan became more sophisticated. One of the team's owners, Walter Cook, a white Trenton, New Jersey, businessman, set salaries for players, for example, ranging from twelve dollars per week for infielders (plus expenses) to fifteen dollars for outfielders and eighteen dollars for pitchers and catchers.[15] Setting salaries helped establish baseball as a legitimate, respectable occupation within the black community, though the players worked other jobs, as well, to make ends meet.[16]

At the same time that professional baseball was emerging, company- and organization-sponsored teams were multiplying in increasingly populated urban black communities. Black porters, or redcaps, sponsored a team at Philadelphia's Broad Street Station, for instance, as did black employees of the city's Central Post Office, YMCA, and leading black newspaper, the *Philadelphia Tribune*.[17] Historian John Betts explained part of this phenomenon when he wrote that "no single agency gave a greater impulse to sport than the formalized athletic club of the metropolis."[18]

Three New York City businessmen founded the New York Athletic Club in 1868, inaugurating "a new era in athletics," and in the 1870s, several more New York City clubs organized, including Staten Island, Manhattan, American, and Pastime clubs. Similar groups formed in Chicago, New Orleans, and San Francisco. The 1880s saw clubs spring up in Philadelphia; Baltimore; Pittsburgh; Cincinnati; Cleveland; Detroit; Chicago; St. Louis; and Providence, Rhode Island, clubs that helped inspire neighborhood and institutional athletic societies, as well.

Several black professional teams followed the Cuban Giants' lead, including the Pittsburgh Keystones, Cuban X-Giants (Mostly made up of former Cuban Giants), Norfolk Red Stockings, St. Louis Black Stockings, New York Gorhams, Boston Resolutes, Chicago Union Giants, and Lincoln Giants of Lincoln, Nebraska.[19] Less than two years after the Cuban Giants organized, enough black teams were playing to attempt an all-black league, the League of Colored Base Ball Clubs, the first of many financially challenged and, therefore, short-lived segregated leagues.[20] Prior to attempting league play, the teams had cobbled together mostly free-lance schedules made up of games versus any team that would play them. Contests were lined up with other black teams and white teams, alike.

Without the Cuban Giants, which refused to join, the new league opened its first season in New York in May 1887 with, according to *Sporting Life* magazine, "a grand parade and a brass band concert."[21] New York's Gorhams beat Sol White's Pittsburgh Keystones, 11–8, in front of 1,200 paying fans. Though the league had teams representing New York, Philadelphia, Boston, Washington, D.C., Baltimore, Pittsburgh, and Louisville, it was forced to shut down just thirteen games into its inaugural season due to a lack of operating funds, the same reason cited for most black league and team failures throughout the history of black baseball. There were at least three other similarly unsuccessful attempts to organize black leagues prior to 1920.[22]

The Cuban Giants' refusal to affiliate highlights another recurring theme in the history of black baseball. Already profitable and, therefore, in no need of federating, the Giants refused to pay the league fee for membership, even though a stronger league could perhaps have better served the Giants' long-term interests. With few exceptions throughout the sport's segregated history, teams acted in their own short-term interests, often to the detriment of the sport as a black-owned enterprise.

Like the teams' cash flow, press coverage during this formative period proved difficult to generate. Historian Neil Lanctot found that black teams in the late 1800s and early 1900s were ignored by the white press, even while the same newspapers devoted significant amounts of coverage to white semi-professional clubs. The tendency of white newspapers to refer to black teams and players in derogatory ways also discouraged coverage by making it less likely that black teams would send information in to those newspapers—an example of what Elisabeth Noelle-Neumann has described as a spiral of silence.[23]

All-black teams were late in starting relative to white teams in part because of the end of Reconstruction and the subsequent proliferation of segregationist laws, policies, and practices. After a relatively brief period of integrated play in the mid-1800s, later in the century blacks were forced off teams and out of leagues, leaving white players and owners with established teams and leagues all to themselves. Black and white players played together in the major leagues as late as 1884, when the color line was established in professional baseball. While black teams were just getting started in New York City, Philadelphia, and elsewhere, major league baseball was winnowing its ranks of players of color.

By the end of the 19th century, as many as ninety percent of blacks lived in the South, which rapidly expanded Jim Crow laws intended to enact the white view "that Negroes should occupy a permanently inferior place in society," wrote John Hope Franklin. "The experience of enacting these laws provided Southern whites with an opportunity to think through and formulate a position that they would not readily or willingly relinquish."[24]

A bare-handed black catcher from Mt. Pleasant, Ohio, Moses Fleetwood Walker, represents both the beginning and end of the first era of integration at the major league level.[25] Before enrolling in the University of Michigan's law school, Walker was the first black to play at baseball's highest level, suiting up in 1884 for the Toledo Blue Stockings of the American

Association. The American Association competed with the National League in the late 1880s before becoming the American League in 1900. Because many American Association team owners were brewers, National Leaguers referred to their rival league as the Beer Ball League.

More significantly, Walker also was the last black in major league baseball. He played only the one season for Toledo, seeing action in forty-two games. His brother, Welday Walker, also played for the Blue Stockings that season, but got into only six games.[26] The Walkers' departure from the American Association initiated more than six decades of segregation for major league baseball, though white and black players, including Fleetwood Walker, played together at the minor league level for another five years.[27]

It is interesting to note that like others of his generation, Walker, a mulatto, gave up on democracy in America and instead advocated the emigration of blacks to Africa, even where it would require forced emigration. Walker published, *Our Home Colony: A Treatise on The Past, Present and Future of the Negro Race in America*, in 1908, a forty-eight-page document that argued for emigration a full decade before Marcus Garvey, publisher of the *Negro World*, launched his "back-to-Africa" campaign. The same year as Walker's publication, Fleet and his brother started a black nationalist newspaper, *The Equator*.[28]

Of the approximately seventy black players in organized baseball between 1878 and 1889, only Walker and his brother played in the major leagues. Fleet Walker continued to play on mostly white teams at a high level of organized baseball until 1889, when he was cut by the Syracuse Stars of the International Association, the league Jackie Robinson would dominate in 1946 prior to joining the Dodgers for the 1947 season. As such, Fleet Walker also was the last black to play in a highly competitive, integrated league. It was not racism, or at least simply that. When he was released on August 23, 1889, Walker was hitting .216 and was ranked no better than twentieth defensively out of the league's twenty-one catchers.

Mainstream newspapers responded to the disappearance of blacks from professional baseball with tribute rather than outrage, and they did not explore or anticipate the broader implications of the sport's blanket segregation. At a time when the number of lynchings was on the rise, the national sporting publications, *The Sporting News* and *The Sporting Life*, offered little more than eulogies on baseball's re-drawn segregation, though *Sporting Life* did publish a letter of protest sent in by Welday Walker.[29] The former catcher argued in the letter that a player's exclusion from the sport should result from "some broader cause" than skin color, reasons such as "want of ability, behavior, and intelligence."[30]

The Origins of Black Baseball

Efforts to "cleanse" major league baseball date to the sport's earliest attempts at organization. Professional baseball's first structured, national organization—white or black—formed in 1867 as the National Association of Baseball Players, and a clause in that organization's constitution set segregation of the sport by specifying that no club applying for membership be "composed of persons of color."[31] When the league re-organized in 1871 as the National Association of Professional Baseball Players, the clause was left out and did not appear in written form again. Instead, white baseball owners adhered to what became known as the "Gentleman's Agreement," a verbal oath that barred black players until Robinson's signing in 1945.[32]

The existence of such an unspoken, unwritten "color line" was noted by the press at least as far back as 1895. An article in *Sporting Life* in June of that year remarked that "nothing is ever said or written about drawing the color line in the [National] League. It appears to be generally understood that none but whites shall make up the League teams, and so it goes."[33] Sol White wrote in his 1907 history of black baseball that in "no other profession has the color line been drawn more rigidly than in base ball."[34]

Though white baseball had no need for blacks, black baseball nonetheless depended upon whites. The precarious financial state of teams and leagues explains why participation in the various leagues by whites was common, as does white ownership of nearly all of the playing venues in the country throughout black professional baseball's timeline. White businessmen often represented an important fiscal resource at a time when securing capital was difficult for minority-owned businesses. Just as black businessmen sought to capitalize on the black community's love of baseball and the importance socially and culturally of the mostly weekend games, white businessmen, too, hoped to make money on the Negro leagues, sometimes by owning teams and, more often, by booking games, renting out ballparks, and selling concessions.

Lanctot described white interest in black baseball as having been driven "solely by profit," by individuals with "little interest in the progress of black baseball or the welfare of its players."[35] This description is supported by the almost complete absence of blacks among the employees of the white promoters off the field, including the ranks of ballpark personnel. By 1906, white promoters controlled three of the four major black teams in the East: the Cuban X-Giants (E. B. Lamar), Philadelphia Giants (Walter Schlichter), and Original Cuban Giants (John Bright).[36] The lone black-controlled team was the Brooklyn Royal Giants. Attempts to avoid white control included incorporating and selling stock, the latter a method employed by the Leland Giants (Chicago), Dayton (Ohio) Marcos, St. Louis

Giants, Winston-Salem (N.C.) Giants, Pittsburgh Giants, Baltimore Black Sox, Madison Stars (Philadelphia), and Louisville Giants.

P. L. Prattis, a long-time writer, editor, and executive with the *Pittsburgh Courier* described the limited fiscal options available to a segregated, impoverished segment of America: "Whites who represent the going culture, the culture that flows freely among themselves and other like peoples, have the money that counts," he wrote.[37] Since the black community was structurally and systematically deprived of investment capital, starting up any business, be it a baseball club or a newspaper, proved daunting. This same scarcity of capital justified for Prattis the newspapers' willingness to accept advertising from, among other companies, the producers of skin whiteners and hair straighteners. "The Negro publisher, deprived of advertising revenue from the sources which are open to the dailies, is often forced to take what he can get in order to continue in business," Prattis wrote.[38]

Evidence of the fiscal reality faced by what was a segregated black business community can be found in the very beginnings of professional black baseball. Sol White, a star player in the late 1800s and one of black baseball's first historians, turned to two white sportswriters in 1902, or six years after the "separate-but-equal Supreme Court decision in *Plessy v. Ferguson,* to form one of the earliest dominant black teams, the Philadelphia Giants. One of the two sportswriters, Walter "Slick" Schlichter, sports editor of the white *Philadelphia Item,* both managed the team and served as its press agent.[39] Schlichter later became White's publisher for the former player's history of early black baseball, *Sol White's Official Base Ball Guide.* White's history still is a key text, a valuable primary source that chronicles black baseball's first twenty years and provides a personal memoir of one of the sport's earliest players. Interestingly, after a lengthy playing career that finished in 1909, White went on to write for two black newspapers in New York City, the *New York Age* and the New York *Amsterdam News.*

Coincidentally, another white journalist, Robert Teamoh of the *Boston Globe,* launched a black league in Boston. Teamoh's league played the 1903 and 1904 seasons before being forced to shut down because of lack of money, adding it to an increasingly long list of short-lived black baseball federations.[40] The league's roster included the Medford Independents, Boston Royal Giants, Washingtons of Cambridge, Malden Riversides, and West Newton Athletics.[41]

Black baseball began routinely making the black newspapers' front pages in 1901 when the black press began covering the Negro leagues in a fashion similar to how the mainstream press covered the major leagues.[42] In Chicago, a city one historian called "ideal" to examine when seeking to understand the sport's dynamics as a black-owned, black-run enterprise, the key figures were Frank Leland and Andrew "Rube" Foster.[43] The Chicago Leland Giants were one of the earliest black clubs to dominate a region and, as a result, they were the subject of blanket coverage by the *Chicago Defender*.[44]

Leland in many ways was perfectly suited for the role of spokesman for black baseball. He played for Washington, D.C.'s entry into the National League of Colored Base Ball Clubs in 1887, and nine years later he gave Chicago its first professional black team, the Unions. A member of the Republican Party, a Cook County commissioner, deputy sheriff, and successful businessman, Leland represented a new generation of black leadership in the city's South Side.[45]

According to historian Michael Lomax, Leland "marked the start of black entrepreneurs making concerted efforts to exploit Chicago's growing black market."[46] He did this by organizing in 1898 a championship between his Giants and the Cuban X-Giants of New York City. The black "world series" sparked interest in the sport among black businessmen in Chicago and in New York, and a business that would become one of the largest for segregated northern blacks had formed. Some of this interest Leland probably did not want. John W. Patterson, who in 1899 organized the Columbia Giants in Chicago, dueled Leland's Giants for local fan patronage into 1900, when Leland won the turf battle and the Columbia Giants shut down.

As a business venture, the Leland Giants present in microcosm much of what Chicago's black business community was endeavoring in the early 1900s to accomplish. Leland joined with two other black businessmen in incorporating the team in 1907. They included in the new corporation a summer resort, roller skating rink, and restaurant, with a goal of establishing "a black professional league on a national scale."[47] Leland's partners were postal officer and publisher Major Robert R. Jackson and an attorney, Beauregard F. Moseley, whose clients included the Olivet Baptist Church, home to Chicago's largest black congregation.[48]

Like so many of black baseball's elite, Moseley also was a journalist. In the early 1890s he launched *The Chicago Republic* newspaper, a "lusty journalistic youngster," according to another Chicago newspaper, the *Broad Ax*. Moseley published "fearlessly and successfully" until the paper's closing in 1896, when he left journalism for "the more lucrative field of law."[49] Moseley's daughter, Bertha Moseley, married Cary B. Lewis, a long-time black sportswriter with the *Indianapolis Freeman*, the *Louisville Courier Journal*, and the *Chicago Defender*. Lewis served also as the *Defender*'s third managing editor and as the first secretary of the Negro National League.

In an advertisement in Julius Taylor's weekly, the *Broad Ax*, the Giants' announcement of incorporation included an offer of stock options in order to generate capital to build a stadium at 69th Street and Halsted. One of the chief variables in determining the fiscal health of a black ball club was whether it owned or otherwise controlled a venue. Few did, leaving most black teams in the position of negotiating with white teams and their owners or with the white booking agents that controlled many of the better parks in the Midwest and in the East. The advertisement presented a plea for racial solidarity and uplift: "Are You In Favor of The Race Owning and Operating This Immense And Well Paying Plant, Where More Than 1,100 Persons Will Be Employed, between May and October each year, where you can come without fear and Enjoy The Life and Freedom of a citizen unmolested or annoyed?"[50]

Leland's plans for a baseball-centric entertainment complex demonstrate the priorities of early twentieth-century enterprises walled in and walled off by segregation. These include the priorities of uplift, of establishing distinctly black institutions and entertainments, and of celebrating and projecting racial pride. Leland's designs also point to the "world within a world" existence forced on a segregated black community. The *Defender*'s publisher, Robert Abbott, shared Leland's vision, and it is this vision that explains much of the *Defender*'s early coverage of and involvement in baseball.

Coincident with Leland's efforts in Chicago, a press-business partnership in Indianapolis worked to develop baseball as a business, specifically the National Colored League of Professional Baseball Clubs. The Indianapolis partnership joined Elwood C. Knox, business manager of the *Indianapolis Freeman* newspaper and son of the paper's publisher, with Ran Butler, owner of black baseball's Indianapolis ABCs.[51] Knox and two of his reporters, David Wyatt and Cary B. Lewis, made the *Freeman* a full partner in the baseball enterprise, much as the *Defender* positioned itself in Chicago.[52] As evidence, a photo in a 1907 issue of the *Freeman* united Knox, Rube Foster, ABC co-owner C. I. Taylor, and J. D. Howard, owner of another black newspaper, the *Indianapolis Ledger*. The photo's cutline: "Four of the Most Interested Factors" in black baseball.[53]

Lewis's is a name that appears many times in several capacities in black baseball's history, most often as a baseball beat writer. He was one of the *Freeman*'s primary writers covering major news events. The paper's page-one lead stories often carried his byline, which appeared alternately as Carey B. Lewis and Cary B. Lewis. David Wyatt also figures prominently early in black baseball history. A former player who competed with and against Rube Foster, Wyatt was the *Freeman*'s writer in Chicago and primary baseball reporter. Wyatt's and Lewis's base in Chicago explains in part why the Leland Giants got more coverage in the *Freeman* than the newspaper's local team, the Indianapolis ABCs.

The *Freeman* published weekly updates on the proposed league and hosted the organization's meetings in its Indianapolis offices. The newspaper solicited inquiries of interest from businessmen with weekly notices in its pages, and it lobbied readers and business leaders for support for the new league.[54] At the first meeting Lewis was elected secretary, setting another important precedent.[55] He would be elected secretary of the first enduring black league, the Negro National, in 1920, as well. Knox and Butler jointly advocated a stock offering to raise money for the team, taking their roadshow to eight midwestern and southern baseball teams, but to no avail.[56]

The league failed to materialize, and in a June 1908 article, the *Freeman* determined that success had eluded the league because "many of the towns mentioned were entirely out of place," or in places that simply could not support and sustain a local team.[57] The ABCs' refusal to join likely doomed the league more than anything else, however. Indy's most successful black team could not abide by the league's prohibition on Sunday games, which the league enacted to conform to local ordinances in place throughout the Midwest.[58] The loss of Sunday games paired with the lack of night baseball would, in C. I. Taylor's view, present daunting scheduling challenges.

Weakened by the failure of the National Colored League, Leland saw his influence on Chicago's baseball scene wane, and his loss was Rube Foster's gain. One of black baseball's most celebrated pitchers, Foster began managing before his playing days ended. He quickly became one of the sport's most successful, most feared managers and, with Leland's downfall, he added "team owner" to his resume. Wherever he went, Foster quickly amassed a loyal and growing following, and almost without exception his supporters included writers and editors in the black press.

Coverage in a 1907 issue of the *Freeman* illustrates the press's reflex to praise Foster whenever and wherever possible. In an age before middle relief pitchers and closers, Foster single-handedly pitched the Leland Giants to four wins in six games against a group of major league all-stars, according to the newspaper. Reporter Frederick North Storey gushed when describing Foster's feats:

> It ended Friday in victory for the Leland Giants, and so heavily have the colored population been realizing on their victory that it is said there has been a veritable famine in chicken and water melon on the South Side. As for Rube Foster, well, if it were in the power of the

colored people to honor him politically or to raise him to the station to which they believe he is entitled, Booker T. Washington would have to be content with second place. . . . Rube Foster was the whole thing, and, what is more, he knows it.[59]

The *Freeman* began turning its sports pages over to Foster himself with some regularity in 1910 when the Chicago magnate began his own campaign to start a national association of black baseball clubs. Proving again they could be counted on as partners with black baseball, the *Freeman*'s publisher, George L. Knox and his son, Elwood C. Knox, put the paper's full weight behind Foster's efforts. In April, the *Freeman* published a special four-page supplement on baseball in support of Foster's efforts, an extraordinary amount of coverage for the sport at a time of twelve- to fifteen-page news weeklies working with limited resources.

Called the "First Annual Base Ball and Sporting Number," the publication was added to the paper's regular sports coverage, which typically amounted to about a page.[60] Justifying the extensive coverage, the newspaper proclaimed its intention to "give the public the first creditable publication ever published by Afro-Americans in the interest of those who not only promote, manage, own and play the great national game, but for the enthusiastic fans and admirers of the race as well."[61]

In the supplement's lead story, Foster proclaimed "the time is now at hand when the formation of a colored leagues [sic] should receive much consideration. In fact I believe it is absolutely necessary."[62] Wyatt wrote in another article in the supplement that "too much credit cannot be given to this able journal for coming to the front in the interest of the great national game and the Negro who is struggling under adverse conditions for recognition. THE FREEMAN can well be classed as the savior of the Negro in a profession which is an honor to the country."[63] The *Freeman*'s self-praise was not unusual. Throughout black baseball's history, newspapers rarely passed up an opportunity to claim credit for any successful venture or to pass along criticism of any endeavor that failed.

The *Freeman* supplement is a remarkable artifact in its unqualified support of the attempts to hatch the league. In addition to Foster and Wyatt, the supplement included Danville, Illinois, businessman J. M. Batchman, who wrote a lengthy story on how the league's financial success would benefit the race. Absent is any challenge to the status quo; the all-white major leagues are scarcely mentioned. Batchman argued that "accumulated wealth in Negro purses is the goal" and that baseball could accomplish it since the sport "commands more attention at present than any other pastime."[64]

Despite the generous amounts of space and latitude the *Freeman* gave Foster, his and the paper's campaigning and lobbying brought no direct results. The blueprint for a league uniting teams from the South and Midwest had been laid out, however, and the partnership between the *Freeman* and black baseball had been further cemented. Foster and the *Freeman*'s primary baseball writer, David Wyatt, wrote in concert on the issue for years, lobbying other team owners and mobilizing a fan base to support league competition. What would be good for Foster—a new league—also was deemed beneficial for the black community at large, including its newspapers.

Foster left the Leland Giants in 1911 to form his own team, the Chicago American Giants, and in the wake of Foster's departure, his former partners cobbled together an alliance of Chicago's black businessmen and community leaders to re-organize as the Leland Giant Booster Club. A portrait of partnership and collaboration in Chicago's segregated business circles, the club included as its members Jesse Bolling, whose restaurant, the Burlington Buffet, served as the club's meeting site; T. W. Allen, a city inspector; Robert Abbott, publisher of the *Chicago Defender*; and Julius F. Taylor, publisher of the Chicago *Broad Ax*.[65]

Developing a "race consciousness" and responding to the injustices of segregation were chief purposes of the black press of the 1920s.[66] Coming out of World War I the black community's agenda was bold, with goals that included the integration of society, equal access and opportunity, and full participation in democracy. The segregation of soldiers by race and discrimination in promotions and assignments set the stage for a protest movement, especially in the context of such harsh living conditions for so many blacks in urban areas. In this so-called "black belt" between 1917 and 1920, a racially motivated bombing or arson attack occurred every twenty days.[67] The rhetoric, then, of protecting and extending democracy in Europe juxtaposed with inordinate numbers of blacks dying on the battlefield and suffering at home served to embitter large numbers of blacks and to make the poor living conditions at home less tolerable. Historian William Jordan put the desire for change in the context of disappointment with W. E. B. Du Bois's call for accommodation during the war, equating that call to a betrayal in the minds of many black community leaders.[68]

The war brought together large numbers of blacks from different classes, geographies, and backgrounds in ways perhaps no other event could, and this helped to forge a group consciousness of sorts.[69] Historian Charlotte O'Kelly wrote that the discriminatory wartime experiences and sacrifices made for the war effort served to plant the seeds for a "large-scale social movement to carry forward the black cause."[70] For these same reasons, the National Association for the Advancement of Colored People became more active in the protest movement, an activism enabled in part by the passing of Booker T. Washington.

An advocate of self-help, Washington wielded great influence on black press editors, enlisting them to promote his version of accommodation with whites.[71] He believed that hard work would be the salvation of the African American people, not protest, and he saw labor as the means through which African Americans could gain respect and acceptance. Such gradualism was predicated on faith in the paternalism of southern whites and on at least a tacit acceptance of white supremacy, a view with diminishing support in the early part of the century. According to O'Kelly, with Washington gone and his influence over newspapers removed, the NAACP could more closely ally with the black press.[72]

It is no coincidence that several significant black publishing concerns began at a time when black protest of segregation and of the poor working and living conditions it created, too, was gathering strength. The Kansas City *Call*, for example, started up in 1919 to serve the growing black community in Kansas City, Mo. The *Call* was a pivotal leader in pushing for the integration of baseball.[73] The Associated Negro Press also launched in 1919 and, unlike its many competitors, managed to foster cooperation among what were hyper-competitive papers.[74]

Also underpinning the expansion of the black press was the "Great Migration" of blacks from the rural South into the urban North and Midwest. Considering that before 1910, 90 percent of blacks lived in the South, the migration north was numerically staggering.[75] In response to Jim Crow laws and policies in the South, which were part of a long-term deterioration of conditions for blacks in the South, nearly 800,000 southern blacks had migrated to the North and West by 1920, according to the Washington *Colored American,* while only 47,000 born in these regions went the other way and moved into the South. The 1920 census showed that for the first time more Americans lived in cities than in rural areas.[76] In Chicago, for example, between 1910 and 1920 the black population swelled nearly 150 percent to more than 109,000.[77] These migrations helped produce ghettos, segregated cities within cities, which created housing shortages, overcrowded schools, and a scarcity of jobs.[78] The population shifts also meant that black newspapers in northern cities inevitably grew in reach and power.

A more self-sufficient black community liberated its newspapers to some extent, supplanting white readers and advertising dollars from white-owned businesses. The many new black institutions increasingly could advertise, putting into the newspaper pages new businesses, churches, schools, and fraternal organizations. According to O'Kelly, the Great Migration "gave rise to a black middle class dependent on their fellow blacks. The growth of a market among blacks was, of course, important for the establishment of independent black newspapers."[79] For transplanted southern blacks, these institutions were alien. The concentrations of racially and ethnically defined groups in the big cities enabled the establishment of institutions impossible in the low-density populations that characterized the South.

The Great Migration coincided with World War I, which also fomented protest. Dissatisfaction with the U.S. government's hypocritical treatment of blacks, who the government was not reluctant to send onto the battlefields of Europe, provided the ideological argument to complement the more practical demands for adequate housing, better work conditions, and more equal protection and provision under the law. The black press, "the only medium in America by which the black leadership can send an unedited message to the masses," in the words of one historian, gave voice to these demands.[80] Historian E. Franklin Frazier credited black newspapers with exerting a great deal of influence on the attitudes of black readers at the time.[81] After six decades building itself into a vital part of the developing black communities of America, these newspapers were ready to join and in some cases lead the protest. Another historian, Martin E. Dann, called the black press of the period the "focal point of every controversy and every concern of black people, representing as it did the strengths and reinforcements which united the black community."[82]

In his study of the black press in the World War I era, Frederick Detweiler found black newspapers to be most concerned, at least in terms of frequency of content, with racial conflict and injustices. This top priority was followed in order of importance by welfare efforts on behalf of blacks, the progress of specific race movements, such as the NAACP, and black crime.[83]

Activism by the press continued long after World War I, as a consumer campaign waged by the New York *Amsterdam News* in 1929 underlines. Promoted under the banner, "Don't Buy Where You Can't Work," the campaign sought to raise awareness of the prejudicial hiring practices of New York City merchants. Joined by the Chicago *Whip* and the Los Angeles *Sentinel*, among other black papers, the campaign succeeded in winning blacks jobs in previously all-white workforces, particularly in retail.[84]

Within this context of protest and social activism, it is logical that the black press would assert itself in the effort to force the integration of professional baseball, first by helping to create and sustain a Negro league and later as a principal voice of protest when the major leagues continued to resist integration. In this context, the black press naturally partnered with black business leaders to found baseball leagues and to help fan public interest in their games.

The 1920s have been called the golden age for newspapers, for newspaper readership, and for sports and sports writing in general. During this time, one of the biggest beneficiaries of the migration, the *Chicago Defender*, became the country's largest black weekly in terms of circulation. Attorney Robert S. Abbott founded the paper in 1905 after failing to secure enough legal work in Chicago's black community to succeed as a lawyer. Abbott drew up the plans for the *Defender* in his living room, referring to the newspaper in those plans as the "World's Greatest Weekly Newspaper."[85]

Active in many fraternal and business organizations, Abbott was a member of at least one baseball-centered civic organization, the Leland Giant Booster Club, which allied black businessmen in support of one another's enterprises and, in particular, the Leland Giants baseball club. This membership explains in part why Abbott's paper served as a chief promoter of Chicago's black baseball teams for so long and with such loyalty. As Chicago's baseball teams expanded their influence by barnstorming, the *Chicago Defender*, too, looked nationally for profit and prestige.

By 1920 the *Defender* distributed more than two-thirds of its weekly issues outside of Chicago, primarily via Pullman porters, who were unofficially the newspaper's circulation agents. Chicago already was one of the nation's busiest transportation hubs, with the Mississippi River and major rail lines converging in the city. This increasingly national influence and awareness among blacks would dramatically expand the impact of a crusading black press, and it would carry news of the Chicago American Giants baseball team to communities throughout the United States. This awareness made it possible for the Giants to embark on extensive road trips and tours that pitted them against black teams and white all-star squads, alike.

By 1925 the *Defender* had a circulation of a quarter-million, which set a new standard for black newspapers. With a pass-around readership of between four and five people, the true number of readers perhaps numbered more than a million, explaining in part how the *Defender* could inspire and persuade so many blacks to leave the South as part of the Great Migration.[86] As the *Defender*'s influence grew, so also did that of its allies and beneficiaries.

Baseball, too, benefited from larger social forces. During a decade in which people "knew more about athletes and entertainers than they did about politicians and world leaders," baseball became an appealing business opportunity.[87] The popularity of sporting events stemmed in part from many post-World War I Americans' desire to return to normalcy. Technology played a role, as well, as the advent and quick adoption of radio put baseball within ear's reach of millions. Fans also could re-live the games in newspaper coverage written by prolific sportswriters such as Grantland Rice, Damon Runyon, and Heywood Broun.[88]

The *Defender*'s success provided a model for other black papers around the country and a precedent for heavy involvement in and promotion of black professional baseball. Abbott looms large in the development of the black press both for the commercial success of the *Defender* and for the professional standards he set for newspapering in general. The *Pittsburgh Courier*, which in the late 1930s would supplant the *Defender* as the most widely read black newspaper, took its cues from the *Defender* in building a national circulation and distribution network and in establishing itself as an advocate for the black community.

The *Courier* was founded in 1910 by a group of businessmen led by Robert L. Vann. After overtaking the *Defender* in readership by the late 1930s, the *Courier* remained at the top through the 1950s. In 1947, for example, the *Courier* was a $2 million business with a circulation estimated at 330,000. The paper operated twelve branch offices, published fourteen editions to cover the country, and employed 165 workers.[89]

The late 1930s and 1940s represented the heyday not only for the *Courier*, but for black newspapers in general. Circulation figures peaked, advertising revenues flowed as black businesses proliferated, and several important publications printed their first issues. During this decade the Negro Newspaper Publishers Association and *Ebony* and *Jet* magazines all were founded. Combined, these trends in black publishing gave "the Negro protest its widest currency . . . an orchestrated crescendo just before" the *Brown v. Board of Education* Supreme Court ruling in 1954.[90]

Just as the *Defender* spearheaded protest during and after World War I, the *Courier* criticized the practices of the U.S. Armed Forces during World War II. The highest circulating black paper during the conflict, the *Courier* launched what became known as the "Double V" campaign, which advocated a fight for victory for blacks at home along with military success abroad. Beginning in the *Courier*'s February 7, 1942 edition and continuing weekly until 1943, the campaign demanded that African Americans serving in a war against fascism and racial discrimination abroad receive full citizenship rights at home.[91] Included in this campaign, for which the newspaper designed a special logo, were articles, editorials, letters, and drawings. Hundreds of Double V clubs organized throughout the country as a result, which helped the *Courier* enlist other black newspapers into the campaign.[92]

The Double V scored many successes, but one of the more important tangible results came on July 26, 1948, when President Harry S Truman signed executive order No. 9981 officially ending segregation and discrimination in the military.[93] The black press, especially the *Courier*, had established itself as an effective and powerful voice for reform and social justice. Simultaneous to the Double V was another *Courier* campaign to end discrimination, the crusade to integrate major league baseball.[94]

Though civil rights as an issue had not been a priority for several years, the defeat of Nazism gave new strength to the movement. Fighting in segregated units, black soldiers had helped defeat fascism. At the end of the war, the question of black rights in America again became relevant. Opinion leaders asked via the black press how black soldiers could die on the battlefield but not be allowed to play centerfield on a major league ball field. Major league baseball had retreated from race as steadily and as completely as the rest of the nation during the first forty years of the twentieth century, but it was being called to account by black newspapers in New York City, Boston, Pittsburgh, Chicago, and Baltimore.[95]

Chapter Two
"We Are The Ship . . . All Else The Sea"

The new Negro league's numbers were modest at first but its ambitions were not. Less than a year after the race riots of the summer of 1919, on May 7, 1920, Rube Foster's American Giants traveled four hours to Indianapolis to play C.I. Taylor's ABCs. The Chicago team won the game 4–2 in front of approximately 8,000 fans, and the Negro leagues were born. A *Chicago Defender* writer described the otherwise ordinary game as "the most important and far-reaching step ever negotiated by the baseball promoters of our Race." The writer, Dave Wyatt, a former black ballplayer himself, was not far from the truth.

How was 1920 and the group that assembled in Kansas City different from the many other years and numerous other groups who had previously attempted to form lasting black baseball leagues? The answer is complex, but it begins with one very large man: Andrew "Rube" Foster. The son of a Texas minister and one of black baseball's all-time pitching and managing greats, Foster practically willed the league into existence by sheer force of personality and dogged determination. The motto he chose for the league, words he had painted on his office door, signaled the barrel-chested man's big mission: "We are the ship. . . . All else the sea." In partnering with other businessmen, black and white, and in enlisting key members of the black press, Foster assembled a group that was larger and in important ways more diverse than any previous founding coalition.

The time proved propitious, as well, at least for black baseball. White baseball in early 1920 was just learning of the Black Sox scandal that "fixed" the 1919 World Series.[1] Following years of debate among black leaders over whether to fight for assimilation and integration or to pursue instead self-help, uplift, and success within the increasingly segregated cities of the north, by 1915 consensus had emerged that separation was a fait accompli. It was time to advance the race by developing within the black community its own civic institutions, businesses, political organizations, and social agencies.

A blacks-only baseball league grew out of the greater structural and societal priorities. Less than a year before black baseball's organizing meetings in Kansas City, riots in Chicago made clear that the racial divisions and white hostility that created the black ghetto of the city's South Side were hardening.[2] On the Sunday after the worst of the riots, the pastor of Olivet Baptist Church declared from the pulpit that "we should hasten to build up our own marts and trades so we can give employment and help to provide against such a day as we are now experiencing."[3] The ghetto in the 1920s could flower into a "black metropolis" only by turning inward.[4]

A leader in turning attentions away from integration to building from within was Robert Abbott, founder of the *Chicago Defender*. Not particularly ideological in his views, Abbott saw power in closely allying to build up black businesses. It is not at all surprising, then, to find the *Defender* so sympathetic to the efforts in Kansas City to put black baseball on solid financial footing. The former attorney practiced what he preached from the pages of his newspaper, building the paper into a national success story. Begun in 1905 as a four-page publication, the *Defender* quickly became a galvanizing force in black communities nationally and, like Jesse Binga's Binga State Bank, also in Chicago, one of the larger black businesses anywhere. Abbott was, in one historian's description, a "model of Negro business achievement and self-advancement."[5]

The *Defender*'s success and black baseball's best chance at stability were in part a result of the newspaper's own self-fulfilling prophecy. A fierce advocate of black solidarity, Abbott used the *Defender* to aggressively promote and publicize the Great Migration of southern blacks northward. By 1920, this "Great Northern Drive" had brought tens of thousands of blacks from throughout the South into Chicago.[6] The newcomers needed jobs, diversions, and, most importantly to Abbott, a sense of race consciousness and racial pride that would some day set the stage for black nationalism and a more militant push for equal rights and equal access.

Abbott's approach in his newspaper pages—simultaneously arguing for a race consciousness and solidarity while at the same time protesting the structures, policies, and practices that put blacks together in the first place—was the strategy of the founders of the Negro National League, as well. By being self-sufficient, the league could create jobs in the black community, build up black-owned businesses, and serve black-only clienteles. In building viable businesses and providing top quality play on the field, the league could challenge major league baseball's exclusionary policies by its very existence.

In piecing together accounts of the founding meetings it is clear that in February 1920 six team owners and at least five sportswriters for the black press convened in the black section of Kansas City. Just two days in length, the series of meetings and social events ended more than two decades of false starts in black baseball ventures and ushered in an era of professional organization that would last more than a quarter-century, or until Jackie Robinson crashed through baseball's color barrier in 1947. The portrait that emerges from black press coverage of the meetings is one of commercial vitality, entrepreneurial vigor, and a spirit of cooperation—all hallmarks of the black metropolis. In organizing baseball, this natural business partnership produced a vibrant thread in the social and commercial life of urban blacks that previously has been only episodically researched.

At the center of those meetings was the larger-than-life Rube Foster, and based on several accounts, in the center was where Foster often found himself, where he felt he belonged. He quickly cultivated loyal followings wherever he went and in whatever ventures he pursued. By the early 1920s, many considered Foster the best known black in Chicago.[7] Almost without exception his many supporters included members of the black press—publishers and writers who promoted him throughout his career. As one black baseball historian wrote, "The affection afforded the father of organized black baseball [Foster] demonstrated the importance of the sport and the Negro National League held for the African American community."[8] Effa Manley, the flamboyant, controversial co-owner of the Newark Eagles, described Foster in her memoirs as "one of the most revered names in Negro baseball history."[9]

Black press support for Foster began during his playing days in Chicago, when he acquired the nickname "Rube" by outpitching Philadelphia Athletics ace Rube Waddell.[10] This support continued long after his swift fall and abrupt death just before Christmas 1930 with a campaign to enshrine him in the National Baseball Hall of Fame.[11] When his Leland Giants swept the Indianapolis ABCs in 1907, Foster was described in the *Indianapolis Freeman,* the ABCs' hometown paper, as "one of the best pitchers in the country." The article's writer claimed that if Foster were white, he "would belong to the biggest league in America."[12] The *Freeman*'s coverage points to a practice common in sports coverage of the time, which was to compare top black stars with their white counterparts, and in so doing, it implied the insufficiency of merely rating first among peers in a segregated, separate world.

That the *Freeman*'s baseball writer was David Wyatt explains in part why the newspaper covering the hometown ABC's would be so lavish in its praise of the visiting manager. A Chicago-based sportswriter and the *Freeman*'s chief baseball correspondent from 1907 until 1920, Wyatt played with Foster as a Chicago Union Giant and as a Cuban X-Giant before turning to journalism. He augmented his newspaper pay by also serving as the Leland Giants' official scorer.[13] (Such obvious conflicts of interest were at the time for black newspapers neither rare nor frowned upon.) "Only praise for the Giants was heard, with Foster, hardly surprising, coming in for the lion's share," Wyatt wrote, after a Giants victory over the ABCs in September 1907.[14]

Perhaps because of their shared background, Wyatt was unabashedly a Foster booster, a status made clear in the very public battle for control of the Leland Giants. The duel pitted Foster against Frank Leland and Major Robert R. Jackson, the latter a powerful businessman and politician in the black community and a frequent writer for the *Chicago Defender*.[15] Wyatt prematurely described Jackson a "has-been who has out-lived his usefulness."[16] The prominent Republican politician survived both Foster and Wyatt, becoming Negro National League president in 1937 at the age of 67.

Frustrated by having to share power, Foster left the Leland Giants in 1911 to form his own team, the Chicago American Giants, which in its first year became front-page, column-one news in the six-year-old *Defender*. Foster's profile and the Giants' success on the field landed the team on the front pages with regularity. Rube Foster had "the confidence and respect of the press and fans. . . . No man in baseball has more influence," according to Cary B. Lewis, a sportswriter for the *Defender* who, prior to 1917, covered sports and national news for the *Freeman*.[17]

After just two years as owner and general manager of the American Giants, Foster had become, at least from the perspective of the *Defender*'s sports editor, the "world's greatest black ballplayer, manager and owner." If Chicago crowned Foster, wrote the editor, Fay Young, "the rest of the nation would follow."[18] Young, the longest serving sports editor during the Negro leagues' history, proved to be one of Foster's most ardent and public supporters throughout American Giants' owner's life.[19] Foster's team, Young wrote, did "more to put Chicago on the baseball map than the three 1916 major league teams in Chicago," a reference to the National League Cubs, the American League White Sox, and the Federal League Chicago Whales.[20] After Foster's death in 1930, Young assumed the role of chief protector of his memory and legacy, comparing all future baseball luminaries to Foster, or, more accurately, to Foster's legacy as Young remembered it.

Foster turned also to the *Freeman* for support, and invariably he got it. In 1915 and 1916, Foster wrangled with another powerful team owner, the ABCs' C. I. Taylor. As with Jackson, Foster would later turn to Taylor to launch the Negro National League, but for three months in 1915 the highly competitive pair traded accusations with abandon, writing broadsides and rebuttals in the *Freeman*'s and *Defender*'s sports pages on almost a weekly basis.

Sparking the feud was a midsummer series between the Giants and ABCs in Indianapolis. The five-game set was marred by several shoving matches and at least one bench-clearing melee. For Foster, the "disgraceful series of games" was cause to write open letters to the *Freeman* and the *Defender* accusing Indianapolis police of striking one of his players with a gun, using racial epithets, and threatening to blow out Foster's brains. Foster further charged Taylor with stealing players, calling him a "stool pigeon," "a liar and a jackal," "the Ingrate . . . of the lowest kind." Taylor's own brothers refused to play for him, Foster wrote.[21]

The *Freeman* published Foster's letters juxtaposed with a studio portrait of a dapper, almost regal Foster wearing a derby hat, tie, and tails, and smoking a victory cigar. The portrait's caption proclaimed that the sharply dressed manager was "held high in the estimation of the base ball public all over the world by both white and colored," an endorsement that no doubt added weight to Foster's case against Taylor in the war for public opinion.

Foster's "explanation" of the fight-marred series required approximately one thousand words. Taylor's response a week later, also in the *Freeman*, ran even longer, occupying all of the paper's eighth page, the *Freeman*'s regular sports page.[22] Taylor blasted the black papers for being "bamboozled" by Foster, for "deifying" him, and for being the means for one person to so malign the character of another. Foster's diatribe was for Taylor grounds for a "libel suit in the Federal courts," he wrote, plaintively asking the newspaper's readers for at least some of the credit for building up black baseball.[23]

Taylor's response gives an inkling of the frustration many must have felt watching Foster so easily, so magnetically attract attention. To his credit, Taylor, unlike Foster, used his lease on editorial space in the *Freeman* to also describe and discuss the state of black baseball in 1915. In cataloging its ills, Taylor lobbied once again for cooperation, and he argued for organization as the cure for those ills. As evidence of his support, Taylor submitted a pair of letters he wrote to Foster prior to the magnates' clash in August. Taylor's letters, which the *Freeman* printed in their entirety, proposed a league and endorsed Foster as that proposed league's president.[24]

Later that year, another flurry of open letters from Foster and Taylor was published by the *Freeman*, this round contesting the title of world champion. Each felt his team deserved the honor, so the two took turns stating their cases and criticizing the other's organization. Each used his hometown newspaper, Foster the *Defender* and Taylor the *Freeman*.[25] Foster said he would not go "far enough to say that the Freeman and [Indianapolis] Ledger are not reputable newspapers, or the sport writers [sic] of their papers, as probably they have wrote as they have been informed by the A.B.C. management."[26] But, Foster claimed that the Indianapolis newspapers had been "hoodwinked." For his part, Taylor admonished the *Defender* for giving Foster "cheap notoriety" and for prematurely crowning the American Giants as champions.

Foster actively sought space and support in the black press. In return, he awarded season passes to black sportswriters, allowed correspondents to travel with the team on road trips, and on at least one occasion presented a sportswriter—the *Defender*'s Fay Young—with the same championship belt given to the players of the American Giants.[27] (Players on championship teams routinely got gold belt buckles in a ritual similar to the championship ring ceremonies for professional sports champions in the twenty-first century.)

Limited resources forced black newspapers to rely on press releases, box scores, and other information submitted by the teams, which were inconsistent at best in making the information available, particularly when on the road or after losses. Those organizations more opportunistic in feeding the newspapers, like Foster's Giants, not surprisingly enjoyed the most coverage. Following the 1917 season, for example, the managing editor of the *Philadelphia Tribune*, G. Grant Williams, praised Ed Bolden and his Hilldales for their "business-like methods," the team's use of publicity, and "for everything they have accomplished."[28]

Like Leland, Foster, and Taylor, Hilldale owner Ed Bolden was among his community's more active advocates. A member of several black fraternal organizations, including the Elks, Masons, and Shriners, Bolden also participated in the Citizen's Republican Club, a local black business and professional group, and he frequently delivered speeches on race consciousness. His perennial champion Hilldale baseball club donated to black causes, participated in charity events, and advertised heavily in the *Tribune*. In another similarity to Foster and Taylor, Bolden regularly sought to generate interest in his Hilldale team and to influence public opinion with first-person accounts in his community's weekly, the *Tribune*.

The wave of baseball leadership that followed Foster, Taylor, and Bolden learned from their predecessors. Cumberland Posey and Gus Greenlee, to name two baseball barons and black businessmen of the 1930s, frequently wrote first-person accounts in and opinion pieces for the *Pittsburgh Courier* and *Chicago Defender*.[29] The son of one of Pittsburgh's wealthiest blacks, Posey co-owned the Homestead Grays in Pittsburgh. He wrote the weekly column for the *Courier*, "The Sportive Realm," a column that was also published by other black papers. That Posey's father, also named Cumberland Posey, was once president of the *Courier* could explain the son's access to and freedom in writing for the newspaper.[30]

The support the black press gave Foster, however, was in many respects unique. Upon taking baseball into the small towns and rural communities throughout the Midwest, the "great" Foster was credited with "spreading the gospel of blackball."[31] His American Giants were praised by the *Defender* for setting the national stage for organized black baseball. To their credit, the American Giants logged 20,000 miles on a single barnstorming tour in 1916, traveling from Chicago to Omaha, Denver, Los Angeles, San Diego, and even Cuba. The *Defender* reported from every stop along the way to a growing national audience increasingly interested in sporting matters.[32] Because the *Defender* was distributed throughout the Midwest and in the South and West by Pullman porters, Foster had help spreading the baseball "gospel" and in so doing extended his influence from his base of power in Chicago.[33]

The American Giants' epic road trip in 1916 laid the groundwork for preliminary talks a year later on another attempt to organize a "colored baseball league." Several veterans of black baseball appeared ready to become charter members of the new league. These owners planned to exclude whites from every facet of their enterprise, from owning the playing venues to booking the games to umpiring the action, according to David Wyatt, reporting in the *Freeman*.[34] Wyatt wrote that

> No white men are to have anything pertaining to a controlling interest. The white man who now and has in the past secured grounds and induced some one in the role of the "good old Nigger" to gather a lot of athletes and then used circus methods to drag a bunch of our best citizens out only to undergo humiliation, with all kinds of indignities flaunted in their faces, while he sits back and grows rich off a percentage of the proceeds.[35]

This vision, of a baseball world inhabited only by black owners, players, umpires, scorekeepers, reporters, and writers, had been articulated by Foster and championed both by Foster and Wyatt since the latter had become a journalist in 1907.[36] The vision also was an impossibility.

In summarizing the aims of the new colored league, Wyatt foreshadowed the stated ambitions of the Negro National League that formed three years later. Only when the black community is able to match the all-white major leagues in terms of quality, Wyatt wrote, "will the colored people be able to acquire a standard that will give them a base or means of comparison in baseball, with the other race."[37] Both Wyatt and Foster believed that a product on the field equal or superior to major league baseball would force integration. Foster also believed integration would occur by adding an entire all-black team, and he had every intention of being the owner and manager of that all-black major league entry.[38]

After a very good 1917 season for the American Giants, Wyatt credited Foster with nothing less than saving black baseball through touring and by booking games with professional, semi-professional, industrial, and club teams throughout the Midwest. "We know it to be a fact that he was the meal ticket of practically every colored club making a bid for recognition for the season of 1917," Wyatt wrote.[39] As a booking agent with connections in both white and black business worlds, including links to the Chicago Cubs and White Sox, Foster was indeed invaluable to the health of black baseball in Chicago and beyond. He hints at his own influence in a November 9, 1918 *Chicago Defender*, when he implores black fans to behave at ball games. Foster was trying to persuade the Chicago Cubs to agree to an exhibition game, which they eventually did, and as part of that campaign, Foster moved to clean up fan behavior. In addition to the public plea, he announced that unruly fans would be banned from American Giants games.[40]

The difficulties barnstorming in 1916–1918 likely inspired Foster to again lobby for cooperation among owners toward the creation of a league, and again Foster turned to the black press as his primary channel of influence. His timing was good, not only because of conditions within the segregated black ghetto but due to a perceived national need for diversion following the miseries of World War I. Americans were plunging themselves into sport and leisure.[41] Sports programs initiated in army training camps helped engender "a more truly national appreciation of sport," wrote one historian.[42] Postwar prosperity and a shorter work week afforded Americans with more leisure time for baseball, which saw its attendance figures pushed to record highs in 1919, the same season the sport would find its credibility threatened by the Black Sox scandal.

The war also revealed the appalling extent of America's hypocrisy. Fighting for freedom in Europe in a war during which blacks served with distinction both as soldiers abroad and in factories at home, America did little to prevent a hardening of the racial divide on its own soil. Unrest uncoiled throughout the country in 1919 during a "Red Summer" that saw twenty-five race riots break out in many American cities. No city in America was more afflicted by "political trickery, chicanery and exploitation" than Chicago, wrote the NAACP's secretary, Walter F. White. Implying that the patience of blacks was running out, White pointed to a new spirit aroused in the oppressed by the inequity of their wartime experiences and their difficulties at home.[43]

Black baseball benefited, as well, and black newspapers saw opportunity in the sport. Many expanded their sports coverage, which fanned support for and loyalty to the black teams. The newspapers "helped many a team to survive," according to one historian, by serving a readership that could not find anything on their teams in the white dailies.[44] Black teams received no publicity for or notice of upcoming games in the white papers.[45] In an age before radio or television, the black weeklies provided *the* vital link between the teams and their fans. In his autobiography, longtime Negro league veteran Buck O'Neil wrote that he:

> read about [black baseball] in the *Chicago Defender* or the *Amsterdam News* or the *Pittsburgh Courier*; my father subscribed to those weekly papers mostly so I could learn about the Negro baseball teams. When the mail arrived on Monday [most weeklies published on Saturday], all the kids were at my house, reading about Dick Lundy . . . or the legendary John Henry Lloyd.[46]

The three major white Detroit dailies of the period—the *Detroit News, Free Press*, and *Times*—sometimes published box scores of Detroit's professional black team, the Stars, but the coverage was inconsistent at best.[47] In fact, much of the history of the Stars is lost because only a few scattered issues of the black weekly *Detroit Contender* survive from the 1920s.

The teams were sources of pride, uplift, and solidarity for their communities, and they united businessmen, community leaders, and a growing urban working class. An April 1918 letter from Ed Bolden to white booking agent Nat Strong, which was published in its entirety by the *Tribune*, hints at this solidarity. In the letter, Bolden rebuffs Strong's attempts to dominate black baseball and to intimidate its team owners: "The race people of Philadelphia and vicinity are proud to proclaim Hilldale the biggest thing in the baseball world owned, fostered and controlled by race men," he wrote. "To affiliate ourselves with other than race men would be a mark against our name that could never be eradicated."[48]

Baseball at this time was establishing itself as the nation's game of preference, as its national pastime. Factors included expanding press coverage; a growing playground movement and increase in school athletic programs and park programs; growing interest among women, which signified the game's propriety; popular songs and humor devoted to the sport; and the automobile. Movie houses began showing World Series films in 1916, while the advent and mass adoption of the telegraph and electric scoreboards began keeping fans in America's cities updated on game action.[49]

These many factors created in some respects the ideal time to form a black league. So, in an April 1919 issue of the *Defender*, Foster again pleaded his case for league organization. He urged other club owners to unite in "not allowing white men to own, manage, and do as they feel like doing in the semipro ranks with underhand methods."[50] Though Foster himself would court white partners, such as J. L. Wilkinson, owner of the Kansas City Monarchs, and John Schorling, owner of Schorling Park, where Foster's Giants played home games, he crusaded in concert with Wyatt against what he described as the corruptive "white" influence. The insults mainly were directed at the white booking agents operating out of New York City and Philadelphia who controlled nearly all of the top playing venues in the East. These promoters, led by Strong in New York and Eddie Gottlieb in Philadelphia, took home between five and ten percent of the gate for booking the games.[51]

Foster was relentless in his lobbying. Beginning in November 1919, then writing weekly in the *Defender* through January 1920, Foster explained in installments why a league was the only solution to the difficulties facing black baseball. If club owners wanted to stop players from jumping for even the smallest of salary increases, if they wanted to have any kind of bargaining power with the parks and stadiums they leased for their games, if they wanted to turn a profit, they would have to join him in organizing, he wrote.[52]

In addition to the space allotted him for his weekly column, "The Pitfalls of Baseball," the *Defender* provided editorial support in articles and columns by the newspaper's own writers. The paper even published Foster's business address so interested owners could contact him. *Defender* writer Ira Lewis wrote of the need for a segregated league that would make money and keep the capital within the black community.[53] Lewis's argument conformed to Robert Abbott's belief in self-advancement and business achievement.

Abbott's and Foster's harmony on how to advance the race explains the abundance of space made available to Foster for his curious blend of opinion, history, advice, and political spin, as well as for the seemingly total editorial freedom Foster enjoyed in filling that space. First and foremost a businessman, Abbott was not doling out free newspaper pages, however. The *Defender* benefited in publishing the exclusives penned by Foster. Foster's stature in baseball and in Chicago's black community and the popularity of Foster's standard-setting American Giants added to the credibility and prestige of the *Defender*, as well.

Abbott's newspaper was far from alone in positioning itself closely with black baseball's elite. *Courier* publisher Robert L. Vann, too, allotted

"We Are The Ship . . . All Else The Sea"   35

generous space to the sport in his new monthly magazine, *The Competitor.* Published in Pittsburgh to complement Vann's weekly *Pittsburgh Courier* newspaper, the magazine offered a general interest mix of features and stories. Savage competition among magazines of the period made a startup's success unlikely, however, and *The Competitor* published for only two years.[54] During its brief run, however, *The Competitor* supported black baseball with almost evangelical fervor, turning its pages over to magnates such as Taylor and Foster in roughly half of its issues.

The February 1920 *Competitor* coincided with the Negro National's organizing meetings in Kansas City, which gave C. I. Taylor the opportunity to set the stage for the meetings by arguing for baseball's organization. Cooperating was the "intelligent beginning of all things," he wrote.[55] By collaborating, the owners could create a showcase for the accomplishment of the race, and "the sooner we as a race recognize this fact, the quicker will we be acknowledged by other people; and the greater will be our strides in the game of life," Taylor wrote.[56] In the lengthy, four-page article, Taylor used economics to bolster in his argument, a tactic which Abbott, Vann, and Foster also frequently employed. Taylor estimated that had his team, the Indianapolis ABCs, been white instead of black, he could have sold it for $100,000. As a black team, it did not "net me a single penny," he wrote.[57]

Six team owners answered the call, booking rooms at the Streets Hotel in Kansas City for a series of meetings in February 1920. A first-rate hotel catering to the black community, the Streets hosted at least a dozen dignitaries for the meetings, which were held two blocks away at The Paseo Street YMCA.[58] In addition to Foster, the ownership group included the ABCs' C. I. Taylor, Detroit's John "Tenny" Blount, Joe Green of the Chicago Giants, Lorenzo Cobb of the St. Louis Giants, and J. L. Wilkinson of the Kansas City Monarchs, who was repeatedly (and erroneously) identified in the *Defender* as J. W. Wilkerson. Not represented, at least according to newspaper coverage of the meetings, were the Dayton (Ohio) Marcos, which were owned by John Matthews.

Cobb was the St. Louis Giants' secretary, a position he would later hold with the ABCs and with Cleveland Hornets, as well, and he, too, frequently wrote columns for the black newspapers. (The Giants were owned by Charles Mills.) Cobb also served as a league official in various capacities from 1920 through 1934, and he was secretary of the Southern League in the 1930s. Other journalists known to have attended and participated were David Wyatt of the *Freeman* (though by June he would be writing for the *Defender*); Elwood C. Knox, business manager of the *Freeman* and son of its publisher; Cary B. Lewis of the *Defender*; Q. J. Gilmore, who wrote for the Kansas City *Call* and was secretary to the Monarchs; and J. D. Howard and Arthur D. Williams of the Indianapolis *Ledger*.[59] During the first day of meetings, Lewis was elected secretary of the new league, a development the *Defender* trumpeted in its sports pages.[60] The subhead for the Lewis article was "Sporting Editor of Defender Elected Secretary," and the only photo that ran with the story was Lewis's head shot. Lewis also had been elected secretary of the failed league in 1907. Arthur D. Williams was later elected secretary of the Eastern Colored League.

Further underlining the collaboration of newspapermen and baseball's businessmen, writers from the *St. Louis Argus* and Kansas City *Call* served as the founding meetings' official hosts.[61] The Monarchs' Wilkinson hosted a ten-course dinner one night, according to items in the *Defender*'s social pages, while the *Call*'s and Monarchs' Q. J. Gilmore hosted a banquet and smoker the following night.[62] Speakers during the evenings' entertainment, in addition to Foster, included the *Defender*'s Lewis and the *Freeman*'s Wyatt.[63]

Perhaps most significantly from the perspective of press involvement, it was the sportswriters who drafted the league's constitution and bylaws. Effa Manley, co-founder and co-owner with her husband, Abe Manley, of the Newark Eagles, credited Lewis and Wyatt, as well as attorney Elisha Scott of Topeka, Kansas, with drafting the league constitution.[64] The *Defender* recognized four for writing the organizing documents: Lewis, Wyatt, Scott, and Knox. The paper reported that the four "were up all Friday night and part of Saturday morning framing the baseball 'bill of rights' to guide the destiny of the future league."[65] According to one veteran of the black press, the owners perhaps felt comfortable yielding so much responsibility to the sportswriters because the magnates had such an abiding respect for blacks who proved competent and intelligent wordsmiths.[66]

The journalists also determined club rosters and the structure of the league, roles difficult to imagine with twenty-first century notions of journalistic ethics and the big business environment of contemporary sports in mind. The managers and owners had little input, at least according to the *Defender*, which reported that "the newspapermen had the day at the meeting. . . . No manager had aught to say about players. They were selected on account of their RELATIVE STRENGTH to each team. The newspaper men will form an arbitration board to settle all disputes and act as publicity agents for games."[67] (There is no evidence of such a board ever meeting to arbitrate.) Foster's own accounts of player selections, as recorded by his biographers, offer a quite different view, one that not surprisingly has Foster functioning as league architect and mastermind.[68]

According to the *Defender*'s reports, which mostly came from Cary B. Lewis, Foster stated the aim and purpose of the meetings, then stepped aside and allowed "the newspaper men" to "decide all questions," including player selection, league structure, rules and bylaws, and a schedule for organizing. According to Lewis's account, this delegation of authority by Foster to the sportswriters was quickly assented to by Taylor and Blount.[69] Despite the *Defender*'s claims on much of the credit, plenty still remained for Foster. Reporting on the meetings from Kansas City, the *Freeman*'s Wyatt called Foster "the Moses to lead the baseball children out of wilderness."[70]

The new league would need credibility and propriety, and the newspapers obliged. When the league's founding owners were announced, the *Defender* described Detroit's John "Tenny" Blount as a "typical" black businessman. The article described him, while erroneously spelling his name as "Blunt," as "one of the most popular and best liked sporting men in the country. Mr. Blunt is well known from coast to coast, having been manager of the famous Keystone Hotel and buffet of Chicago."[71] What the article omitted was that Blount, like many black baseball club owners during the century's first half, ran rackets in gambling and prostitution. Even a year later, a column by Fay Young about Blount described the way he ran his businesses as an "example for all managers to follow." Young did not name any of Blount's illicit businesses.[72] Other than his vocations, very little is known about Blount. At the time of the league's founding he was a man in his thirties with "an unremarkable past," according to one historian.[73]

Association with gambling and rackets was among the black leagues' thornier issues, dependent as these leagues were on successful black businessmen. Numbers games were simple, typically inexpensive amusements in which a bettor put down a penny or nickel on a specific three-digit number. Winning numbers were announced in the *Defender*, appearing in cartoons and in columns. The "Old Dan the Numbers Man" cartoon, for example, was used by Abbott's paper to announce winners in the early and mid-1920s.

Gambling kingpins who also owned black baseball teams included Gus Greenlee of the Pittsburgh Crawfords, Cum Posey and Rufus "Sonnyman" Jackson of the Homestead Grays, also in Pittsburgh, Abe Manley of the Newark Stars and later, of the Newark Eagles, Robert A. Cole of the Chicago American Giants, Ed Semler of the New York Black Yankees, Ed Bolden of the Philadelphia Stars, Tom Wilson of the Nashville and Baltimore Elite Giants, and Alex Pompez of the New York Cubans. These men virtually dominated the Negro leagues during the 1930s, when as a group they made a big move into professional sports. Greenlee led this pack. In the 1920s, however, only Blount, the Cubans' Pompez, and Philadelphia promoter Ed Gottlieb were involved in numbers games and gambling.[74]

Since Blount's precise ownership stake in the Stars and role in running the team are unknown, it is possible Rube Foster had a controlling interest in the team and merely installed Blount as his agent. This would explain why Foster stocked the Stars with his own players, a move Foster publicly described as an effort to help the Stars become competitive and the league achieve parity.[75] The press also helped the new league by pledging to place correspondents in every city in the new league in order to report and promote its "comings and goings."[76]

Vann's monthly magazine, *The Competitor*, trumpeted the league's formation a month after the meetings. Included in the magazine's coverage was a two-page feature on the reconciliation of Foster and Taylor for the good of the sport. Foster, in particular, deserved readers' respect, according to the magazine, because of the sacrifice he was making by linking his profitable American Giants with several weaker teams. After all, Cary B. Lewis wrote, Foster "controlled the situation pretty much not only in Chicago, where baseball is the fourth meal of the day, but in the Middle West," as well.[77]

In the article Lewis presented the magnates' plans as a model for other black-owned business cooperatives. "The workings of this league will be watched with more than passing interest by everyone," he wrote. "If it is successful, as we all hope, look for a further merging of colored business interests on a national scale."[78] In putting a premium on the league's financial success, Lewis turned up the pressure on the athletes. Unstinting loyalty and "100 per cent effort will be required of them on and off the field," he wrote, arguing that gentlemanly conduct was every bit as important as athletic competition in making the new league a success. This notion of propriety in all spheres of life, not just in the competition on the field, was emphasized by sportswriters throughout the history of the black leagues, realizing as the writers did that mainstream society might be watching.

In the April 1920 issue of *The Competitor*, Dave Wyatt also filled two pages. His team-by-team preview of the season introduced readers to each of the team owners by providing short biographies.[79] This business-owner-as-hero model marks a sharp contrast to sportswriting common in the mainstream or white press of the period. Writers such as Grantland Rice and Jimmy Cannon helped usher in the era of the "Big Event" and the "Famous Sports Hero," an era that coincided with the celebration of black baseball's businessmen in the pages of the black press.[80] In the mainstream press, the athlete often provided the focus; Babe Ruth, boxer Jack Dempsey, and golfer Bobby Jones are prime examples. They were among mainstream society's heroes, and their chroniclers, therefore, have been described as "myth makers." For the big city dailies, these "heroes" made the 1920s a "Golden Age for sport."[81]

Had baseball card collecting been popular in the 1920s, fans of the nascent Negro leagues likely would have coveted the cards of Foster, Taylor, and Bolden. Because these men were team owners and not players, the backs of the cards would have presented lists of businesses owned and positions held in the local black church and in business and social federations like the Persian Temple of Mystic Shriners. There would have been no baseball cards of the players, who were considered mere employees. Players would not supplant owners as heroes to and role models for the black community until the mid-1930s.[82]

The black press model does, however, bear a striking and provocative resemblance to fifth century B.C. epinician poetry, particularly to Pindar's *Olympian* odes. Pindar and his contemporaries praised the owners of the chariots but never their drivers. Even the horses got more poetic attention than the "athletes" of the period. These poets, according to one classical poetry scholar, "read into the poetic record the great power and wealth of their patrons, but they seek to do so while implying that their patrons do not pursue the wealth for its own sake." The criteria and context for heroic action were similar for the black press in the first half of the 1920s, which portrayed the owners as patrons uninterested in their own gain but instead in the uplift of the entire black community.[83]

Uncritical support of the owners continued in the *Competitor*'s July issue in the form of an energetic attack on other Midwest black newspapers for failing to give their full support to the new league. "It is almost inconceivable and unbelievable that an effort to promote the colored baseball league would awaken only half-hearted interest and support from the colored press," read the article, which, interestingly, carried no byline.[84] It is possible that one of the team owners wrote the piece, which might explain the absence of a byline, and the leading candidate is, of course, Foster. He is described in the article as "that indomitable leader."[85] The *Competitor* article also noted the "wonderful progress" made by the league three months into its first season.

The Great Migration so aggressively promoted by the *Defender* was perhaps the biggest difference between the prior, unsuccessful attempts to start a league and Foster's organization in 1920. The migration of southern blacks after World War I produced the population densities necessary to fill the stands of ballparks hosting Negro league games, ballparks that almost always belonged to white businessmen. By 1910, African American communities were thriving in Chicago (44,000 blacks), New York (92,000), and Philadelphia (85,000). Philadelphia's black population multiplied fifty-nine percent between 1910 and 1920 to 134,229, while in Chicago during the same period the jump was nearly 150 percent, to more than 109,000 blacks.[86] In total, one and a half million left the South and headed for northern cities between 1910 and 1930.[87]

These population shifts fueled the establishment of separate businesses, including banks and newspapers, hospitals and funeral homes, hotels and restaurants, ballparks and theaters. By 1906 in Philadelphia, for example, there were nine professional black baseball teams operating within one hundred miles of the city.[88] The rapid growth provided unprecedented business opportunities, such as Philadelphia's Hotel Dale, Dunbar Theater, and the Brown and Stevens Bank, all black-owned. In Chicago, South Siders started the Binga State Bank, the first black-owned and black-operated state bank in the country, as well as the prestigious Appomattox Club, and Grand Hotel. And in Washington, D.C., the Old Rose Social Club, Little Harlem Café, and Café De Luxe served a black clientele in neighborhoods near Griffith Stadium.

Chicago was becoming, in one historian's words, a "Mecca of Negro business enterprise." In addition to Jesse Binga's bank, the Douglass National Bank, Liberty National Insurance Co., and the Arcade Building opened up for business during this period.[89] Robert S. Abbott, the *Defender*'s publisher, was a stockholder and director on the board of the Binga State Bank, and he served with Binga in several associations and clubs. Abbott's newspaper celebrated the bank as a commercial center by and for black Chicagoans, which for the paper signaled a new era for black businesses.[90]

Foster, too, associated with several different businessmen in a range of ventures. In addition to running the American Giants and the agency that booked all of the Negro National League's games, Foster managed Schorling Park, owned by Charles Comiskey's son-in-law, John Schorling, and he co-owned the American Giants Garage, "South Side's Finest Public Garage" and a regular advertiser in the *Defender*.[91] Foster also owned the lease to Detroit's Mack Park, home to the Detroit Stars for most of that team's league membership, which is another indication that Blount was in reality Foster's lieutenant, not principal owner of the Stars.

Three months after the founding meetings, the league opened its inaugural season, when Taylor's ABCs beat Foster's visiting American Giants 4–2.[92] It was a very good start. Decades later, Effa Manley wrote in her biography that that first game marked Negro baseball "coming into its own" as a black-owned, black-run industry.[93] In June, a game at Chicago's Schorling Park between the American Giants and the New York Cubans pulled more than ten thousand people in through the turnstiles. The American Giants went on to shatter attendance marks at several parks, including Kansas City's American Association Park and Detroit's Navin Field. For the season, about one third of the league's total attendance saw its games at Schorling Park, pointing to the phenomenal success of the Giants, Foster's control over the scheduling, and the relative weakness of the rest of the league's teams and baseball markets.[94]

Though Foster's blueprint for baseball was being realized, he had grander visions still, including a plan for a new league in the South and with it a two-circuit organizational structure similar to the major leagues. According to the *Defender*, Foster was considering a trip in March 1920 to Atlanta to consult on the new Southern Circuit. David Wyatt and Cary B. Lewis also were scheduled to go on the trip and to help form the new league, but the trio never left Chicago. It is not known what prevented Foster from taking the next step, and coverage in the black newspapers is confusing. In one report, which declared that "all of the baseball magnates who attended had great praise for the sport page of the Chicago Defender," the meeting in Atlanta was set and the prospects for two circuits looked good.[95] But the *Defender* did not report on the plan again.

Regardless, the Southern League flourished as a stand-alone league, albeit at a less-than-major-league level and with no formal ties to the Negro National. Because of the size of most its member cities and towns, the Southern retained semi-professional league status throughout its history. Teams were in located in New Orleans, Atlanta, Chattanooga, Tenn., and Montgomery, Ala. A forerunner to the long-lived Southern League, the Southern League of Colored Base Ball Clubs organized in 1886 as perhaps the first semi-professional Negro league. It united teams in Charleston, S.C.; New Orleans; Savannah; Jacksonville, Fla.; Atlanta; and Memphis.

At the top level, Negro National teams other than the American Giants struggled to make a profit, a predictable problem that with prodding from Foster led David Wyatt to write an article for the *Defender* that implored fans to support the Negro National. Further indicating cooperation between Wyatt, the *Defender*, and Foster, Wyatt wrote that fans should prepare to pay more for game tickets. Almost unimaginable with contemporary sensibilities, this lobbying by Wyatt on behalf of Foster was not uncommon. The same article lionized Foster, crediting him with having made "more sacrifices for the good of the game than all the [other] managers together" and for breaking up his own team in order for Detroit to be able to field a club, albeit a mediocre one. Fans were urged to help Foster realize his "life's dream," which meant that an "increase in the price of admission must be met by the public," Wyatt wrote.[96]

Wyatt's urgings signal an extraordinary influence by Negro league baseball officials and perhaps access by the press into the financial records of the clubs. It was not the first time, after all, that the paper had defended ticket price increases. Following the close of the 1913 season, Foster and the American Giants announced an increase for 1914 that angered the team's fans. The

Defender's response: Fans will "have to pay for quality and they have certainly got their money's worth lately, referring to the colored championship."[97] Sportswriters continued this practice into the 1930s. The *Pittsburgh Courier*'s Wendell Smith took fans to task in 1938 for failing to offer up enough money when a hat was passed on behalf of the Pittsburgh Crawfords, blaming fans in his weekly column for "poor sportsmanship." Smith advised readers to "pay for what you see. . . . Let's vindicate our inherent faith in humanity."[98]

Reinforcing the perception that the black press routinely served as the league's publicity arm was an incident in August that created the first public relations crisis faced by the new league. In a game between the Bacharach Giants and an unidentified Negro National League team, a Bacharach pitcher unleashed what the Giants claimed was a wild pitch. Thrown too close to the batter to go unnoticed, the pitch nearly ended the game because of the arguments and scuffling that followed the errant throw. After delays on four different occasions, the game finally ended with a Giants' win, according to an unbylined article in the *Defender*.[99]

Possibly written by Foster or by Young for Foster, the *Defender*'s report warned players against such behavior and advocated that players caught fighting be barred from the league.[100] At the very least, such players should be banned from playing in Chicago, according to the article, though no players were banned for the August fight or for any other fight for that matter. The article previewed a theme recurrent in baseball coverage from the 1920s through the late 1950s—fan behavior and propriety at games. The article also demonstrated that the black press would be available to owners and managers seeking to address their teams' fans, access that was routinely taken advantage of by baseball's officials.

In all, the 1920 season proved to be a financial and sporting success, with all of the teams making it to the finish line and game attendance that on occasion had been spectacular. When Negro National League owners gathered in November in Indianapolis for their first round of annual meetings, they voted to expand, bringing Philadelphia's Hilldale into the fold. Hilldale owner Ed Bolden's decision to join in some ways vindicated Foster's vision. A perennial powerhouse in Philadelphia, Hilldale had a loyal following and represented a key market. The owners also decided to move the Dayton franchise to Columbus and under the control of Sol White. Perhaps most importantly, the league approved a reserve clause intended to prohibit players from jumping teams, as well as to prevent teams from taking the field against clubs that had pirated players.[101] Players following the money wherever fatter paychecks could be had would remain a nettlesome issue throughout the Negro leagues' existence, a problem exacerbated by many teams' failure to contractually bind their players.

One reason that teams failed to use player contracts was the fear of insulting players by inferring that a man's word was somehow insufficient. Such a concern points to a position of weakness, and as such it presaged a difficult twelve-year existence for the league. The balance of power never swung fully in the owners' direction and away from the players, who for the most part played when and for whom they liked. A lack of control over playing venues, too, severely restricted the owners' ability to turn a profit. The first few seasons were particularly difficult for the league, with only the Kansas City Monarchs and Foster's American Giants showing a profit.[102] Weather and a down economy contributed, as well, with a resulting dip in attendance of twenty-five percent during the second season compared to the first.

Heading into the 1923 campaign, the league faced another challenge, one equal to if not greater than any external economic factor: A rival league run mostly by white booking agents looking to cash in on black baseball. Once again, Foster could count on the *Defender*. In the newspaper Foster published a series of attacks on the Philadelphia-based Eastern Colored League, which united the Bacharach Giants, Baltimore Black Sox, Brooklyn Royal Giants, Lincoln Giants, and Hilldales. His principal charge was that the rival league's teams were raiding Negro National clubs of players, but Foster also somewhat hypocritically accused the upstart league of corrupting the sport with "racially impure" influences, the white booking agents. His race-based claim ignored J. L. Wilkinson's membership in the Negro National, as well as the many white stadium owners that Negro National teams depended upon for playing venues, most importantly John Schorling and Schorling Park. Foster's public relations campaign against the ECL continued in the *Defender* and, to a lesser extent, the *Freeman* throughout the early 1920s.

Foster's columns, which regularly occupied roughly a third of the *Defender*'s opening sports page, provided the magnate with a tool with which to burnish his reputation and recast the past. In his columns he took credit for, among other good deeds, organizing the league and sacrificing personal success for "the good of the Race."[103] He claimed responsibility for making baseball socially and professionally reputable, and he criticized his fellow owners for failing to pay their league dues.[104] An equal opportunity accuser, Foster blamed players for "ruining the game" by jumping from teams, leagues, and even countries for higher pay.[105]

Foster also used the column to defend himself against accusations that the Negro National was unwilling to hire black umpires, a recurring criticism seen in black press coverage during the league's first several seasons.[106] Before Foster reluctantly hired black umpires in 1922, all league games were officiated by white umpires—another instance of racial hypocrisy on Foster's part. In fact, his basic defense in the umpire controversy would ironically re-emerge in the 1940s when it would be used by major league baseball to explain why professional baseball remained segregated. Foster claimed in December 1920 that the necessary "qualifications are sadly missing in the [black] umpires that I have seen perform."[107] This basic claim—that ability, or lack of it, presented the only barrier—was repeated by several major league managers and owners twenty years later when declining to sign or even grant tryouts to black players.[108] Several major league team owners, including Clark Griffith of the Washington Senators and Larry MacPhail of the New York Yankees, declared in the 1930s and 1940s that they would integrate if they could, if only there was talent to justify it. Though he signed several Cuban players, Griffith argued against integration in 1937 because he said it was "unreasonable to demand of the colored player the consistent peak performance that is the requisite of the game as it is played in the big leagues."[109]

Notably the *Defender* broke ranks with Foster on the issue of umpires. In an October 1920 issue, an op-ed piece proclaimed that the "public demand for umpires of color will get all the support of this paper."[110] The *Defender* began raising the issue in June 1919 before the league was formed, and periodically returned to it until 1922 when Foster hired one-half dozen black umpires. In the October 1920 editorial, the newspaper protested that it was not right to watch a game between "two teams of Race men . . . and have two white men umpiring our games crammed down our throats." By contrast, the writer argued, the White Sox would never hire black umpires. Conspicuously again, the critique carried no byline.[111]

The *Defender*'s protest against white umpiring is consistent with the paper's advocacy of self-help and support of the rights of blacks to administer their own affairs. Implicit in the protest, however, is acceptance of an all-white major league baseball. The White Sox's refusal to hire "one or two gentlemen [umpires] of color" is not challenged, nor is the segregated state of professional baseball. For the *Defender*, white baseball is the standard that black baseball was endeavoring to achieve. Only later would the black press's role become more of an activist one that challenged the sport's segregation rather than affirmed it with silence by focusing exclusively on the Negro leagues.

Also emblematic of this acceptance is the coverage of an October 1919 clash between Bolden's Hilldales and a collection of major league all-stars, including Babe Ruth, a favorite in the black community. The game presented the *Defender* with an ideal opportunity to challenge baseball's segregation, particularly since Hilldale won. The newspaper declined the opportunity, however, instead remarking on the crowd's disappointment that Ruth had failed to hit one of his famous home runs.[112] Ruth's presence and performance, even what he did *not* do, took precedence over the achievement of the all-black Hilldale nine.[113]

Also not mentioned was the fact that in winning the Hilldales established some solid evidence that black players measured up to the quality of players in the major leagues. As baseball historian Bruce Lenthall pointed out, in the 1920s Negro league ballplayers were considered great based on what they accomplished against white major leaguers.[114] This conservatism in the coverage reflected the philosophy and politics of the *Defender*'s publisher. For at least the time being, in the 1920s, Robert Abbott resisted the more militant stances taken by his competitors, the Chicago *Broad Ax* and the Chicago *Whip*.[115]

The close ties and symbiotic relationship fostered and enjoyed by the press and baseball's hierarchy in forming the Negro National, ties that have been largely ignored in scholarship, held until shortly before Jackie Robinson broke professional baseball's color barrier in 1947. This partnership delegated to the newspapers and their writers and editors the duties of league governing body; public message board for owners and managers; public relations arm, principally for Foster; and statistics and league standings bureau. The writers also acted as advocates or referees of fairness, sportsmanship, and professionalism. The black press connected the teams with their fans, especially when those teams played on the road. There was no other way to keep up with the teams. Radio and television were media of the future, and the white dailies ignored black baseball almost entirely. It is for this reason that black newspapers remain the most important source documents for histories of Negro league baseball and, therefore, snapshots of a time, a place, and a people.

Chapter Three
From Fraternity to Fracture

So many baseball fans filled Detroit's Mack Park on a chilly Sunday afternoon in May 1920 that the very structural integrity of the stadium had quite possibly been compromised. There were not enough seats for the more than 15,000, who, according to the *Chicago Defender*, "did everything except riot in their quest for entrance."[1] Those that managed to get inside Mack, including many who elbowed past security guards and the "hundreds perched" on the park's fence like "rows of sparrows," watched the Detroit Stars beat Havana's Cubans 7–2.[2] As the Negro National League's first season opened, the future of black baseball looked bright.

Baseball in the 1920s offered a community ravaged by the Depression much more than mere diversion. In the words of *Pittsburgh Courier* publisher Robert L. Vann, the Negro National's promise offered blacks "an economic and civic institution" capable of enabling a shared sense of identity and purpose.[3] It is little wonder that more than a quarter-century after Jim Crow's legalization, the major black weeklies, such as the *Courier* and *Defender*, considered themselves important partners with black entrepreneurs in helping to make organized baseball a reality for what was a completely segregated community.

In the 1920s, themes in the black press's baseball coverage included the significance of the sport as a way to create jobs and income within the black community; the moral obligation for blacks to support their own leagues; the symbolic importance of black baseball in terms of civic pride and solidarity; and the opportunity to demonstrate blacks' economic and athletic achievement to mainstream society. Implicit in each of these themes is an acceptance of or acquiescence to white-enforced segregation and the nether world for blacks it created. Founded to fight legal race discrimination of all kinds, the NAACP marked its first decade in 1920, while the re-formed Ku Klux Klan, which aimed to enforce race discrimination, was but five years old.

Based on coverage, the baseball-press partnership of the 1920s can be described as passing through three phases: close coordination in the early and middle parts of the decade, mounting skepticism and criticism from the writers beginning in the mid-1920s, and rapprochement in the latter part of the decade as black baseball's prospects dimmed. The coverage reveals newspapermen more interested in promoting the interests and welfare of the black community than in twenty-first-century journalistic values such as objectivity and accuracy. For an activist press, this should not surprise, and the writers' priorities underscore their newspapers' role as validators of the black experience.

Early in the decade, the *Defender* boasted of its participation in and support of the league, promising its readers a "correct version" of the comings and goings of the Negro National League. The *Defender* claimed in 1922 to be "the newspaper which has done more for baseball and sports among our people than any three papers published."[4] This self-congratulation explains in part how the *Defender* could choose during this phase of black baseball's history not to criticize the league or its owners even though this group routinely failed to address, much less solve, the sport's structural problems. Throughout the first half of the decade, the newspaper emphasized what it called the owners' "church-like harmony," a description that research proves tragically comical. The club owners rarely agreed on anything throughout the leagues' four-decade history, including where or even whether to hold annual meetings.[5]

The relationship of the newspapers with the league they helped start was complex and conflicted. The many "official" roles of writers at baseball's annual meetings in 1922 are emblematic. Ira F. Lewis, the *Pittsburgh Courier*'s managing editor and its president, perhaps best represented these complexities and the coalition that created them. Lewis covered the meetings for the newspaper, writing both news articles and opinion columns. He also helped officiate the meetings as league secretary, an elected position that was second-most powerful in the league's hierarchy. Finally, Lewis took part in votes and deliberations as the chief representative for the Pittsburgh Keystones baseball club. Viewed through twenty-first-century eyes, these are prima facie conflicts of interests, making unbiased news coverage an impossibility. The greater priority, however, was the league's success, and for an activist press endeavoring to lift a segregated people, objective news reporting simply was not a goal.

Another member of the press that January was Q. J. Gilmore, a contributing sportswriter both to the Kansas City *Call* and Kansas City *Sun*.

Gilmore's first responsibilities, however, were as full-time secretary and business manager of the Kansas City Monarchs baseball team. Gilmore's abilities to gather information and write made him attractive to the newspapers, which saved money by paying Gilmore for his coverage rather than absorbing the costs of sending a correspondent to the Chicago meetings.

While gathered for league business, united as they were for the financial success of the young league, the sportswriters in attendance agreed to form the National Sport Writers' Association. In electing the *Defender*'s Frank "Fay" Young as the association's first president, the group likely was recognizing both Young's tenure and the *Defender*'s reach. In a May 6, 1922 issue (page 20), the newspaper claimed 1.1 million weekly readers and 58.1 million readers for 1921, or more than half the black population in the country at the time. Even in 1922, Young's elder status was established. He is considered the first full-time black sportswriter in the country and the first to report on black college athletics. He supervised the nation's first full page of black sports, and he wrote under many bylines: "Frank Young," "Frank A. Young," "Fay Young," and "Mister Fan." The nickname, "Fay," was created using the initials of his full name. Joining Young on the executive committee were Lewis (vice president) and the *Indianapolis Ledger*'s A. D. Williams (secretary). Dave Wyatt, Q. J. Gilmore, Elwood Knox, and Earl Hord also were charter members of the association.

Among the sportswriters' stated goals was fostering a "fraternal feeling" among the respective newspapers. They aimed to "to work in complete harmony along sports lines" to give the nascent Negro baseball league every chance of succeeding.[6] Though the group did provide some reporting of away games, the coverage suggests that these reports were neither frequent nor regular.[7] There is no evidence of the association ever formally meeting again, though the same small group of men had no dearth of opportunities to informally gather.

Opportunistic, optimistic, participative journalism was common for black newspapers of the period, and in the mainstream press, as well. Robert Abbott wrote a column in September 1922 on the *Defender*'s front page urging blacks to "pull together" to "promote various causes and programs—college campaigns, health campaigns, and so forth."[8] Abbott not only wrote about cooperation, he used the influence of the *Defender* to foster it. In the 1920s he founded the Chicago Defender Goodfellows Club, which allied South Side businessmen, including several gaming kings, to raise money for the needy, particularly at Christmas time.[9] There is no indication that the newspapers' involvement in these campaigns was considered a conflict of interest. Quite the contrary, such involvement was considered being a good corporate citizen. Furthermore, the black newspapers saw themselves as a "fighting press," one committed to the uplift of its readers, which was a goal shared by black businessmen in baseball and beyond.[10] Such cooperation may have helped develop a sense of common understanding that excluded the view of such close ties as a conflict of interest.

In the mainstream press, the 1920s represented the "Golden Age of Sports," a time when writers such as Grantland Rice, Damon Runyon, Heywood Broun, and Paul Gallico turned athletes into mythic heroes and their athletic contests into epic battles.[11] Just a decade later, Gallico lamented the myth-making style of sports journalism of which he was such a big part. He and his fellow writers of the period, Gallico said, created "egoists out of normal young men and women by writing too much about them. . . . We create many [heroes] because it is our business to do so, but we do not believe in them."[12]

The black sportswriters' optimism and unflagging support were obvious at least through 1924 when the press-baseball alliance showed its first cracks. Until then the writers glossed over baseball's problems and instead encouraged and in some cases demanded support for baseball from "the Race," for the good of the Race, on the basis of supporting a black-owned business. The papers continued to give team owners seemingly unlimited access to their sports pages, as well, including weekly columns both in-season and out. Several un-bylined articles on topics important to the owners were almost certainly penned by the owners themselves. In addition to the articles-cum-editorials, the likes of Rube Foster, C. I. Taylor of the Indianapolis ABCs, and Cum Posey of Pittsburgh's Homestead Grays all wrote regular columns for either the *Defender* or *Courier*. Foster wrote for both.

Foster used his column primarily to claim credit for what he and his fellow black team owners were able to accomplish given the scant resources with which they had to work, resources especially slight when compared to those that owners in the major leagues could access. Where big league owners had "wealth counted in millions," Foster and his fraternity had "only the faith in the weather man. . . . We are willing and know what can be done, but have nothing to do it with," he wrote.[13] To succeed where so many of his predecessors failed, Foster pooled resources with other Chicagoland—or "Bronzeville"—businessmen, black and white. Of course in his columns he only mentioned his and the Giants' black business partners.[14]

Symbolic of the close-knit business fraternities in baseball's cities were the many banquets, smokers, and celebrations baseball's owners threw for one another, events almost always attended also by newspapermen, business associates, and black politicians. At one such banquet in honor of Rube Foster in early 1923, those gathering at Cleveland's Coleman Restaurant included officials of the Cleveland Tate Stars baseball team; the editor of the Cleveland *Whip*; a director of the Empire Bank; a vice president of the Starlight Realty Co.; and other local businessmen.[15]

The group that collaborated to organize YWCA Day at Chicago's Schorling Park that same year perhaps best illustrates the mutual ties and interests of Chicago's business and political elites. The event's organizing committee teamed *Defender* publisher Robert Abbott; Jesse Binga, owner of the Binga State Bank; Oscar DePriest, Chicago's first black city council member, successful real estate broker, and numbers king; Frank L. Gillespie, founder and president of the Liberty Life Insurance Co., which claimed to be the first "legal reserve company ever incorporated north of the Mason-Dixon line"; and Frank Young, the *Defender*'s sports editor.[16]

Both Binga State Bank and Liberty Life were major advertisers in the *Defender*, and Abbott served as a director on the Binga Bank board. Both were members and officers of the Appomattox Club, which united Chicago's black Republicans, and the Associated Business Club. Abbott was president of Associated Business; Binga was secretary. A. L. Jackson, associate editor of the *Defender*, served as vice president of the Appomattox Club in 1924, when P. L. Prattis of the *Courier* acted as the association's corresponding secretary.[17]

Rube Foster, Taylor of the ABCs, and Bolden of the Hilldales in Philadelphia were card-carrying members of these business coalitions; they were businessmen and community leaders first and baseball men second. Taylor, for example, was a member of and a deacon in the Bethel A.M.E. Church; a member of the Persian Temple of the Mystic Shrines, among other branches of the Masons; and owner of a billiards parlor and social club in Indianapolis, where some of Taylor's players worked in the off-season.[18] According to his obituary in the *Freeman*, Taylor was a man "active in all civic matters . . . and in all charitable drives."[19] Foster and Bolden had similar business and civic résumés.

As the guest lists for the various social functions suggest, the press-baseball relationship was reciprocal. Team owners bought advertising in the black newspapers, offered newspapermen seats on the teams' corporate boards, and made them partners in the founding and running of their leagues. There is little evidence, however, of direct financial investment in any of the baseball teams by newspaper publishers or the writers that covered the teams, although it is a possibility given their many associations in the various business fraternities. The only direct financial tie discovered went the other direction. A reference in Cum Posey's obituary describes him as a principal owner of Pittsburgh's Homestead Grays and a shareholder of the *Courier*. Posey's father was the *Courier*'s first president and a founding director. The extent of the younger Posey's investment in the *Courier* was not specified.[20]

Because baseball's officials and members of the press enjoyed prestige and power through their affiliation, they made their ties very public. When the Chicago American Giants opened their 1917 campaign, black Chicago alderman Louie B. Anderson joined Abbott, the *Defender*'s publisher, to form the pitcher-catcher battery for that season's ceremonial first pitch.[21] Anderson, a World War I veteran and attorney, joined Abbott to watch the game from a special box reserved for them by Foster, a section that also included alderman Edward H. Wright, founder of the Appomattox Club and an attorney, and two other black businessmen.[22]

Part of the explanation for the fast partnership lies in the fact that the mentalities of Foster, Taylor, and Bolden, and those of *Defender* publisher Robert S. Abbott, *Indianapolis Freeman* publisher George Knox, and *Pittsburgh Courier* publisher Robert Vann, were so similar.[23] Each subscribed at least in part to the views and methods of Booker T. Washington, who preached a gospel of self-help and accommodation with whites through achievement and hard work. When Bolden incorporated his Hilldale Baseball and Exhibition Company, for example, he employed his former players to run it. To get more of Hilldale's fan base in the Darby area of Philadelphia out to games, Bolden arranged with the local black-owned transit company to add Hilldale Park to its trolley lines and to run extra cars before and after the games.[24]

Foster's columns repeated Washington's prescriptions. A common refrain in the manager-owner's weekly writings posited that black baseball *had* to succeed if for no other reason than for the jobs it could create for blacks. Fans naturally were obliged to give the league their "healthy patronage and support," he wrote, because baseball helped "so many hundreds of our own in a material way."[25] Baseball was unique in this respect. Other sports did not have the commercial impact within the black community that baseball provided, principally because of the large number of baseball games in any one season.[26] In a page-one *Courier* editorial, Vann contrasted baseball's fiscal importance with that of football, which, given the disparity in the numbers of games played, could "not assume the economic proportions known to baseball."[27]

This emphasis on baseball as a business meant that what happened at the gate and in the front office overshadowed what occurred on the field, at least as reflected in newspaper coverage. In a January 1922 column in the *Defender*, for example, sportswriter Dave Wyatt supported Foster's stated desire to weed out the league's lesser businessmen and to find "those who are fit," a common cry in the *Defender* and in the *Courier* during the 1920s.[28] Owners less adept than Foster at business matters would have to go, Wyatt argued, "in order to make the game more profitable to those who are fit." For emphasis, Wyatt used a barnyard phrase repeated by sportswriters throughout the 1920s, 1930s, and 1940s in reference to the fortunes of the Negro leagues. Wyatt prematurely called black baseball "the goose that has laid the golden eggs."[29]

Tracking who the press felt was responsible for safe-guarding the golden egg-laying goose oddly is a convenient way to mark shifts in coverage. Protection of the gold production first rested on the shoulders of fans, who were called on to support what the owners were trying to do to build up the sport. Later, when it became clear the owners could not overcome their own greed and acrimony, this responsibility shifted, at least from the perspective of the black press, to the owners themselves. Next, in the 1940s, writers assigned custody of the goose to the players in warning them against fighting and in demanding that they more consistently play hard. Finally, in the 1950s, the goose's fate was returned to the fans, who were rallied to support an evanescent entity that had produced the likes of Jackie Robinson, Roy Campanella, and Monte Irvin.

Wyatt's zealousness in supporting Foster perhaps blinded him to the magnate's obvious preference not merely for top businessmen, an elite that included rivals J. L. Wilkinson in Kansas City, who was white, and Ed Bolden in Philadelphia, but for those willing to yield to his ways and wishes. The mercuric baseball career of Detroit's John "Tenny" Blount is evidence. Foster controlled the roster of Blount's Detroit Stars, as well as the lease on the Stars' venue, Mack Park. When Blount cooperated with Foster, he was described in the press as "an example for all managers to follow," Foster's "most trustworthy lieutenant," and "one of the best known and most popular owners that the game has produced."[30] When Blount's support wavered, however, the *Defender* and *Courier* joined Foster in casting Blount out of baseball and censuring him "for not playing league games and because players claimed he had stopped paying their salaries."[31] Blount asked sportswriters to intervene, daring anyone to find anything inaccurate in his accounts. Foster offered to resign, knowing his offer would be rejected, and Blount was voted out of the league.

Wyatt's zeal for and blind loyalty to Foster was not an anomaly. Though difficult to envision in a modern era populated by the likes of George Steinbrenner, Peter Angelos, and Bud Selig, black baseball owners were *the* heroes in the sports pages of the 1920s, not ball players, which offers a sharp contrast to mainstream sports journalism of the period. The owners were often referred to as magnates or captains of business. The most frequently praised magnate was Rube Foster, though, to be fair, it was often Foster himself penning the praise. To the *Defender,* no one "worked more faithful [sic] than the Chicago 'chief' to make the meeting possible," a reference to Foster's involvement organizing the league.³² Anticipating the inaugural season beginning in April 1920, Wyatt hailed Foster as having "made more sacrifices for the good of the game than all the managers together" and as "the rock against which many a wave of adversity has been dashed to nothingness."³³

A controversy in 1923 about scheduling shows the lengths the black press was willing to go in this early phase to burnish the image of its heroes. Since ballpark ownership was rare in the Negro leagues, team schedules were dependent on the pleasure of other, usually white teams, including major league, minor league, and even white semi-professional teams. Most black clubs had to lease parks when the home teams of those venues were either on the road or idle, and they usually had to pay steep rental fees that eroded already thin operating margins. Rube Foster, who composed the schedules, claimed that since only four of the league's teams controlled their venues, he was forced to schedule a disproportionate number of weekend dates in the parks black teams controlled, most notably his own.

Foster used his weekly *Defender* column to explain why the Negro National schedule so heavily favored his own Chicago American Giants, but he omitted in his explanation the five percent cut he claimed as a booking fee, a fiscal fact the *Defender* conveniently overlooked, as well. Frank Young had to have known about the fees since in February 1920 he helped draft the league's constitution and bylaws, documents that gave Foster the authority to charge a commission. Under the byline "Mister Fan," Young argued that there was "no possible way to arrange schedules other than [the way] they have been arranged." Young threatened unsupportive fans with the loss of baseball: "If President Foster withdraws his financial support from the league or the association—up in the air it goes."³⁴

The lack of black-owned venues prevented the black leagues from functioning as top rank professional organizations. The teams' league schedules all were different in number, sometimes dramatically so, and each team could schedule as many "exhibition" games as it wanted, with league and non-league foes alike. Most also barnstormed liberally, playing in small towns and against semi-pro and even industrial teams both black and white. If a league member played fifty to eighty league games, it likely played roughly one hundred exhibition games, as well, none of which counted in the league standings.

Foster's five percent take for booking the games was perhaps to be admired since the owners were above all lauded for their business acumen, or for what the writers credited to them as business acumen. When Cleveland's George Hooper bought a baseball park for the Tate Stars, he was celebrated for "saving" the team, according to the *Defender*, which depicted him as "one of the really remarkable men of the Race." Hooper invested in the game not to make money, but rather "from a purely unselfish motive—from a desire to be of service to an enterprise dedicated to the good of the members of his Race," according to the newspaper.[35] Only a passing mention was made a month later when the Stars failed to come up with the $1,000 league deposit and, therefore, closed down.

The owners' presence in and commitment to their urban communities offered a sharp contrast to the complete lack of such activity by the white bookmakers at the helm of the Negro National League's primary competition, the Eastern Colored League, which was organized in December 1922 in Philadelphia. This black-white contrast was picked up as a theme in the newspapers covering Negro National teams, publications that routinely described the upstart ECL and its members as "outlaws," comparisons that only added to the luster of the Negro National's "Race men."[36] The target of much of the writers' ire was the ECL's principal owner and backer, New York bookmaker Nat Strong. As owner of the black Royal Giants, the white Brooklyn Bushwicks, and Dexter Park in Brooklyn, Strong chose not to establish links with black businessmen in Harlem, where his Royal Giants played.[37] Strong did not seek favor or coverage from the black newspapers the *New York Age* or *Amsterdam News*. He hired only white ticket-takers and white umpires, and he worked collusively within the ECL and with stadium owners to virtually lock Negro National teams out of New York, the city with the nation's largest black population at that time.[38]

Another white ECL team owner reviled in the black newspapers, Charles Spedden of the Baltimore Black Sox, also spurned the local black business community by refusing to hire stadium workers of color. Spedden added insult to his injuring of Baltimore's black working class by describing its members as less than satisfactory "in the rapid handling of change . . . [and] short when the count up is made."[39] Spedden and Strong provided the perfect foil to black baseball's "Moses," Rube Foster, and Strong's and Spedden's exploitation of black baseball made support for the ECL a moral issue for Foster and his fellow NNL owners. In the pages of the *Defender*, Foster described Ed Bolden's affiliation with the rival league as "racial treachery."[40] In Pittsburgh, Ira Lewis wrote that Strong's control of black baseball in the East placed black players in a "condition of almost abject slavery," in contrast to Foster's Negro National, where baseball had "shaken off the yoke of white man's control."[41] From the perspective of writers such as Lewis, Young, Wyatt, and others, an owner's interest in building up baseball as a distinctly black enterprise was the central issue. Strong and his partners were white profiteers little interested in the welfare of the black community, men each willing "to sell his right leg if the price is right," Lewis wrote.⁴²

A power struggle between Strong and James H. Williams, owner of the Penn Station Red Caps, underlines the racially based method of determining the virtue or ill of an owner's or even an entire league's decisions. The Red Caps were one of the hundreds of semi-professional teams that enjoyed corporate sponsorship. In his struggle with Strong over the rights to players, Williams and the Red Caps were portrayed by the *New York Age* as victims in the struggle, even though Williams had raided Strong's Royal Giants of its top players. When Williams tried to arrange the club's games, Strong blocked him just as Foster routinely blocked teams accused of raiding the NNL of players. The *Age* criticized the bookmaker for trying only to "get the colored public's money," while doing nothing to "get involved in community affairs."⁴³

When an NNL team scooped up players from an ECL club, just as the Red Caps had done, the theft somehow defied definition as a player raid in the descriptions of the black press. As practiced by the NNL, a raid was somehow benevolent in providing rival teams with a "friendly warning" that until and unless they came into the racially pure NNL, they would have to suffer the consequences.⁴⁴ "Unless Manager Bolden comes into the fold, he may find his club wrecked," the *Defender* stated, in an unbylined article. "In union there is strength."⁴⁵ Because of scuffles over players and the personality clashes among owners, the league rivalry was described as war, one in which "the very future of baseball as a commercial enterprise among our group hangs in the balance," according to the *Defender*.⁴⁶

The NNL's commercial viability was paramount to the weeklies, and the newspapers' emphasis of commercial achievement was most conspicuous during the first Colored World Series in 1924, a poorly attended ten-game affair that represented a truce in the war between the Negro National and the ECL.⁴⁷ After feuding and fighting for most of the 1923 and 1924 seasons, Foster, Bolden, and Strong cobbled together an armistice that pitted the champions from the two leagues in a series of games that required a fortnight to complete. If newspaper reports are to be believed, fans began demanding a Colored World Series but, judging by the coverage, the newspapers themselves wanted such a series every bit as badly as the fans. The *Defender*, for example, lobbied for a series as a way to accomplish a peace between the rival leagues.⁴⁸

Whether fan support or press demands came first is difficult to discern. In August 1924, Ollie Womack of the Kansas City *Call*, for example, urged black fans to demand a championship, writing that he believed the black community could and should offer up a parallel to white baseball's

World Series. "Why should not the black players enjoy the advantages as white players in the majors do?" Womack wrote, urging the magnates to settle their differences.[49] Womack argued that if major league players are afforded a chance to take home post-season winnings of $3,500 per player, why shouldn't the "pioneers" of black baseball?

The *Defender* and the *Courier* each claimed being "deluged" with letters from fans asking why there was no series. If the magnates did not appease the fans, the *Defender* warned that they risked alienating those upon whom they depended.[50] For Foster and Bolden to preclude a series because of personal animosities was, for the *Courier*, a "BABY ACT" involving "ABOUT TWO PERSONS," a juvenile dispute that had gone on long enough.[51] The pressure worked, and Foster and Bolden negotiated arrangements for the first Colored World Series to pit Bolden's Hilldales, once again champs in the East, versus Wilkinson's Monarchs, defending titlists in the NNL.

Newspaper coverage of this first postseason stressed gate receipts and the financial impact of the games, not the performances on the field or the outcomes of the games. Detailed accounts of revenues and disbursements were published in the *Defender* and the *Courier*, both of which sided with owners and against players in a controversy about whether the Series' participants could have made more money barnstorming.[52] Even holding the Series was hailed mainly for the potential financial windfall. The *Courier*'s Philadelphia-based correspondent, W. Rollo Wilson, wrote during that first Colored World Series, which was won by the Monarchs, that, "like the white man, the 'brother' is beginning to see the folly of falling out of things that concern his financial well-being."[53] Another story in the *Courier* anticipating the Series is remarkable in the detail it provides of the financial arrangements, including which parties were entitled to a share of the revenues, how expenses would be assigned, and even who should receive complimentary game tickets.[54] The story appeared on the *Courier*'s front page.

For the black press, the Colored World Series became a symbol of progress, if only for a year. The Kansas City *Call* celebrated it as a "long step forward" for baseball among blacks, while the *Philadelphia Tribune* championed Taylor and Foster for organizing the sport and, therefore, making possible such a "symbol of race progress."[55] The *Defender* and *Courier* trumpeted the Series on their front pages in the only instances during the early 1920s that baseball made page one, and they provided blanket coverage of the games in the sports sections, even after the event began foundering in 1925. After losing money in 1925, 1926, and 1927, the Colored World Series was discontinued.

Just as the black press ignored the major leagues, the Negro leagues normally were invisible to the white dailies. The Series changed this, if only for a few weeks. Fay Young, who in addition to covering the games for the *Defender* served as one of the Series' two official scorers, credited white dailies in Philadelphia and Kansas City "for giving front-page space and carrying the scores play-by-play. The [Kansas City] Journal-Post went so far as to use the pictures of [Nip] Winters and [Bullet] Rogan in the Sunday morning edition, the first time in history of the papers that a Colored man's picture . . . found its way into print unless he had committed a crime," Young wrote.[56] Through coverage in the dailies, white baseball fans were awakened to the existence of two fully functioning black leagues, organizations that at least in some ways resembled major league baseball. As the *Defender* noted, the Series did "more to gain the fans' attention in the national pastime as regards to our group, than anything that has been done in recent years."[57] The *Call* was even more enthusiastic, arguing that "Negro sport has done what Negro churches, Negro lodges, Negro business could not do." The Series had "shown that a Negro can get attention for a good deed well done, and that publicity is no longer the exclusive mark of our criminals."[58]

The Colored World Series could not overcome its own unwieldiness, however. Too many games in too many cities, poor weather, and gate receipts insufficient to reward players for giving up lucrative post-season barnstorming schedules doomed the event after only four editions; the last was held in 1927. Series players each received less than $100, which in fact was far less than barnstorming could have paid them.[59] With so many games over such durations, played in multiple cities, fans found it difficult to sustain interest in the Series' outcome. The fact that the black newspapers were published weekly added to the difficulty of keeping up with the teams' fortunes.

The one exception to otherwise universally supportive coverage concerned an evidence of hypocrisy perhaps too glaring to overlook, particularly given the stated objectives of the league and the journalists' very public involvement in the league's affairs. The league's umpires all were white. In spite of their own rhetoric about building a black business by and for the black community, Rube Foster resisted hiring black officials and, therefore, erected a color barrier of his own. Young picked the issue as an important one as early as 1920, the year of the Negro National's founding, and he increased pressure on black baseball as the decade progressed. In a 1922 column, for instance, he called on the league to begin hiring black umpires, specifically "Jamison in Baltimore" and "two in New Orleans." (The Jamison reference was to Caesar Jamison of New York, who umpired throughout the East and South.) In response, Foster foreshadowed a rationale used by major league owners to bar black players from the big leagues. He claimed there were no qualified black umpires. Young chided in response, "Train them, I say. Train them. . . . If you can train a chimpanzee to do things then you can train men."[60]

Foster eventually hired eight black officials in April 1923, enough to handle most of the league's games, and the *Defender*'s response indicates that newspaper's readiness to forgive. The paper published a column by one of the umpires hired, Tom Johnson, a former player for the St. Louis Stars. Johnson attempted to recast history in favor of Foster by describing him as having "long been determined to install an umpire system," despite protest and resistance. Johnson did not identify the protesters and no evidence of resistance is found in the black newspapers other than that from Foster himself. But, the magnate's "courageous" stand made him no less than "the Race's greatest leader . . . the 'father' of a movement which is destined to be the Race's greatest achievement of all time," Johnson wrote.[61] The *Defender* also published a column by another of the umpires hired, Billy Donaldson, who wrote a similarly glowing tribute to Foster.[62]

The ECL also wrestled with the umpire issue, and it faced mounting criticism in the black press. Bolden hired black officials first in 1925 but, at a time when jobs in the black community were scarce, he named a white sportswriter, William Dallas, a personal friend, to supervise them. Though Dallas had the experience—he previously supervised both baseball umpires and basketball referees—his hiring piqued black sportswriters. Seeing Bolden's move as a ploy to get publicity in white newspapers, the *Afro-American* linked the ECL's success to the publicity it enjoyed exclusively in the black press.[63] A cartoon in the *Philadelphia Tribune* depicted Bolden as an Uncle Tom seeking favor from the white man.[64]

Rollo Wilson, who Bolden passed over in appointing Dallas, reminded Bolden that the owner was running the "Mutual Association of Eastern COLORED Clubs." Wilson also pointed out that the white Philadelphia Baseball Association had never appointed a colored man in charge of its umpires.[65] Interestingly, Wilson did not object on the grounds that he was not selected, even though Wilson had years of experience as a sports official in various capacities. The decision to hire Dallas perhaps was the result of Bolden's priority as a business man first and a Race man second. He hoped to get mention in the white dailies and, therefore, to attract white fans to games; Dallas's hiring could be seen as part of that larger effort. Bolden's efforts fell flat, however. The white newspapers paid little notice; white baseball fans, too, remained unmoved. Officiating did not improve, perhaps even worsening during the 1925 season.

The Dallas episode provides evidence of an increasing willingness on the part of the newspapers to challenge the leagues' owners. Earlier in the decade, it is possible if not probable that the writers would have worked with league officials privately to determine the racial composition its roster of officials. It is also probable that prior to Bolden's umpiring debacle Bolden himself would at least have been given the option of publishing an explanation in the *Philadelphia Tribune*.

In contrast to the frequent and favorable coverage of owners, the players were largely ignored. Most player mentions in the newspapers during the decade included only last names, even on first reference, as Young's description of the Colored World Series demonstrates. Stories about players often criticized their behavior, both on and off the field, in sharp contrast to the treatment of the owners. A former player himself, the *Defender*'s Dave Wyatt nonetheless was a frequent critic of the players. Echoing Foster's own critiques, Wyatt described them as greedy and self-serving. These descriptions served indirectly to keep salaries down, favoring the owners' business interests. In a February 1922 article, Young refers to outfielder Clarence Smith as "property of Detroit Stars," an ironic choice of words given slavery's long-fingered legacy.[66] When players groused over pay in 1923, the *Defender* called them "Monshine [sic] drinkers" slated to be either cut or traded.[67] Later in the decade, Young criticized the Chicago's black players for not being in shape and for being too easily enamored with "whiskey, white mule, synthetic gin," and "riotous living. . . . If the players can't be handled, baseball is doomed."[68] For Young the lack of dedication on the part of the players trumped mismanagement by the owners as the chief threat to the game.

Players existed in newspaper coverage largely as chits or pawns and rarely as individuals each with a vested interest in the fate of the leagues themselves or as human beings with families, lives outside baseball, and hopes and dreams of their own. This treatment would continue throughout the 1920s and change only in the next decade, with the stardom of pitching great Satchel Paige and hard-hitting catcher Josh Gibson, both of whom are enshrined in the National Baseball Hall of Fame. Boxing great Joe Lewis and Olympic gold medalist Jesse Owens also re-focused attention on individual athletes.

The newspapers' approach in regular game coverage was boosteristic, at least through the first half of the 1920s. The *Defender* reported many stories under the byline "Mister Fan" to offer a fan's perspective. Almost certainly written by Young, the stories used colorful colloquialisms and hyperbole to effuse unbridled and unabashed enthusiasm for the games. Before the 1923 season, for instance, Mister Fan predicted it would be "one of the greatest in the history of the league," despite heavy financial losses suffered by owners in the 1922 campaign.[69] The Mister Fan column repeated the rosy prediction in 1924, describing the American Giants as training "as no club that has ever left Chicago has ever trained." The Giants were working to become "a smooth working combination, the best that has ever represented the South side lot," according to the *Defender*.[70]

Trumpeting large crowds was a hallmark of week-to-week season coverage, with attendance figures often appearing in a story's headline. In fact, it was not uncommon for the turnstile total to appear in a game story's headline but for the score and even the game's winner to be excluded. In May 1923, 11,000 people "jammed into every available space" to see the Kansas City Monarchs beat the Chicago American Giants, according to the *Defender*.[71] A week later the newspaper ran the headline, "Ten Thousand See Detroit Opener at Mack Park," and in June, "17,000 See Foster Win."[72]

Game statistics, rankings, and even league standings, however, were problematic. Only a few teams regularly sent in results, even fewer when they lost. Fans often complained, as did the writers, and with increasing volume during the decade. The *Courier*'s Wilson lamented the void in June 1925, pointing out that the newspapers could not distinguish which games counted as official league games and, therefore, could not generate accurate statistics themselves.[73] The lead story in the *Defender*'s sports page in a January 1926 issue acknowledged that the newspapers had been accused by fans of withholding results out of bias against the league. The truth, according to the *Defender*, was that "there never has been a record kept of results," and no fines levied for this breach by the league.[74] This negligence probably contributed to the partnership's fracture later in the decade and, presumably, to waning interest on the part of fans unsure of their teams' rankings in the league standings.

While major league baseball and the ECL were virtually ignored, both the *Defender* and the *Courier* published regular coverage of the Negro Southern League. The *Defender* also reported regularly on Chicago's Sunday Church League, while game summaries of industrial league and semi-professional play appeared in both papers. The *Courier* published extensive Southern League game coverage and more semi-professional coverage than did the *Defender*, including a regular column on the perennial semi-professional champion Homestead Grays. During the off-season, fans were treated to stories almost weekly on some of the NNL's teams, usually the American Giants, either from the annual meetings or in anticipation of the start of spring training in the South. A regular column in the *Courier* by former player Dizzy Dismukes on how to play the sport also served to keep baseball on readers' minds throughout the year.

As baseball wound down its season, the black press turned its focus and resources to football among the historically black colleges like Tuskegee, Wilberforce, Howard, and North Carolina A&T. The Tuskegee-Wilberforce game, for example, routinely made the front pages of the *Defender* and the *Courier*, both before and after the rivalry's annual renewal. Basketball, boxing, and track and field, all of which integrated before baseball, also were major sports in terms of black press coverage.

Sportswriters' participation in the annual business meetings provides a convenient indicator of the health of the baseball-press partnership during the decade. At least through 1924, the writers were full participants, granted unrestricted access to the owners and even seats at the table during proceedings. From the 1924 meetings Young reported that he, Q. J. Gilmore, and the *Indianapolis Ledger*'s A. D. Williams, who would replace Lewis as league secretary in 1926, were the three newspaper men "who were really qualified to speak their opinion" on the Negro National because they "sit in the league meetings . . . know all the workings, the plans, the trials of the league."[75] By late 1924, however, the league's messy state of affairs was such that the owners felt they required secrecy for the first time. End-of-the-year meetings, which assembled officials from both the NNL and ECL for the first time, were described by Young as "closed—really closed—even to the newspaper men and the publicity man of the league having to sit out in the anteroom" of the Appomattox Club.[76] The press-baseball partnership began to splinter as the league's problems proved stubborn and as an internecine blame game among the owners forced all officials and writers to pick sides. The sportswriters would never again enjoy the full access to and participation in league affairs that characterized the early 1920s.

The exit of sportswriters from the league's organizational meetings did not immediately turn positive coverage into criticism, however. The league's survival and success still were paramount, explaining in part what can only be described as distorted reporting on the league's affairs. The writers continued to describe attending games as a civic obligation and to characterize the league's business in unflinchingly positive terms. Though the December 1924 meetings pitted Foster and Blount against each other for control of the Detroit Stars, a thoroughly one-sided fight that left Blount out of the league, the *Courier* nonetheless described the meetings as enjoying a "praiseworthy spirit" and displaying "a wide range of good feeling and satisfaction." The meetings, according to the newspaper, ensured that the 1925 season would "go down in history . . . as the league's greatest."[77]

The 1925 season of course was not the greatest. The league made less money, and attendance for the second Colored World Series sagged well below that of the first year.[78] The 1926 campaign proved no better and by late season Frank Young could no longer abide the internal dissension among the owners and that disunity's undercutting of what the Negro leagues were founded to do. Young lashed out in September, challenging the owners to "lay their petty ambition and jealousy aside and get down to business." Because of the ceaseless bickering among the "magnates," Young wrote that the time had come to negotiate territorial boundaries similar to those used by big league baseball.[79] The *New York Age* and the *Afro-American*, too, began criticizing the white-controlled ECL, accusing league leadership of operating primarily in its own best interests and, therefore, of being "not interested in the welfare of the entire league."[80] The criticism marked a significant shift in coverage and a break from the boosterism that had characterized most of the first six seasons of Negro league play.

The 1926 Colored World Series provided little relief. After what was an eleven-game marathon, the *Courier*'s Rollo Wilson wrote that in business terms the Series was "not worth a nickel," while Young called the games "a joke" in light of their paltry payouts.[81] The entire ECL shut down in mid-1928, while in the west the Negro National struggled to hold together. Rube Foster suffered a nervous breakdown in 1926, in part because of the stresses of governing such a fractious group. He never fully recovered from the breakdown, and he did not rejoin black baseball's governing elite.

A column by Young in late 1928 marked another turning point in the *Defender*'s support for the leagues and a change in the paper's impulse to blame fans and players when things went wrong. In the November 3 issue, finally, for the first time, the lack of support among fans pointed to the problem and no longer represented the problem itself. "The fans aren't getting what they want and we know it and the interest is lagging in the league," Young wrote. If the owners did not change their ways, "there won't be a league and one bright morning they will wake up to find that they have killed the goose that laid the golden egg."[82] Threats to the goose's life came for the first time from owners, not the fans, "who must be satisfied or they will go somewhere else," Young wrote.[83] In July 1929, when he observed more black baseball fans filing in to see the White Sox than the number paying to watch the American Giants game that same day, Young pointed to the poor product on the field offered by the then white-owned American Giants, an assignation of blame difficult to imagine during the decade's first half.

Far from the lofty ambitions of February 1920, the Negro leagues had become burlesque. An afternoon in August 1930 at Schorling Park, once the crown jewel of the league's ballparks, represented the league's ills in microcosm. The only fans in the stands for a double-header between the American Giants and the Birmingham Black Barons were family of the players. Rowdyism had chased away most all others. The Giants held up the first game for ten minutes to protest an official's call, and the Black Barons threatened to walk off the field. During the second game, three fights among players gave those few fans who had remained more than enough cause to leave.[84] Fights on the field were increasingly common. Arguments with umpires, the games' slow pitching, and the lazy fashion in which teams took the field and switched sides contributed to delays, as well, as did players who were not in shape or, according to the *Defender*, were too enamored with alcohol.[85]

Conditions were no less grim off the playing fields. The first signs of recession appeared for the black community in the middle of the decade and, according to one labor historian, this community already was in the throes of the Depression by the end of 1926.[86] Young blamed the 1927's season of disappointment on bad weather and "the lack of employment among our folks."[87] When the stock market crashed in October 1929, thousands of blacks had already lost their jobs as the structural problem for baseball worsened. At a time when the national economy was weakening, player salaries, park rentals, and travel expenses all were rising.

Fiscal challenges and Foster's absence necessitated the involvement of white businessmen, which alarmed the black writers. The pitch to fans all along had been to support the Race and the baseball businesses it controls and from which it benefits. Young gave voice to the fear that the Negro National was ceding control to non-black interests. After Foster's commitment to a mental health institution, the American Giants went to a white businessman, William Trimble. The Monarchs, St. Louis Stars, and Detroit Stars, too, were owned by white men, making the league, in Young's terms, a "50–50 proposition," racially.[88] (The league re-organized again as an almost all-black-owned, black-run organization 1932.)

Game reports, columns, analysis—all coverage was devoted to the Negro National League to the exclusion of the rest of professional baseball. Except when being described as an adversary of the NNL and, therefore, as being against the best interests of black baseball, the ECL was rarely referred to and its games were not covered by black newspapers in Negro National League cities. This changed in late 1924 when the two leagues reached an armistice for the purposes of staging the first Colored World Series. During the year of the ECL's founding, for example, the *Defender* mentioned that league only twice, and in both instances the paper celebrated Ed Bolden's defiance of its leadership.[89] In 1923, during the ECL's first season of play, the *Defender* again referenced the ECL but twice, once to criticize the "Eastern association raid" on NNL players and a second time to call the new league's limited schedule a "real laugh."[90] Even major league action failed to get a mention in the *Defender* during the 1922 season until Frank Young's season-ending roundup column.[91] The only other references to "organized baseball" were stories in October anticipating exhibition games between major league and Negro league teams.[92]

Also absent in coverage throughout the period is any discussion of integration. It was not an issue for blacks or whites, at least not as it related to professional baseball, not yet. The pendulum of race had swung so dramatically toward separation that the black press and baseball's "magnates" busied themselves with building up the sport as a business and not directly challenging, in historian Donn Rogosin's words, "the inherent irrationality of American segregation."[93] The newspapers, too, were focused on promoting the interests and welfare of the black community as a discreetly separate world within a world, socially, culturally, and economically segregated from the mainstream.[94] One of the only references to the exclusion of blacks from "organized baseball" was made by the *Courier*'s Ira Lewis in Vann's short-lived monthly *Competitor* magazine. Lewis observed that major league baseball seemed to approve of Cubans, "provided they do not come too black," Chinese, Indians, "and everyone else under the sun . . . except the black man." He mused that "Perhaps, some day, a Regular American baseball man will establish a precedent—maybe."[95]

Even on the many occasions when Negro league teams and squads of major leaguers played against each other in exhibition games, the hypocrisy that black players were prohibited from playing in the country's "National Game" drew little mention, much less debate or protest.[96] These exhibition games for the black press were instead reasons to celebrate since getting the two colors on the same field was more important in the 1920s.

The emphasis on building up black baseball and, more generally, on improving the lot of black Americans perhaps explains also the lack of criticism regarding the practice of many major league teams to hire blacks as trainers and mascots, and only as trainers and mascots. It is possible that these subservient roles fueled racial prejudice, and they most certainly helped to foster stereotypes that later players, including Jackie Robinson, would find difficult to break. In the 1920s and 1930s, trainers served only as equipment managers, with no medical, nutritional, dietary, or physical training responsibilities whatsoever. Even these limited roles were important to the black community, however. Bill Buckner, a long-time trainer for the Chicago White Sox, was portrayed as a sort of hero in the pages of the *Defender*, which ran features on the black barbershop owner and reported on his travels with the Sox. When he was reappointed the Sox trainer in February 1922, fans flooded the *Defender* with letters of congratulations.[97] In March, when Buckner accompanied the Sox to spring training, he reported back via the *Defender* on the "plentiful" Ku Klux Klan buttons worn by residents of the Lone Star State.[98]

Blacks also joined major league teams as mascots, a position that often required providing some comic relief. Mostly, however, mascots served as good luck charms. The *Courier*'s Wendell Smith wrote in 1939 of the New York Giants' mascot, Cecil Haley, a thirteen-year-old "new luck piece" who was expected to "put his mystic powers to work by some supernatural method."[99] Nashville of the American Association employed a black mascot nicknamed "Rubber," while the Philadelphia Athletics under Mickey Cochrane had a black bat boy and a mascot nicknamed "Black Cat."[100] Like the trainers, black mascots were celebrated in the weeklies—an indication of how much the newspapers would have to change philosophically and how dramatically priorities would be re-ordered before the campaign for baseball's integration could begin in earnest in the late 1930s. The hiring of "Black Cat" was hyperbolically hailed in the *Amsterdam News*, for instance, as "the most radical move any major leaguer has made in the annals of baseball."[101]

Sportswriters in the 1930s would not only call for change but would launch initiatives designed to challenge the status quo and to get major league baseball's leaders to the negotiating table. In the 1920s, however, since there was no formal ban on players of color in writing and, therefore, nothing that could be litigated or protested, the black press first had to win from organized baseball even the admission that there indeed was such a policy. The publishers, editors, and writers of the *Defender* and *Courier*, among other newspapers, saw in the Negro leagues, therefore, a great opportunity. The sheer number of games promised significant economic gains for a hardscrabble community. Build it and the fans would come, the journalists believed, and they would come in such numbers as to make mainstream society take notice and, ultimately, begin discussing integration.

The black businessmen funding this great hope encouraged this agenda and often supplied its rhetoric. This served the owners' own purposes, which were largely about making profit and acquiring power and prestige. They, too, articulated their enterprise in moralist terms and, with the help of obliging newspapers, used bylined weekly columns to cast themselves as humanitarians. They were fulfilling Booker T. Washington's philosophy of self-help and uplift and, therefore, accepted white society's belief that with a little work, anyone could escape poverty and better themselves. The Negro leagues' very name attests to this tacit acceptance.

First seen as agents of change, the owners were gradually seen as obstacles to it. The newspapermen would have to wait for another generation of businessmen to turn black baseball into a profit-making enterprise and, therefore, a black institution viable enough to force recognition of the hypocrisy of segregation in athletics and, by extension, throughout American society. But never again would black team owners be allowed to so freely and frequently use the black newspapers as their own personal soapboxes from which to lash out at adversaries and rivals or to demand fan attendance. Young in Chicago and Lewis and Wilson in Pittsburgh would from this point cheer far less and increasingly make demands that black baseball do better at organizing and in providing a good product. The intimacy shared in smoke-filled banquet rooms and in black-only hotels during the Negro National League's founding meetings was gone for good, shattered by the owners' malpractice, avarice, and inability to see beyond their own selfish interests. This fracture would produce reporting less wedded to the individual agendas of businessmen within the black community and more trained on winning civil rights and ending segregation. It would also shift emphasis from the baseball's back rooms to its playing fields, setting the stage for players to become the heroes of the 1930s and 1940s.[102]

Chapter Four
Transitions

On a sunny Sunday in August 1934, tens of thousands of people from all over the Midwest filed into Chicago's Comiskey Park for a day of song, pageantry, and, of course, baseball. Many arrived on trains in the days leading up to game day, using the trip as an opportunity to shop in the big city. Others streamed in strictly for the baseball, for that day's game featured many of the finest black ballplayers in the country, including Satchel Paige, Cool Papa Bell, and Oscar Charleston. Between 25,000 and 30,000 saw Paige pitch his West all-stars to a 1–0 win in a pitching clinic that quite possibly marked the high point of Negro league baseball.[1]

Pittsburgh Courier city editor William G. Nunn wrote in a front-page article that that glorious weekend, culminating with the all-black all-star game on one of white baseball's biggest stages, "made me proud that I'm a Negro and tonight I'm singing a new song. . . . I felt proud tonight that I was a member of a race who had achieved."[2] *Courier* sports editor Chester Washington described the East-West Classic as a "perfect baseball day . . . a success from every possible standpoint." The inter-racial goodwill "heralded a new day in Negro baseball," Washington wrote, uniting roughly 5,000 white fans and 20,000 or so blacks who, at least for a day, "forgot the color line before the great god of sports."[3]

The years 1930–1936 saw the collapse of the Negro National League, the first truly professional all-black league of substance, and then its rebirth. It was a period of fundamental shifts, including a generational change in team owners and a transition in sports coverage leadership at both the *Chicago Defender* and the *Pittsburgh Courier*. During this time Pittsburgh replaced Chicago as the power center of both black newspaper publishing and black baseball. In the context of what was an economically depressed decade for most Americans but in particular black Americans, the cooperation from and among newspapermen to ensure financial success and athletic achievement in black baseball was part of a larger effort to establish credibility before the mainstream from which the black community was systematically excluded. It was this period of self-help and uplift that made possible the activist reporting and campaigning for the desegregation of baseball that characterized the late 1930s and early 1940s, a phase of activist journalism led by black writers such as Wendell Smith at the *Courier*, Sam Lacy at the *Baltimore Afro-American,* Joe Bostic at the *People's Voice,* and Lester Rodney at the *Daily Worker.*

The Negro leagues and the black press were the fulfillment of Booker T. Washington's prescription for cooperation within and among black businesses "as separate as the fingers, yet one as the hand in all things essential to mutual progress."[4] Black businessmen encouraged each other and their constituencies to band together. "We have the Numbers, we have the Urge, we have the Knowledge, we have the Ambition, we have the Activity and we have the Opportunity," wrote Major Robert R. Wright, Sr., founder and president of Pittsburgh's Citizens & Southern Bank & Trust, president of the National Negro Bankers Association, and once an owner of the American Giants. "A spirit of self-sacrifice and cooperation is very necessary in order to build up business. We can never enjoy the benefits of our purchasing power, unless we are willing to unite and altruistically help competent and worthy Negro business men," Wright wrote in the *Courier.*[5]

From the perspective of a fighting press that was allied with business for the purposes of uplift, the Negro leagues *had* to survive, and for many of the reasons Wright outlined. As an economic model and incubator of young black baseball talent, Negro league baseball became the hammer with which to chip away at baseball's color barrier. This was the plan from the beginning. League co-founder Rube Foster told the *Indianapolis Freeman's* Elwood Knox in 1920, "We have to be ready when the day [of integration] comes."[6] Two decades later, team owners Gus Greenlee and Cum Posey declared that the Negro leagues had "a definite object in view. That object is entrance of Negro Leagues into White Organized Baseball and entrance of Negro Players into the Major Leagues."[7] Integration would be the culmination of Negro league history, but only after the leagues developed into an enterprise substantial enough and of enough material value to major league baseball to merit its attention.[8]

In one of the significant transitions during the period, newspaper readers witnessed a passing of the baton from long-time sports editor Fay Young at the *Defender* to Al Monroe, an inferior writer far less inclined to take strong positions on issues and less able to articulate those positions when he did.[9] In Pittsburgh, leadership of the *Courier's* sports pages shifted in the 1930s from Ira F. Lewis, who became the paper's business manager, to Chester Washington. Like Monroe, Washington favored cooperation over confrontation, and even in his own weekly "Sez Ches" column he was reticent to criticize. A battle between John L. Clark, secretary of the Negro National League, and Cum Posey, an owner of the Homestead Grays, that was waged with bylined articles in the *Courier* throughout 1933, demonstrated Washington's predisposition toward détente.

Clark, who also was secretary of the Crawfords, the inter-city rivals of Posey's Grays, accused Posey of raiding other NNL teams for players. Washington ran articles by both league officials on an almost weekly basis. He pledged that the *Courier* sports department would "reserve its opinion" until "all of the evidence in the case has been turned in." [10] In the meantime, he wrote, "the opinions of both Mr. Clark and Mr. Posey will be published under their own names." But Washington's verdict on the controversy was never offered. (The league, however, sided with Clark, voting to evict Posey's Grays in midseason.) Washington was, therefore, an unlikely candidate to launch a high-profile campaign against segregation. Active protest would have to wait for the arrival of Smith, Lacy, Rodney, and Bostic later in the decade.

New in the mix were the *Amsterdam News*, which began regularly covering Negro league baseball during the 1930s, and the communist newspaper, the *Daily Worker*, which was also based in New York City. The *Worker* added a sports section after the 1936 Olympics in Berlin. The *Amsterdam News*'s new sports editor, Romeo Dougherty, had already earned distinction as a noted film and theater critic, and he brought a fresh voice to sports coverage and unabashed support of black baseball and its powers.[11] In Washington, D.C. in 1934, Sam Lacy took over as sports editor at the *Washington Tribune*, installing a powerful new voice for baseball's integration in the nation's capital.

Monroe and Washington, in particular, only rarely challenged the status quo. Priority instead was placed on self-help and uplift. Like many distinctly black enterprises after the Depression, Negro league baseball had to be re-built. It is not surprising, then, that race relations took a back seat in sports coverage through the early part of the decade. In fact, rather than challenge white baseball's leaders, the black papers treated them with deference and respect. Charles Comiskey refused to integrate his Chicago White Sox throughout his ownership of the team, yet he was hailed as a friend of the Race for renting out Comiskey Park for Negro league games. Like other major league baseball owners who loaned out their venues, Comiskey took home nearly a third of black baseball's take. The practice richly profited the White Sox because of the East-West all-star game, played annually in Chicago beginning in 1933. The Sox's share of the gate during the decade ranged between 25 percent and 40 percent.

From the perspective of the black press, Comiskey was courageous for daring to comment favorably on the caliber of Negro league talent. Washington quoted the "Old Roman" as saying, "You can bet your last dime that I'll never refuse to hire a great athlete simply because he isn't the same color of some other player on my team."[12] Monroe, too, burnished Comiskey's image, writing "that no Race players wore the colors of the White Sox was hardly the fault of Comiskey."[13] Monroe did not identify who *was* responsible for the "blackout," and the Sox did not integrate until Cuba's Orestes "Minnie" Minoso, the "Cuban Flash," made the roster in May 1951, *after* the team was sold to Bill Veeck.

Across town, chewing gum magnate and, in 1934, the new owner of the Chicago Cubs, Phil K. Wrigley was celebrated in the *Defender* as "democratic" and "fair" for merely pledging to treat black and white fans alike at Cubs games in Wrigley Field. In 1934, promises and pledges—mere rhetoric—satisfied. As for black Cubs on the field, that decision was field manager Charlie Grimm's, Wrigley said, a response good enough at the time for the *Defender* and a common refrain from major league owners.[14] Owners routinely deflected questions about players to their managers, who in turn passed the buck back to the owners. The Cubs would somehow manage to delay the team's integration until the late stages of the 1953 season.[15]

Perhaps reflecting a sense of inferiority or supposed inferiority vis-à-vis mainstream society, the *Defender* and *Courier* noted any and all inklings of openness from baseball's powers regarding integration, which marked a significant change compared to coverage in the 1920s. The newspapers did not, however, seek to hold this elite accountable. As the Yankees prepared to take on the Cubs in the 1932 World Series, for example, Monroe noted at the end of his weekly column the lack of black players on both teams, but he was careful to note that his observations were not "intended as a slap at the Cubs or Yanks. Far from such a thing."[16]

Eager to receive due recognition for its players and teams, the black press in the early 1930s marked any positive statement from outside the black community regarding the quality of play in the Negro leagues. When Babe Ruth talked about the "colorfulness" of black baseball and the "sparkling brilliancy" of Negro league play, the comments went into the *Defender*'s sports pages with a large photo of the Babe, who was described in the caption as a "friend of the Race."[17] After a Canadian newspaper far from readerships in Negro league cities similarly lauded black baseball, the *Pittsburgh Courier* reprinted the praise in total.[18]

Coincident with the changes in leadership of sports coverage was a shift in that coverage, albeit short-lived, toward more objective reporting.[19] The unbridled boosterism and optimism characteristic of black baseball coverage in the 1920s gave way to a slightly more neutral stance. Signaling the switch, sportswriter Dan Burley used his column in the *Defender* to promise readers "impartiality, unbiased opinion and clear-cut, straightforward [sic] presentation of the game." This objectivity, never achieved, was intended to replace "the partisan spirit that used to characterize all athletic comment by writers of our group," he wrote.[20] Burley claimed readers had demanded this non-partisan coverage, though there is no evidence in the newspaper of any such demand. Letters to the editor did not reflect it. Mainstream sports journalism was being transformed, as well, becoming more objective, with greater attention paid to individual athletes. For mainstream papers, new competition from radio for game accounts put more emphasis on human interest angles.[21]

For the black press, the assumption of a less partisan perspective was not altogether voluntary. Sportswriters less regularly attended league meetings compared to the decade prior, and when they did, the writers enjoyed far less access to the business being conducted. Gone was a seat at the table for the black press, and with it an eyewitness account of how the league was being run. Operating on the outside forced more of a dependence on press releases and correspondence. Monroe, who was based in New York rather than Chicago, did not personally know Robert A. Cole, for example, who in 1932 was the new owner of the American Giants and Schorling Park.[22]

This lack of familiarity provides quite a contrast to the partnership that welded Fay Young and Rube Foster in purpose and plan.[23] The second generation of journalists and owners was not as small a social circle as the one that bonded the likes of Young and Foster, and the new generation of owners had significantly more capital at its disposal than did Foster and his group. The new owners, therefore, did not need the writers as much as their predecessors had, so a separation was perhaps inevitable. Demonstrating the lack of familiarity more common in the 1930s, Monroe frequently misspelled the names of then Negro National commissioner Judge William C. Hueston and Kansas City Monarchs' owner J. L. Wilkinson.[24] Monroe spelled Hueston's name as Houston and Wilkinson as Wilkerson. Monroe even botched the name of Oscar Charleston, a heavy-hitting phenom and one of Negro baseball's all-time greats, and on more than one occasion, writing "Charlestown" instead.

For the most part, however, Burley and Monroe endeavored to reflect more objectivity and, therefore, less partisan perspectives. At the *Courier*, Chester Washington and W. Rollo Wilson did as well, at least in regular weekly baseball coverage. Not surprisingly their columns varied, with some, like Wilson's, remaining unapologetically partisan, but others, such as Burley's, Monroe's, and Washington's striving to stay on the sidelines. Monroe, in fact, would remain fairly neutral for most of the decade, before switching almost exclusively to boxing coverage upon Fay Young's return to the paper from the Kansas City *Call* in 1937. Though the *Courier*'s Wilson also pledged neutrality, little change can be seen in his columns over time.[25]

Many of the regular columns were written by the team owners themselves and, thus, could not be considered objective at any level. Cum Posey, co-owner of the Homestead Grays and, importantly, a shareholder in the *Courier*, wrote three different columns for the Pittsburgh paper.[26] Gus Greenlee, too, often wrote of league business in articles published both by the *Defender* and *Courier*, among other papers. And former player and manager Dizzy Dismukes regularly reported on the Negro National for the *Courier*, coverage that was predictably sunny and uncritical. John L. Clark, secretary of the NNL and of the Pittsburgh Crawfords, had two regular columns in the *Courier*, one in the sports pages and, in the news pages, a column on city life called "Wylie Avenue." Clark had almost a lifetime affiliation with the *Courier*, writing several columns for the paper during his career. After Greenlee and the Negro National faded from black baseball in the 1930s, Clark moved to Washington, D.C., and wrote a political column for the newspaper.

Another reason for the new generation's reticence to confront was interdependence. In the difficult economic circumstances of the 1930s, division was a luxury the black community could ill afford. Penny-pinching in American households nearly devastated Negro league baseball, which had to rely almost exclusively on weekend dates because of the work schedules of most of its fans. Some players called the profitable doubleheader weekend dates "getting out-of-the-hole" days.[27] Negro league organizers convened in early 1930 to prevent a repeat of what was a dismal 1929 season, a year the *Defender* called "the worst in the history of the league's eleven years of existence."[28] (It is unknown what the paper considered the eleventh season—the NNL began in 1920.) A raid on players by an upstart circuit, the Texas Oklahoma Louisiana League, combined with the withdrawal of several Negro National teams unable to finance another season to cripple the Chicago-based league. The owners discussed the challenges but, according to the *Defender*, could not agree on their solutions.

Like many black leagues, the Texas Oklahoma Louisiana League was semi-professional and, therefore, not a "major" professional league. The Negro Southern League was the largest of these second-tier Negro leagues. The Texas Oklahoma Louisiana was the brainchild of former Kansas City

Call sportswriter and former Monarchs business manager Q. J. Gilmore, who held the title of league president. The circuit opened its first season on April 27, 1929, with the Dallas Black Giants defeating the Shreveport Black Sports 4–0 in front of 3,500.[29] Similar to the Negro National's founding nine years prior, the black press joined with Gilmore to start the league, meeting at the Pythian Temple in Dallas in early 1929.[30] A.D. Williams of the Kansas City *Call*, Roscoe Dunjee of Oklahoma City's *Black Dispatch*, Clarence Starks of the *Dallas Express*, and Robert White, who wrote for "a white daily of his city," Shreveport, La., helped to start the league. Later, in 1938, Gilmore returned to baseball's forefront in an effort to organize a minor league for the black leagues "for the betterment of the game."[31]

The measures the NNL owners did draw up for 1930 were merely cosmetic. Owners vowed, for instance, to put much more effort into publicizing games and reporting results, obligations observed far more in their breach than in their fulfillment throughout the nearly forty-year history of the leagues. Just a few years later, in July 1933, the secretary of the newly re-formed Negro National League, John L. Clark, indicted owners for failing to provide a record of performance and for not playing "fair with the press." These failures prevented the league from any claim of equality with the major leagues, Clark wrote, a criticism Brooklyn Dodgers president Branch Rickey would echo a dozen years later to justify failing to compensate the Kansas City Monarchs for Jackie Robinson.[32]

Signaling the deep roots of the problems, the league failed to finish the 1930 season and simply faded away. Judging by coverage in the *Defender* and *Courier* or, more accurately, by the lack of coverage on the league's disappearance, there was no formal closure. The league merely ceased functioning, its owners scattering. One of those owners, the Homestead Grays' Cum Posey, said he feared the worst: "The 1931 baseball season among the colored clubs of the nation has never had a more dreary outlook."[33] One of the Negro National's premier clubs, the Hilldales in Philadelphia, announced it was shutting down. Owner Johnny Drew explained much of the league's woes in describing those of the Hilldales: "Fans do not have the money to spend on baseball."[34]

In February 1931 the *Defender*'s Dan Burley lamented that subsequent to the league's annual business meetings the month prior, business meetings from which the public and the press were barred, "nothing in the line of news has been heard . . . they might have been swallowed by an earthquake." Burley wrote that fans "don't even know the names of all the managers [or] who won the league pennant last year."[35] In fact, by late 1931, black baseball had regressed to its pre-1920 wilderness existence, with unaffiliated teams playing games wherever and whenever they could find them.

With no Negro National League to cover in 1932, the *Defender* and *Courier* reallocated resources to college, high school, and even community sports. The newspapers also focused on basketball as their sports section's dominant topic longer into April and May than in previous years. Ashley B. Carter, president of the Union Church Athletic Association in Chicago, for example, regularly covered his association's games and events for the *Defender* during the NNL's dark period. His byline, absent before and after this period, appeared on coverage of the city league's baseball, basketball, track, and bowling. Both newspapers also published more on the Texas Oklahoma Louisiana and Negro Southern leagues, which were looked to by the black press to sustain the sport's future. The *Courier* covered the Southern League's meetings and games much as it had Negro National and Eastern Colored leagues prior to 1931, and the *Defender* published several articles with the byline of L. S. N. Cobb, who at the time was secretary of the Southern League.[36] Previously, as secretary to the St. Louis Giants in 1920, Lorenzo Cobb participated in the NNL's founding in Kansas City, and he served as secretary to the ABCs and Cleveland Hornets and in various capacities in the Negro leagues from 1920 through 1934.

The void in baseball coverage also was filled simply by creating events. The *Defender* sponsored several large athletic and social events throughout 1932 and covered them extensively in its news and sports pages. The events were more a response to the punishing economy than to the dearth of black baseball games, but these tournaments fulfilled several of the same roles as the Negro leagues and, unlike the Negro leagues, they were hugely, predictably successful. A Labor Day Weekend youth baseball tournament in 1932, for example, counted 2,000 participants. A softball tournament for girls the same summer attracted "thousands" of players, according to the newspaper, which called its program a "city-wide move to interest youths in a program of outdoor activities."[37] This civic involvement explains in part why the newspapers remained steadfastly behind black baseball even though the likes of Rube Foster, president of the Negro National League, and C. I. Taylor, owner of the Indianapolis ABCs—both black church and civic leaders in the 1920s, outspoken in their moralist proscriptions—yielded in the 1930s to a decidedly less respectable ilk of black owner in numbers runners Gus Greenlee, Rufus "Sonnyman" Jackson, John "Tenny" Blount, Tom Wilson, Robert Cole, Alex Pompez, and Abe Manley. The turnover in league leadership and team ownership is among the fundamental changes that occurred during the first half of the 1930s, and among those that saved black baseball from obliteration.

After a dark period that lasted more than a season, the Negro National League re-emerged in January 1933. An organizational meeting in Pittsburgh attracted twenty prospective owners, but only six ultimately fielded a team: the Crawfords, Grays, American Giants, Nashville Elite Giants, Indianapolis ABCs, and Baltimore Black Sox. The early going foretold of significant organizational challenges. The ABCs almost immediately relocated to Detroit, while Chicago moved its home games to Indianapolis, replacing the ABCs and leaving Chicago without a league entry. The Black Sox pulled out just weeks into the season, while the Grays were bounced out of the league in June for raiding Detroit for a pair of players. The Columbus (Ohio) Blue Birds did not have the financing to continue the season, so Greenlee consolidated the team with two others to form the Cleveland Giants.

In a wildly inaccurate rewriting of history, Monroe described the reorganized, Gus Greenlee-run league as profoundly challenged compared to the gleaming structure built up by Rube Foster. In the *Defender*'s casting of history, that first Negro National "had no general problems," while "today it has nothing but. The passing of Foster introduced problems into the sport."[38] In reality, Foster's empire tottered and fell as a house unceasingly divided against itself, but at least Monroe did not presume business and athletic success for the new league or, unlike previous commentators, uncritically predict that the upcoming season would be black baseball's "best ever." Monroe's coverage of 1933's "closed door meetings" put responsibility for safeguarding the sport this time in the trust of the athletes rather than with the owners, and he called on players to take steep pay cuts to ensure the viability of the league. A $1,600 monthly salary cap enabled a lowering of ticket prices to twenty-five and thirty-five cents in 1933 from the previous range of seventy-five cents to one dollar.[39]

Demonstrating the power shift eastward, to Pittsburgh and away from Chicago, the 1933 organizational meetings were held in the Steel City rather than Chicago, Indianapolis, or Kansas City. After Rube Foster's death, the Chicago American Giants drifted and ultimately collapsed. Though they were later revived under black businessmen Robert A. Cole, a former Pullman porter, and Clifford O. Stark, Foster's partner in a garage and automotive parts business, the American Giants would never recover the prominence they achieved under Foster. Gus Greenlee's Pittsburgh Crawfords were the heirs apparent.[40] Kansas City's decision not to join the league also signaled a generational change since the Monarchs were the last of the league's founding members from the inaugural 1920 season.

From Foster's Schorling Park, the sport's locus of power shifted to Gus Greenlee's Greenlee Field, one of the first and finest Negro league-owned ballparks. Built in six months at a cost of between $75,000 and $100,000, the ballpark served, in one historian's words, as "a particular point of pride" for Pittsburgh's black Hill District since it was one of the very few black-owned playing venues.[41] Black-owned ballparks were rare throughout the history of the Negro leagues, forcing most black teams to play when a field's home team, almost always white, played on the road. When Greenlee Field opened, it was the league's only venue controlled by the team. Nashville's Elite Giants had to play in a minor league park, Sulphur Dell, home to the Southern Association Nashville Vols. The ABCs began the season in Perry Stadium, which opened in 1931, renting it from Indianapolis Indians' owner Norman Perry. The venue situation was so bad that the Grays, bitter rivals of the Crawfords, were forced to play home games on the Craws' home field, forcing Cum Posey to pay Greenlee for the privilege.

Greenlee Field's turnstiles admitted baseball fans for the first time on April 29, 1932, and to dedicate black Pittsburgh's new gem, *Courier* owner and publisher Robert L. Vann delivered the speech of dedication and threw out the first pitch. Ches Washington wrote that "all the color, glamour and picturesqueness that usually attends the opening of a big league ball park was in evidence."[42] *Courier* writer William G. Nunn celebrated the fact that the field had been "erected by a Negro, for Negroes, with Negroes as participating factors."[43] Nunn watched the five games between the Crawfords and Homestead Grays, a series between black baseball's elite teams, and wrote that the Craws were "a major league diamond outfit." The Pittsburgh team's major league-caliber play, equipment, field, and fans gave evidence to Nunn's evaluation.[44]

Official league power transferred through the chairmanship, which went from Rube Foster to Judge William Hueston, who began serving in the late 1920s, then again to Greenlee. A numbers king hard-wired into Pittsburgh's political, social, and civic scenes, "Big Red" Greenlee bailed out the *Courier* at least once financially, explaining in part the editorial freedom he enjoyed in the *Courier*'s pages. Greenlee's financial help was not uncommon. With limited access to capital, particularly from white-owned financial institutions, black entrepreneurs realized that economic cooperation was necessary in building up businesses in the black community.[45]

Greenlee used his famous Crawford Grill on Wylie Avenue to essentially control commerce on Pittsburgh's south side. Teaming up with Woogie Harris, owner of the Crystal Barbership also on Wylie, Greenlee "ran the city's rackets" and "earned his reputation from being fair," according to a history of black-run numbers games.[46] Leveraging his power, Greenlee became chairman of a re-formed Negro National League in late 1932 and set organizational meetings for early 1933. Much like the Chicago

American Giants before them, Greenlee's Crawfords were the best outfitted team in terms of uniforms, equipment, and transportation, and also like the Giants they were perennial champions. The Craws traveled in a seventeen-passenger Mack bus with a six-cylinder, seventy-nine-horsepower motor capable of generating speed of sixty miles per hour, according to the *Courier*.[47] For a team dependent on barnstorming, owning and controlling the means of transportation was no trifling matter.

Like Foster a dynamic personality and physically imposing man, Greenlee also shared Foster's entrepreneurial vigor. The Crawford Grill, a three-story restaurant and cabaret on Wylie Avenue, flourished as a social and entertainment hub much as the Cotton Club did in Harlem. Patrons included George Benson, Duke Ellington, August Wilson, Miles Davis, Dizzy Gillespie, and Louis Armstrong. When Satchel Paige married Janet Howard, a waitress at the Grill, in 1934, Bill "Bojangles" Robinson served as best man and provided tap dancing for entertainment. Lena Horne, among others, began her career at the Crawford, where she first sang "Stormy Weather," her signature song.[48]

Greenlee also managed and promoted light heavyweight boxing champion John Henry Lewis, among other fighters, occasionally using Greenlee Field as the fight venue. The *Defender* and *Courier* frequently mentioned Greenlee's proprietorship of the Grill and his involvement in boxing, but without exception avoided reference to his numbers businesses. In the black press, it is as if they did not exist. A tribute in Wilson's "Sports Shots" column is typical. Praising Greenlee on the 1933 season, Wilson thanked the magnate for sacrificing time and money "all because he feels he is honor bound to keep faith even though his associates fall by the wayside." Wilson made no mention of Greenlee's main source of income, the "Policy wheels," as the numbers games were called.[49] This reticence is ironic since the *Defender* itself participated in the illicit business by clandestinely publishing the winning numbers for at least a dozen different numbers games. The paper used some of its single-panel cartoons to display the numbers and sometimes printed winning combinations seemingly randomly in the text of stories and columns.[50]

Omitting the burgeoning business of gambling points to the importance of noting what the black press left out of its coverage. Numbers games became, according to one historian, one of the largest black businesses in the decade, reaching revenues of $100 million.[51] Flush with cash, the "policy kings," as the number runners were called, were empowered in the 1930s to make an aggressive move into professional sports. In basketball, the Chicago Crusaders and the Savoy Big Five are examples of successful professional teams backed by gambling money. Robert Abbott secretly supported the numbers runners because they were by some measures the biggest philanthropists in the black community.[52] As it did for Greenlee's profile, the newspapers burnished the images of Detroit Stars owner John "Tenny" Blount and Newark Eagles owner Abe Manley. For the *Courier*, Manley was "the man who has invested more in the game, as a sport and as an investment, than anyone," a "quiet-spoken business man," and a "lover of the game [with] unbounded faith in the future of the game."[53] Manley's numbers ventures also were not mentioned.

The only instances of coverage of the numbers games in either the *Courier* or *Defender* in the 1930s, at least in connection with black baseball, are one by Posey in his "Posey's Points" column and another in a front-page story on the extradition of New York Cubans owner Alex Pompez, a principal in the Eastern Colored League. Posey argued that lotteries should not be considered illegal, at least not in the same way as burglary and "other major crimes" since the backers of lotteries, including Posey, did not compel individuals to play.[54] Pompez was extradited by Cuba to New York to face a number of charges related to his gambling concerns. In its coverage of the high-profile investigation, the *Courier* estimated Pompez's annual revenues from his numbers syndicate at five million dollars.

One reason for the *Defender*'s silence on the prominence of gambling-generated financing for black baseball was the friendship of Al Monroe with some of Chicago's biggest numbers runners, the Jones brothers, including Ed, George, and McKissack (Mack) Jones. Monroe accompanied the brothers on trips, writing some of his "Everybody Goes When the Wagon Comes" columns from the road during the decade.[55] The Jones brothers were indicted by a federal grand jury in March 1940 for tax evasion; they settled with the government in May by agreeing to pay $500,000.[56]

The same economic and demographic realities underpinning Greenlee's and the Crawfords' rise explain why during this same period the *Courier* displaced the *Defender* as the nation's largest black weekly. The *Courier* began challenging the *Defender* in the late 1920s and early 1930s, and sports coverage was a factor. Louis received more front-page mentions, more headlines, and more coverage than any other individual in the 1930s as boxing took on an important symbolic role in black communities nationally. Louis, who became world heavyweight champion in 1937, was featured in the *Defender* eighty times between 1933 and 1938; the second-most referenced individual in the paper during the same period was Haile Selassie, leader of Ethiopia, which Italy had invaded. He was mentioned twenty-four times.[57] Coverage of Louis and black baseball, including the local Crawfords and Grays, helped carry the Pittsburgh paper to the top in its silver anniversary year, 1937.[58] According to an official audit that year, an audit that *Courier* publisher Robert L. Vann finally agreed to cooperate with, the newspaper had a weekly circulation of 250,000, a high water mark reached by the *Defender* more than a decade earlier. When pass-around circulation is added, actual *Courier* readers probably numbered around one million. The *Defender*'s audited circulation, meanwhile, slipped to 100,000 in 1933 and to 73,000 in 1936.[59]

The *Courier*'s success came during a decade especially cruel to baseball, both white and black. According to one historian, "one minor league after another was folding up and the framework of the professional baseball world was giving signs of complete decay."[60] Seeing the sport's role as an important tonic during difficult economic times, President Roosevelt told the *New York Times* that baseball "had done as much as any one thing in this country to keep up the spirit of the people."[61] Roosevelt's tribute coincided with the suggestion from the National League's president that 1933 might "put to the acid test" the popularity of the sport. People "will budget their expenses and choose only what promises them the most enjoyment," John A. Heydler wrote.[62]

With the return of the Negro National League, the business-based rationale for professional baseball's integration became more prominent in black press coverage. This argument presented several exhibits of blacks' readiness to enter the mainstream, all of them from the early and mid-1930s: the East-West Classic all-star game started in 1933; Negro league participation in the previously all-white semi-professional tournaments in the Midwest; the supremacy of boxing titan Joe Louis; the four gold Olympic medals brought home by Jesse Owens; and a vibrant black entertainment scene populated by the likes of Armstrong, Ellington, "Bojangles" Robinson, Horne, Josephine Baker, and Marian Anderson. White society simply could not ignore these talents.

The money generated by big events such as the Negro leagues' annual all-star game, the doubleheaders between quartets of black teams in major league parks, and Louis's fights, which filled venues such as Comiskey Park and Yankee Stadium, provided concrete evidence that integration was in everyone's best business interests. Major league baseball at the same time very publicly lamented its sagging attendance and lack of profits.[63] In fact, according to White Sox owner Bill Veeck, only one of major league baseball's sixteen teams made a profit in 1933. The fiscal logic of integration was not lost on at least a handful of major league owners, who as early as the late 1930s began plotting to begin hiring black talent.

Exhibit A in the argument for integration's economic benefits was the East-West Classic, an all-star spectacle inaugurated in 1933 that was unlike any other in baseball, white or black, and, other than Joe Louis's fights, the biggest sporting event in black America.[64] Though newspapers and baseball would never again reproduce the close partnership used to found the Negro National League in 1920, they did join forces to make the Classic possible. The annual showcase began in August 1933 and quickly added a second edition in New York City that same year. It endured into the 1950s and often outdrew the major league all-star version. Long-time Negro leaguer Buck O'Neil described the Classic in his autobiography as "something very special." While the big leagues left the choice of players up to the sportswriters, the Negro leagues left it up to the fans. "After reading about great players in the *Defender* and *Courier* for so many years, they could cut out that ballot in the black papers, send it in, and have a say," O'Neil wrote. "That was a pretty important thing for black people to do in those days, to be able to vote, even if it was just for ballplayers, and they sent in thousands and thousands of ballots."[65]

The game was principally about racial pride. Blacks came from all over every year, scheduled their vacations around the event, and required that extra passenger cars be added to the Illinois Central and Union Pacific trains.[66] "We kept the game in Chicago because it was in the middle of the country, and people could get there from all over." O'Neil wrote. "In Chicago, all the black stores would sell tickets to the game. . . . Ben Franklin Department Store, Monarch Tailors, Harry's Men Shop, the South Center Department Store, they'd all have a big sign out, EAST-WEST TICKETS SOLD HERE."[67]

The East-West game owed its existence to the black press. Greenlee, Posey, and writers Roy Sparrow (Pittsburgh *Sun-Telegraph*) and William G. Nunn (*Courier*) collaborated to stage the all-star game. Greenlee provided the necessary marketing muscle and financial backing, and he hired Sparrow to coordinate publicity.[68] Sparrow sent press releases to fifty-five black weeklies and ninety white dailies, which succeeded in generating coverage nationally. The black press relentlessly promoted the event. The *Courier* ran four stories on the upcoming game in its August 4, 1934 issue, then another five stories promoting it in the August 25 issue. The league also bought advertising for the Classic in the *Defender* and the *Courier*, among other papers. Only the big weeklies could get the word out beyond Chicago and into the heartland. The *Defender* and the *Courier* exclusively administered fan voting for player selections, printing the clip-out ballots weekly and doing all the tabulations. Their writers acted as official scorers for the game. Their publishers officiated, throwing out the games' first pitches and spectating with Chicago's public officials. Their sports sections and front pages celebrated the event as evidence that black society had all that white society boasted and that black baseball talent belonged in the major leagues.

Perhaps because of the newspapers' cooperation in staging the event, cooperation that gave them a stake in its success, flirtations with and public commitments to objective reporting ended with the campaign to make the all-star Classic one of the black community's premier events. According to one account, the two newspapers split a five percent cut of the gate, though it is not clear if the money was a quid pro quo, rewarding the papers for the publicity and promotions.[69] Certainly the payoff incented the newspapers to do what they could to make the event a success. The *Defender* reported in anticipation of the first all-star game that it was "gaining daily in momentum as its popularity sweeps the nation like a relentless hurricane," a description that given the share of the take the *Defender* was to get points to a clear conflict of interest.[70] The five percent share also explains in part how the Chicago paper could cooperate with the *Courier*, its primary competition for readership. The *Defender* described the alliance as an effort to "make this venture one of the greatest success stories in sporting history."[71]

By all accounts, the inaugural East-West game in 1933 proved a triumph, a gleaming gem in the rough of another economically difficult black baseball season. Despite rains and the Depression, a "howling, thundering mob" of 20,000, almost all black, turned out to watch the West, led by Rube Foster's half-brother, pitcher Willie Foster, beat the all-stars from the East.[72] When combined with the "O Sing a New Song" pageant of music and dance held annually at Chicago's Soldier Field, the August weekend could plausibly be described, as the *Defender* put it, as the "biggest event in the history of the Race."[73] More than 150 black vendors, ticket takers, ushers, and concession operators worked the game.

The East-West accomplished what the Colored World Series could not. In bringing together so much of the black community, and in presenting an undeniable quality of play on a stage normally used to showcase major league talent—Comiskey Park, the East-West Classic attracted positive attention in mainstream society, from mainstream media, and among white professional baseball's leadership. The black press catalogued this attention and added it to the case for acceptance and for the right to an opportunity to "make the grade," a phrase the *Courier*'s Wendell Smith would frequently use to refer to integration. Monroe, for instance, noted that while the all-star teams played before 20,000, the Cubs played across town that same day before 8,000 fewer fans.[74]

The *Courier*'s Ira Lewis observed in an impassioned critique of daily newspaper coverage of blacks that the attention from mainstream media on this lone occasion centered on something positive and not on the criminal. "We are not only persecuted but crucified, as it were, before the bar of public opinion by the city editors of the daily press, who symbolize the word Negro with crime, Lewis wrote."[75] A story distributed by the Associated Negro Press and picked up by the *Courier* and *Amsterdam News*, among other papers, reprinted *Chicago Daily News* reporter Henry L. Farrell's praise of three all-star game participants—Dick Lundy, Oscar Charleston, and Mule Suttles. According to Farrell, one of the few in the daily press to comment on the first Classic, the three players were "good enough to play in the white major leagues," if only they were "a lighter shade." The losing East team could have replaced the lowly Reds or Red Sox in the major leagues, Farrell wrote, and done quite well in their stead.[76]

In 1935, 60,000 attended the musical pageant, or enough to fill "all the hotels," including the black Grand Hotel at 51st and South Parkway and "every train" coming into Chicago. About 30,000 filed into Comiskey the next day for the all-star game, 10,000 more than witnessed the major leagues' version that same season.[77] The pageant-game combination quickly became a showcase for blacks nationally, and it demonstrated that sports and the arts could bring the races together. The *Defender* made this argument after the 1936 Classic, which 30,000 attended, that the time for integration had come, and the newspaper encouraged fans again to write Commissioner Kenesaw Mountain Landis.[78] For Ches Washington the game also demonstrated the caliber of Negro league play, proving to fans of both races "that there are several stars in colored baseball who could make the grade in the major leagues."[79] Nunn shared Washington's appraisal, writing from the Comiskey Park press box that the players on stage at the Classic "had the stamp of 'major league' quality written all over them." Nunn also complained that the game lacked proper announcing and was not broadcast.[80]

John L. Clark emphasized the East-West Game's success in business terms, pointing out that ten people were paid full-time to organize the game, another ten to run it, and fifty to one hundred young people to sell tickets and concessions. Forty ball players, six coaches, two managers, and four umpires also benefited from the profits, all of which "passed through the hands of Negroes," he wrote, forgetting the rents paid to the White Sox for the use of Comiskey Park.[81] For Clark, the game was a model of business success for the black community. The *Courier*'s columnist in Philadelphia, Rollo Wilson, also saw the all-star game's impact in its balance sheet. In fact, Wilson emphasized the importance of a sound business foundation for black baseball perhaps more than any other writer during the decade, a priority expected from Wilson's position as commissioner of the league in 1934. Part of his income, therefore, was derived by the league's and all-star game's successes.

Two weeks after Clark's 1934 accounting, Wilson correctly argued that economics and only economics would open up big league baseball, and that the East-West Game provided the "opening wedge." People would notice the $4,700 pocketed by the White Sox for use of their park. Scouts had observed superstar players Satchel Paige and Mule Suttles. Fans had witnessed "a new, all-time high" for Negro baseball, Wilson wrote.[82] The Classic's big numbers and smooth operation gave Negro league baseball a measure of credibility. Harry Grabiner, vice president of the White Sox, told the *Defender* that he "unhesitatingly approved" of the men running the Classic, men who had "not once fallen down on promises or put up arguments just for the sake of arguing."[83] Grabiner's words gave black baseball's owners reason to hope because many of these businessmen aspired to join big league baseball when their players gained entry.

Even before the Classic, white sportswriters began raising the level of debate on baseball's exclusionary policies. The *Defender* specifically credited the New York *World-Telegram*'s Heywood Broun, who wrote in February 1933—six months before the East-West game—a lengthy article critical of the major leagues' patent unfairness.[84] His column was a reaction to a racist sketch performed at the New York Baseball Writers Association dinner that month, a dinner at which Broun also delivered a speech criticizing baseball for prohibiting blacks. Reprinted in full by the *Defender* and syndicated to hundreds of white dailies, Broun's column provided a blueprint of sorts for the argument the black press would make in the next decade, an argument centered on athletic and financial viability. In his article, Broun highlighted the talent on Negro league team rosters. He also quoted the major leagues' official position of having no "set rule" against players of color. He cited Paul Robeson's success as an All-American football player at Rutgers and called black sprinter Eddie Tolan "almost a team in himself." If Tolan could compete against international opponents, Broun asked, why couldn't a black play professional baseball?[85] Adding blacks to the major leagues would in Broun's opinion provide a more "colorful" style of play and "attract a number of Colored rooters."[86]

The black press would pick up on each and every one of the columnist's points in its crusade to crack the color barrier. Ches Washington followed up Broun's widely read polemic with a four-month-long "symposium" presenting the views of big league baseball's owners, managers, players, and sportswriters. In asking why blacks were barred from the major leagues, Washington was indirectly challenging the Gentleman's Agreement among baseball's owners not to integrate, an unwritten pact to which Broun's article drew attention. Among those Washington interviewed were National League president John Heydler; Charles Comiskey; the secretary-treasurer of major league baseball, Leslie O'Connor; and Gerry Nugent, president of the Philadelphia Phillies. Though Washington's summer symposium spurred no concrete action, it flushed out into the open the positions of some of baseball's top officials, showing some with seemingly open minds and others trying to avoid the issue altogether.[87] The *Defender* also saw opportunity in the awareness Broun had created and advocated a letter-writing campaign to put pressure on major league baseball. The paper urged readers to write Landis, providing his full mailing address to encourage response.[88] The Commissioner's office subsequently was "overrun with letters," according to the *Defender*, with several hundred readers answering the paper's call.[89] Neither Landis nor baseball's all-white owners responded to the letters or to the *Defender*'s public campaign.

Despite Landis's silence, there were some signs of openness, and from unexpected places. *The Sporting News*, for example, a publication that served practically if not officially as the voice of major league baseball, declared in its pages in January 1934 that some of the best baseball players were not eligible to play "but for the color line!," an endorsement of black baseball talent and a dramatic admission in print to the practice of exclusion. The weekly's statement drew headlines in the black press, which repeated its pledge to continue to push for at least a chance for black players to make big league rosters.[90]

In the mid-1930s, Shirley Povich of the *Washington Post*, Dan Parker of the New York *Daily Mirror*, Jimmy Powers of the New York *Daily News*, and other mainstream writers also began criticizing baseball's segregated state. Westbrook Pegler had called baseball to account as early as 1931. The black press often reprinted large portions of these supportive columns, which were almost without exception more critical of major league baseball than anything written by black press sportswriters. A Los Angeles *Post Record* column in July 1935, for example, grilled the "master minds" of baseball for "pretending that the only people who have a right to play baseball, or watch it being played, are whites." The writer, Gene Coughlin, wrote that the major leagues' refusal could not be explained sociologically, democratically, or economically, especially with big league ball in such need of a drawing card.[91] The *Defender* and Al Monroe were not nearly as pointed as Coughlin, Povich, and the other mainstream newspaper columnists. One month before Coughlin's critique, Monroe merely "wondered" why and how major league baseball could explain away its unwillingness to open up to Race players.[92]

Eager to use baseball's hypocrisy as a critique of capitalism, the Communist press, too, joined the struggle and in 1936 this support was welcomed by black sportswriters. The Communist press seized on the issue, seeing in baseball a microcosm of what Chris Lamb and Kelly Rusinack described as "all that was wrong with American capitalism."[93] When Wendell Smith and Sam Lacy realized, however, they would be considered guilty by association by major league baseball, they began distancing themselves, their newspapers, and their crusade from socialism and, specifically, from the *Daily Worker* newspaper. Rusinack and Lamb researched involvement by the Communist press, specifically the *Daily Worker*, which published hundreds of articles in its campaign to integrate baseball, and they found that while the Communist Party was certainly interested in using sports to advance its own political philosophy, "its most effective effort to influence American society—the campaign against segregation in baseball—emphasized democracy, not communism."[94] Still, the taint of communism was enough to inspire the black writers to distance themselves from the *Worker*.

Beginning in the latter part of the 1930s, writers such as Smith at the *Courier*, Lacy at the *Afro-American*, Joe Bostic at the *People's Voice*, and Lester Rodney at the *Daily Worker* took their protest to the offices of major league baseball. The campaign to integrate would move in this time period from the sports pages to the front pages as the black press turned more activist. The campaigning would not have been possible had it not been for the attention brought to black athletic achievement by mainstream media, which was prompted by black press efforts to build up and to promote Negro league baseball.[95] In the late 1930s black sportswriters could count many more allies in their struggle than when the decade opened.

Chapter Five
Interventionism

A snub on a sandlot introduced Wendell Smith to baseball's inviolable color line. A high school senior playing American Legion baseball in Detroit, Smith pitched his team to a 1–0 playoff victory. After the game, a top scout for the Detroit Tigers, Wish Egan, signed Smith's catcher and boyhood friend, Mike Tresh, to a major league contract. Tresh would play sixteen seasons of big league baseball. Egan also secured the services of the losing pitcher. He did not offer a contract to Smith.

"I'd sign you, too, if I could," Egan told the young pitcher. Decades later, after a celebrated career in journalism, Smith cited Egan's words as inspiration to dedicate himself to contributing "something on behalf of the Negro ballplayers." Fortunately for the black press, and for black baseball, Smith chose to make his contribution through a conspicuously activist journalism that sought better treatment of blacks everywhere, beginning with those on the baseball diamond.[1]

A freshly minted graduate of historically black West Virginia State College, Smith roared onto the baseball scene and into the sports pages of the *Pittsburgh Courier* in October 1937, writing with a force and flair that immediately distinguished him from his colleagues. Unlike Ches Washington, who Smith would replace as the *Courier*'s sports editor in 1938, the young writer did not reflexively accept segregation and with it the implicit subordination of blacks. Smith and his counterpart and contemporary at the *Afro-American*, Sam Lacy, not only covered Negro league baseball's efforts to force integration, they became directly involved themselves. This direct participation on the part of sportswriters during the late 1930s and early 1940s marks this phase of the integration campaign as starkly different from those of the 1920s and early 1930s, and it offers a sharp contrast to mainstream sports journalism of the period, as well. Mainstream journalism by this time no longer emphasized or embraced campaigns or crusades. In

1946, a leading journalism textbook, for example, declared that the "days of writing crusading stories are far past."[2]

For much of the previous two decades, black sportswriters preached to the converted. In the late 1930s and even more so in the 1940s, Smith and Lacy combined eloquence in print with activist intervention and dogged persistence to expand the campaign beyond the black community. They took the campaign to the white major league baseball owners, where ultimate power to bring down the bar resided, and in this they enlisted support from white sportswriters at the big dailies.

The crusade grew especially active during and after World War II, a period during which black Americans became significantly more active and confrontational on social and civil rights issues. Though economic conditions for blacks deteriorated during the years between the wars, the period saw growth for the black press in terms of readership and influence, growth that fueled an expansion in the black protest movement. As a minority group press, the newspapers of the period served to define concepts of race and racial struggle. "Its writers were thus sincerely involved in the race's problems," wrote black press historian Charlotte O'Kelly.[3] The late 1930s also was a period during which the country was, according to Smith, "turning fairly liberal, a time when people became very conscious of the fact that Negroes were not playing in the major leagues."[4] The black press generated much of this awareness by making first-person intervention a natural response if not an implicit duty. A content analysis of coverage during 1944 and 1945, for example, reveals that among Smith's goals of the black press writer were economic opportunity and full integration.[5]

Smith's involvement in this new interventionism was multi-dimensional. In 1938 and 1939, for example, his second and third years with the *Courier*, he canvassed nearly fifty big league players, managers, and executives specifically on the issue of integration. He argued frequently and forcefully in his columns and in his regular beat coverage for an end to the unwritten rule that banned blacks from big league rosters. Smith arranged face-to-face meetings between members of the black press and top officials of major league baseball. In the mid-1940s, Smith arranged tryouts for Negro league players with big league teams. Perhaps most crucially, he specifically recommended Jack Roosevelt Robinson, a shortstop with the Kansas City Monarchs, to Branch Rickey, president of the Brooklyn Dodgers, as the black player who could "make the grade" in the major leagues and take black baseball to the promised land.[6]

Like Smith, Sam Lacy first became involved in efforts to integrate baseball in 1937, as sports editor at the *Washington Tribune*, a relatively small black paper in his native Washington, D.C. He joined the paper full-time in 1934 and, according to one historian, was, at least initially, "ambivalent toward major league integration."[7] This ambivalence changed to activism in November 1937 when Lacy wrote baseball's commissioner, Kenesaw Mountain Landis, to recommend that baseball's owners "express themselves" on the absence of blacks in the big leagues. Landis's response not surprisingly was silence, so Lacy worked locally, meeting instead with Washington Senators owner Clark Griffith and covering and promoting the city's Negro league team, the Homestead Grays. Lacy's December 1937 meeting with Griffith was cited by historian Brad Snyder as "the beginning of Lacy's campaign to integrate baseball."[8] For the seven months following the conference, Lacy penned a column in the *Tribune*, "The Pro and Con on The Negro in Organizational Baseball," in which he included letters of support for integration written by prominent Washingtonians and quoted reactions from white sportswriters.[9] Lacy's influence and reach widened considerably when he joined the larger *Afro-American* in 1939 as a sportswriter and columnist.[10] After a brief flirtation with professional sports—he spent the 1941 season managing the black basketball team, the Washington Bruins—and parts of 1942 and 1943 with the *Chicago Defender*, Lacy returned to the *Afro-American*, where he remained for more than fifty years.[11]

Like Smith, Lacy was guided and motivated professionally by personal experience. He grew up working part-time jobs at Washington, D.C.'s Griffith Stadium, which served as home to both the Senators and, off-and-on, to the Homestead Grays.[12] Lacy helped with daily Senators practices, did odd jobs at the ballpark, and sold concessions during games. He also played baseball for several seasons for black teams in Washington and Connecticut. Lacy was, therefore, an ideal candidate to confront Griffith with the hypocrisy of keeping blacks out of America's game, which Lacy regularly used his weekly column to do. Also like Smith, Lacy arranged meetings with major league baseball officials, and he helped to form a committee with the big leagues to study how best to accomplish integration.[13] He conducted surveys and wrote to and about white sportswriters to widen the campaign beyond the black community.

It is important to note also what Smith and Lacy did not do. Unlike Joe Bostic at the *People's Voice* in New York City or Nat Low at the Communist paper, the *Daily Worker*, both of whom regularly and directly confronted major league baseball and, specifically, the Dodgers' Branch Rickey, Smith and Lacy believed in quiet cooperation, particularly during the early part of this interventionist phase of the integration campaign. Though they often were aggressive in print, they also celebrated any development they viewed as progress and the people they credited with that progress. Behind the scenes, their direct involvement occurred without intimidation or threat of protest. "Through all of this I always tried to keep it from becoming a flamboyant, highly militant thing," Smith said, shortly before his death, of his involvement in the campaign. "I think that's why it succeeded. If there had been picketing . . . this thing wouldn't have developed the way it did."[14] In arguing against a proposed boycott by blacks of Griffith Stadium in 1939, Lacy wrote that picket lines would be "misplaced."[15] Smith and Lacy saw the owners more as the agents of change than as the chief obstacles to it. They reserved that ignominy for baseball's commissioner, Landis, who Lacy characteristically—and accurately—described in 1939 as "the big reason why no play has been made for colored performers."[16]

Smith naturally became the point person in the campaign because, according to Robinson scholar Jules Tygiel, in the 1940s Smith was "the most talented and influential of the black sportswriters."[17] Smith also had at his disposal the influence of the *Courier*, which in the late 1930s and throughout the 1940s was the largest black weekly in America. Its reach and readership gave Smith significant leverage when negotiating with and attempting to influence major league officials.[18]

Along with Lacy, Bostic, and the *Courier*'s Randy Dixon, Smith seemed to thrive on controversy, at least in print, and to much the same degree as his predecessors, Chester Washington, Al Monroe, and Fay Young, seemed eager to avoid it. Cum Posey commented on this difference in a January 3, 1942 guest column. Paying tribute to Washington, Posey wrote: "Going over his columns we have found that [Chester Washington] has never criticized a Negro athlete or a Negro athletic enterprise. . . . We must name him the 'Diplomat of Sports.'"[19] The young writers were victims of segregation in much the same way as the players and owners they wrote about, and in the 1940s a greater understanding of the costs of that segregation was developing.

Repeatedly turned down for membership to the all-white National Baseball Writers Association and barred from major league press boxes, this generation of sportswriters saw crusading and campaigning as their rightful roles. This perspective in part explains their often unorthodox methods, such as Smith's role as an employee of the Brooklyn Dodgers during Jackie Robinson's first year with the team, a time when Smith still performed the duties of *Courier* sports editor.[20] It also explains the black writers' solidarity in pressing for integration and in criticizing Negro league baseball. This solidarity in August 1940 produced the American Sport Writers Association, which elected Fay Young as its first president.[21] The association's list of officers reads like a Who's Who of black press sportswriters of the period. In addition to Wendell Smith, elected vice presidents were Art Carter of the

Afro-American, Eddie Burbridge of the *Louisiana Weekly*, Richard Jackson of the *St. Louis Argus*, and Herman Hill, the *Courier*'s correspondent in Los Angeles. A protégé of Lacy, Carter was a sportswriter for both the *Afro-American* and *Tribune*. He also worked in the 1940s as a part-time publicity director for the Homestead Grays and in 1946, at 34, became publicity director for the Negro National League. Russell J. Cowans of the *Detroit Tribune*, who would replace Young as sports editor of the *Defender* in the 1950s, was elected secretary of the new association, and Ed Harris of the *Philadelphia Tribune* treasurer. Board members included Dan Burley of the *Amsterdam News*, E. B. Rea of the *Norfolk Journal and Guide*, Bill Bagby of the Kansas City *Call*, Lucius Jones of the *Atlanta Daily World*, and Ken Jessamy of the *Cleveland Call and Post*. What the association accomplished is not known; the association's affairs were not reported in either the *Defender* or the *Courier*.

The willingness on the part of the new generation of writers to mix it up with the power elites was in evidence almost as soon as they arrived. Soon after joining the *Courier* in October 1937, Smith became harshly and colorfully critical of Negro league baseball's leaders and, in another departure from previous sportswriters, did so by name rather than hiding behind general statements and vague pronouncements. In one of his earliest "Smitty's Sports Spurts" columns, for example, Smith smartly ridiculed as "strange and inconsistent" the capricious decisions handed down by "Chief Justice [Gus] Greenlee" and "Justice [Cum] Posey," the "High Tribunal of Negro Baseball."[22] However, just as Lacy did in East, Smith allied with black baseball for the stated goal of integration. In 1938, for example, Smith sided with owners in criticizing his "strange tribe" for its support of major league baseball since the money they spent served only to perpetuate segregation. "Major league baseball does not want us," he wrote. "Despite the fact that we have our own teams and brilliant players, the most colorful in the world . . . we go elsewhere."[23]

This paradoxical position—of simultaneously calling for black separateness and distinctness *and* for the integration of society—would define much of Smith's writing for the *Courier* during this period. Though fully committed to and engaged in the struggle to integrate and, therefore, to make blacks full-fledged members of the dominant society, Smith also called on blacks to build up their own enterprises.[24] It is as if he wanted the pendulum between separation and integration to impossibly swing simultaneously in opposing directions, and at equal speeds.[25]

Smith's and Lacy's criticisms of black baseball's owners and officials, expressed as they were in the context of an obvious affinity for and friendship with the sport's players, can in part be explained by the writers' ages.

Smith and Lacy were contemporaries with the players and, therefore, not with the owners. The writers socialized with the players, so it should not surprise to see in the same columns praise of the athletes' play *and* scathing commentary on the leagues' shortfalls. The deficiencies, from the perspectives of Smith and Lacy, were primarily those of ownership, and they included a lack of organization and planning, a dearth of comprehensive or regularly kept statistical records, the need for an independent commissioner, the lack of a working press or publicity office, inconsistency in the staging of championships or world series, and the lack of a balanced schedule.

As part of his self-styled campaign to win baseball's integration, Smith proposed in January 1939 an organization similar to the NAACP and pledged to fight segregation with the association's members "until we drop from exhaustion."[26] This distinctly black organization would paradoxically labor for its own uselessness and irrelevance as the voice for an oppressed and excluded minority, a parallel with the self-immolating goals of the black press itself. If and when Smith's stated goals were realized, there would be no need for black baseball, a dilemma perhaps only the hindsight of history can put in relief. Smith demonstrated little awareness of this dilemma in his *Courier* coverage, and the same was true of Lacy and Young.

In the late 1930s and early 1940s, Smith's distinctive style and insight as a columnist rapidly matured. With the world at war, the young reporter and columnist compared the treatment of blacks in the United States with that of Jews in Nazi Germany. Because baseball in America was celebrated as a paradigm of democracy, of American moxie and fair play, the exclusion of blacks for Smith and Lacy made the sport an emblem for American hypocrisy.[27] Smith called the "closed door policy" in baseball a "great American tragedy" and "a blot on the Statue of Liberty, the American flag, the constitution."[28] When the United States entered the war, Smith reminded all-white major league baseball that it was "perpetuating the very things thousands of Americans [including a disproportionate number of blacks] are overseas fighting to end, namely, racial discrimination and segregation."[29]

One of Smith's more important contributions in the crusade to integrate came before America's involvement in the war—a series of interviews with forty players and all eight National League managers on whether blacks should be admitted into major league baseball and, if admitted, whether they could survive at the sport's highest level. Among those interviewed were players for the Pittsburgh Pirates, New York Giants, and Brooklyn Dodgers. Called the "Most Exclusive, Startling and Revealing Expose, of the Attitude of the Major League Players and Managers Themselves, Ever

Written," Smith's series weekly occupied a full page and sometimes two full pages of the *Courier*.[30] The campaign was but one manifestation of the *Courier*'s sense of mission. "The [newspaper] always had some kind of program going, a crusade for something of consequence," Smith said, reflecting on his career for Jerome Holtzman's book, *No Cheering in the Pressbox*. "I started in 1938 a crusade or campaign for the inclusion of Negro league ball players into the major leagues [and] the paper was elated. It got me raises. It really got me on my way [and] gave me a name in the sportswriting business because these stories were a revelation."[31]

Barred from major league press boxes, Smith instead conducted most of his interviews in the lobby of Pittsburgh's Schenley Hotel. His intent was to use his campaign to expose and, by exposing, eliminate one of the major leagues' most frequently stated excuses for failing to integrate, which was the belief that major league players, a large percentage of whom hailed from the South, would simply refuse to play with blacks. Smith's survey revealed the opposite—seventy-five percent were in favor of integration, a few players and managers enthusiastically so. Brooklyn manager Leo Durocher, for example, said he had played against blacks "who could play in any big league that ever existed," players including Satchel Paige, George "Mule" Suttles, and Josh Gibson. Years later, when asked if he would play Robinson should Rickey sign the shortstop, Durocher responded, "Would I use him? Hell yes. I'd sleep with him and watch him like a mother watches her newborn baby."[32]

If seventy-five percent were in favor, a quarter either opposed or refused to state an opinion. Casey Stengel, in 1939 manager of the Boston Bees, was in the latter category, uncharacteristically deferring the question to the owners. Bill Terry, manager of the New York Giants, flatly stated that blacks would never make the majors, a prediction the *Courier* put on its front page.[33] The prominent placement, however, reflected the minority of Terry's position, as well as the importance of Smith's efforts from the perspective of the paper to flush out the truth. Smith found most of Terry's own players in favor of ending the color ban.

Smith did not merely survey the players and managers but attempted to persuade them, as well, a role not inconsistent with a fighting press's mission. In his conversation with Terry, for example, Smith said he argued the Negro league player's position and tried to convince Terry that even "social mingling" of white and black players would not be a problem. He told Terry that blacks "travel all over the country with college football teams and encounter few difficulties."[34] Smith even recommended the players most qualified to make integration a reality—Buck Leonard of the Homestead Grays and Josh Gibson of the Pittsburgh Crawfords.[35] (When baseball's doors did finally open six years later, Rocky Mount, N.C., native Buck Leonard, arguably the best hitter and best first baseman in Negro league history, and Josh Gibson, almost certainly the Negro leagues' all-time best power hitter, were considered too old to make the jump.)

The launch of Smith's series coincided with the annual burst of publicity in the black press that preceded the East-West Classic all-star game. Smith's interview coverage dwarfed the space devoted to the all-important Classic, an imbalance that demonstrates the importance the *Courier* placed on Smith's campaign. White major league officials reported they were reading, and "with great interest," said Jimmy Long, publicity chief for the Pittsburgh Pirates. Long said he was speaking both for himself and for William E. Benswanger, president of the Pirates. Long also said Benswanger supported the admittance of colored players.[36] William Harridge, president of the American League, "admitted that he had been following the Pittsburgh Courier's expose," according to the *Courier*'s Ches Washington.[37]

Smith's survey clearly had an effect. Many white fans, perhaps even a majority, were not even aware of baseball's color line prior to Smith's surveys, which were picked up by, among others, the Pittsburgh *Post-Gazette*, *The Sporting News*, and the Associated Press, which fed hundreds of newspapers throughout the country. The survey series raised awareness of the Negro leagues and of the color bar, and it led to increased support for the crusade among white sportswriters and columnists.[38] Secondly, the survey's results showed that a majority of white athletes would either support integration or, at the very least, not oppose or protest it. Ches Washington called Smith's discoveries "revolutionary" in revealing how owners falsely "pass[ed] the buck" and blamed their players for the ban's continuance.[39]

Coincident with Smith's survey coverage was an incident involving New York Yankee outfielder Jake Powell, an event that galvanized the black community and revealed how systematically ignored blacks were in the white press. A guest on WGN Radio's pre-game show in Chicago, Powell told host Bob Elson that he spent the off-season in Dayton, Ohio, as a policeman, keeping in shape by cracking "niggers" over the head. As historian Richard Crepeau found, "the white press gave the incident and its aftermath considerably less space than did the black press."[40] The black community's anger over Powell's racism and major league baseball's and the Yankees' mild response to the player's misconduct were almost completely ignored by the dailies. The Chicago *Daily News*, for example, published only a small item on the bottom of the second page of its sports section.[41] *The Sporting News*'s coverage is particularly revealing. Commentator Dan Daniel wondered on page 1 whether the "Negro fans of New York" would forgive the Yankee player or "carry on the feud," framing the controversy as a test of the black community's ability to forgive and move on rather than as an example of baseball's institutional racism and insensitivity.[42] Daniel's story carried the headline, "Powell Slur To Bring Bar Against Impromptu Broadcasts By Players," suggesting that the import to *The Sporting News* was radio's accessibility to players and not any slight felt by America's blacks.

In contrast, the black press pounced on the Powell incident as evidence of professional sport's close-mindedness. The *Defender* argued that if blacks had been allowed entrance into major league baseball, the Powell incident would not have happened, "for as in Congress, legislatures and city councils, wherever we have elected officials, the presence of our men reminds—and demands—respect."[43] Two weeks after the WGN broadcast, the *Defender* reprinted in full Powell's statement of apology, a statement that included an offer to visit the newspaper to issue an apology in person.[44] While the *Defender* called for a boycott of the beer brewed by Yankee owner Jake Ruppert, in New York the *Amsterdam News* collected more than 6,000 signatures on a petition demanding Powell's unconditional release. Similar to Senate majority leader Trent Lott appearing on BET television to explain his pro-segregation remarks at Strom Thurmond's 100th birthday celebration, in 1938 Jake Powell toured Harlem with one of Harlem's civic leaders, Hubert Julian. He issued apologies and explanations at every stop, including at the offices of *Amsterdam News*. Neither the *Defender* apology nor the Harlem tour were reported in the white dailies.[45]

The Powell affair and Smith's groundbreaking reporting were overshadowed in the American consciousness by a world again at war. Powell quickly was forgotten, even by the black press, and Smith's campaign receded to the margins of the newspaper's sports coverage. In fact, the *Courier*'s sports pages from 1940 through the first half of 1942 infrequently referenced the color bar at all. Smith mentioned the ban only twice in 1940, once in May to compare major league baseball's undemocratic behavior to that of Hitler and the Nazis, and in August when he ridiculed big league baseball for prohibiting exhibitions against Negro league teams. "They have been embarrassed too many times!" he wrote, claiming that the "embarrassments" had made the case that "our teams have proven their worth in exhibition games [with] more dash, fire and hustle."[46] (Smith included in this same column mention of the "nation's greatest all-around athlete," a collegiate who "sparkled in baseball, football, basketball, and track"—Jackie Robinson. In addition to being a star running back for UCLA alongside Kenny Washington, Robinson was in 1940 the Pacific Coast Conference's top scorer in basketball, an all-conference shortstop, and a national collegiate broad jump champion.)

After the survey coverage ran, Smith turned his attention to boxing and football. Smith's switch may have had something to do with the ascendancy of football as a national sport and perhaps with residual frustration with big league baseball and its recalcitrance. His interest in boxing most likely had to do with that sport's growing importance to the black community, a popularity that rivaled and, on fight nights, eclipsed that of black baseball. Joe Louis, Sugar Ray Robinson, and a host of other talented champion black boxers were among the most famous black celebrities. Championship prizefights were plum assignments for black sportswriters, assignments a young, ambitious writer like Smith naturally would jump to get. He became the newspaper's primary boxing writer and, as a result, the *Courier*'s commentary on Negro league baseball was left to Randy Dixon, formerly sports editor for the *Philadelphia Independent* and briefly the Negro National League's secretary.

Dixon's columns for the *Courier*, "The Sports Bugle," were almost uniformly critical of the Negro leagues, and in them Dixon condemned with an intensity previously rare in the *Courier*. When combined with Smith's and Lacy's unvarnished if infrequent assessments of league affairs, the colorful criticism marked a break from previous eras of coverage. "The Negro National League is much ado about nothing," Dixon wrote. "Does the league accomplish anything at its meetings? No."[47] Because of leadership's inability to cooperate, Dixon recommended that the league "be added to the antique collection in the nearest museum" as a relic lacking any utility.[48] Another of Dixon's columns, from early 1940, roasted the magnates, a group the columnist often called the "the mag-nuts," in part because newspapermen had been excluded from the league's annual meetings that year in Philadelphia. Newspapermen were, however, prominent in the meetings, and as participants rather than as correspondents. C. B. Powell, chairman of the *Amsterdam News*, was nominated to become league president. (He did not win.) Dan Burley, also of the *News*, and Al Monroe of the *Defender*, also were nominated for league positions.[49]

A 1941 column by Dixon alluded to owners' efforts to have him muzzled and his column dropped, and Dixon did lower the heat in response. But he remained critical of a league he felt had become "its own worst enemy."[50] Whether or not the owners effectively pressured the *Courier* to check Dixon is unknown; only the indirect reference to owners' complaints appears in the newspaper's sports pages. Dixon continued to spotlight the owners' neglect in submitting to the black newspapers news, statistics, and game reports. The owners did not understand the "magic of printer's ink," he wrote, complaining that most of the news sent in had more to do with disputes between the owners than with the action on the field. News and bulletins that could have been "calculated to set John Fan to talkin'" were instead "conspicuous by their absence," Dixon wrote in May 1941, saying he would settle for a regularly published schedule and some box scores.[51]

Despite Dixon's weekly harangues, the *Courier* remained for the most part a friend to the leagues' top officials, particularly the Negro National League's Pittsburgh-based owners. The *Defender*, too, provided access to owners, especially Greenlee, Effa Manley, and Memphis Red Sox owner and long-time Negro American president, J. B. Martin.[52] Several articles on Martin and his troubles with Memphis police appear in the *Defender* in 1940 and 1941. A prominent pharmacist in the black community and civic leader, Martin was hounded by Memphis's sheriff because of Martin's political views and his position as the city's chairman of the Negro National Republican Committee. The treatment, which included "molesting" and searching "from head to foot" customers of Martin's pharmacy, eventually forced Martin and his brother, physician W. S. Martin, out of Memphis and northward to Chicago.[53]

Cum Posey continued to write his near-weekly "Posey's Points" column for the *Courier*, and in 1941 served on a committee to raise money for a memorial to honor *Courier* publisher Robert L. Vann, who died the year prior. Posey called the committee work "a pleasure." To honor a man he knew "not as a great journalist, or a business executive, or a political power," but as "just a regular fellow," was gratifying, the Grays' owner wrote.[54] Posey's committee financed the building of the Robert L. Vann Memorial Tower, which still stands at Virginia Union University in Richmond, Va., in front of the L. Douglas Wilder Library. Vann died in October 1940.

Gus "Big Red" Greenlee, owner of the Pittsburgh Crawfords, also had the *Courier*'s full, unremitting cooperation. When he announced that he was re-organizing his team in 1940, Greenlee got the lead story and a column of support from Smith.[55] Crawfords games were promoted, as was Greenlee's Crawford Grill on Wylie Avenue. Greenlee on at least one occasion loaned money to Vann and the *Courier* trust, and Vann and Greenlee were members of many of the same business and fraternal organizations. Regular Negro league game coverage was largely positive, as well. Opening day in 1940, for instance, was celebrated in the *Courier* with a half-dozen stories, all of them exuberantly positive, even as Dixon wrote in his column of the year as the league's "Showdown" season, describing the Negro National's very existence as a "nuisance."[56] Two of the more optimistic articles carried the headlines, "Expect Record Throng At Opener for Memphis" and "Cubans Have Players To 'Write Home About.'"[57]

The decade's first season did provide showdowns, including those between Pittsburgh and New York City for primacy in black baseball and between ownership factions—one led by Posey in Pittsburgh and another by the Manleys in Newark. The civil war divided the Negro National League and placed the black press again in the middle. Owners looked to the black papers as a mouthpiece in the battle for public opinion and as a weapon with which to bludgeon the opposition. In June 1940, as Jackie Robinson was breaking national track and field records at UCLA, the Manleys organized a meeting with sportswriters to state their case, principally as it related to their battle with the Crawfords and Grays for the services of pitching great Satchel Paige. Attending were Dixon, Dan Burley, Art Carter of the *Afro-American*, and Oliver "Butts" Brown of the *Newark Herald News*.[58]

Posey struck back, using his own column in the *Courier* to ridicule the Manleys' attempt at influencing the press and thanking the *Courier*, *Chicago Defender*, *Afro-American*, and *Philadelphia Tribune* for supporting black baseball "for years and years." Absent from Posey's tribute was the *Amsterdam News*, New York's top black paper and a publication Posey had liberally praised in the 1930s as a welcome alternative to the *Courier*.[59] In the 1940s, Posey possibly viewed the paper as too close to the Newark-based Manleys, who were from New York City and still drew a significant number of fans from that market. Like Foster, C. I. Taylor, and Bolden before them, Posey and the Manleys found liberal space in the black papers in which to lobby support for their positions.

In Washington, D.C., Lacy also applied pressure on black baseball, criticizing the quality of play on the field and, like Dixon, citing a lack of professionalism among black baseball's owners that prevented them from consistently informing the press and the public and allowed them to continue to raid players from fellow league members' teams. "Perhaps there is something to the contention that we are keeping ourselves down," he wrote in May 1941.[60] Lacy also criticized the Grays' hiring of a white publicity agent, Joe Holman, a writer with the *Washington Times-Herald*, who not only failed to generate coverage of Homestead by the white dailies, but alienated the black press in the process, according to Lacy. The Grays hired "a downtown (ofay, if you please) sportswriter to do their publicity," he wrote. "Ho hum! Incidentally, it was the same scribe who only a few moments before had told me he thought the best chance for colored players to break into the big leagues lay in their ability to 'clown.'"[61]

The Grays' strategy was not unique. In Chicago, a white promoter, Abe Saperstein, was hired by the East-West Classic's organizing committee to generate publicity in the white daily newspapers and on radio. Owner of the Harlem Globetrotters baseball and basketball teams, Saperstein had previously handled publicity work for the East-West game, but he did not specifically cater to white dailies prior to 1941. His hiring was not criticized by black baseball, but it coincided with one that was—the addition to the Newark Eagles' payroll of a white publicity agent, Jerry Kessler, in 1936.[62] (Kessler was replaced in 1940 by Butts Brown, editor of the *Herald News*, Newark's leading black newspaper.) It is possible that because Saperstein brought money into the Negro leagues and was a vital connection in Chicago for black teams that he was not subjected to criticisms. Black baseball approached Saperstein. Bolden and Manley, however, had control over whom they hired, and both opted to hire white men, publicity men who could only aid the leagues indirectly by generating notice.

For its part, the *Defender* in Chicago focused more on repairing black baseball than on the racial divide. Baseball's resurgence on the city's South Side would have to begin with a new ballpark, according to the paper. The American Giants' venue—Schorling Park—burned down on Christmas Day 1940. Called South Side Park before 1911, Schorling was situated in the heart of the black community, on the north side of 39th Street (now called Pershing Road) between South Wentworth and South Princeton avenues. Foster's American Giants began playing in the 15,000-seat, wooden stadium in 1911 after the White Sox moved into the new steel-and-concrete Comiskey Park, and used Schorling as their home field until 1940.[63]

The *Defender*'s lead news columnist, Lucius C. Harper, was a lonely voice on the color barrier, commenting on major league baseball's willingess to hire "convicts, aliens, but no Negroes." No other *Defender* sportswriter mentioned the major leagues in any context throughout 1940 and 1941.[64] A Negro American League in disarray was the problem for Young, who felt it was "in about the worst shape . . . floundering around like a ship with a broken rudder in stormy seas," he wrote, while still serving as secretary to the league.[65] This estimation provided Young with yet another opportunity to memorialize Rube Foster, who he described in a back-handed critique of the Negro National as an iron-willed leader who stood for "peace and harmony" with other leagues. Given Foster's unrelenting wars with rival leagues and even his fellow league owners, Young's description is intriguing, as is his characterization of the owner's demolition of his own American Giants as having been done purely for the benefit of John "Tenney" Blount's Detroit Stars. Foster's American Giants won the Negro National's first three championships; the Stars never won more than a city title.[66] Also intriguing is Young's description of himself as Foster's "publicity agent," which perhaps explains his recasting of organized black baseball's first decade.

On the field, record-breaking crowds during the 1941 season helped raise black baseball's profile and give the sport a product major league baseball could no longer ignore. More than 30,000 gathered for black baseball at Briggs Stadium in Detroit, 20,000 at Yankee Stadium and at Sportsman's Park in St. Louis, and 12,000 each at Comiskey in Chicago and at Oriole Park in Baltimore. Most of these games were played as part of weekend doubleheaders, which became some of the black community's largest gatherings and social events, easily outsizing major league games played on the same days in the same cities. (Other big events for the black community included the Penn Relays in Philadelphia and the Howard-Lincoln football game played each fall over Thanksgiving weekend.) Because these crowds were part of the economic case being made to major league baseball, attendance numbers often took precedence in headlines in the black press, even over the games' final scores.[67]

The biggest jewel in the crowning year for black baseball that was 1941, the East-West Classic drew a record 50,000 and produced a contest several writers called "a dream come true." More than 10,000 were turned away on a day when only 16,000 paid to watch the Chicago Cubs play the New York Giants on the other side of town.[68] Both the *Courier* and *Defender* facilitated voting for all-star participants and provided extensive pre- and post-game publicity. The *Defender* included a four-page insert for the 1941 Classic, providing the event's history, a scorecard for the game, a page of photos, and previews of the mid-August clash.[69] The *Courier* anticipated a game that promised to be "the most spectacular, colorful, colossal extravaganza in the history of Negro baseball."[70]

As a footnote to the 1941 season, it is often overlooked that at this time Jackie Robinson was not major league baseball's likely barrier-breaker. Along with UCLA teammate and fellow running back Kenny Washington, Robinson was, however, a leading candidate to erase the re-drawn color bar in professional football, a sport that at the time enjoyed far less social and cultural status in America than baseball. Robinson starred in the annual college all-star game against the reigning professional champions, the Chicago Bears. Robinson "sparkled" in front of 90,000 in the all-stars' 37–13 loss to the Bears. He also led UCLA as its leading scorer in basketball. A September 1941 column by Dixon, for example, used Robinson's exclusion from pro football, not pro baseball, as Exhibit A in his case against America on charges of hypocrisy.[71] Even at this early date, the black press was helping to create Robinson's persona for his later breakthrough in baseball. Hot-tempered and the possessor of a keen sense of justice, Robinson was described by Randy Dixon as having "meritorious deportment." Six months later, Robinson was among the handful of black baseball players coming out of college who were cited as innocent victims of baseball's "unwritten law" against blacks.[72]

The *Courier*'s famous Double V campaign launched in 1942 provided a larger theme under which the goal of baseball's integration naturally fit. With the banner of winning victory at home as well as victory abroad, blacks protested for and demanded an end to discrimination in all walks of American life, including serving in the armed forces, securing jobs, obtaining insurance, and playing on the baseball diamond. As the Depression faded and blacks began to feel more empowered, and as the United States fought a war in the name of democracy abroad, blacks more stridently protested the denial of democracy and its benefits at home. The sports pages reflected this new boldness. When Satchel Paige's Monarchs played and defeated Dizzy Dean and his All-Stars at Wrigley Field in May 1942, for example, the first time a black team had been invited to Wrigley, the *Defender* used the occasion to call for an end to Jim Crow in baseball and to organize an interracial committee to lobby baseball's commissioner.[73] Young pointed to the 30,000-strong, integrated, mostly black crowd as proof the races could get along and that fans would pay to see integrated play. "These brown baseball fans are baseball hungry," Young wrote, hoping that the front office in Wrigley Field would "sit up and take notice."[74]

The paper assembled a group that included a prominent white hotel owner, William Harrison of the Grand Hotel, which served annually as headquarters for the East-West Classic; two attorneys, C. Francis Stradford and William Patterson; and the *Defender*'s Fay Young. The case the quartet made hinged on three factors: the demonstrated willingness of black and white athletes to work, play, and even room together; big league baseball's need for players in the wake of the war draft; and the testimony of big league players that they would play with and compete against black teammates.[75] (Precedents for interracial competition included industrial league basketball, college football, and college track.) Interaction between the races on the playing fields remained a theme for Young throughout the 1940s. The 1942 College All-Star football game, with its mixed race rosters and Southern white players, proved to Young, for example, that baseball's excuses for keeping the races separate were merely that. The newly organized National Basketball League, with its pair of integrated teams, also provided Young with a model to present to major league baseball.

Always immaculately dressed, the *Defender*'s sports editor embodied the philosophy of the newspaper, which was to show what the Negro could do and to show him at his best. This philosophy manifested itself in Young's critique of player behavior throughout his career, his urgings of fans to mind their manners at the ballpark, and his disdain for the constant bickering among Negro league team owners.[76] The philosophy also helps to explain why he would agree to serve as secretary to the Negro American

League for five seasons while directing his paper's sports coverage of the same league.

After the buildup to the war, both the *Defender* and the *Courier* refocused their attention on the integration of baseball in mid-1942 with a campaign that rapidly gained supporters within major league baseball and in organized labor, the clergy, and the Communist party. The campaign's renewal meant less attention on the Negro leagues in general, including their many organizational and structural flaws, but only for that 1942 season as attention shifted to the Double V campaign.

Even a casual reading of the leading black newspapers during this period reveals changes in the national mood vis-à-vis fair employment practices and equal rights. In June 1942, the National Maritime Union and the International Workers Order demanded that Landis drop baseball's color bar. Also in June a leading Catholic prelate in Chicago called for an end to the ban, and the International Open golf tournament in Chicago integrated for the first time, providing for baseball a "stirring example" of inter-racial harmony, Smith wrote.[77] In August, the New York City-based Catholic Interracial Council unanimously passed a resolution that called on the major leagues to integrate, a resolution that was described as a "plea for democracy."[78]

Summer 1942 also saw a demand from the National Athletic Commission of the International Workers Order, which represented 155,000 workers, including "several thousand Negroes," that the Chicago Cubs immediately integrate, a demand echoed by the Chicago Joint Council of Packing House Workers.[79] (Speakers at the union's meeting included the *Defender*'s Fay Young and Dave Malarcher, a long-time Negro league player and manager.) The United Furniture Workers of America, based in New York City, joined the movement in August by calling for blacks in professional baseball in a resolution passed "as an expression of the democracy we are fighting for" in Europe.[80]

Cracks of light were opening up in the previously solid wall put up by major league baseball. Philadelphia Phillies owner Gerry Nugent declared having "no objections" to signing qualified Negro leaguers, while Philip K. Wrigley, owner of the Cubs, told reporters the major leagues could accommodate blacks. Until and unless the public demanded change, however, Wrigley said the Cubs would remain white-only, and they did, for another full decade. It was Wrigley's declaration, made at a businessmen's luncheon, that prompted the International Workers Order in New York City to demand that the Cubs integrate.[81]

The black press got more than a helping hand from the Communist New York newspaper, the *Daily Worker*, which in March launched its own campaign: "Can You Read, Judge Landis?" Responsible for spawning several different petition drives and for sparking protests at premieres of the film, *Pride of the Yankees*, the *Daily Worker* campaign generated more than one million petition signatures by July and elicited the first comments directly from Landis on baseball's policy regarding integration.[82] Since the Communist party did not claim a million members, its petition drive successfully reached outside its core constituencies for support. The party had a booth at the East-West Classic, for example, at which members collected signatures. Historical scholarship on baseball's desegregation has for the most part failed to credit the *Daily Worker*, including its editor Lester Rodney and sports editor Nat Low, and the hundreds of articles the *Worker* printed in protest of baseball's color bar.[83]

In a statement printed by daily newspapers and the black press, Landis responded to the Communists' campaign by declaring for the first time that "there is no rule" against Negro players and that none had ever existed. He said that as many as twenty-five black players were probably good enough to play in the major leagues and that "Negro players are welcome." Black press sportswriters almost uniformly discounted Landis's statements, saying they did not represent any change in major league baseball's position. The *Defender*'s Harper, for example, wrote that no matter what Landis had said, "the old line is still there." The Commissioner's statements, Harper wrote, were designed merely to shift blame for the line and responsibility for its removal from Landis to the owners. Importantly, the commentator observed that it was not race that barred black players from the major leagues, but merely skin color. Mulattoes, after all, had "slipped in" and onto South Atlantic League teams. Gus Bonno, once a Negro league pitcher, briefly played in the major leagues, but as an Indian.[84] Young, too, believed that whites simply could not reconcile themselves to paying blacks the same salaries they paid their own. "Judge Landis decision? Bosh!" Young wrote.[85]

For the *Courier*'s Ches Washington, Landis's statement was an opportunity to credit Smith and the newspaper for the series of survey stories, the first of several such opportunities for self-congratulation, seemingly none of which the *Courier* passed up. Washington wrote that Landis had put the "matter of discrimination" on the owners, clearing as it did any owner to sign players of color.[86] On numerous occasions, the *Courier* and *Defender* each claimed primary responsibility for the fight to rid baseball of Jim Crow.[87] Smith chose instead to share credit with other sportswriters, black and white, for eliciting Landis's seeming new openness on race. He lauded white writers Jimmy Powers, Dan Parker, and Lloyd Lewis for "keeping the flame burning." Smith also credited Ira Lewis, Ches Washington, Rollo Wilson, Bill Nunn, and Cum Posey, all of the *Courier*; Sam Lacy and

Bill Gibson of the *Afro-American*; and the *Defender*'s Young. Sensing new momentum, Smith called on the NAACP, the Urban League, and the Elks to "shoulder arms . . . and carry on!"[88]

Landis's proclamation, coming on the third anniversary of Smith's survey series, appeared to have an effect, though likely one he did not intend. The Pittsburgh Pirates offered to grant black players tryouts, perhaps sensing a new environment and attitude toward integration and providing evidence that the previously solid front indeed was cracking. William Benswanger was quoted by the *Daily Worker* as agreeing to tryouts for black players on July 27, 1942.[89] Benswanger denied this to the *Pittsburgh Courier*, but he agreed to allow Smith and the *Courier* to select four black players for a tryout at Forbes Field sometime in late August or early September.[90] Benswanger's concession was celebrated with banner headlines on the *Courier*'s front page and sports pages and in several of its weekly columns. Prematurely, the Pittsburgh newspaper framed the tryouts as a climax to its long campaign to integrate baseball.[91] In what would become a formula for the treatment of major league moguls acting in support of the campaign, Smith devoted an entire column to pay tribute to Benswanger, calling him "unwavering, unselfish," the "Greatest Liberal in Baseball History," and the "Wendell Wilkie" of baseball. Other adjectives included "compassionate and benevolent," sincere, forward-thinking, and democratic.[92] The gushing praise perhaps explains why when Benswanger failed to follow through on his offer by never granting the tryouts, the *Courier* did not follow up on the story or hold the Pirates accountable. Embarrassment meant that, for the *Courier*, the story simply disappeared.[93]

It is unclear why the Pirates did not go through with the tryouts. Smith later said Benswanger simply got cold feet, and it is possible Landis pressured Benswanger not to hold the tryouts. Since the *Daily Worker* publicly took credit for securing them, it is also possible if not probable that Benswanger did not want to risk any association with Communists, a group he energetically and vocally opposed.[94] Benswanger is quoted by the *Courier* disparaging the *Daily Worker*, its sports editor, Nat Low, and Low's tactics. The Bucs' owner charged Low with putting words in his mouth.

Smith's initial stories on the Pirate tryouts were picked up by the Associated Press and daily newspapers throughout the country, which perhaps added to the newspaper's embarrassment when the club reneged. The *Defender*, however, noted the "run-around" given the Negro leagues by the Pirates, and Fay Young personally followed up with the Pirate organization and with major league baseball officials. His wires went unanswered, and his attempts to meet with club presidents at the Palmer Hotel, site of joint major league meetings, were dashed.[95] Young attended the annual meetings anyway, even though he was not invited. He spoke with sportswriters from the dailies and learned that "the general impression" among major league baseball officials was that the Communists were behind the move to integrate, a sentiment that, if genuinely held, cast millions of black baseball fans and the black press in the same boat politically as the Communist party. "How the Chicago Defender and millions of baseball fans of color could be classed as Reds simply because they demanded a fair deal for all?" Young asked.[96] The perception played into Landis' hands, however, allowing baseball to resist the inevitable for a few more years.

Recognizing the taint of guilt by association, the black press distanced itself from the *Daily Worker*, which previously had been treated as a welcome partner in the campaign. One *Courier* article in 1938, for example, celebrated Lester Rodney, editor of the *Daily Worker*, for "joining The Courier and Sam Lacey [sic], of the Washington Tribune, and Jimmy Powers, of the New York News, in their crusade against the racial bar in the big leagues."[97] In August 1947, however, Wendell Smith felt the need to "get straight for the record" how "Communist propaganda" was obscenely distorting the historical record on how the major leagues integrated. According to Smith, "the Communists had nothing to do with getting Negroes into the major leagues. . . . They are trying to take credit so they can sell even more vicious propaganda to millions of Negroes."[98]

One of the more important tasks undertaken by the black sportswriters was to reveal the various smokescreens major league baseball created to hide its policies on race, distractions that included painting the black and Communist presses with the same brush. Young in response asked owners in person and in print how millions of Negro league baseball fans could be lumped together with a political party. He called Brooklyn Dodger president Larry MacPhail on his statement that the Negro league owners themselves did not want integration for fear of what it would do to their livelihoods. The owners "have no such fear," Young wrote in his weekly *Defender* column, citing a lengthy interview with J. B. Martin, in 1942 the president of the Chicago American Giants. "I am for it wholeheartedly," Young quoted Martin as saying. "I cannot see where it would injure our baseball one bit and if it did I am still for it. . . . I can't figure who the Negro league officials are whom McPhail [sic] talked to."[99]

In fact, a major league baseball committee in 1946 was formed to look at "the Race Question," producing a confidential document that became public in 1951 at congressional hearings on baseball's monopoly powers and anti-trust immunity. Written by Larry MacPhail, who was in 1946 president of the Yankees, the document shows a group of businessmen concerned about losing the revenues generated by renting big league parks to black teams on weekends.[100] The report provides a startling historical document of racism at professional baseball's highest levels. According to the committee, blacks possessed "natural ability" but lacked "the technique, the coordination, the competitive attitude, and the discipline which is usually acquired only after years of playing in the minor leagues." Contradicting its own claims about the deficiencies of black players, the report also feigned fear for the Negro leagues' vitality: "The Negroes who own and operate these clubs do not want to part with their outstanding players," MacPhail wrote, knowing the professions of J. B. Martin and others to the contrary.

The lone voice in either the *Courier* or *Defender* preaching caution and declaring the growing movement to integrate baseball a challenge to the Negro leagues' vitality came from Cum Posey, a magnate long accustomed to minority-held positions. The Grays' co-owner used his weekly "Posey's Points" to warn readers of integration's potential harm to black baseball. He presciently wondered how a handful of blacks in the majors could be worth risking all of Negro league baseball: "We're more concerned about the 200 other colored players in this league and with our own investments," he wrote.[101] In an odd similarity to MacPhail, Posey felt that the many letters being written to Commissioner Landis, good-intentioned though they were, could strip the Negro leagues of the major league venues upon which the leagues depended. Clinging to Booker T. Washington's five-finger-as-one-hand philosophy, Posey wrote that it would be far better to "help build a major Negro baseball league playing every day baseball."[102] Though they were inconsistent with the newspapers' aims, Posey's views were not criticized in either the *Courier* or the *Defender*.

In another example of direct black press involvement, a New York City assemblyman, William T. Andrews, helped to organize a meeting with MacPhail at the Dodgers' offices in Brooklyn. Meeting with MacPhail for nearly two hours to discuss integration were, among others, Dan Burley of the *Amsterdam News* and Joe Bostic of the *People's Voice* of Harlem. Former Negro league commissioner Ferdinand Q. Morton and Fred Turner of the NAACP also attended, getting from MacPhail an acknowledgement that "Negroes are ready for the big leagues," which flatly contradicted the Dodger executive's testimony before Congress. They did not get any concrete concessions or timeline from the Dodger president, however.[103]

The *Defender*'s page-one columnist, Lucius Harper, summed up the obstacles to baseball's re-integration, predicting that it would require another "thirty years or so." Harper blamed Landis, the "southern influence" on organized baseball, and the white fan's failure to see baseball merely as sport rather than as "an event to vent his spleen on racial supremacy." Only when these three things changed, Harper wrote, could baseball "truly become a national sport worthy of its name."[104]

The 1942 season ended amidst profound concerns for the health of baseball in America, both black baseball and white baseball. Challenges included gas and tire rationings, a government prohibition on private bus use, and the loss of many players either to the war abroad or to defense industry production at home. Players leaving because of the war drained both the major leagues and the Negro leagues of talent. The major and minor leagues, diluted though they were in terms of quality on the field, clung to their refusal to play blacks or even to grant them tryouts. Even though major league baseball had featured a one-armed player, Pete Gray, the Pacific Coast minor league reneged on an offer to grant black players tryouts, just as the Pirates had done.[105] For Young, "things look[ed] dark" for baseball.[106]

Figure 1. From a December 1916 issue of the *Indianapolis Freeman*, the cartoon shows the disunity and division that plagued the Negro leagues. The Chicago American Giants' Rube Foster and C. I. Taylor of the Indianapolis ABCs are depicted fighting over the "World's Colored Championship," which Taylor's ABCs won in nine games.

Figure 2. The Black Sox scandal in 1919 gave the Negro leagues reason to celebrate "crooked" baseball's color bar. (From the October 11, 1924 *Pittsburgh Courier*)

Figure 3. Black newspaper publishers claimed that they had to accept ads for products like skin whiteners and hair straighteners just to survive, to bring in enough in advertising revenue. This "Sanitary Slicker" ad appeared in the July 1920 edition of the monthly *Competitor*, a newspaper supplement published by the *Pittsburgh Courier* in 1920 and 1921.

Figure 4. Barrel-chested Rube Foster virtually willed the Negro leagues into existence, leading the launch of the first successful Negro league, the Negro National, in 1920. National Baseball Hall of Fame Library, Cooperstown, N.Y.

Figure 5. The Paseo Street YMCA in Kansas City's black district, where the Negro National League was founded in 1929. Today it is a merely an eyesore, a blighted brick building located just two blocks from the gleaming Negro League Museum.

Figure 6. The Blue Room restaurant stands where The Streets Hotel once thrived as a nexus of black community life in 18th-and-Vine section of Kansas City.

Figure 7. The Birmingham Black Barons, including centerfielder Willie Mays, played their games at Rickwood Field in Birmingham, built in 1910. The ballfield is still used for city recreation league games and for the annual Rickwood Classic.

Figure 8. For white Birmingham Barons games in the 1950s, blacks had to sit in this right-field section of Rickwood Field.

Figure 9. Long-time sports editor of the black weekly *Pittsburgh Courier*, Wendell Smith is the forgotten man in the narrative of Branch Rickey's signing of Jackie Robinson. National Baseball Hall of Fame Library, Cooperstown, N.Y.

Figure 10. The *Afro-American*'s Sam Lacy, left, Dodger pitcher Dan Bankhead, and the *Courier*'s Wendell Smith wait for a flight in Daytona Beach. After Robinson's signing by the Dodgers, Lacy and Smith covered "The Jackie Robinson beat." National Baseball Hall of Fame Library, Cooperstown, N.Y.

Figure 11. No player contributed more to the success and, therefore, the longevity of the Negro leagues than Satchel Paige. He was the first Negro leaguer inducted into the National Baseball Hall of Fame. National Baseball Hall of Fame Library, Cooperstown, N.Y.

Figure 12. Jackie Robinson wrote his own epitaph, which reads: "A life is not important except in the impact it has on other lives." National Baseball Hall of Fame Library, Cooperstown, N.Y.

Figure 13. By the 1949 season, when this photo was taken, black teams had to resort to barnstorming to survive. The Indianapolis Clowns, which produced Henry Aaron, was the last Negro league team to play a full season. National Baseball Hall of Fame Library Cooperstown, N.Y.

Figure 14. Dr. J. B. Martin, seated center, was the longest-serving Negro league president, and he held the Negro American together into the 1950s. To his left in the February 1953 photo is Dr. W. S. Martin, Martin's brother and owner of the Memphis Red Sox. To his right, Tom Baird, an owner of the white-owned Kansas City Monarchs. Also pictured, standing, are William Bridgeforth of the Birmingham Black Barons, left; Syd Pollock, owner of the Indianapolis Clowns; Bill Margolis, Chicago American Giants; and Ed Gottlieb, owner of the Philadelphia Stars. (From the *Chicago Defender*)

Figure 15. This ad for upcoming White Sox games appeared in the *Chicago Defender* in June 1953, giving evidence of the South Side's affinity for the Go-Go Sox. No ads for the all-white Cubs appeared in the *Defender* in the early 1950s.

Chapter Six
Preparing the Way

Black baseball's buccaneer, who faced all-comers with a cutlass in his teeth and a twinkle in his eye, commanded attention both on and off the field in such an entertaining fashion that writers quickly realized they had a gold mine in quotes and story angles. An unimposing physical specimen—180 pounds evenly distributed over a six-foot, three-inch frame—Satchel Paige was so clearly superior to his opposition, black *and* white, that he became a sort of pulley for the sport, capable of dramatic ups *and* downs but used mostly to lift black baseball. Regard for black achievement appreciated—and to no small degree—as a result of this one player's stunning and sustained achievement.

Paige single-handedly re-oriented baseball coverage in the black newspapers. Prior to his emergence as a star pitcher in the mid-1930s, game coverage consisted mostly of straightforward accounts of play with scant little on the players. In most cases, in fact, only last names were used to refer to players, a practice that has made compiling an accurate statistical record of Negro league play difficult.[1] Only on the rarest of occasions did the weeklies run a feature story on an individual athlete, at least until the emergence in the 1930s of Joe Louis, Jesse Owens, and Satchel Paige, in sharp contrast to mainstream sports coverage. The dailies embraced personality-driven sports reporting during the decade, using it to sell newspapers, to supply fans with heroes, and to counter the popularity of radio, which offered listeners an immediacy the papers could not provide.[2]

Of undetermined age, and unwilling—perhaps unable—to give his age, Paige rarely lost to major league all-star teams, and with a variety of pitches uncommon for any pitcher of any color in any era, he often dominated them. Paige's bag of tricks included his hesitation pitch, so named because of a slight delay before releasing the ball; the "nothin' ball," which was a straight changeup; his be ball, because he made sure it "be where I want it;" the bat dodger, four-day rider, and midnight creeper.[3] Though his statistical record is incomplete, like those of most Negro leaguers, he is known to have pitched sixty-four consecutive scoreless innings and to have won twenty-one straight games. Nicknamed after carrying luggage—satchels—at a Mobile, Ala., railroad depot as a young boy, Satchel posted a 32–7 record in 1932 and went 31–4 in 1933. While playing for a Bismarck, North Dakota, team, Paige was impossibly credited with 134 wins out of 150 games. He was the logical choice to become in 1971 the first Negro league player inducted into the National Baseball Hall of Fame.[4]

Fans embraced what Ches Washington described as Paige's "mound manner and his cockiness."[5] A February 1936 tune-up game against major league all-stars is typical in the coverage Paige received and for the numbers of the fans he pulled into the park. The sold-out game in Oakland equaled "one of the greatest exhibitions of pitching witnessed by the writer in nearly a score of years," wrote white sportswriter Eddie Murphy.[6] Paige struck out a dozen and allowed but three hits, one of them surrendered to New York Yankee great Joe DiMaggio. The Yankee Clipper described Paige as the greatest pitcher he had ever faced, praise that vaulted the pitcher onto the front pages once again, and praise that remains one of Paige's more important credentials.[7] One of white baseball's biggest stars and best hitters publicly lauding black baseball's premier pitcher was big news, and the coverage in the late 1930s demonstrates again that the priority for the black writers was not yet to directly challenge the color bar. The priority was instead on establishing black players' capabilities.

Paige remained the biggest baseball story in the early 1940s, as well. The black papers heavily promoted his appearances whenever he came to town, and without exception he drew the season's largest crowds.[8] Fay Young credited the pitcher's brilliance for giving the Negro leagues in 1941 "its best season."[9] "Satchell Paige Day" at Wrigley Field highlighted the 1943 calendar, the same year Paige's divorce made the *Defender*'s front page. When he returned to Chicago in December 1943 to judge a band contest, the *Defender* championed his celebrity and called black baseball's highest-paid player "the greatest single drawing card in baseball today."[10] These stories were not aberrations. A content analysis revealed that for several seasons, "Satch" received as much or more coverage than a majority of the Negro league teams.[11]

Newstands in the 1940s exposed mainstream society to Paige, as well. In 1940 he was the subject of a lengthy feature article in the *Saturday Evening Post*, the first instance of Negro league coverage in a leading monthly magazine.[12] The *Post* article elicited a variety of reactions. Lucius Harper, writing on the *Defender*'s front page in 1940, asked readers to overlook

Post writer Ted Shane's "rather Negroid" depiction and instead "give him due credit for putting the cause of Negro baseball up to a vast, white audience."[13] The payoff of attention from mainstream society was worth the stereotyping Shane liberally used in his descriptions and accounts, at least to Harper. Shane described Paige as having "apelike arms," "canalboat" feet, and a "Stepinfetchit accent," and he proclaimed that "Harlem says: 'he's that famous. He do jes' like he please, and nobody can say nuttin'!'"[14] The *Courier*'s Rollo Wilson, however, objected both to the stereotypes and even more so to the story's many errors. Neither the *Post* nor Shane acknowledged the errors or Wilson's protestations. Long-time black baseball veteran Buck O'Neil said players at the time celebrated the *Post* piece, even though it portrayed the Negro leagues like a "circus" and Paige as a baseball "clown," because, like Harper, the players recognized that the magazine could raise awareness of and interest in the leagues. "It was more important to us that this was the first time a magazine like the *Saturday Evening Post* had ever written about black baseball," O'Neil wrote in his autobiography. "We felt this might open the doors in the major leagues for some of the fellas. . . . We had to be discovered first."[15]

Less than a year after the *Post* piece, Paige was the focus of feature stories in *Life*, *Time*, and *Sport* magazines.[16] The *Time* piece, titled "Satchelfoots," piqued Paige, who felt the nickname made him sound like a clown. "I ain't no end man in no Vaudeville show," Paige told biographer Hal Lebovitz. "I don't like it, I don't want it, and I don't care who knows it," he said.[17]

Paige also got exposure on WGN Radio and in several white dailies. It could be argued that without Paige, Negro league baseball itself might have folded much sooner than it did. When 18,000 people turned out to see Paige and his Monarchs defeat the Chicago American Giants on opening day 1943, Fay Young wrote that black baseball was "in for a good season." Lucius Harper agreed, saying that in 1942, despite war-related hardships, organized Negro baseball had "passed through one of its most dramatic and successful years."[18] But Paige's prowess on the mound could compensate for only so much, and the conflict and contentiousness among owners that characterized the 1943 Negro league season nearly killed the very entity that was to produce Jackie Robinson two seasons later.

The internecine warfare among the owners during the 1943 season occurred against a national backdrop of strife and race-based division. As World War II raged in Europe, race riots in midsummer swept through several U.S. cities as blacks responded en masse to discrimination in employment, housing, and political representation, particularly in urban areas.[19] In sports, the Professional Golfers Association voted to remain open only to whites, and the All-American Girls Professional Baseball League, a brainchild of Cubs' owner Philip K. Wrigley, began play with four teams and an unwritten rule prohibiting blacks.[20] It is interesting that Wrigley, concerned as he was about losing revenues due to the war, would invest in an entirely new women's league rather than acquire even one black replacement player for his Cubs. Wrigley ultimately lost $200,000 in the women's league and backed out after two years.[21]

Perhaps the most divisive issue for black owners concerned competing claims on the rights to certain players. Officials in Pittsburgh, St. Louis, New York, Cleveland, and Philadelphia traded charges that other teams had stolen their players, but only Homestead's Cum Posey in Pittsburgh had a weekly bully pulpit in the black press from which to preach, and he used it throughout the season to tell his side of the story and to charge other owners with misconduct.[22] Once again, the papers were used by an owner for the purposes of power plays and the manipulation of public opinion.[23] The controversy, which dragged on through April, May, June, and July, was merely the latest in a series of disputes over player commitments, which were exacerbated by the absence in many if not most cases of written player contracts.[24] Owners feared offending even recreant players by demanding a signed legal document. Players liked the flexibility the lack of contracts provided, giving them the freedom to jump teams, leagues, and even countries in the hunt for a bigger paycheck.

Signaling in 1943 the decline of the Negro American League in terms of importance to the black community was the inclusion of the Cincinnati Clowns, later relocated and renamed the Indianapolis Clowns. Owned by controversial white promoter Syd Pollock, and famous for face-painted, tap-dancing players, the team's entry was yet another cause for division among league owners. Like the magazine coverage of Paige, the Clowns served to perpetuate—and even create—stereotypes of black athletes.[25] Consensus on the Clowns' admittance finally was reached, but the Clowns had to agree to no minstrel shows or clown acts.[26] Faced with such discord, and concerned more with the war raging in Europe than with provincialism in baseball, neither the *Defender* nor the *Courier* mentioned or otherwise confronted the color line during the 1943 season. The two papers did not even note the *existence* of the major leagues, leaving the lion's share of baseball coverage to the internal squabbles within the black leagues. It was not positive attention. For Smith, it was time for the Negro National to "clean up its filthy house" or risk killing "the goose that laid the golden egg."[27] He wrote that he had become fed up with the squabbles over players, about the need for an independent commissioner, and with the sorry state of the sport's "make-shift promotions," a reference to the continued unwillingness on the part of the teams to keep the newspapers informed of scheduled games.[28]

Yet again, the East-West Classic provided relief, if for only a short time. The event attracted a "roaring throng" of 51,723 to Comiskey Park for a "gigantic and successful sports extravaganza," Smith wrote.[29] The season still ended in utter turmoil, however, with irregularities and disputes marring a Colored World Series that pitted the Grays against the Birmingham Black Barons. The Series was so poorly conducted that Wendell Smith and William G. Nunn at the *Courier*, Sam Lacy at the *Afro-American*, and Fay Young at the *Defender* offered in 1944 to form the World Series Arbitration Committee to settle disputes among the owners, who did not take the trio up on their offer (only league president J. B. Martin voted "yes").[30]

The baseball event of 1943 occurred during the off-season, in December—a meeting of more than forty major league owners, general managers, and league officials in New York City. After a great deal of lobbying by Sam Lacy, Commissioner Landis invited a delegation of black leaders to the annual meeting, issuing the invitation under the auspices of the Negro Publishers Association.[31] Though the meeting failed to produce tangible results, it marked the first time integration was included on big league baseball's formal agenda, and Landis's invitations were major league baseball's first issued to men of color. That black newspaper publishers were invited by baseball's highest office underlines the efficacy of the campaign of the black press's writers and editors, and of the direct involvement in the campaign by the black press. Curiously, Landis did not include any Negro league owners or players, or those presumably closest to the drama and those with the most at stake. Instead, in addition to the publishers and writers, Landis invited controversial actor, athlete, and activist Paul Robeson, a public supporter of the Communist party. Many believe Robeson's presence was orchestrated to provide white baseball's owners with an excuse for not engaging in the talks. It was unlikely, after all, that a group of conservative white businessmen would have much to do with a flamboyant, black Communist sympathizer.

Black press coverage of the meeting was substantial. The *Courier*, which sent business manager Ira Lewis and Wendell Smith, published three stories on the meeting and a photograph of Smith interviewing Landis, and it reprinted Lewis's "epochal" speech to major league baseball's owners in full. In his roughly ten minutes of remarks the newspaper executive decried the color barrier in personal terms, telling baseball's elites that he had felt "the bitter pangs of sorrow and disappointment over the unfair and unjust attitude of organized baseball toward Americans of color."[32]

He called instead for fidelity to "American tradition" and action in the name "of all that we love, in the name of democracy."[33] He attempted to persuade the owners that football, track, basketball, boxing, and entertainment had proven that blacks and whites could co-exist without "disturbing the public."[34] Perhaps most importantly, Lewis exposed Landis's obfuscation of the Gentleman's Agreement, essentially calling the Commissioner a liar for denying its existence. The *Defender*, which sent its publisher, John Sengstacke, also extensively covered the meetings. Sengstacke, who also was president of the NPA, joined Lewis in blasting baseball for allowing the Gentleman's Agreement to stand, calling it an insult to democracy.[35] Lewis and Sengstacke were accompanied by Howard Murphy, business manager of the *Afro-American* chain and secretary of the NPA, who also spoke, as well as C. B. Powell of the *Amsterdam News*, William O. Walker of the *Cleveland Call and Post*, Louis Martin of the *Michigan Chronicle*, and Raymond Campion, a white pastor in Brooklyn's largest black parish. Oddly, Sam Lacy was not invited, and Robeson's presence might explain why. Unlike Smith, Lacy shunned any affiliation or cooperation with communists, including the *Daily Worker*. Lacy might also have been blacklisted because of the discomfort he was causing Clark Griffith in Washington over the Senators owner's race policies.

Given the presence of Robeson and mere platitudes from the publishers, perhaps it should not surprise that the twenty minutes of presentations from Sengstacke, Lewis, and Murphy sparked no questions from the sixteen owners and twenty-eight other officials in attendance. According to Smith, the executives did not react at all.[36] The black attendees never heard from the owners or from Landis again. The owners had been exposed to an eloquent case for integration, however, one that explicitly identified and attacked the unwritten ban, and the meeting provided the black press and the daily press with another occasion to discuss the color line's incompatibility with democratic ideals and values.

It is worth noting that rather than making an economic case for integration, an approach the black owners likely would have taken had they had the opportunity, the publishers instead stressed the more vague notions of democratic principles. It seemed to sportswriters such as Smith and Lacy that arguing the potential financial benefits of allowing blacks into baseball would have been far more persuasive than polemics about democracy and American tradition.[37] Smith and Lacy knew that economics were a significant reason that several major league owners were resisting integration, owners who were profiting richly from renting out their stadia to Negro league teams when their own clubs were playing on the road.

If the publishers missed their opportunity, the writers used post-meeting coverage to capitalize on weaknesses in the owners' solidarity. Wendell Smith made sure in describing the meetings afterwards to establish that it was not the Negro league owners who were the primary obstacles to progress, by default implicating the owners in the majors. This began Smith's counter to arguments from teams such as the White Sox, Senators, and Yankees for the preservation of Negro league baseball, revealing that Charles Comiskey of the White Sox, Clark Griffith of the Senators, and Larry MacPhail of the Yankees were not acting in the interests of the black community, but to protect their revenue streams generated by renting their playing fields. These rents generated tens of thousands of dollars for owners who merely opened up their ball parks and "three hours later collect[ed] ten grand," Smith wrote.[38] Owners in Washington, D.C., Philadelphia, Pittsburgh, Cleveland, Cincinnati, and Boston also benefited from the high rents. Griffith counted profits of about $100,000 in 1943 from renting Griffith Stadium to the Grays, for example, while the Yankees made money leasing out not only Yankee Stadium, but the organization's minor league parks in Norfolk, Newark, and Kansas City.[39] It is perhaps no coincidence that the first to integrate, Branch Rickey's Brooklyn Dodgers, did not have such an arrangement with the Negro leagues for Ebbets Field. Smith also turned the tables by putting Negro American League President J. B. Martin on record as declaring "absolutely no opposition" on the part of the league to integration. Martin told Smith, as he had said to Young, that, "I want it clearly understood that we are not opposed to any move which would advance Negro players to the major leagues."[40] The article served also to set the stage for future business dealings with major league baseball since in it Martin asked that black team owners be given "the same consideration in regards to the acquisition of these players that they give to the minor leagues."[41]

Major league owners ultimately rejected Martin's and Negro league baseball's claims to legitimacy, however, and Smith inadvertently provided them with the cover to do it. In a column published just one week before Martin's statement of unqualified support for integration, Smith warned that if the Negro leagues did not do a better job organizing and administering their affairs, then "a major league owner is in no way compelled to recognize the contracts and agreements which ordinarily apply to trades and sales of ball players."[42] This same rationale became the outline for the argument Branch Rickey used two years later in defense of appropriating Robinson from the Kansas City Monarchs without paying anything in compensation to the Monarchs' owners. In 1943 Smith wrote that Negro league owners would have to "tighten the business strings within their organizations and prepare for the future."[43]

Smith's unvarnished criticism and patronizing columns are likely reasons the Negro American and Negro National leagues passed on the writer's offer in December 1943 to compile statistics for league games in 1944 for a fee of $5,000.[44] Though Newark Eagles' owner Effa Manley supported Smith's plan, the other owners felt the sum was too high. The Negro National went instead with the Monroe Elias Sports Bureau, at a cost of $425 per month. The Negro American chose the Howe News Bureau, also a white-owned company, at a rate of $300 per month. The selections were viewed as "an insult to Negro sports editors," and the *Courier* hinted that the black papers might boycott the two statistical services in protest of the Negro National's "anti-Negroism." The newspaper described the leagues' decision as "an affront to Smith's ability," "an affront to the entire Negro press," and a bypassing of "the biggest opportunity to . . . play ball with the Negro Press which in more ways than one, is responsible for its tremendous success today."[45]

While Smith and the *Courier* pressured major league and Negro league baseball, Fay Young worked locally. He interviewed several Chicago Cub officials simultaneous to the meetings in New York City, including Philip Wrigley and his general manager Jim Gallagher, to press them on whether the Cubs were planning or preparing to sign a black player. While calling integration inevitable, Wrigley provided no timetable, and Young did not criticize the owner for failing to make an explicit commitment. Gallagher predicted that black players would first integrate the minor leagues, pointing out that even among white players, only one had ever gone straight to the major leagues—Frankie Frisch of the New York Giants and St. Louis Cardinals.[46] While Gallagher's prediction was logical, it also served to buy time for major league baseball and, more specifically, for the Cubs. It typically took a few years for a prospect to work his way through the various tiers of the minors and up to the big leagues, as the Cubs' own Gene Baker demonstrated before joining Ernie Banks in integrating Chicago in 1953.

As World War II continued in Europe and in Asia, efforts to integrate sports at home brought mixed results. In 1944, Sportsman's Park in St. Louis, home to the Cardinals and Browns, became the last major league ballpark to de-segregate its seating. In professional football, however, the color barrier was just going up, walling off the likes of Kenny Washington and Jackie Robinson.[47] Much like major league baseball's ownership group, professional football's owners agreed in unwritten terms not to sign black players. The agreement could not be found in any bylaw or constitution, and, as in baseball, its shadowy existence made it more difficult to confront or overcome. No blacks played in the National Football League from 1933 to 1946, though black athletes like Robinson and Kenny Washington were allowed to play for predominantly white colleges. The fact that other sports were seemingly following the example of big league baseball provided yet another reason why baseball's barrier was considered by the black sportswriters to be "so vicious and dangerous . . . and must be torn down," Smith wrote.[48]

The armed services claimed many major league players, depleting professional baseball's rosters and forcing teams to look to American Legion players and even high school teens. African Americans were still off limits, but little attention was paid the hypocrisy.[49] Civil rights would return to the nation's consciousness only after the defeat of Nazism in World War II. Absent the rhetoric of civil rights activism, baseball coverage in 1944 was not unusual. The focus was on regular game coverage and on the excitement surrounding the late-summer East-West Classic. Smith's columns did not tackle the color bar for the most part, and the *Defender* devoted far less space to sports in general and baseball in particular, weekly providing less than a full page of sports throughout the year. The *Defender* did not reference the color line or major league baseball in any context during the year. In short it was a year of quiet before the tremors of 1945, when Smith, Rickey, and Robinson conspired to integrate baseball. As 1944 drew to a close, black baseball's elites were still being urged to clean house and to more resemble the majors in structure and in day-to-day operations. At the annual meetings, the *Courier*'s managing editor, William G. Nunn, addressed the owners and called for the establishment of a commissioner's office, the development of a Negro league farm system, and an honest and public accounting of player salaries so that their escalation could be held in check.[50] In Chicago, meanwhile, self-help was still the emphasis. Fay Young urged the black public to "generously support" the clubs, and to "go to our own ball games and help build" this distinctly black business. "The other fellow takes our dollars and cents and gives nary a Negro player a chance to even tryout [sic] for a major league team," he wrote.[51]

One of the integration campaign's most significant events punctuated 1944's close—the death of Commissioner Landis and, therefore, an end to a quarter-century of resistance to racial reconciliation in baseball from sport's highest office. Wendell Smith mixed praise and criticism in his column paying tribute to the legacy of the man the black press called "the Great White Father." He lauded the "iron hand" Landis wielded against gambling of any sort. On the issue of race, however, Smith lamented that Landis "never used his wide and unquestionable powers to do anything about the problem" and instead played a subtle "fence game."[52] Without exception other black press writers paid tribute to Landis, perhaps because they did not wish to spoil the opportunity his death presented for integration. With the

December 1943 meeting still a fresh memory, they wrote instead of their gratitude for the access he provided them.

Landis's passing was propitious, for at the same time the membership rolls of civil rights organizations such as the NAACP and the Urban League were swelling. The NAACP's size grew nearly ten-fold during the war, for example, while the Urban League tripled in size.[53] During the war, blacks across the political spectrum pushed for equal participation and equal access. Campaigns such as the Double V, the petition drive aimed at major league baseball, and Philip A. Randolph's March on Washington were examples of the new activism. At the forefront of this movement was the black press, which was described at the time by influential sociologist Gunnar Myrdal as "the greatest single power in the Negro race."[54] By war's end, the black press reached 1.8 million subscribers with a pass-around readership of as many as ten million.[55]

With public opinion changing, the time proved ripe for a resumption of direct participation in the crusade by the black sportswriters, involvement that provoked, pushed, and enabled baseball to travel the last mile to integration, or at least to its beginning point. Integration cannot, after all, be accomplished with the signing of a single player, and it perhaps can never be declared "finished." Even in 2006, the sport continues to "integrate" with the additions of Japanese, Chinese, and Korean players, for example, even while it is flush with talent from Latin America, Central America, and the Caribbean.

Player tryouts in 1945 proved to be the hinges on which the door to black players finally swung open. The ways these tryouts were handled demonstrate the very different philosophies or mentalities among the writers about how best to exact change and finally break through the membranes of conservatism and racism. Two sets of tryouts occurred in April 1945, making the month pivotal for the crusade. April also saw the appointment of a new commissioner for baseball, a former senator from Kentucky, A. B. "Happy" Chandler. Though Chandler opposed anti-discrimination legislation in his home state, he quickly announced plans to study integration for baseball. Shortly after being named Landis's successor, Chandler told the *Courier*'s Ric Roberts that he believed if a black man could fight in Okinawa or Guadalcanal, "he can make it in baseball."[56]

With major league and Negro league teams in the South for spring training, Wendell Smith and Joe Bostic of the *People's Voice* in New York separately, using very different approaches, worked to secure tryouts. Bostic confronted baseball; Smith worked behind the scenes. Bostic wrote of the tryouts as the goal; Smith saw them as merely a means to an end, or one front among many in the war against segregated play. Bostic had a powerful new weapon in a fair employment law passed in February 1945 in New York. Newly elected Governor Thomas Dewey passed the Ives-Quinn Anti-Discrimination law, which penalized private institutions for discrimination in their hiring practices. The fair employment law applied to New York's three major league teams—the Yankees, Giants, and Dodgers, so Bostic seized on the bill as an opportunity to challenge baseball's color ban by forcing a team to grant players a tryout.[57]

Bostic teamed with Nat Low, sports editor of the *Daily Worker*, to take two aging black players to the Brooklyn Dodgers' Bear Mountain, New York, training camp. Unannounced, the writers demanded tryouts for Dave "Showboat" Thomas, a first baseman, and Terris McDuffie, a pitcher, and they cited the new employment law in making the demand. If Rickey and the Dodgers denied the players the opportunity, Bostic promised to charge them with discriminatory hiring practices, so Rickey allowed a tryout the next day, April 7. Though they were the first public workouts granted black players by a major league baseball team, Rickey later said he resented having been backed into a corner. On the day of the tryout, Rickey received Bostic and his party "with cold fury," according to the *Daily Worker*. The Dodgers did not sign either of the players.[58] Lester Rodney, editor of the *Daily Worker*, summarized his newspaper's role in the fight to integrate as that of agitator, spurring action and sparking debate, and it was an accurate description. The role of the Communist party was an important one, but only until other forces took the lead, including "the better sportswriters," Rodney later said. "By 1945, we were only a minor part of the movement."[59]

Wendell Smith's better known choreography of tryouts in April 1945 with the Red Sox offers a sharp contrast to the confrontation orchestrated by Bostic and Low.[60] After reading about a white city councilman in Boston running for re-election in a precinct with a significant black population, Smith said he got the idea of enlisting that councilman's support in pressuring the Red Sox. Smith phoned Boston's Isadore Muchnick and pitched the potential benefits of joining Smith in pressing the Sox for a tryout for Negro league players. Muchnick agreed, but his reasons for doing so are mysterious. According to historian Howard Bryant, Muchnick ran unopposed in 1945 in a district with less than one percent non-white residents and in a city with a black population of less than ten percent.[61] In his own notes of the events, Smith presents Muchnick's re-election as the motivation for the local politician to join Smith in pressing the Red Sox for the workouts, and this depiction of events is repeated throughout most of the scholarship on and re-tellings of the Boston tryouts. It is possible if not probable, however, that Muchnick acted out of conviction, as Bryant suggests. Muchnick was quoted by the *Courier* as saying that he did not understand baseball's "pre-Civil War attitude toward fellow American citizens because of the color of their skin." In his campaigning for the tryouts, Muchnick threatened the Red Sox with a vote against the team's city permit for Sunday games, which was by quirk of law an annual requirement of both the Red Sox and Boston Braves.[62]

On April 16, four days after FDR's death, three players hand-picked by Smith went through hitting, throwing, fielding, and running drills at Fenway Park. In addition to working with Muchnick to secure the tryouts, Smith drove the players to the ballpark, arranged for their accommodations at the *Courier*'s expense, and sent information prior to and after the tryouts to Boston's newspapers, both black and white. Smith selected Marvin Williams, second baseman for the Philadelphia Stars, Sam Jethroe, outfielder for the Cleveland Buckeyes and the Negro American League batting champion of 1944, and Jackie Robinson, who had not yet played his lone Negro league season for the Kansas City Monarchs. Jethroe did later integrate Boston's professional baseball scene, with the Boston Braves in 1951.

Smith selected the three players because they were everyday players young enough to be able to endure in the minor and major leagues.[63] Josh Gibson and Satchel Paige, the best known black baseball players, were deemed too old, according to Smith. In April 1945, Gibson was 34; Paige was probably 39. In addition, Cum Posey and the Homestead Grays refused to surrender Gibson, their top drawing card, offering a hint of the Negro league obstructionism to come. And because he was a pitcher, Paige would only play every five days; Smith wanted an everyday player, someone on the field and in front of the mostly white fans each and every game. Robinson was selected not because he was the best player. He clearly was not. But Robinson was an army officer, a college man (though he did not graduate), a four-sport letterman at UCLA, and, perhaps most importantly, a name the American public already recognized. Robinson had already played on integrated teams and against major leaguers on the West Coast. The public knew him primarily for his feats in college football, including those in a year-end all-star game against professional football's champion Chicago Bears. Additionally, his older brother, Mack Robinson, won a silver medal to Jesse Owens' gold in the 200-meter sprint in the 1936 Olympics.

The three players drilled in front of Sox management for an hour and a half, with mostly high school players. Most of the Red Sox players were on their way north following spring training and, therefore, did not witness the tryouts.[64] Because they were not publicized, the workouts were not witnessed by sportswriters from the dailies, either, nor did they draw much comment from the city's black press. The *Boston Globe*, for instance, failed to report on the tryouts. With the transition in the White House from FDR to Harry S Truman, there remained precious little attention in the public consciousness for three blacks hitting and fielding baseballs on a cold day in Boston. The lack of attention likely aided the Red Sox in resisting pressure to integrate, and the team's apathy was confirmed when the Sox failed to contact Smith or the three players. Smith and Muchnick offered a team frequently accused of systemic racism with the opportunity to be the first to integrate in the cradle of abolition. Instead, in 1959, the team earned the ignominy of being the last major league team to integrate, signing Elijah "Pumpsie" Green.[65]

Even casual baseball fans might wonder why Boston, the City on a Hill, the cradle of liberty, could be so resistant to integration. Several factors contributed, including a significantly smaller black press compared to New York City, the entrenched racism at the highest levels of decision-making in the Red Sox organization, and the extreme to which Boston's blacks were walled off from the rest of the city. The city's black newspapers, such as the *Boston Chronicle* and the *Guardian,* were much smaller than either the *Courier* or *Defender.* Mabray "Doc" Kountze, a black writer with the *Chronicle*, began lobbying the Red Sox and Braves to integrate as early as 1935, when he met with Red Sox officials to discuss a tryout for black players. In 1938, he met with Boston Braves management to attempt to persuade the club to play against black teams.[66]

Almost as an afterthought during the busy week in Boston, Smith telephoned Branch Rickey before returning to Pittsburgh to inform the Dodger president of the tryouts. Rickey suggested that Smith stop by Ebbets Field the next day to discuss the players Smith had in mind, the players the Sox had seen. When the two met, a momentous meeting completely unreported at the time and still under-appreciated, Rickey confessed little knowledge of Robinson as a baseball player, recognizing him instead as a football and basketball star. "We talked a long time about the respective merits of the players I took to the tryout," Smith recounted nearly twenty-five years later. "He was primarily interested in Robinson [because] he was already a known name."[67] Though Smith knew his huddle with Rickey in Brooklyn was "a good story," he agreed not to write anything of either the meeting or of Rickey's plans to have Dodger scouts shadow Robinson during the 1945 Negro league season. "I knew that would ruin the whole thing," Smith said. "When we talked on the telephone, we didn't use [Robinson's] name. He was 'the man from the West.'"[68]

Smith's cooperation with Rickey in not reporting on potentially the biggest story of his career was consistent with Smith's and the *Courier*'s involvement throughout the campaign, and it signals 1945 as very different in terms of black press coverage of and involvement in baseball. The access Smith had to Rickey—phoning him while traveling from another major league city—is remarkable. Smith's efforts to arrange tryouts and meetings, endeavors for which there was no obvious potential compensation, also are notable. Smith's reporting and columns were in the tradition of the black press as a "fighting" press and, as such, he never claimed or even sought to be purely objective. As Chris Lamb and Glen Bleske described it, Smith was "willing to put his personal beliefs ahead of his journalistic instincts."[69] Smith himself wrote that he would have done whatever Rickey requested as long as it meant baseball would integrate.[70] Rickey appreciated Smith's efforts to keep the Dodgers' plans out of the news and the agitators at bay, Smith wrote. "I think that's why we got along as well as we did," the writer recounted.[71]

While Smith collaborated with Rickey, Lacy sent a letter to all sixteen major league owners recommending that a committee be formed to determine the best method of and timetable for integration. In contrast to Bostic but like Smith, Lacy made no demands, writing that he "realized that achievement of the goal is going to be a slow and tedious process, and one which will require a maximum of understanding and careful planning." Though Lacy viewed the committee's formation as a compromise to his preferred route of more concrete action, he wrote that at the very least it "will be a step in the right direction."[72] The letter won him a spot on the owners' agenda for their annual meeting in Detroit in May 1945, where he more fully presented his ideas. The owners approved the formation of the committee and appointed Rickey and MacPhail, president of the Yankees, to lead it and to name additional members. The *Afro-American* celebrated Lacy's success, but, yet again for the black press, the claim was premature.[73] MacPhail never attended the meetings called by Lacy and Rickey, the latter of whom of course simultaneously was working with Smith and scout Clyde Sukeforth to scout and sign Robinson. Rickey, therefore, likely acted at a pace somewhat less than urgent. Negro league owners, too, refused to participate with the new committee, a recalcitrance that was embarrassing to Lacy. "Don't ask me to explain the basis for the opposition," he fired back. "That like everything else regarding colored baseball's attitude toward progressive action, is woefully unexplained."[74]

Smith's cooperation with Rickey continued throughout the 1945 season. As the *Courier*'s sports editor, he had the Negro league schedules and game results, or at least most of them, at his disposal. Rickey stayed in close contact so Smith could inform the general manager of where Robinson was playing and even where he was staying on road trips. Smith wrote no stories on Robinson or Rickey until September, telling the *Courier*'s readers then, for the first time, of Rickey's contacts with Robinson. Even in September, Smith did not mention the season-long evaluation or, more significantly, the fact that Rickey had already signed Robinson to a minor league contract.[75] Though Smith probably did not know of the signing at the time he wrote the September article, he did find out well before its public announcement in late October. On October 23, the Montreal Royals, Brooklyn's top farm club, announced Robinson's signing, and brought to a close nearly sixty years of segregation in major league baseball. Smith had known for more than a month what Rickey and the Dodgers were conspiring to do but held back out of fear of derailing Rickey's plans and out of respect for the Dodger president. Once the signing was announced, the black press began celebrating. Black writers seized on the event's social significance and its historical context, on the human drama for Robinson, and upon the need to continue supporting Negro baseball.[76]

Robinson's drama was told in part in his own words. The November 3 issue of the *Courier* featured the first of his many bylines for the newspaper—"'Glad of Opportunity And Will Try to Make Good.' Robinson."[77] The newspaper simultaneously pledged "not to jeopardize the best interests of Negro organized baseball in any way," even though the signing of Robinson "transcended anything else at this particular time" and, as Posey predicted years earlier, marked the beginning of the end for black baseball.[78]

Despite its promise to the Negro leagues, the black press immediately and comprehensively shifted resources to coverage of Robinson and the Dodger organization and away from the black leagues. The white press, however, exhibited little awareness of the signing's import and, by extension, of the extent of prejudice and racism in America. In their analysis, Lamb and Bleske found white mainstream press coverage of Robinson and baseball's integration "limited, both in content and context," and devoid of appreciation of the potential impact on the emerging civil rights movement.[79] Bill Weaver's analysis, too, concluded that black newspapers immediately picked up on and highlighted the historical magnitude of what the Dodgers had done, while mainstream newspapers treated it as "relatively unimportant."[80] Weaver's analysis was supported quantitatively by William G. Kelley, who found that the black press covered the signing "with more fervor and emotion" than did the metropolitan newspapers, which "tended to take the story as another occurrence in the sports world."[81]

The black press realized what the white mainstream dailies did not, that the moment the ink of Robinson's pen dried on Rickey's contract, baseball's history was cleaved into periods of "before" and "after," just as *Brown v. Board of Education* in May 1954 marked eras in the nation's schools.[82] It was, the black newspapers recognized, segregation's soundless detonation.

The *Pittsburgh Courier*, *Chicago Defender*, and *Afro-American*, among other black papers, in contrast to mainstream media, reported with emotion and as participants in the drama, framing the event as part of the narrative that began with Moses Fleetwood Walker's exclusion from American Association play in 1889. Robinson and Rickey immediately emerged in the black press as heroes in the bitter battle for equal access and equal participation. In one column, for example, Wendell Smith placed Robinson in the context of baseball's history by tracing that history back to Walker, who, like Robinson, was "well educated and a gentleman of the highest quality."[83] Smith's description conveniently omits Walker's jailing on charges of murder and the former player's legendary—and ultimately fatal—drinking problems.

A study of coverage of the period reveals that the Communist *Daily Worker* and white columnists were important allies to the black press, though beat writers for the mainstream dailies only sporadically commented on baseball's color barrier and the efforts to erase it. These writers reached an audience far greater than did black sportswriters, however, so even with less comment they exerted pressure on major league baseball the black press could not. In agitating, confronting, and directly involving itself in the campaign to integrate, the *Daily Worker*, too, provided instrumental assistance, which the black press initially welcomed and championed. As a political party operating in the fringes of society, however, its role was inevitably limited.

The direct involvement and participation of the black press, which marked the beginning of the campaign's final phase in 1939, with Smith's interviews of major league players and managers, proved critical not only in facilitating a black player's entry into big league baseball, but specifically in selecting Jackie Robinson as the player to do it. Rube Foster did not envision in 1920 at the founding of the Negro National League the addition of a lone black player, and a relative newcomer to the Negro leagues at that. In the 1940s, however, just such a signing meant success to a crusading press eager to use baseball as a springboard into other realms of society, culture, and the human concourse. Foster also did not envision resistance to integration and even obstructionism on the part of some Negro league team owners. In holding back Josh Gibson and penning warnings to black baseball in his weekly column, Homestead's Cum Posey hinted at this stonewalling, which would give the black press an opportunity to distance itself from the Negro leagues, their erstwhile partners in the great crusade. As a study of the final period in the Negro leagues' history shows, it was an opportunity the black newspapers did not forgo. The period 1940–1945 was the Negro leagues' last as the focus of sports coverage in the black press, beginning an evanescent decade for these leagues, whose very name was increasingly viewed as a source of shame.[84]

Chapter Seven
The Promised Land

By signing Jackie Robinson to a contract with Montreal without compensating the Kansas City Monarchs for their loss, Branch Rickey presented the Negro leagues with a wrenching choice. As businesspeople and capitalists, the black team owners naturally were outraged by Rickey's "theft" of one of the leagues' better players and fearful he might take more. They hurriedly met in Pittsburgh to determine how to best protect their interests. The other option, of course, was to facilitate integration in any way possible in fulfillment of their leagues' founding mission and to move yet closer to the larger social goals of the black community at large. In short, the owners could either publicly endorse the color barrier's breach and, therefore, encourage further dilution of their product, or they could fight for fair compensation and face condemnation from all quarters of the black community, including the black press.

In some ways, the black press faced the same dilemma. Writers could sympathize with the owners' concerns and perhaps even intervene to try to win at least some financial compensation for the players the major leagues wanted. Forgiving the black leagues' past sins, the writers could possibly lobby for a formal alliance with major league baseball in an arrangement not unlike that baseball had with its minor leagues. Such an arrangement might legitimize the black leagues' perpetuation, at least for a while longer, for a transition period during which black owners could reorganize and rebuild. Based on their actions of the late 1930s and 1940s, the writers obviously viewed intervention and activism as right and natural, even as duties and responsibilities. Or, as ultimately they elected to do, black sportswriters could press on toward full integration and cast off all that hindered the race, including its own recalcitrant owners, even if that approach meant ending thirty years of partnership. The writers' dilemma was one manifestation of what W. E. B. Du Bois called the American Negro's double-consciousness, a psychological rift in the black soul: "One ever feels his twoness," Du Bois wrote in 1903, "an American, a Negro, two souls, two thoughts, two unreconciled strivings; two warring ideals in one dark body, whose dogged strength alone keeps it from being torn asunder."[1]

Sam Lacy signaled early the response most black sportswriters would make, in a November 1945 *Afro-American*, by declaring "little sympathy" for black owners who were griping about being overlooked. Lacy reminded readers that he had offered the magnates help in "the recognition of their rights as legitimate club-owners" when he formed a committee with major league baseball to study how to accomplish integration, an offer the owners flatly turned down. Not only that, the owners had criticized Lacy for what they perceived as his "effort to run [their] business," an accusation to which Lacy and Wendell Smith had grown accustomed.[2] The magnates ignored similar entreaties from the *Pittsburgh Courier* and evaded attempts to hold them accountable for what was increasingly a bunker mentality. The articles and the owners' response (or lack of response) to them in some ways explain why the black press viewed the Negro leagues in the late 1940s and 1950s as obstacles to progress.[3]

Dr. J. B. Martin, president of the Negro American League, publicly and repeatedly declared unqualified support of Robinson and any other black player able to matriculate into the major leagues. Martin released a statement congratulating Rickey on his "moral courage" and claiming that he, Martin, could speak for America's fifteen million blacks in saying they were with Rickey "one hundred percent."[4] Behind the scenes however, owners of both Negro American and Negro National teams huddled with Martin and Tom Wilson, president of the Negro National League and owner of the Nashville Elite Giants, to determine how to stop or at least slow the flow of players out of the leagues.[5] J. L. Wilkinson and Tom Baird, owners of the Monarchs, also publicly stated their desire to "see Jackie make good," declaring that they would "never do anything to mar his chances." Wilkinson nevertheless told Smith that white baseball had to be prevented from "just stepping in and taking our players without giving us some kind of consideration."[6]

In previous eras, it would not have been unusual for the black press to publish the owners' declarations of support while simultaneously working behind the scenes to help those same owners recoup their losses. In fact, for many of the writers, it would have been in their self-interests, given the numbers of black press members who held office in the leagues and kept score and/or directed publicity for the teams. In the 1920s, the writers, editors, and publishers were integral in the founding of the Negro

National League, cooperating under the banner of building up a black-owned business.

For their part the owners circled the wagons. Less than a month after Robinson's signing was announced, the owners met to draft a letter to the new commissioner of major league baseball, Happy Chandler. The letter declared the owners' rights based upon their leagues' constitutions and the existence of player contracts, which were not universal but, in the mid-1940s, neither were they rare. The letter called for "deals" to be brokered with the Negro league teams for the rights to individual players, arguing that after all the black teams were those that had developed and prepared the players for big league play.[7] The owners' co-signed letter testified to the Negro leagues' professional status of fifteen years by citing their constitutions, schedules, rules, and minutes of their many meetings.[8] Chandler ignored the pleas. Wendell Smith reacted quickly and forcefully, addressing both the letter and the accompanying press release from J. B. Martin. The *Courier*'s sports editor mocked the irony of Negro league owners "running like mad" to the commissioner of white baseball for help after stubbornly resisting for years the creation of a powerful and independent office to oversee league affairs, a concept Lacy and Smith had presented the owners with more than once. Rickey in fact cited this deficiency as a chief reason why he did not consider black baseball a legitimate professional organization or one worthy of negotiating with for the rights to players. Whether Smith realized it or not, his column significantly bolstered Rickey's claim that the Negro leagues in fact did not qualify as a viable professional federation and, therefore, Smith indirectly encouraged major league baseball to raid the black teams for talent. Smith's condemnation clearly weakened the black club owners' bargaining position.[9]

In Chicago, Frank Young collected and examined reactions to Robinson's historic signing and not to the objections raised by Negro league owners. For readers of the *Defender*, there was no controversy over compensation, at least not in the initial months after the signing. Young did not mention it, nor did he do any enterprise reporting on the issue. Perhaps because of his age and declining health (Young would be hospitalized less than two years later), *Defender* coverage was limited to a roundup of excerpts, mentions, and reactions that had previously appeared in other newspapers. In the October 27, 1945 issue, the responses gathered were from throughout professional baseball, including ones from former St. Louis Cardinal player and manager Rogers Hornsby, Clark Griffith, Negro American League president J. B. Martin, and others. The November 3 issue followed up with a roundup of coverage appearing mostly in Southern newspapers. In both issues, the vast majority of opinions on Rickey's move was positive, with a few voicing skepticism as to whether Robinson could make the grade.[10] A newspaper in San Antonio, for example, declared discrimination "at an end in sports and entertainment," while another in Spartanburg, S.C., lobbied for segregation's continuation in sports "as in all other activities," according to Young.[11]

In mid-December 1945, the black owners met to conduct business long neglected before integration. They adopted uniform, universal player contracts much like those transacted in major league baseball, and, for the first time, they instituted a player reserve clause. The owners scurried to sign their players to these contracts because Robinson had not been contractually obligated to the Monarchs. Rickey had no legal obligation to compensate Wilkinson and Baird, therefore, and there is evidence the Dodgers made certain this was the case before signing Robinson.[12] These self-preserving moves, coming so late, combined with the euphoria over a black ballplayer in Brooklyn, inspired the *Courier* to lay bare the growing gulf between the black press and black baseball. According to the newspaper, owners "uncorked some atomic shots at its long-time friend, the Negro press" and blasted the black newspapers for being "too vocal" on integration.[13] The black owners even contemplated a lawsuit against Rickey but decided instead that "such a move might be construed by the public as an effort to keep Negro players from entering the majors." According to the *Courier*, the owners spent more time at their annual meetings denouncing Rickey and the black papers than on "revamping the weak structure of their organization."[14] Such condemnations in the black press further strengthened Rickey's position vis-à-vis the black leagues.

Though Robinson was an unqualified success with Montreal in the International League in 1946, leading them to the league championship and winning for himself most valuable player honors, major league teams balked at adding more black players. Their resistance was almost comical. The Washington Senators, for example, fielded Cuban players, granted a tryout to a player of Chinese descent, and suited up a one-legged pitcher, Bert Shepard. He lost a leg fighting in World War II. The St. Louis Browns played a one-armed infielder, Pete Gray, and for more than half the 1945 season. Gray lost a limb in a childhood accident. The Phillies, too, were open to fielding players with handicaps, granting a tryout to a nineteen-year-old with one hand. "Anyone except a known colored man is welcomed into the big leagues," declared the *Courier*'s Rollo Wilson.[15]

Nevertheless, as 1945 closed, the black press was jubilant, even while black team owners hunkered down for a fight. The brotherhood ties were once again severing. Forced to choose between greater integration and the preservation of a conflicted black league, the black press did not hesitate in voting against segregation of any kind. As historian Bill Simons has noted, negative images of the black leagues proliferated in both the black press and mainstream media, but they "possessed an almost visceral intensity" in the black newspapers. Long gone was the shared pride in a flowering black institution.[16] An unlikely, de facto alliance against Negro league owners, therefore, had formed in Rickey, Chandler, and many if not most of the black sportswriters. Emblematic of his part in this alliance, Smith would draw equal-sized paychecks in 1946 from the *Courier* as sports editor and from the Dodgers as a traveling companion, chauffeur, and secretary for Robinson.[17] Officially, Smith was on Brooklyn's payroll as a scout. Practically, he helped arrange housing for Robinson in the segregated South during spring training and on the road during the regular season. He also served as Robinson's Boswell, chronicling his first two seasons weekly and ghostwriting for Robinson.

The *Courier*'s photographer and entertainment writer, Billy Rowe, also was paid by the Dodgers to accompany Robinson, especially during spring training. Being so closely allied with major league baseball, even being paid by major league baseball, was not seen as a conflict of interest by Smith or by black sportswriters in general. In covering a story in which they themselves were participants, the black writers for the most part believed in accomplishing baseball's integration by almost any means available. As Lamb and Bleske wrote, these writers also believed that a counter balance had to be offered to the mainstream press, which was seen as apathetic to Robinson's quest, perhaps even against it, and certainly ignorant of black baseball in general.[18]

Realizing that they might find themselves completely shut out financially, Negro league officials in early 1946 signaled a change of heart. Precisely as Lacy had recommended more than a year earlier, well before Robinson's signing, the owners began campaigning for some sort of minor league-type of affiliation with major league baseball and petitioned Chandler to this end.[19] According to Wendell Smith, the Negro leagues called on the Commissioner to stop major league baseball from raiding the black teams in a letter drafted at New York's Theresa Hotel. The officials said they were "protesting the way" Robinson was signed, explaining that black teams had "gone to so much expense to develop players and establish teams and leagues."[20] This time the commissioner fired back. During a series of meetings in January, Chandler emphatically told black baseball: "Get your house in order," making reorganization a requirement before the Negro leagues could approach big league baseball for any type of negotiations or officially sanctioned status.[21] While Chandler condemned black baseball, Rickey defended his decision not to pay the Monarchs for

Robinson: "There is no Negro league as such as far as I am concerned. Negro baseball is in the zone of a racket and there is not a circuit that could be admitted to organized baseball."[22] If no Negro league existed, there could be no contractual obligation requiring Rickey to pay the Monarchs for Robinson's services, just as Smith had foreshadowed, however unintentionally.

It is easy to imagine a black press of the 1920s or 1930s rushing to the defense of Negro league owners in reaction to Chandler's and Rickey's indictments, demanding compensation for top players, and holding lily-white major league baseball accountable for its Jim Crow legacy. When the priority was on building up black baseball, in making it viable and vital, such a reaction would have been considered an obligation. In 1946, however, the *Courier* and *Defender* used banner headlines to proclaim Chandler's charges and wrote columns repeating, even supporting and amplifying his demands and criticisms. The writers catalogued and elaborated the problems Chandler said plagued the black leagues, analyzing each and every one, and often offering solutions.

Chandler's charges were the lead sports story in the *Courier*'s January 26 issue and the focus of Smith's "The Sports Beat" column that same week. The columnist slammed the owners for "protecting their own selfish interests" rather than seeking to improve the status of black players. In Smith's colorfully articulated view, the "Negro Press" and "other forces interested in the general welfare of Negro baseball" found themselves pitted against the owners, who sought "first, last, and always" to protect the "shaky, littered, infested segregated baseball domicile."[23] Smith even adopted Chandler's rhetoric, wagering in a February 16 column that the owners would never "get their house in order" because of in-fighting and "the many evils" within black baseball.[24] Smith quoted Chandler again in June to accuse the owners of failing to keep the public informed and, therefore, for failing to even begin attempting to get their "house in order."[25]

When the Newark Eagles walked off the field in July after a dispute with the umpire, the behavior and the subsequent lack of a reaction from league presidents J. B. Martin and Tom Wilson substantiated, at least from Smith's perspective, the charge from Branch Rickey "that the Negro leagues do not actually exist."[26] The only counterbalance to Chandler's charges and the *Courier*'s support for those charges was a four-inch response in the February 2 issue from J. B. Martin, distributed by the Associated Negro Press wire service.[27] Sam Lacy went so far as calling Chandler's accusations "arrogant," but he justified them by saying that "no less should be expected what with colored baseball leaders behaving as they are." The early 1946 article also gave Lacy another opportunity to remind readers of his efforts to get the black owners to begin preparing for integration and for some type of alliance with major league baseball.[28]

As Lacy's comments indicate, the black press saw itself as the primary force driving the integration of baseball and, specifically, the signing of Robinson. Lacy, Young, and Smith each referenced their and their papers' roles in baseball's integration at seemingly every opportunity. In abstracting the year athletically, Smith wrote that his newspaper was "particularly proud of Robinson's brilliant achievements, because it was this paper that recommended him to Branch Rickey"[29] Jackie Robinson affirmed the writers' intervention himself, telling the *Afro-American* at the time of his signing that he knew it was "obtained only through the constant pressure of my people and their press. It's a press victory, you might say."[30] Each of the three newspapers—the *Courier, Defender*, and the *Afro-American*—viewed itself as the leader in the crusade, or at least attempted to portray itself as the principal.

Not only did the writers grill the owners, they gave critics such as Cum Posey plenty of ink and column inches with which to scold. Smith and the *Courier* gave the enigmatic, vituperative Cum Posey frequent and high-profile opportunities to take on black baseball's leadership, even though, as secretary to the Negro National, Posey himself was a member of that elite. The lead story on January 5, 1946, written by Smith, echoed Posey's complaints, which centered on Martin's and Wilson's vicissitudes and their failure to correct "the many flaws within Negro baseball." Posey wrote for himself in a February 2 column that again catalogued for readers the black leagues' ills, including poor scheduling, conflicts of interests among league officials, and poor organization throughout the leagues.[31] Though it could not have been his intent as secretary of the league, Posey nonetheless provided further evidence yet for Chandler's and Rickey's claims of amateurism on the part of the black leagues. Posey's upbraiding was one of his last public acts; he died in April 1946.[32]

As businessmen and job creators, the owners had legitimate concerns. The vitality of their businesses was being threatened, and their monopoly on black baseball talent ending. It is surprising, then, that neither the writers nor league officials gave more published contemplation to the post-integration reality for black baseball. At least some ruminating on the extinction of black baseball was done by Smith in the late 1930s, during his celebrated series of interviews with major league managers and players. Smith acknowledged "many letters" from readers who wrote that they were concerned about the Negro leagues should the color barrier come down. These readers believed, according to Smith, that integration would "automatically spell doom for both the Negro American and National leagues." One reader presciently noted that the major leagues likely would take only the "cream of the crop. Then—what would the Negro public do for its heroes on Negro teams?"[33]

Smith's reaction to those readers' concerns provides a valuable articulation of the newspapers' struggle and of their naiveté regarding the Negro leagues' post-Robinson future. Presumably speaking for the *Courier* staff or perhaps, more broadly, for the black press, Smith wrote that, "we believe that anything done by the majors to improve the status of Negro players will prove beneficial and advantageous to Negro baseball in every way."[34] Big league teams would have to gain sanction from Negro league owners to sign players, Smith wrongly predicted, and then pay owners the price those owners set. Rickey infamously did neither, and Smith, who would become inextricably linked with Rickey's maneuverings, not surprisingly excused him and provided him cover. Smith's blindness to the potential damage to the Negro leagues could in part be attributed to a new optimism developing among blacks. As the 1940s began, the civil rights movement was entering a new phase. World War II returned blacks to war and into the armed services, and again they fought for democratic ideals on foreign soil. In this context, racial discrimination at home quickened the country for action. Also promoting the movement were the economic gains, advances in education, and progress in voter registration among blacks in the North. The NAACP, for example, sharply increased its membership rolls and ramped up fundraising efforts.

Still relatively new on the job in 1939, Smith also suggested that the money made on top players could be plowed back into the leagues to make them better, a prescription that ignored two decades of avarice on the part of the owners and the growing impossibility of segregated play juxtaposed with increasingly integrated major league play. If black baseball could "line up with the majors and serve as recruiting grounds," as a sort of minor league system, owners would "profit in every way and the Negro player also."[35] Lucius C. Harper, a regular front-page columnist for the *Defender*, wrote that fans believed integration would "boost 'Negro baseball' and attract better material with the hope that it may graduate into better salaries and work under better facilities."[36] According to Harper, it was the owners and not the fans who harbored the fears, believing integration would "do harm to the interest of their clubs."[37]

In the sunset of his lengthy career, Lacy told historian Jim Reisler that he had known integration would begin the black leagues' demolition but that after Robinson, "the Negro leagues was [sic] a symbol I couldn't live with anymore."[38] It is unclear if Lacy devoted much thought to this inevitable denouement since evidence of such anticipation is not found in Lacy's sports writing throughout the leagues' history. Eight years prior to Robinson cracking the color barrier, Vic Harris, captain of perennial Negro league champion Homestead Grays, did tell Lacy that if big league teams began signing black players, it would mean the end for the Negro leagues: "We do have some good ballplayers among us, but not nearly as many fit for the majors as seems to be the belief. But if they start picking them up, what are the remaining players going to do to make a living? Our crowds are not what they should be now. . . . How could the other 75 or 80% (of black players) survive?"[39] (Harris was right, even in his math. A total of seventy-five players moved from Negro leagues to major league teams. Many more played in the minor leagues, but of 500 on Negro league rosters in 1945, only about 10 percent ever found work in the big leagues.[40])

Before actively working toward integration in 1945, Joe Bostic of the *People's Voice* in New York defended the existence of the Negro leagues in 1942 as being a critical part of the black community's economy and culture. In this context, integration represented a direct threat. Bostic wrote in a July 11 column that year that the issue, like most others, was ultimately about money:

> Since all baseball prognostications are made under the sign of the dollar mark . . . why shouldn't the fledgling that is Negro organized baseball take the same attitude. The whole (integration) discussion breaks down into the query, "Would Negro baseball profit or lose by the entry of Negroes into the American and National leagues?" *Scoreboard* feels that the net result would be written in red ink on the ledgers of Negro baseball.[41]

But concerns such as Bostic's were not entertained by the black press in the months before or after Robinson's signing, not by Smith or Lacy, and not even by Bostic himself. It would be more than two years before the press began constructively addressing the problems for the Negro leagues created by the departure of many of their best young players.

For the mainstream press, the drama of Robinson's signing did not include the Negro leagues as a prominent part, even though the event represented the culmination of the mission of those leagues and vindicated in some ways their quarter-century of existence. Shirley Povich, for example, a noted columnist with the *Washington Post* and an ally with the black press in the early 1940s in pushing major league baseball to integrate, recounted in 1953 how baseball had opened its doors. As the *Courier*'s Ric Roberts noted, Povich's narrative omitted Wendell Smith: "No complete saga of the eventual abolition of the ban can be offered without a recording of Wendell's lone voice which, as early as 1938, crystallized into a delegation."[42] The dailies' distorted version of history endured long after Robinson and Rickey, which, as Rogosin wrote, is a testimony to Rickey's success at myth-making. Some of the blame for the black leagues' omission in the narrative should also go to Robinson, who was often negative in describing the Negro leagues, even though he spent but one season in them, in Kansas City. In one autobiography, Robinson devotes only three pages to his Negro league experiences.[43]

If the metropolitan newspapers ignored black baseball, it was the major leagues that existed on the periphery for the black community prior to Robinson joining the Dodger organization. Black press coverage reflected and reinforced this status. The *Defender*, for example, did not run a single story on the major leagues during the 1945 season, or until Robinson's signing was announced in October.[44] Black press coverage of the Negro leagues, however, resembled that of major league baseball by, say, the *New York Times* or *Chicago Tribune*, including news on player moves, accounts of league meetings, box scores and game coverage, schedule information, and feature stories.

Representative of baseball coverage before Jackie Robinson's life as a Dodger, the *Defender* promoted the East-West game in 1946 on its front page with an eight-column headline predicting it to be the "Most Colorful in History."[45] The advance story was forty-three column inches, the longest baseball story in the *Defender* that year, and with it appeared lineups, four photos, and nine other Negro league stories. A pair of one-inch stories on Robinson and catcher Roy Campanella toiling in the minor leagues represented in total the coverage of major league organizations in the *Defender* that same issue. (Campanella was signed by the Dodgers in 1946, assigned that season to Nashua, New Hampshire, Brooklyn's Single A farm team.)

White society, culture, and athletics—the white world—existed in the periphery of the black press much as the black community resided in the margins of mainstream media coverage.[46] This imbalance remained until Robinson joined the major leagues in 1947. After Robinson's move to New York City, the imbalance reversed, with major league baseball pushing the Negro leagues into the shadows. A content analysis of *Defender* and *Courier* baseball coverage indicates that the amount devoted to the Negro leagues sharply declined in 1946 as Robinson's major league debut approached and continued to diminish, both qualitatively and quantitatively, during the 1947 and 1948 seasons.[47] Conversely, coverage of the major leagues increased during the period, and to remarkably similar extents as coverage of black baseball constricted. An example: For the two newspapers combined, the number of issues in which the majority of baseball coverage was on the Negro leagues dropped from twenty-four in 1945 to ten issues for each of the 1947 and 1948 seasons.[48] On the other hand, the number of issues in which the majority of baseball coverage was on the major leagues went from four issues in 1945, including three *Courier* issues, to sixteen in both 1947 and 1948.[49]

Only one major league story in the black press was accompanied by a photo in 1945, the story on Jackie Robinson's signing in October. By 1947, the total of major league baseball articles appearing with a photo was thirty-five, or almost double the number of Negro league stories that appeared with at least one photo. These disparities occurred despite a much larger well of stories for the Negro leagues versus that for the major leagues, especially in 1945 and 1946, since only one previously white team had a black player, the Montreal Royals.[50] Major league stories in the black press also were much more likely to carry a byline than those on the Negro leagues, indicating on-site reporting and a shift in the allocation of the black press's always limited human resources. Newspaper staffs were notoriously small. Sam Lacy told author Jim Reisler that, "The average reporter in those days might cover courts in the morning, a luncheon or ball game that afternoon, and perhaps a dinner or meeting in the evening. You had to be well-rounded because the job required you to cover everything."[51]

With Robinson in a Royals uniform, the black newspapers relied even more on the Negro league teams to send in their own results. The increase in the overall number of stories is a tribute to the writers' productivity. In 1945, six Negro league stories carried bylines compared to four for the major leagues. In 1947, with Robinson playing a full season in Brooklyn, the ratio of bylined stories swung in favor of the major leagues by a margin of twenty-four to two.[52] The attentions of Smith and Young, too, shifted before and after the color barrier's break. Examining the weekly columns of both sports editors, eleven focused in 1945 on the Negro leagues while five centered on the major leagues. By 1947, twenty columns written by one of the two sports editors centered on the major leagues versus just six on the Negro leagues, indicating not merely a shift but, with the eve of integration, more attention on baseball in general.

There is evidence the newspapers were attempting to keep up with both leagues, at least in terms of day-to-day beat coverage. After a 105 game summary stories combined in 1945, all of them on Negro league games, because integration still was a year away, the papers printed 121

Negro league game summaries in 1946, 97 in 1947, and 71 in 1948, all while coverage of major league action was on the rise. The number of major league game summaries climbed from zero at the beginning of the period studied to 34 in 1948, even though only a handful of big league teams had integrated.

After 1946, editorials and columns in the black press commenting on the Negro leagues focused either on the ineptness of league officials and owners or, paradoxically, the need for fans to continue supporting the leagues for the purpose of completing baseball's integration. With involuted logic black newspapers called on readers not to turn their backs on the Negro leagues while the newspapers did precisely that, at least in terms of amount and type of coverage. In May 1947, Ric Roberts, the *Courier*'s Washington, D.C.-based writer, urged fans to rally around black baseball, which was "at its lowest leevl [sic] in history," he wrote. Both the terms and the tone of Roberts' column were typical during the period following Robinson's signing:

> It is important, therefore, that our baseball fans should remember that (the Negro leagues) is the lone channel through which Jackie Robinson, Roy Campanella and Don Newcombe might have traveled to the hitherto lily-white side. . . . Now, more than ever, the leagues need your support, and none of the smart-alecky disdain that some fans seem to be developing . . . the golden egg is wonderful . . . but let's not forget the goose that laid 'em.[53]

Within a few weeks of Roberts' column, Smith issued an equally emphatic call for fan support, saying that Negro league owners deserved consideration due to their sizeable investments over the years to keep black baseball going.[54] "The lush days haven't been here long," he wrote, referring to the banner 1946 season, "and they won't be here much longer." As late as May 1948, Fay Young at the *Defender* was simultaneously crusading to integrate the Cubs and White Sox *and* urging black community support for the up-and-down, Martin-owned Chicago American Giants. Young's tone was similar to that of a parent trying to talk a child into taking medicine:

> It is only right that all of us roll up our sleeves now and give the team our fullest support. It is all right to yell for what we want but it sure wouldn't be right if we didn't patronize the club when it appears to be what we asked for. It takes money to run a first class ball club. If we want Chicago to have one we have to attend the ball games. There is no other way around it.

The column was prefaced with an anonymous poem, "The Purpose of Life," which read:

If you never made another have a happier time in life;
If you've never helped a brother through the struggle and his strife;
If you've never been a comfort to the weary and the worn—
Will you tell us what you're here for in this lovely land of morn?[55]

The illogicality of Young's exhortations is revealed in an account by another venerable black sportswriter, Doc Young, who in the 1950s served as sports editor at both *Jet* and *Ebony* magazines. He wrote in the *Defender* in 1948:

Go to a barbershop, a bar, a home, a newsstand during the season; listen to the men and women as they cheer when [Lou] Boudreau hits or makes a fancy play [for the Cleveland Indians]. . . . Then, for contrast, stand around when someone says, "Well the [Cleveland] Buckeyes lost a doubleheader today!!" Somebody is likely to say, "Oh, them bums!"[56]

The Indians integrated also in 1947, signing Larry Doby of the Newark Eagles in July.

Black press sportswriters reasoned that continued fan patronage was more important in the late 1940s than ever before because the black leagues finally had become a breeding ground for major league talent. Thus, after decades of persuasion based on the purported quality of the black game, a quality obviously being diminished by the flight of talent, fans in the mid-1940s were being urged in paternalistic tones to get behind this crepitate product for the greater good of the race. *Courier* columnist Mal Goode, for example, in lamenting the loss of black business ownership with what he termed the "death of the Negro leagues," wrote that the gain was "greater—we got our self-respect back—and you have to have been black to understand what we meant."[57]

This exultation overshadowed the growing recognition that black baseball's days were numbered, and that the number was not large. Anticipating Robinson's first action in a Dodger uniform in Ebbets Field, Smith wrote it would be a day he could truthfully say, "Mine Eyes Have Seen the Golry! [sic]."[58] And an obituary tone is evident in Doc Young's column from the *Defender* in 1949: "Many of our writers have been willing to consign [black baseball] to the ash-can and to burlesque if to an extreme degree. . . . Despite their shortcomings, they have done tremendous good. They filled a void; they provided a showcase; they satisfied the baseball hunger."[59]

Black papers seemingly wanted their cake and the luxury of eating it, too, chronicling Robinson's every move in Montreal and Brooklyn but simultaneously pleading with fans not to let black baseball fade away. Long-time black radio personality Jack Saunders wrote a column in a September 1948 *Courier* that celebrated the new big leaguers, but it included a plea to readers to support black baseball:

> For God's sakes, fans, don't let Negro baseball die. . . . I know you want to see (Robinson, Doby, and Campanella) play. . . . I, too, make a bee-line for Shibe Park whenever the Dodgers and Indians come to town. . . . But if Negro fans don't start supporting those teams again, they will fold up! . . . The way I see it, Negro fans are doing Negro baseball, future Negro stars and potential major leaguers a great injustice by withdrawing their support. . . . How will major league scouts be able to look over Negro material if there are no Negro teams playing?[60]

Shibe Park in 1948 barred black sportswriters from its press box. Only members of the Baseball Writers Association of America were allowed, and membership in the BWAA required affiliation with a *daily* newspaper.[61]

The utilitarian view of the press toward the Negro leagues, which were looked to for more capable black talent, was motivated at least in part by the desire to gain full status for blacks. Equality was the goal, Wendell Smith so frequently wrote. When Robinson first saw action in white baseball, playing for Montreal in April 1946, the headline for the *Courier*'s front page read, "American Way Triumphs in Robinson 'Experiment,'" and the story was attended by verse from Robert Browning that declared, "God's in His Heaven—All's right with the world!"[62] In June of Robinson's first major league season, as the Dodgers got set to play in Boston on Memorial Day, Smith was inspired to pair Robinson's "blow at big league hypocrisy" with Revere's ride "to fight those who would deny them the rights of America."[63]

In an important way, the tables had been turned. Rather than the owners using the papers for their own purposes, manipulating writers and editors and persuading readers, in the mid-1940s the writers were attempting to prop up the black leagues for their purposes, which they cast as a "noble experiment." The Negro leagues were merely facilitators, a farm system to be judged on its crops rather than a grand showcase of and for the Black Metropolis. In this new economy, the currency was baseball players capable of success at the major league level. "The Negro Leagues simply became a vast source of cheap ballplayers with enormous talent," Donn Rogosin wrote.[64] After Rickey's pickpocketing of the Monarchs, however, the new currency was paid for with the old. In July 1947, Bill Veeck and the Cleveland Indians compensated the Negro league's Newark Eagles $15,000 for the services and contract of Larry Doby, who integrated the American League. Soon after, the St. Louis Browns shelled out $20,000 for two former Monarch players, and Branch Rickey acquired the contracts of pitchers Roy Partlow (from the Philadelphia Stars) and Don Newcombe (from the Eagles), both "bargains" at $2,000 apiece. "Obviously, there is gold in them thar bronze stars," Smith proclaimed.[65] The "bargain basement" sale of players by the Negro league owners can be viewed as a final, self-immolating exploitation by those black team owners, as well as the beginning of the black players' exploitation by major league baseball.

Early in "the noble experiment," it appeared that the doomsayers had over-reacted. The season prior to Robinson's first with the Dodgers—1946—was perhaps the Negro leagues' most successful in their history, both on the field and in fiscal terms, as well. With the war over, game crowds frequently ranged between 12,000 and 15,000, though, as historian Robert Peterson surmised, the black press was more interested in how Robinson, Roy Campanella, Johnny Wright, Don Newcombe, and other black players were doing in the minor leagues.[66] The season's largesse even prompted B. B. Martin's Memphis Red Sox to announced plans for a $250,000 ballpark.[67]

More than 45,000 people attended the East-West Classic in August 1946, enough to spur a second all-star game in Washington, D.C., which attracted another 17,000.[68] Integration was coming, but with the geography of Robinson in Montreal, Roy Campanella and Don Newcombe in Nashua, New Hampshire, and Johnny Wright in Three Rivers, Quebec, there was no direct competition yet for paying fans in Negro league cities. That would come a year later, and Robinson and the Montreal Royals hinted at what the future might bring. With Robinson as its chief attraction, Montreal drew one million fans in 1946 for the first time in the franchise's history, breaking attendance marks both at home and on the road. The *Courier*'s writer in Montreal, Sam Maltin, reported that Robinson was surrounded by admirers at home, at the ballpark, in restaurants, and on streetcars.[69]

The Newark Eagles, who beat the Monarchs to take the 1946 Negro World Series, had the organization's best year ever, both athletically and financially, according to Smith, who put the team's World Series' winnings at $25,000.[70] Another *Courier* writer, Ric Roberts, went so far as to predict new interest in the Negro leagues because of black baseball's banner season combined with the beckoning of the major leagues. "The game will go on—it will improve," he wrote, in the 1946 *Negro Baseball Yearbook*, which was published by the *Pittsburgh Courier*.[71] Of course it could not improve; the insuperable loss of talent would be too great, and the progress of Robinson and Campanella and Newcombe took money and space in the sports pages away from the black leagues for good. As James Overmyer noted in his history of the Eagles, the Negro leagues "were doomed" in a newly integrated baseball world.[72] The solid financial footing gained in 1946 proved fleeting and was nearly wiped away just a year later. The 1947 season saw ten of the twelve black teams lose money.[73] Attendance at Negro league games plummeted, much of it redirected to big league parks.[74] The Newark Eagles, playing in Brooklyn's backyard, counted 120,000 patrons for home games at Ruppert Stadium in 1946 but only 35,000 in 1947. The club was forced to shut down after the disastrous '47 season.[75]

Direct competition for black teams as the result of integrated major league play affected Brooklyn (Dodgers), Cleveland (Indians), and St. Louis (Browns) in 1947; New York (Giants) in 1949; and Chicago (White Sox) in 1951. Special rail fares were advertised in the black newspapers for carriage from throughout the Midwest to St. Louis and Chicago for games in those cities against Jackie Robinson and the Dodgers.

As interest in and coverage of Negro league baseball was trending down, Smith claimed in June 1947 that no one in either league was willing to keep the public informed, a complaint that in important ways excused the *Courier*'s omission of regular, comprehensive league coverage.[76] The press and the public had been "forgotten" due to the inability of the leagues to funnel information to the black papers, Smith wrote, citing this failure as the source of the crack in the "very foundation of Negro baseball." The *Courier*'s shift in allocation of resources to major league coverage was not reckoned, and those who faulted integration for their woes at the turnstiles were "simply dodging the issue," according to Smith. The black writers can be fairly charged with kicking the leagues while they were down. Integration marked open season for fault-finding. The *Defender*'s Fay Young, for example, used his weekly column to grill Negro league "would-bes" for failing to supply the news and to defend the abundance of coverage devoted to Larry Doby and Jackie Robinson:

> We haven't any white complex. When the news is of importance, it gets space—the same is of pictures. The columns are not for sale. Our business is to cater to John Q. Public, who buys the newspaper, not to the promoter or the coach. But when either the publicity man, the coach or the promoter fails to get us the news when we want it, the kind we want and the pictures—he is a very foolish man.[77]

Young defended issues of the *Defender* like one in October 1947 in which Jackie Robinson's game-winning home run was front-page news and the subject of three page-one photos, a twenty-one-inch bylined article, and extended coverage on the sports pages.[78] In contrast, the story of the Cubans winning the Negro World Series against Cleveland was buried in a page-fifteen, eight-inch article.[79] Johnny Johnson at the Kansas City *Call* described Negro baseball as "the only going concern that has never seen the wisdom of utilizing qualified publicity agents. Just anybody can write their . . . copy and judging from the kind of releases that are usually received, just about anybody does."[80]

Other page-one *Defender* stories on baseball that season included the signing of Robinson by the Dodgers in April, Robinson's favor among fans in May, Larry Doby's signing by the Indians and the St. Louis Browns obtaining Willard Brown and Henry Thompson in July, the major leagues scouting eight Negro league players in August, and the progress of the Dodgers' Dan Bankhead, also in August. No stories on the Negro leagues appeared on the *Defender's* front page that 1947 season.[81]

Black newspapers and fans turned their attention to the major leagues and away from the black leagues throughout baseball's integration, an incremental process that required more than a dozen years to merely add one black player to each of the sixteen major league rosters.[82] Like the Eagles, most black teams quickly began losing money as their ticket sales dropped and as the black press reduced coverage to make room for updates and statistics about Robinson and other black players as they were signed. The black teams became increasingly irrelevant for a community eager for a greater, fuller, more open democratic society. As Smith wrote, the "big league doors suddenly opened one day, and when Negro players walked in, Negro baseball walked out."[83]

Robinson was seen as a lever in this struggle as even the name—Negro leagues—became an unwelcome reminder of minority social and economic status. Effa Manley, co-owner of the Negro National League's Newark Eagles, wrote in her memoirs, that "erstwhile black baseball followers—who for years had been rabid fans of the all-black outfits—now found themselves becoming far more interested in the daily doings of Jackie Robinson and the Brooklyn Dodgers, than in the happenings within the Negro leagues. . . . There was a growing swell of racial pride that was sweeping headlong across Black America."[84] Even the Negro leagues tried to capitalize on Robinson and his immediate popularity in the black community, putting the one-year veteran of their leagues on the cover of the 1946 *Negro Baseball Yearbook* rather than an established league star.[85] In the late 1940s, the Philadelphia Stars, a black team, featured Robinson wearing his Dodger blue on their own program cover.

In the meta narrative, of Robinson as Moses and big league baseball as the promised land, overlooked are the great sacrifices made by blacks. Negro league baseball sacrificed at the altar of integration was a stiff price, indeed, as writer and activist Amiri Baraka, wrote decades later. For Baraka, the false hopes of integration did not merit the killing of the Negro leagues:

> To rip off what you had in the name of what you ain't never gonna get. . . . We're going to the big leagues. Is that what the cry was on those Afric' shores when the European capitalists and African feudal lords got together and palmed our future?. . . . So out of the California laboratories of USC, a synthetic colored guy was imperfected and soon we would be trooping back into the holy see of racist approbation. So that we could sit next to drunken racists by and by. And watch our heroes put down by slimy cocksuckers who are so stupid they would uphold Henry and his Ford and be put in chains by both while helping to tighten ours.[86]

For Baraka, baseball's "integration," as a badge for the black's integration into American society, was artificial, infelicitous, a perfidy, and a farce. "But many of us fell for that and fell for him, really," he wrote.[87] Robinson certainly believed in his cause. When filling out a questionnaire the Montreal Royals had all its players complete, in answer to the question, "What is your ambition?," Robinson wrote: "To open doors for Negroes in Organized Ball."[88]

Chapter Eight
Staying Away in Crowds

Jackie Robinson's breakthrough in Brooklyn is one of the most celebrated, researched, written about events in American history. As scholar Bill Simons described, Robinson's pioneering first season still stands as "one of the most widely commented on episodes in American race relations," an irresistible story of grace and dignity that has become sacrosanct in American folklore.[1] It has been told and re-told in film, on Broadway, and in enough books to fill entire sections in bookstores and libraries.[2] More relevant here is the fact that a great deal of industry has gone into documenting and analyzing newspaper coverage of Robinson during his first year as a Dodger, including studies of coverage by the black press, by mainstream media, and on the differences between the two.[3]

In examining black press coverage, it is clear that for the black weeklies and, by extension, the black community, Robinson *had* to "make the grade" and break the long-held racial barrier in the major leagues. The newspapers emphasized Robinson's more positive attributes and experiences and conveniently ignored or omitted those that were less felicitous. The black press excised from the narrative, for example, that Robinson's father had deserted the family, that Robinson did not graduate from UCLA (he attended for two years), and that the player had been court martialled while in the Army.[4] Instead, in the pages of the weeklies Jackie Robinson was a college man and an army officer, a superior all-around athlete who in childhood managed to overcome the absence of a father.[5] This careful editing of the Robinson narrative began as early as spring training 1946, before the player's season in Montreal. After an Odyssean journey from Los Angeles to Sanford, Florida, a racially divided town like most in Florida in the mid-1940s, he, Smith, and *Courier* photographer Billy Rowe were told by the local sheriff to be out of town by nightfall. The sheriff claimed that a hundred townspeople in Sanford had asked him to, "get the niggers out

159

of town."[6] They fled to Dodgers training headquarters in Daytona Beach. Smith reported nothing of the incident, however, and Robinson and Rickey, too, kept quiet.

Throughout the 1947 season, Smith routinely emphasized the positive and comprehensively filtered out the negative. Objective reporting was not an option as far as the sports editor was concerned, given what he felt was at stake for his readers. The *Courier*'s coverage, therefore, contrasts sharply with that in the mainstream media. Though the daily newspapers published far less on Robinson in general, the white press also emphasized Robinson's virtue, but almost exclusively his virtue as an athlete. The dailies paid little attention to his race or to the experience of being a lone black man in a white world. Ignored also was Robinson's life outside of baseball. In short, mainstream media sports coverage for the most part did not change as a result of Robinson's presence in major league baseball. The big metros continued to treat Dodger games as athletic contests devoid of social or political consequences, and their writers saw Robinson merely as one of nine Dodgers on the field.[7]

For the black press, however, major league baseball had become "the Robinson beat." For Wendell Smith, the shorthand had multiple meanings. Just as he did during spring training in 1946, Smith drew a salary from the Dodgers throughout the 1947 season. At the same time, as sports editor for the country's largest black weekly, he cast Robinson's first year as a universally upbeat experience. Smith published positive comments and descriptions, endorsements, and statements of approval of Robinson from all quarters of professional baseball. He traveled to Cuba for the Dodgers' spring training and from Havana reported weekly on Robinson's and Roy Campanella's progress, including praise of that progress from Dodger manager Leo Durocher and others.[8] When Montreal manager Clay Hopper, whose racism was common knowledge, praised Campanella, it became the lead story for a March issue of the *Courier*.[9] Smith recounted Robinson's heroics with the Royals the previous season, and he documented the player's more recent feats during spring training in 1947 as Smith followed the Dodgers throughout Latin America.[10] In early April, Smith conducted a poll of Dodger players on whether Robinson should join the big league club, and the *Courier*'s reporting of that poll is emblematic of Smith's approach to coverage that first season. The newspaper published the results in Smith's "Sports Beat" column of April 12 and with them remarks from some of Robinson's detractors (Dodgers Eddie Stankey and Dixie Walker, for example). Smith did not report, however, on the near mutiny of the Dodgers against Durocher for determining that Robinson would play first base.[11] Players passed around a petition saying they would refuse to play with Robinson, mirroring the racism that gripped the nation in racial crisis. Mainstream media did not report on the rebellion either, but the white dailies did not have writers in Havana. Smith was on the scene, so it is difficult to believe he would not have known of the planned walkout.

Throughout spring training, with Smith on site, Dodger coverage dominated the *Courier*'s sports section. News on the Negro leagues, therefore, moved to the margins to make way for the new "Robinson beat." When the regular season began and Robinson's status as a major leaguer had been made official, the shift in coverage became even more evident. Smith's Dodger coverage moved to page one.[12] In the April 19 issue, the *Courier* gave readers twenty-two photos of Robinson, or more photographs than were published as part of Negro league coverage during any one full season since 1920.

An important part of the Robinson success story, at least for the black press, was the impact financially for the Brooklyn organization. Smith, therefore, emphasized ticket sales and the numbers of blacks flowing into Ebbets Field, statistics that were nothing less than phenomenal. In one of Smith's most quoted articles, a May 31 column on the Dodgers' record-breaking crowds, Smith began the piece with a clip of verse: "Jackie's nimble, Jackie's quick, Jackie's making The turnstiles click!"[13] The story detailed the "record-breaking crowds" following the Dodgers, who had become in Smith's words, even though the Negro leagues still were playing full schedules, "the team to see." Another story, celebrating in its headline the 95,000 "cash customers" Robinson had helped draw in four spring training games, Smith said the new Dodger "is definitely box office."[14]

Throughout that first season, Smith presented readers with a picture of racial harmony even though the writer almost certainly knew of the deep dissension among the team's members over the Robinson's presence. It was not uncommon during that 1947 season to see in the *Courier* a photo of Robinson standing, playing, or shaking hands with a white teammate. Off the field, in *Courier* coverage at least, Robinson was the perfect family man, effortlessly balancing the roles of husband, father, ballplayer, and barrier breaker. Signifying the importance the newspaper placed on these portrayals, of a Robinson seamlessly fitting in in all respects, the April 26 issue reported in its news pages the birth of Robinson's and his wife's first child, Jackie, Jr.[15] What is absent in Smith's coverage, again, is significant. An April "Sports Beat" column, for example, included excerpts from letters sent to Robinson in Brooklyn. All of the letters reprinted came from well-wishers, even though, as it has been thoroughly documented since, Robinson's mailbag was weighted down also with hate mail, including death threats. "The fans have been wonderful to me," Smith reported Robinson as saying about his fan mail.[16] In his various autobiographies published later during and after his playing days, including one Smith helped to write, Robinson described receiving a large amount of hate mail throughout that first season, though no evidence of this can be found in Smith's or Robinson's own writing in the *Courier* throughout 1947.[17]

Smith's April 26 mailbag column also hinted at the intimacy between Smith and Robinson. The writer did not deem it necessary to explain to readers how it was that he had such unfettered access to the player's mail and the blanket permission to reprint it in a national weekly. The collaboration between the two extended to a first first-person column Robinson wrote for the *Courier* beginning in the April 5 issue and continuing weekly throughout the 1947 season. How much Smith ghostwrote for Robinson is not known, but, judging by the consistency of the columns' content and emphases with Smith's own reporting, the level of the sports editor's involvement would seem to have been quite high. Robinson wrote, or cooperated to produce, twenty-four exclusive "Jackie Robinson Says" columns for the newspaper his rookie season, and they were uniformly positive. Bursting with enthusiasm for the game, Robinson's weekly reports were characterized by a "gee-whiz" American wholesomeness and optimism. Centered in the column title appeared a body-less cutout of Robinson's face, which bore a toothy grin that stretched from ear to ear. Completely absent in the columns are complaints or even mentions of the hate mail, death threats, cold treatments from opponents and teammates, or of the segregated conditions Robinson endured off the field and on the road.

Robinson's inaugural "Jackie Robinson Says" column set the tone for the columns that followed that first season. "Whenever I hear my wife read fairy tales to my little boy, I'll listen," he wrote. "I know now that dreams do come true."[18] The four-sport letterman was in his own words just an ordinary guy who had been granted a shot at greatness. In later weeks, Robinson wrote about how wonderful the fans were in Brooklyn, "baseball's greatest city."[19] In May, trying to quell rumors in the press of discontent among the Dodgers over his presence, Robinson wrote that on the contrary, "everyone I have come in contact with since I joined the Dodgers has been all right."[20]

Of course all was not right, as a mid-April incident against the Phillies in Ebbets Field made clear. Philadelphia's conduct toward Robinson presented in microcosm a picture of the treatment he had to endure throughout the season, including and even especially during spring training. During the series between the two teams, Philadelphia's Alabama-born manager, Ben Chapman, viciously and unrelentingly heckled and taunted Robinson. Chapman also enlisted at least three Phillies players to do the same, and he instructed his pitchers that whenever they had a 3–0 count against Robinson, to bean him rather than risk walking him. Many years later, Robinson remembered the experience as something akin to "torture," writing that of all the unpleasant days in his life, that cold day in front of the home crowd, with Chapman in his ear, "brought me nearer to cracking up than I ever had been."[21] But Robinson published nothing of his true feelings in his weekly column, and if he had, Smith likely would have edited them out. The "noble experiment" was to the black press as it was to Rickey about much more than one player. Later in the season, when the Dodgers asked Robinson to have his picture taken with Chapman in an effort to smooth over differences and present a positive image to fans, Robinson wrote in his *Courier* column that he was "glad to cooperate" and that Chapman impressed him as a "nice fellow" who did not mean the things he shouted.[22] Robinson's autobiographies remember it much differently. The smiling, apparitional head of Robinson sitting atop his fictional accounts of the 1947 season, therefore, was symbolic. Smith, too, had to keep smiling. The sports editor's "The Sports Beat" columns were in complete harmony with Robinson's weekly depictions.

As the road show continued, Robinson described his first trip to Pittsburgh as "very enjoyable" and his visit to Cincinnati as "a nice experience."[23] In St. Louis, where he and his wife Rachel received death threats, he "never ran into difficulties with the Cardinal players. They were nice to me." In reality, the Cardinal players were consistently abusive, as Robinson described in later, more nuanced recollections. When the Cards visited Brooklyn in early May, some St. Louis players reportedly threatened to strike rather than share the field with a black man.[24] It is also interesting to note how in his weekly column Robinson (and/or Smith) went out of his way to laud some of major league baseball's more infamous racists. After praising Ben Chapman in May and the Cardinals on two occasions in June, Robinson saluted his Montreal manager, Clay Hopper, *The Sporting News* publisher J. G. Taylor Spink, and even the sport's most notorious and nefarious Negro-hater, Ty Cobb.[25] Providing a one-two punch in positive publicity, Smith, too, emphasized the season's more celebratory episodes. In mid-season, for example, Smith chronicled how Robinson's white teammates invited both the first baseman *and* Smith to join them for a round of golf. "There is harmony and unity on the Brooklyn club," Smith wrote, "and Jackie is part of it."[26] (The golf outing did in fact contribute to goodwill toward Robinson from his teammates.)

Another weekly feature, "The Robinson Box Score," was added in May in order to provide Robinson's weekly statistics and season-to-date totals in capsule form. In the May 31 issue, two more weekly features were added: "Dodger Dust," a collection of notes about and details on the Dodgers' season, including trivia such as, "the train was two hours late getting into New York from St. Louis;" and "Diamond Confetti," which consisted of game notes on action during the previous week. One such "Diamond Confetti" note documented Robinson's first home run at the Polo Grounds. Because the *Courier*, like most black newspapers, published weekly rather than daily, roundups were the best the paper could offer in terms of routine game coverage.

Looking at coverage more generally, the tendency during the 1947 season was to ally with major league baseball, which required a distancing from the Negro leagues. A litany of criticisms enabled this stiff-arming, while prominently placed praise of big league baseball's top officials gave at least the appearance of cooperation among major league baseball and the big black weeklies. After the Chapman incident, for example, when the photo opportunity with Chapman and Robinson was arranged, the *Courier* praised Commissioner Happy Chandler for taking "the bull by the horns," action that was in Smith's estimation one of the new commissioner's "most momentous steps." When the Cardinals threatened to stage their strike rather than share the field with Robinson, National League president Ford Frick acted "quickly and firmly" to squash the revolt, charging into the fray with "official guns blazing."[27] Bill Veeck's signing of Larry Doby was cause for the *Courier* to hail Veeck as an owner who kept his word. (The newspaper also took credit for recommending Doby to Veeck in much the same way Smith had recommended Robinson to Rickey.)[28]

The newspapers were supported in their myth-making by a relatively new and already important force within the black community, *Ebony* magazine. Launched just as Robinson signed in 1945, the monthly magazine put the new Dodger on its cover for its September 1947 issue. Pictured with his wife, Rachel, Robinson is wearing civilian clothes and holding his baby boy. Everyone in the picture is smiling, and the photo is juxtaposed with the headline, "Family Man Jackie Robinson." The article's lead sentence refers to the first black major leaguer as, "Ex-Sunday School teacher John Roosevelt Robinson," a man who reporters were amazed to find is "a malted milk devotee who insists he's just 'a home boy' with simple ambitions." A "loyal family man," Robinson was "warmly devoted to his pretty, trim, ex-nurse Rachel Annetta Isum," according to the article. On the Negro league circuit, where Robinson played for only a season, the player was known for his "quiet, modest, yet assured manner," proving himself to be the "exact opposite of all the stereotypes about ball players and about Negroes." (The magazine did not enumerate the stereotypes.)[29] A second story on the Robinson family in the same *Ebony* issue declared that neither Rachel nor

Jackie Robinson smoked or drank and that they did not like nightclubs. Rather, they had preferences and proclivities "typical of the unpretentious life that the Robinsons live." The story did not reference in any way the negative experiences common to the Robinsons since he had joined the Dodgers, which, by September, were numerous. It was more important to portray Robinson as a hamburger-eating, movie-going, vitamin-pill devotee who stressed "the value of good character, dignified behavior and sportsmanship as virtues for all Negro youngsters."[30]

Fay Young performed a similar service for Larry Doby when that player arrived in Cleveland in July 1947 to integrate the American League. In his *Defender* column, Young praised the former Navy man for his service in Guam and for the fact that Doby did not "smoke, drink or swear. He doesn't even drink coffee," Young wrote. "He is married. He has little to say." For once, "things are as they should be—here in America." For signing such a baseball saint Indians management included the "most liberal men" in baseball, according to the *Defender* writer.[31] The *Courier*, too, extolled Veeck and major league baseball for adding Doby, but overlooked the fact that Newark lost its all-time home run king and, therefore, its biggest box office draw.[32] When Effa Manley complained of year-end losses for the team of $20,000, in large part due to Doby's departure, Manley was, in Wendell Smith's words, simply "crying the blues. . . . What [the owners] must realize is that the 'boom' is over and they'll now have to cut salaries and everything else if they expect to keep going." The rather callous attitude also was reflected in what was a common refrain from the black press, including Smith on several occasions, that, echoing Chandler's rebuke, instructed the black leagues to "get their house in order." Smith repeated the advice several times during the 1947 season.[33]

As the Dodgers prepared for the 1947 World Series, Smith, Young, and Lacy each attempted to put the crowning season in historical, societal context. Against this backdrop, the writers also reported on the vast amounts of red ink being spilled throughout the Negro leagues. Looking at the coverage from a macro perspective, it was as if the black press had begun writing the black leagues' obituary in earnest. Smith wrote that heavy payrolls were "killing" the Negro leagues. The owners sought to blame their losses on "everything and everyone but themselves," he wrote, showing no sympathy for the owners or sentimentality toward what had been a fixture in the black community for a quarter-century. "They seem to feel that the world has turned [sic] its back on them and there is nothing they can do about it."[34] W. Rollo Wilson, too, came down hard on owners, who he said had fielded "poor" ball clubs, failed to play according to their schedules, relied on athletes who were too old, and paid players far too much. In his long and varied career, the veteran *Courier* columnist helped to start black teams and leagues, and he served in the leagues' hierarchies in a number of official capacities, including secretary and even commissioner. Worst of all, Wilson wrote, owners blamed major league baseball for their ills rather than taking responsibility for their own deficiencies.[35]

Another key characteristic of coverage in 1947 was the posture toward baseball's black fans, a bloc that was treated more often as a single entity, as if the fans represented a political party united by similar goals and aspirations. Differences in how the *Courier* and the *Defender* spoke to the fans in their sports pages reflected the generation gap between, respectively, Pittsburgh's relatively young sports editor, Wendell Smith, and the dean of all black sportswriters, Fay Young, the first black writer to even have a regular sports column. Smith focused on the game and its players. Young frequently wrote directly to the fans, often in paternal tones. He freely dispensed advice on how to help Robinson and Doby succeed, and just as liberally published rebukes of what he felt was inappropriate behavior at the ballpark, behavior Young feared would diminish mainstream society's opinion of the black community. Young warned fans against drinking, using profane language, and, above all, behaving like "rowdies." Young believed that it was not only Robinson who was on trial, but the Negro fan, as well, making fan behavior "the hot potato dodged by managers who would have taken a chance by signing a Negro player," he wrote. "The unruly Negro has and can set us back 25 years."[36] Anticipating Robinson and the Dodgers in Chicago for a set against the Cubs in late May 1948, the *Defender* warned fans: "Watch your language, no loud voices or clowning, and leave the liquor at home." This game-day advice appeared in a story that ran on the newspaper's front page.[37]

The *Defender*'s paternalism in 1947 certainly was not new. Appearing next to advertisements for whitening cream and hair straighteners, advice on behavior was common in the black press throughout the 1920s and 1930s. It faded from coverage, however, in the early 1940s, returning in 1945 once re-integration neared. Young in 1945 cited fans for playing crap games in the restrooms of Negro league ballparks, using "filthy language," "committing nuisances," and showing disrespect to women in attendance.[38] This posture was not taken by Smith or by the *Courier*'s other writers, nor is it evident in coverage in the *Afro-American*'s sports pages throughout the 1940s.

Robinson's and Doby's major league breakthroughs coincided with high water marks for the black press in terms of readership and circulation numbers and, therefore, influence on and in the black community. Black publishing ventures multiplied during the decade, a boom that included the startups of *Ebony* and *Jet* magazines and the existence of 170 black newspapers. The halcyon days provided "the Negro protest its widest currency," wrote black press scholars Armistead Scott Pride and Clint Wilson, "an orchestrated crescendo just before" *Brown v. Board of Education* in 1954.[39] As part of this protest the black community pressed for fairness and, therefore, looked to shed the emblems and products of segregation. The Negro leagues, therefore, increasingly were seen as sources and reminders of shame, rather than as cause for pride and solidarity. One of black baseball's all-time greats, Homestead Grays first baseman Buck Leonard, said, "After Jackie, we couldn't draw flies."[40]

By the end of the 1948 season, the shift in black press coverage away from the Negro leagues and to major league baseball was complete and irrevocable. In its September 13 issue that season, the *Courier* accompanied a single, six-inch story on the Cleveland Buckeyes winning the Negro American League pennant with blanket Dodger coverage: a page-one promo, a page-two advance on the Dodgers' road trip to St. Louis, a story on Don Newcombe's ailing wife, a story on Roy Campanella's International League-leading statistics, and a roundup of praise of Robinson from the Chicago Cubs' manager. Similarly, in October 1948, the *Defender* celebrated the recently de-segregated Indians with an eight-column, banner headline on its front page, while on page twelve there appeared a single, nine-inch story on the Grays' Negro League World Series title over the Birmingham Black Barons.[41]

Even in baseball's second-tier cities, the black communities there turned toward the major leagues and away from their own teams. In Indianapolis, for example, the emphasis in baseball coverage in the black *Indianapolis Recorder* shifted in 1946 and 1947 away from the hometown Clowns, Chicago's American Giants, and Kansas City's Monarchs and instead to Robinson and the Dodgers. Railway travel packages to take fans to major league cities to see the Dodgers were regularly advertised in the *Recorder*.[42] As they shifted their own attentions and loyalties, the black press's sportswriters hypocritically condemned Negro league owners for giving up. After the fiscally disastrous 1947 season, the Manleys not unwisely sold off their Newark Eagles and exited baseball. Though the Eagles essentially competed with the Dodgers to sell tickets to home games, a competition the Manleys could scarcely win, in the opinion of Wendell Smith, Newark's owners were deserting a black institution in its time of need.[43] The Manleys did not go quietly, however, as Effa Manley lashed out "hotter than horse radish," according to the *Defender*, and blamed the lack of support from fans and from the black press. Both the *Courier* and the *Defender* vigorously defended themselves, providing a glimpse into the collective psyche of the black sportswriters in the context of the great dilemma. Fay Young was apoplectic: "Why blame the Negro Press. . . . Who has helped Negro baseball all these years? Surely not the daily press with all the money spent for publicity men," a reference to the Manleys' hiring of a white publicity man, Jerry Kessler, in 1941. "It has been the Negro Press. Why kick it in the pants now?"[44]

The Cleveland Buckeyes folded after the 1948 season, and Marty Richardson of the Cleveland *Call* reasoned that it was not integration that spelled the team's doom but rather "bad faith with the public by the owners" and poor management.[45] Repeating a familiar refrain found in the sporting pages in the 1940s, Olympian Jesse Owens called on owners and fans in mid-1949 to preserve "the Golden Goose that began to lay golden eggs," the golden eggs being, of course, players like Robinson and Campanella. "If Negro baseball dies, there is no other means of preparing Negro players for the majors," Owens wrote.[46] Ignoring their own transference of allegiances, the *Courier* and the *Defender* pleaded with fans not to forsake the egg-laying golden goose of black baseball. As the Negro American League was set to open its 1948 season, Fay Young wrote, even as he deployed nearly all his newspaper's resources to cover major league action: "It is only right that all of us roll up our sleeves now and give the team our fullest support."[47] In Pittsburgh, the words of the *Courier*'s Jack Saunders reached desperation: "For God's sake, don't let Negro baseball die! . . . I'm not so wrapped up in big league baseball that I've lost interest in Negro baseball! That, I shall never do; my conscious [sic], and my desire to support all Negro enterprises, won't permit me to."[48]

Saunders summarized the great dilemma facing the black press and its readers vis-à-vis the coexistence of a desegregating major league scene and an institution—the Negro leagues—that sprung from segregation and required some degree of it to remain. Which to support? Not surprisingly, in the aggregate, the black newspapers attempted to choose both, at least in terms of their rhetoric. While pressing on for segregation's eradication, the writers and their readers impulsively, reflexively strove also to preserve black businesses and institutions, and the jobs and income they generated. Of course the options were, ultimately, mutually exclusive, and as this became clear, the Negro leagues rapidly declined. Never was the future clearer than in August 1948, when a record number—80,403—crammed into Cleveland Stadium to see Satchel Paige shut out the Chicago White Sox. Meanwhile, across town, the Cleveland Buckeyes, one of the few Negro league teams with the luxury of controlling its own ballpark, failed to draw enough fans to justify another season of baseball. The 3-0 Indians win made the front pages of the *Courier* and *Defender*. The Buckeyes simply could not compete for the black fan's dollar with the integrated Indians, which, with Doby and Paige, not only sold out home games but brought home the ultimate prize, winning the 1948 World Series. More than two and a half million fans bought Indians tickets that title season, which was a record for the club at the time.[49]

After a tortuous 1948 season for black baseball, and anticipating a worse campaign in 1949, Smith wrote the year would determine the black leagues' future. Hinting at his own prediction, he referred to the game as "burlesque," wondering:

> . . . whether we are going to have it in the same gaudy colors and the identical, corny routine. The stage is set and the audience is waiting for the show to go on. The shows in the past haven't been anything to write home about. The theme has been monotonous at times and there have been instances when the cash customers have gotten up and gone home because they refused to accept burlesque after being promised legitimate acts.[50]

Smith's bad theater metaphor followed by a few months a description from the *Defender*'s Young that compared the shoddy Negro league play to bad food and the black press to cooks forced to dish it out. Do not blame the cooks for the bad reviews; blame those buying the food, Young advised.[51] Smith delivered an even harsher rebuke when he described black baseball's owners as more interested in "preservation of their shaky, littered, infested segregated baseball domicile" and the "perpetuation of the slave trade they had developed" than in improving the status of the black ball player.[52] It is difficult to imagine a charge more insulting than to be accused of trading in slaves, a charge made with language that was and is today freighted with associations of the most pejorative, pernicious kind.

The Negro National League folded at the end of the 1948 season because, in the words of one writer, of "crowds which stayed away in huge numbers this past season."[53] The Chicago-based, Martin-led Negro American continued to limp along, but as Robert Peterson wrote, in a post-integration baseball world "few black teams could make money, or break even." The owners quickly moved to sell their good, young players in a last-gasp attempt to recoup their investments.[54] The major leagues, which even by 1953 managed to place but twenty blacks on seven of its sixteen teams, increasingly passed over the Negro leagues and instead signed players directly out of high school and college.

Considering the writers' vituperations, the black press's reaction to the leagues' growing frailty is fascinating. Following a scorched earth policy vis-à-vis coverage and treatment of Negro league officials throughout the mid-1940s, in 1948 the *Courier* and *Defender* separately launched what can only be described as desperate efforts to rescue a despoliated black institution. The attempts were perhaps borne out of remorse, which might explain the fecklessness and futility, even in the near term, of the newspapers' proposals. In a May 1948 issue of the *Courier*, Wendell Smith trumpeted a plan to create "the greatest scouting system ever devised in the history of baseball!," a *Courier*-led campaign to replenish the Negro leagues of talent lost to big league baseball. The paper offered one hundred dollars to any reader recommending a player "who makes the grade" and gets assigned to a Negro league team.[55] The impractical plan signals at least sympathy on the part of the black press with the plight of its erstwhile partner in the fight and perhaps something more profound, like regret or remorse. The same *Courier* issue included no coverage of the very leagues the newspaper proclaimed it was trying to help, however. The *Courier* did publish reactions to the recovery plan from Negro league team owners, who were enthusiastic. That the reactions appeared in the same issue as news of the proposal indicates cooperation between the newspaper and the owners. At the very least, the owners were notified of the plan before publication. Effa Manley called the "Talent Hunt" a "life saver." NAL president J. B. Martin congratulated the paper for its willingness to help the black leagues, and Vernon Green, owner of the Baltimore Elite Giants, expressed gratitude that "some one is going to help find us players."[56]

In another sign or expression of some measure of sympathy, Smith reported that his newspaper would enlist some of the Negro leagues' best former players to serve as "official scouts" in order to find talent. Though many players were invited, however, only one, Elbert "Pops" Turner, agreed to join the campaign.[57] Nonetheless, Smith led the sports section of the *Courier* on three other occasions with essentially the same announcement in a sally of stories that offers more evidence of the sports editor's view of the paper as a participant in and not merely a chronicler of black community affairs.[58] Of course the talent hunt proved an unmitigated failure. In October, Smith confessed that it had been "hard to find Negro baseball talent. . . . They just can't be found and we're going to have to wait until the kids playing in the sandlots around the country develop."[59] There is no evidence in the coverage throughout 1948 of a single reader receiving one hundred dollars or of any "talent" having been found. The *Courier* paid little attention to the Negro leagues in general, focused as it was on Robinson and Campanella in Brooklyn, Paige and Doby in Cleveland, and Don Newcombe and Dan Bankhead in the Dodgers' minor league system.

The *Defender* was no more successful with its scheme, a "National Baseball School initiated and sponsored by the Chicago Defender." The story announcing the concept ran on page one and expressed the newspaper's ambition of finding "the Jackie Robinsons, Satchel Paiges and Larry Dobys of tomorrow" by training young boys and sending them to the Negro leagues.[60] Though the *Defender* claimed cooperation from coaches and athletic directors, colleges and high schools, playground instructors, clubs, churches, fraternal groups, and "sports minded people everywhere," the school never opened.

A controversy in 1949 surrounding a little-known player for the Birmingham Black Barons shows how dramatically the fortunes for young black players had changed just two seasons after Jackie Robinson's big break, as well as the pickle in which the new career potentials placed the black teams. Art Wilson, a shortstop and, in 1948, the NAL's batting champ, was wanted by both the Cleveland Indians and the New York Yankees. Bill Veeck got to him first by signing Wilson while he played winter league baseball in Puerto Rico. The Yankees, meanwhile, negotiated with Black Barons' owner Tom Hayes, Jr., for the rights to Wilson, agreeing to pay $10,000. But Wilson went to the Indians and led the Pacific Coast League in batting in 1949. (He eventually played at the big league level, albeit briefly, for the New York Giants.) Baseball's policy on black players had rapidly changed, Smith noted, "from a 'hands off' agreement to a 'grab 'em quick' pattern."[61] From barring even top black players during wartime, when many of the major leagues' stars left to fight, big league teams in 1949 were grappling over athletes that might or might not play at the highest level.

The loss of talent and resulting erosion in ticket sales quickly cost the Negro leagues three of their most storied and longest-lived clubs—the Homestead Grays, the Newark Eagles, and the New York Black Yankees. The league played on with ten teams in two divisions, but most of these teams were in second-tier baseball cities or markets, such as Memphis, Birmingham, Louisville, and Houston. Again, perhaps out of sympathy, the sportswriters' broadsides were replaced with generally positive coverage. Frank Young anticipated the 1949 season by writing on page one of the owners' promise of a better year, great things, and a bright future, "even though the golden era has passed."[62]

Of the *Courier*'s three sports pages in 1949, the first was devoted to major league coverage, continuing a pattern that began before spring training. Negro league coverage appeared on the second sports page and sometimes even the third. Progress in the integration of the sport was meticulously documented, whether the news came from the Pacific Coast League in California, the Texas League in the Southwest, or the South Atlantic League along the eastern seaboard.[63] Also a part of this blend was regular and oftentimes bylined coverage of sports at the historically black colleges and of city league action, which also served to fill the void left by the disappearing black teams. As part of the continuing campaign to roll out integration in all corners of baseball, the *Courier* in 1949 began protesting the segregated housing conditions endured by black major league players during spring training, a campaign picked up again in the 1950s.[64] In the early 1960s, after being named Chicago's first black columnist with a mainstream daily, the *Chicago American*, Smith used the spring training crusade to establish himself with the paper and among its readers as a champion of the black community.[65]

In columns and editorials mentioning the Negro leagues, gone was the contempt for the owners that had characterized previous years. In its place was passive acceptance of the leagues' news status as artifacts of a fast-fading past. When recounting the color barrier's breaking by Robinson, Smith did not mention the deleterious effects on black baseball.[66] Another editorial early in 1949 called on the Negro colleges to develop big league talent since the black leagues were "operated and conducted in a quaint and unstable manner . . . tottering and leaning toward the chasm of oblivion." Black baseball could no longer be counted on to develop stars, which had become its only raison d'etre in the perspective of the black press.[67] Despite the very public proposals to save black baseball, however, Smith often wrote as if he was embarrassed that the leagues lingered, reminders as they were of a history of subjugation and segregation. In one of his more colorful columns, for example, in March 1949, Smith fabricated a first-person perspective of a former black leaguer recounting his dream-come-true story of playing in the big leagues. In Smith's column-long joke told at the expense of the leagues, the veteran shortstop described his play for the "Black Spasms," members of the "United Consolidated International Benevolent Holy Smokes League."[68] Smith was taking swipes at the up-and-down fortunes of black baseball and the façade of unity the owners so often presented to hide what were in fact deep divisions.

The ridicule was often curiously juxtaposed with calls to blacks for support of Negro league baseball, despite its many flaws. Smith, Ric Roberts, and Jack Saunders, among other writers and columnists, reminded readers ad nauseam that the world would not have Jackie Robinson or Larry Doby if not for the existence of the Negro leagues. As early as May 1949, as marked by a column by Smith, it was enough that the black leagues had furnished major leaguers to excuse the owners for being little more than capitalists, or for failing to be idealists in the Jeffersonian sense. Smith's May column marked a fundamental, cultural shift in perspective.[69] Another cue, albeit a more subtle one, that the Negro leagues had been supplanted is found in a page-one lead column in the *Courier* in summer 1949. Written by society writer Evelyn Cunningham, the article instructs black women going to major league games on how to dress and how to behave.

White fans were "whispering," she wrote, so "girls" had to avoid letting their emotions "run amuck" and make sure they did not "turn epileptic . . . shout race stuff . . . [or] throw ourselves around just a little too much like we are in a conga line."[70] An etiquette column on page one indicates that major league baseball attendance had become de rigeur, even for black females.

The one aspect of Negro league baseball that proved most resilient, because of its social significance on the calendars of blacks throughout the East, Midwest, and even South, was the East-West Classic. Judging by coverage it clearly was the highlight of the 1949 season, even three seasons into Robinson's career. After famously bullying black baseball to "get [its] house in order," Happy Chandler improbably tossed out the Classic's ceremonial first pitch, which marked the unprecedented blending of the two worlds, of white and black baseball. Chandler's very public duties also underline the Negro American League's acceptance of its second-, even third-tier status in the freshly integrated baseball world. Smith noted this "unofficial tie" between black and "organized" baseball, implying in the contrast, perhaps unknowingly, that black baseball was not organized.[71]

Though the *Defender* and *Courier* extensively covered the major leagues' World Series in 1949, the championship won by the Baltimore Elite Giants generated little more than a footnote. The *Courier* devoted all of four inches to Baltimore's four-game sweep of Chicago, while promoting on its front page the upcoming Dodgers-Yankees subway series.[72] After the season, the *Courier* covered the major league meetings in December just as it once covered the Negro league year-end meetings. No story on the Negro leagues' annual conference appeared in the *Courier* in 1949, a season that ended with thirty-six blacks in the major leagues and the Negro league team owners in debt.[73] It was a far cry from previous eras when black writers and black owners dined and smoked together, feting one another at banquets and socializing into the wee hours of the morning in blacks-only hotels.

Chapter Nine
Sunset

Leon Carter: "All those years and all that doubletalk. The white man is finally moving in."

Bingo Long: "I don't care; we're going to rule the league now."

Leon: "Yea man, just as long as the league is still here."

Bingo: "Now what's that supposed to mean?"

Leon: "Ain't no black person gonna pay to see us play no mo, not when they can see kids like Esquire playing with the white boys. No, no, no. This is the end of Negro ball."

Bingo: "When they see Joe do his stuff, they're going to be coming back to see some mo. They like him. They're going to love us."

Leon: "'Fraid not, good buddy. They like a new kind of colored player now. We ain't 19 no more."

Bingo: "Well, that's OK. We in the league now. We the pinnacle of baseball creation. We gonna set it right. New paint and a new scoreboard."[1]

—from *Bingo Long Traveling All-Stars & Motor Kings* (1976)

Determining when Negro league baseball ended is every bit as difficult as pinpointing when it began.[2] For Wendell Smith in early 1950 the Negro leagues were "on the ropes and ready for the killing," a description that preceded "probably the worst [season] in the history of Negro baseball."[3,4] Black baseball historian Larry Lester ends his timeline of the East-West Classic in 1953, even though the all-star game continued in some form until 1963.[5] The 1953 Classic drew only 10,000 people, underwhelming the big league scouts who were on hand to evaluate the fast-shrinking pool of talent.[6] Lester justifies his endpoint with the fact that the 1953 edition was the last to showcase a Negro leaguer on his way to the major leagues—Ernie Banks of the Kansas

175

City Monarchs and Chicago Cubs. Lester's judgment is supported by coverage in the black press, which ended routine, weekly game coverage of the black leagues also after the 1953 season and cast the once-great Classic that year as an also-ran. The *Courier*'s William G. Nunn wrote that year that the midsummer contest and crown jewel of the Negro leagues for twenty years needed nothing short of "an overhauling." The "names" were gone, he wrote, and with them the big crowds, fanfare, celebrities, and high-profile politicians.[7]

Certainly by the mid-1950s the Negro American was semi-professional at best, a shadow of itself compared to a decade earlier. League games were diversions that relied ever more on sideshow entertainment and less on athletic achievement or competition. In some ways this brought black baseball full circle to its beginnings, as sideshow entertainment. The first professional team, the Cuban Giants, used Spanish-sounding gibberish to entertain resort patrons at the Argyle Hotel in New York. In the 1950s, even the entertainment level of league games was, for the black press, somewhere between burlesque and a circus, which affected yet another shift in coverage. Replacing the scalding criticism and ridicule characteristic of coverage a decade earlier were gratitude, tribute, and nostalgia. There were even hints of regret in this pre-civil rights decade, particularly in those Wendell Smith columns that nostalgically remembered black baseball's better days. In Chicago, Fay Young's "Fay Says" column even more frequently recalled memories of black baseball's leaders and star players, especially those of the sport's heyday in the 1920s.[8] Young began regularly reminiscing as early as 1948 when he launched a summer-long series of tributes to "outstanding individuals and events," beginning with Rube Foster, to whom the first four installments were dedicated.[9]

Though not the nationally read newspaper it was in the 1920s and 1930s, Young's *Defender* still wielded great influence in the 1950s. It had no real competition in Chicago after the *Chicago Bee* closed down in 1946. *Muhammad Speaks*, the leading newspaper for black Muslims, did serve Chicago's black community, but sports coverage was not a regular feature in that newspaper. The *Defender* boosted its reach in May 1952 when it acquired the oldest black newspaper still in business, the *New York Age*, but the aggregate circulation of the *Courier*, *Defender*, and *Afro-American* chain declined to 288,000 by 1963, from a high of 661,000 during World War II. Like the Negro leagues, the black press was beginning to lose its top talent to the white dailies as their newsrooms began diversifying in the 1950s. The rapid growth of television also hurt readership. By 1950, one-third of the nation's households claimed at least one TV set.

Sunset 177

Both the *Courier* and the *Defender* frequently used black baseball as a benchmark to measure how successful a black major leaguer had become or how much progress had been made in integrating the sport. When Monte Irvin signed a $25,000 annual contract with the New York Giants for the 1952 season, Fay Young noted that it was five times what the outfielder could have made for his old Negro league team, the Newark Eagles, "plus playing winter ball in South America."[10] Young also congratulated Tom Hayes, owner of the Birmingham Black Barons, when another Giant, Willie Mays, won the National League's Rookie of the Year award. Condolences might have been more appropriate since in Mays the Black Barons lost perhaps the greatest individual of any color to ever play the sport.[11] For the black press, the Negro league players were the currency with which to pay for progress in integrating major league baseball.

Also common to coverage in both the *Courier* and *Defender* were tributes to Foster and Greenlee and the fathers of black baseball, tributes that became more abundant as the number of games dwindled.[12] Smith celebrated the institution as the Eden-like "garden spot" for major league talent:

> Every single Negro player in the big leagues is a graduate of either the Negro American or National Leagues. Ninety per cent of the Negro players in the minors also came from those two circuits. In other words, in the space of six years, the Negro leagues have sent a million dollars worth of ebony talent to the majors and three top minor leagues.[13]

He wrote of the "cherished days" of the roaring 1920s when Rube Foster ruled the black baseball world and of a time that seemed like only yesterday when "a group of enterprising men sat down and dreamed up the [East-West] spectacle."[14] Though an important black economic and cultural institution was dying, for many blacks, especially young blacks, Negro league baseball had become an unwanted relic of a segregated past. Cultural critic Gerald Early has argued that "baseball lost its cultural resonance with the black masses in the 1950s," when integration killed black baseball.[15]

In the larger narrative of integration, therefore, the Negro leagues were increasingly relics of the past. New paint and new scoreboards were not enough. While the major leagues were getting the lion's share of baseball coverage in the black press, space devoted to individual teams depended upon whether or not they had players of color. Race was a far more important variable than even locality or proximity to the newspaper. The Cubs in 1951, for example, were simply nonexistent in terms of *Defender* coverage, and the only mention of the team in 1952 appeared in a Russ Cowans-written season preview in March.[16] In the *Defender* there is little record of the Cubs having even played the 1951 or 1952 seasons, and the trade that sent former Negro leaguer Minnie Minoso to the White Sox further differentiated the North Side Cubs from the South Side Sox. In a letter to the editor published by the *Defender*, a reader noted the "coincidence" of the reversal of fortunes for the Sox and the arrival of Minoso. "Attention you cellar-hanging Cubs," he wrote. "You can't play ball with prejudice, and expect to reach first base."[17]

The *Defender*'s interest in the White Sox only began in 1951 with Minoso's arrival. The "Cuban Flash," who had played for the New York Cubans and the Homestead Grays, came to the Sox that season from the Cleveland Indians as part of a complex, seven-player, three-team trade. The *Defender* published sixty-five stories on the Sox during Minoso's first season, including a three-part feature series on Minoso written by Cowans, who had replaced Young as sports editor of the paper. Cowans's support of Sox management also is telling. The writer defended general manager Frank Lane and field manager Paul Richards against charges that they were holding back two exciting black prospects, calling the accusations "hogwash."[18] No defense of the Cubs was ever offered.

Because the Sox played in Chicago's black community, the city's blacks were pre-disposed to embrace the Sox, an "interracial team" credited by the *Defender* with changing "the racial climate in Chicago."[19] An editorial in the newspaper in 1951 declared that "Win or lose, the White Sox have got the citizens by their hearts," noting that since Paul Richards was "not only a southerner, but a Texan to boot," the team had to be judged as being particularly progressive.[20] Comiskey Park stood "in the middle of the teeming Southside," the editorial writer noted, "perhaps the largest Negro community in the world." Locality determined much of the new loyalty to the Sox, which benefited from a natural—and practical—transfer of patronage for South Side blacks from Negro league teams like the American Giants and Clowns, but only after the Sox integrated.

Even a cursory examination of coverage reveals that race was the key variable in coverage, determining both quantity and quality of coverage. Anticipating the 1952 season, for example, Cowans spent spring training with the Cleveland Indians rather than with either the Cubs or Sox. Cleveland had Larry Doby, Luke Easter, and 39-year-old Quincy Trouppe, while the Cubs still were all white. The Sox had Minoso and third baseman Hector Rodriguez, but no other players of color or veterans of the Negro leagues.[21] Meanwhile, the Negro American could muster just six teams for the sixty-fifth year of black baseball in Chicago. The Baltimore Elite Giants and the New Orleans Eagles shut down after 1951—the Giants because they had no home park and the Eagles because of poor attendance.[22] Two of the remaining six team owners were white, Ed Gottlieb of the Philadelphia

Stars and Syd Pollock of the Indianapolis Clowns. After losing so much top talent to the majors, black teams had only colleges, independent leagues, and Mexican teams to rely upon for replacements. A page-one story in mid-April noted the six former Negro leaguers expected to move up from the minor circuits and into the big leagues for the 1952 season, a crop of players led by the Dodgers' Joe Black and the Indians' Quincy Trouppe.[23] The story noted that the half dozen would push the number of "sepia-toned" big leaguers to eighteen, which meant of course that for a vast majority of Negro leaguers, the job market was shrinking rather than expanding.

In their major league coverage, the black newspapers carefully noted the Race's advances and setbacks throughout the major leagues. As the season began, for example, a mere exhibition game in New Orleans was a major story for the *Defender* in Chicago. Minoso and Rodriguez took the field for the White Sox in the Crescent City in defiance of a Louisiana state ban on integrated play. Attracting the largest crowd in Pelican Park's history, the game against the Pirates earned favor for White Sox general manager Frank Lane, who Cowans credited with "cracking the racial intolerance in New Orleans."[24] The two Cubans did have to dress and shower in separate facilities, but "it was a grand ball game," Cowans quoted Lane as saying, in a page-one story. "When Minoso left the field after five innings, everyone in the park cheered. After that I was proud to be an American," he told the *Defender*.[25]

The minor leagues, too, were desegregating in the early 1950s, and in growing numbers. In June 1952, Mickey Stubblefield, a 24-year-old pitcher for the Pirates, integrated the Class D "Kitty" league.[26] Six of the American Association's eight teams had at least one black player, the holdouts not surprisingly being racially riven Columbus, Ohio, and Louisville.[27] The Texas, Sooner State, and Coastal Plain leagues all dropped restrictions on race for the 1952 season. Even the eight-team Class B Florida International league integrated without incident, a development that caught the attention of the establishment *Sporting News* weekly.[28] The movement gave large cities such as Dallas, Houston, Miami, and Tampa their first integrated minor league contests, and by the end of the year, 104 non-white players appeared on minor league rosters throughout the country.[29] Few of these young players saw action in the Negro leagues.

The end of the 1952 season culminated in a World Series that showcased former Negro leaguers Robinson, Campanella, and newcomer Joe Black, who pitched the Dodgers to two of their three victories, including Game One in only his third major league start. Robinson used the grand stage of the Series to turn up the heat on major league teams that had not yet integrated, especially the Yankees, who he accused of being prejudiced against blacks.[30] The Yankees subsequently leaked to the *Defender* that the club was "racing" the Red Sox to sign pitcher Bill Greason and that the scout who had discovered Mickey Mantle, Tom Greenwade, had been assigned to do it.[31] The unidentified source of the leak assured the paper that New York had "several Negroes in its farm system," though in reality the Yankees did not. The notion of a "race" between the Yankees and Red Sox for a little-known independent Texas league player is far fetched, particularly since both clubs would wait years to integrate, the Yankees until 1955 with Elston Howard and the Red Sox until June 1959 for the ignominy of being the very last.[32] Smith kept the pressure on the Yankees by discussing the team's "definite anti-hiring" policy vis-à-vis blacks. The writer refocused attention on New York every few weeks or so, believing the team to be a pacesetter in the American League. The Yankees' sluggishness did likely retard integration efforts in the American, which lagged behind the National League. Yankees general manager George Weiss did not hide his feelings, saying that he did not want black players because they would attract "the wrong kind of fans."[33]

In 1953 the *Courier* began a series of report cards on the major league teams' progress toward racial integration and their plans to promote minority hires and signings as described by club officials. One of those William G. Nunn interviewed was then-new Cardinals owner, August A. Busch, Jr., who promised to do better in signing more black players for the St. Louis farm teams, a feeder system coincidentally engineered by Branch Rickey in the 1920s.[34] Another *Courier* writer, A. D. Gaither, reported the pledge from Cincinnati Reds general manager Gabe Paul that young black players were "on the way up" through the Reds' minor league system.[35] Both Smith and Young pushed and prodded the Cubs to integrate, and they were specific on how the club should do it—by promoting promising second baseman Gene Baker.[36] When the Cubs did finally bring up Baker in September 1953, at the same time getting Ernie Banks from the Kansas City Monarchs, the black press viewed the moves as belated, desperate, and inevitable, providing a sharp contrast to the newspapers' responses to the signing of Robinson in October 1945. The black papers put news of Banks and Baker in its back pages.

The Cubs indeed were late in integrating, justifying the black press treatment. By the time Chicago turned to the Negro leagues, Rickey had raided them for four rookies of the year.[37] Banks and Baker came to Chicago only a year before *Brown v. Board of Education* and less than two years before Rosa Parks would inspire the civil rights movement in Alabama. The daring of Rickey and Robinson so dramatically contrasts with the desperation of Wrigley and his field manager, Phil Cavarretta.[38] While

Rickey orchestrated high drama, issuing a one-sentence press release just prior to the 1947 season to announce Robinson's new status as a Dodger, the Cubs quietly added Banks and Baker late in an increasingly meaningless 1953 campaign.[39] Former Negro leaguers Robinson, Roy Campanella, Don Newcombe, and Joe Black meant that for the Dodgers, sellout crowds, even on the road, and postseason play were de rigueur.[40] Banks and Baker, meanwhile, came too late to brighten another dark Cub season. Chicago's attendance dropped by more than a quarter-million in 1953, and the team lost $500,000.[41]

Larry Doby and the Indians and, of course, Robinson and the Dodgers were covered wire-to-wire. But until September, the Cubs were largely irrelevant. In the *Defender*'s 1953 baseball coverage, the beginnings of a campaign to get Gene Baker promoted to the parent club is in evidence.[42] The *Defender* noted in March when Baker, a former Monarch, was not promoted and was instead re-assigned to the minor league Los Angeles Angels, but the short article offered no criticism of the parent team.[43] With the Cubs faltering, however, Fay Young in July argued that the team "didn't give a fair break" to Baker in spring training.[44] Cowans joined Young in criticizing in August, writing that the North Siders, "up to their individual and collective necks in the barrel of trouble," could use Baker, who Cowans accurately described as a better shortstop than Cub starter Roy Smalley."[45]

When the Cubs finally promoted Baker from the Angels and signed Banks and Bill Dickey from the Monarchs in September 1953, the *Defender* framed the decisions as coming from a team succumbing to pressure rather than from one proactively making roster moves: "Under extreme pressure from both the fans and newspapers in their respective cities, the Detroit Tigers and the Chicago Cubs have finally signed Negro ball players," wrote an un-bylined writer, most likely Cowans. The article specifically cited "a number of daily newspapers" that had been campaigning for the addition of Baker to bolster a Cub defense that "fell apart" during the 1953 season.[46] Chicago's big move was treated as a trivial piece of news by the *Defender*, which announced Baker's buyout on page sixteen. There were no columns celebrating the move. No credit was claimed by the paper. In fact, far more attention was paid to Robinson's Dodgers, who were gearing up for another Series against the Yankees. Robinson, at 34 one of Brooklyn's "Old Men," was playing at his fourth position for the Dodgers during the 1953 season, putting the Cubs' recalcitrance into some historical perspective.[47]

In the opinions of the *Defender*'s sports writers, the Cubs were late and, therefore, deserved little credit among readers. In contrast, the newspaper hailed St. Louis Browns' owner Bill Veeck, who had integrated the Indians in 1948, and supported him in his fight to keep the team in St. Louis. Fay Young characterized major league baseball's decision to move the Browns to Baltimore as punishing Veeck for integrating the American League in 1948.[48] That Veeck's '48 Cleveland Indians made it to the World Series added insult to injury, or, in this case, injury to insult.

The bulk of newspaper space once devoted to black baseball games in 1953 went to the Sox. The *Defender* covered the team from January through December, with most of the attention going to Minoso. When Rodriguez lost his third base job to Rocky Krsnich in January, the *Defender* led its baseball coverage with the story.[49] The paper placed on page one the benching of Minoso in Memphis for a pre-season game between the Sox and Cardinals because of a local Jim Crow ordinance.[50] And a story on the late-season call-ups of former Negro leaguers Bob Boyd and Connie Johnson featured a three-column photo of the new Sox.[51]

Before he joined the Cubs, Banks provided black fans with a legitimate reason to pay to see a Negro league game. He arguably helped the entire Negro American League stay afloat. The Monarchs' home opener in 1953 versus the Clowns, for example, drew 18,205 fans—a good crowd by even major league standards.[52] The Sunday game gave Missourians and Kansans an opportunity to see the Negro leagues' first female player, Clown second baseman Toni Stone. Though Stone was a good player, she obviously was a sideshow attraction, a strategic roster move designed to sell tickets more than to win games.[53] The former Minnesota high school star gave the Clowns "a road attraction unequalled in Negro baseball," according to the *Defender*, which did not question or criticize the gimmicks and stunts of the Clowns' owner, Syd Pollock.[54]

Stone was joined in July by "the nation's foremost baseball clown," Ed Hamman, a roster move that removed any doubt that Pollock and his "Funmakers" were more entertainers than professional athletes, and this shift came just a single season removed from Henry Aaron's statistically spectacular half-season with the team in 1952.[55] Characteristic of coverage of the Clowns by the *Defender*, the "roster moves" were documented without critique, skepticism, or historical perspective.[56] These player moves also included adding "King Tut," who used a ridiculously large glove and dressed either as an Egyptian pharaoh or in a tux and top hat, and a dwarf named Spec Bebop, who entertained but did not play.[57] The *Defender*'s Clowns coverage read just as one might think Pollock had wanted it to, by announcing upcoming games and celebrating the entertainment values of the "Imps of the Diamond," a "baseball circus really worth seeing."[58] (Pollock, who based his operations in Tarrytown, New York, moved the team several times, a transience that inspired Wendell Smith to refer to it as the Cincinnati-Miami-Ethiopian Clowns.[59])

The newspaper's unwillingness to criticize the "circus" that black baseball had become points to the conflicted position the black press found itself vis-à-vis the Negro leagues as it pressed for fuller integration. In the 1940s black newspapers refused to cover the Clowns, seeing them as "a detriment to Negro league baseball" and as an embarrassment to blacks everywhere.[60] The *Courier*'s Wendell Smith, in 1943, called the Clowns a "fourth-rate Uncle Tom minstrel show."[61] By 1953, novelties, gimmicks, and comedy seemingly were required to attract paying customers. In the late 1950s, all that remained of the Negro leagues were traveling troupes owned by white promoters. The end of segregation meant fewer opportunities for black ballplayers, not more, and black team ownership disappeared for a half-century.[62]

Prior to the 1950s and black baseball's dependence on sideshows, the black press consistently criticized the Clowns. Distasteful to the writers was Pollock's promotion of negative racial stereotypes and what they felt was the trivialization of black baseball for profit. For Pollock, neither the criticism nor its reasons was new. In the early 1930s, Pollock owned the Cuban House of David, one of several crack all-star teams that attracted attention with its "Jewishness," including long beards for its players.[63] In the 1940s, Cum Posey said sportswriters would "always feel disgusted at [Clowns owner] Syd [Pollock] for . . . capitalizing on the rape of Ethiopia when that country was in distress."[64] The *Courier* called white promoter Abe Saperstein a "bad influence" since by booking games for the Clowns he was "ridiculing Negro baseball, Negro players and the race in general."[65] In 1942 the *Defender* called the team "a detriment to Negro league baseball."[66] Wendell Smith did not like the potential effect on the perceptions of whites of black baseball. Whites "like to believe" that the Clowns' slapstick comedy and nonsensical approach "is typical and characteristic of all Negroes."[67] For most of the team's history, in fact, the black newspapers did not cover the Clowns at all, except to serve notice of their upcoming games with Negro league teams. Neither did the newspapers cover similar "clown" acts, such as the Zulu Cannibal Giants, Cincinnati Clowns, Tennessee Rats, or Jax Zulo Hippopotamus Clowns of New Orleans.[68] The Negro leagues prohibited member clubs from playing the Ethiopian Clowns, as the Clowns were known prior to 1943, until the Clowns' profits became too substantial to ignore. The Negro National League invited them in as members in 1943, provided they change their name, which they did, to the Indianapolis Clowns. Because they were a barnstorming team, the Clowns survived through the 1950s.

The year 1954 was predicted by the *Defender* to be "the turning point when baseball truly could [not] ignore racial prejudice," and the newspaper was in part correct. Banks and Baker would play a full season in Wrigley. Minoso again appeared with the Sox in Memphis to play the Cardinals, this time defying that city's racial ban by playing.[69] Cincinnati, Pittsburgh, St. Louis, and Washington would add their first African Americans, leaving only the Phillies, Tigers, Red Sox, and Yankees without a "tan" player.[70] Five more minor league circuits would integrate, including the Southern Association and Georgia State League.[71] And May 17 would become "Decision Day," as it was called in the black press, the day the Supreme Court outlawed "separate but equal" in public schools in its landmark decision, *Brown v. Board of Education*. Previewing the 1954 baseball season in March, the *Defender* covered the spring training camps of the Cubs, Indians, Sox, Giants, and Dodgers. The teams were treated equally, in both tone and in the amount of column inches devoted. The Cubs finally were in the club, relevant, and of interest to Chicago's black community. The Sox, however, clearly were South Side blacks' team of choice, as a page-one season preview story headlined, "Pennant Fever Hits Chicago Again As Fans Await Sox Opener Tuesday," demonstrated.[72] Judging by *Defender* coverage, there were no black fans awaiting the Cubs' opener.

The newspaper's coverage of the Cardinals' integration, however, offers an interesting contrast to that of the Cubs. While the Cubs' owner, chewing gum magnate Philip K. Wrigley, is not mentioned by the *Defender* in the early 1950s and, therefore, is not seen as a sympathetic figure, Cardinals owner August Busch, whom the paper refers to as "Gussie," received entirely favorable coverage.[73] Where the Cubs promoted Baker "under pressure," Busch a season later was characterized as "spear-heading the drive" to integrate the Cardinals organization in acquiring San Diego Padre Tom Alston.[74] One possible reason for the deferential treatment was Alston's high price tag for the Cardinals, who gave the Padres more than $100,000 and four players. An astronomical price for a minor leaguer at that time, it easily was the most paid for a former Negro leaguer. The *Defender* gave Busch credit for "personally negotiating" the deal, and described him as "tickled pink" in acquiring the first baseman.[75] The "Gussie" nickname and colorful descriptions indicate an access to and intimacy with Busch that Cowans and the *Defender* possibly enjoyed, a closeness clearly absent in dealings with Wrigley.

By June, the Cubs were again irrelevant, but for purely competitive reasons. Mired in seventh place, the North Siders lacked pitching and power. Banks' explosive, record-setting slugging was a year away. Fay Young wrote in mid-July a twenty-inch column on the "Cubs Woes," the longest *Defender* story on the team during the early 1950s. Young expressed a lament that contemporary Cubs fans might find depressingly familiar: "Mr. Wrigley has the money. . . . Why don't [sic] he go out and buy players and give us a pennant? . . . Headaches and headaches, and fans yelling 'bloody murder.'"[76] In contrast to the deference paid to Busch, Young faulted Wrigley for overlooking Willie Mays and Junior Gilliam, both of whom played regularly in Chicago in Comiskey Park when their teams—the Black Barons and Baltimore Elite Giants, respectively—came to town to play the American Giants. The Cubs suffered another ignominious season, finishing second to last with just sixty-four wins in 154 games. But Chicago's season proved a picnic compared to that of the Negro American League. Despite all evidence, all odds, and even common sense, league president J. B. Martin predicted "a good season" for the four-team circuit. "In fact, I'm convinced it will be the best season since the war."[77] It was not. That the newspaper did not question Martin's improbable prediction signaled again the conflicted goals of its sports coverage, namely, to advance integration while in contradiction preserving a black institution.

The Indianapolis Clowns, Kansas City Monarchs, and Satchel Paige provided case studies of the sad state of black baseball. Paige signed to play with the Harlem Globetrotters, a traveling squad on the model of the famous basketballers of the same name, both owned by Chicago-based Abe Saperstein. The Monarchs made Toni Stone their highest paid player. And the Clowns added two more female players—Connie Morgan and Mamie "Peanut" Johnson, promising "unmatched comedy."[78] All that remained for black baseball was life on the road. Young, who had covered the first black professional league, the Negro National beginning in 1920, had witnessed and reported on the ebbs and flows of the sport as a black-run enterprise; he knew 1954 marked a low point: "We, who have spent more than half a life time following and helping to create an interest in the game 'are of no use to the game now,' . . . so why worry about it?" he wrote.[79]

Beginning in 1954, another shift in coverage was evident in both the *Courier* and *Defender*. When the words "National League," "American League," or "Spring Training" were used in headlines, they invariably referred to major league baseball and not, as in decades past, the Negro leagues. "Training Camp Scenes," for example, in a March 13 *Courier* appeared with three photos of the Chicago Cubs and Milwaukee Braves at spring training, where the black newspapers had reporters on site. This unannounced and subtle change reflects the assumption made by the black papers that the chief reference point in baseball for the black community had become the major leagues. Later, in 1957, the *Courier* published an eight-page "Baseball Supplement." It included no reference to the Negro leagues in any context and pertained wholly to the major leagues.[80]

Smith described this shift in a startling February 1954 "Sports Beat" column in which Negro baseball was declared "forgotten," a league in which baseball fans were "no longer interested." The black press, once "Negro baseball's most ardent supporter, focused a vast majority of its attention on the major leagues," a switch that for Smith was "understandable" since readers "wanted everything [they] could get about Negro players in the majors." The black press was obligated, then, "to devote as much space as possible to the subject," a devotion that Smith admitted had cost black baseball "its voice."[81] This column provides perhaps the most unequivocal explanation from a black sportswriter for the changes in coverage and the cost of those changes to black baseball. Almost precisely a year later, Smith penned another obituary for the Negro American League, noting that it was down to four teams and had lost even the Clowns. Putting the blame for the league's collapse on the greed and disunity among team owners, Smith indicted ownership for using baseball "as a front, to cover up other means of endeavor and various shoddy enterprises." The column marked the first time Smith noted the common practice in the 1930s of fronting numbers businesses with baseball operations.[82] It was almost as if Smith was shoring up his own defense of the black press for its abandonment of black baseball.

John Johnson, sports editor at the Kansas City *Call*, wrote after the 1955 season that "Negro baseball has served its purpose." Black players in the major leagues "eternally proved that race has absolutely nothing to do with the ability to measure up whenever a man is given a fair chance to make good," he poignantly wrote. Johnson also noted that he could not definitively report which team had won the 1955 Negro league title. This no longer was cause to criticize the teams for failing to send in game reports. In late 1955, it was proof that "there is no longer a need or justification for a Negro league," the editor wrote, a league that had become "a relic of a jim crow period."[83]

Epilogue

As C. Vann Woodward wrote, there is a "twilight zone that lies between living memory and written history," a zone that is one of the "favorite breeding places of mythology."[1] Since so many Negro league histories, including nearly all of those most popularly read, rely upon oral history for their accounts, the black press has become an indispensable primary source in what otherwise might have remained one of the more impressionistic and inaccurate "twilight zones" of legends and lore. The microfilmed pages of the Kansas City *Call*, *Chicago Defender*, *Pittsburgh Courier*, and *Afro-American*, among others, are the primary sources upon which modern-day Negro league scholarship depends. In documenting the history of the black community in the twentieth century's first half, these newspapers are a vital reflector of culture and of daily life, at least for the mostly middle-class blacks who were these papers' primary readers. The black sportswriters who are the focus of this book, the key change agents in this reading of history, provided in their coverage and commentary a comprehensive record of an institution wholly lost in the name of desegregation.

This record shows that direct involvement in locally owned black businesses, including baseball teams, was a natural dimension to and an extension of the newspapers' role in the communities they served. The papers often were participants in and leaders of charity events, fundraising drives for civic causes, and various festivals and events within the black community. These roles were not viewed as conflicts of interest, as they might have been for mainstream daily newspapers, but rather the duty and responsibility of an alternative, minority press, the voice of an oppressed people. This was particularly true in the early years of the period studied here, in the 1920s and early 1930s, when the newspapers joined black business leaders to build up the black community from within. After the desegregation of professional baseball, these newspapers advocated and fought for equal rights and access in all walks of life, in all pursuits and professions, which meant of course advocating a deathblow to many of the businesses with which these papers once partnered. The constant over time was service to the community of readers and to remaining relevant in and through the greater societal changes. Early, this meant working for economic viability and self-sustenance. Later, it produced claims to the black's rightful place in mainstream society and, therefore, separation from or movement beyond the racially defined institutions, enterprises, and expressions segregation had spawned.

One way to track shifts in coverage is to examine the treatment of and access provided to black baseball's team owners over time. After a decade of "boosteristic" support in the 1920s, black baseball's magnates found themselves criticized in the 1930s by writers increasingly frustrated by the owners' avarice, mismanagement, and dissension, among other flaws. Columns and articles of support were still published, but gone in the mid- and late-1930s was the intimacy and camaraderie enjoyed at lavish dinners and clubby smokers just a decade prior. In the 1940s, the crusade to integrate baseball moved from the sports pages of the black press to its front pages, and into the pages of the white dailies and even the Communist press, as well. The Communist *Daily Worker* seized on baseball's ban, seeing in baseball a microcosm of "all that was wrong with American capitalism."[2]

As did many Americans, the black press viewed the nation's spectator sport of choice as an important emblem and barometer of American culture and of its openness to diversity. In some ways, baseball was at the forefront. "What people didn't realize, and still don't, was that we got the ball rolling on integration in our whole society," Buck O'Neil wrote. "Remember, this was before Brown versus Board of Education of Topeka. When Branch Rickey signed Jackie, Martin Luther King was a student at Morris College. We showed the way it had to be done, by just keeping on and being the best we could."[3]

Perhaps no individual black writer was more pivotal than was Wendell Smith, who provided the critical link between Branch Rickey and Jackie Robinson and who actively campaigned for baseball's integration his entire journalistic career. Smith recommended Robinson to Rickey as "The One," and he helped the Dodgers' president keep tabs on and scout Robinson throughout the 1945 season. Smith kept quiet on the biggest story of his career for fear of preventing that story. To give Robinson every chance at success, the writer accompanied white baseball's only black player in spring training and on the road during the regular season. He secured Robinson segregated accommodations, provided the player and his wife with companionship, and carefully crafted his public image in the pages of the *Pittsburgh Courier*, even ghostwriting Robinson's first-person newspaper column throughout the debut 1947 season.

Daily newspapers exhibited little awareness of the significance of Robinson breaking through in the major leagues. A reflector of mainstream culture and its values, these metropolitan dailies demonstrated by omission the extent of prejudice and racism in America, missing entirely the societal importance of Robinson's emergence. The white dailies reported on the new Dodger as merely an athlete. Once Robinson made Brooklyn's roster, the black press immediately and comprehensively shifted resources to coverage of the Dodgers and away from the Negro leagues, sending important cues to a black readership with newly divided loyalties, especially at a time when even use of the term "Negro" in an institution's or organization's name became debatable within the black community.

The newspapers, themselves, exhibited divided loyalties, as well. Once the color barrier had been broken, the peril of the Negro leagues became a frequent topic of discussion in the black weeklies, but, once again, the conduct of the leagues' team owners complicated coverage. With their enterprises threatened, many of the owners fought either to hold on to their players or to get compensation from major league teams for the rights to those players, efforts that were seen by some writers as obstructionist.[4] The owners' actions, therefore, provided sportswriters with an opportunity to distance themselves from their erstwhile partners, and for the most part the writers obliged.

By the late 1940s and early 1950s, however, the black press's scolding softened and gave way instead to tribute and even nostalgia. The sometimes wistful longing for black baseball's glory days underlines the dilemma that divided loyalties can produce for a people desiring to enjoy full access to and participation in greater society while at the same time preserving its unique identity apart from that society. This double-consciousness, as Du Bois called it, produced the wrenching choice between preserving the Negro leagues, which would have meant holding back or retarding the professional growth of their players, in order to maintain separation and subordination, or killing it on the altar of integration, the sacrifice of an institution that had meant so much to so many, a uniquely black enterprise, an important summertime diversion, and an economic engine employing at its zenith more black executives than the number who have made a living in major league baseball since.[5] Like Native Americans before them and native Alaskans since, blacks gave up more than they gained but believed there could be no other way. As black writer and critic Amiri Baraka wrote, the Negro leagues were:

> like a light somewhere. Back over your shoulder. As you go away. A warmth still, connected to laughter and self-love. The collective black aura that can only be duplicated with black conversation or *music* . . . these were professional ballplayers. Legitimate black heroes. And we were intimate with them in a way and they were extensions of all of us, there, in a way that the Yankees and Dodgers and whatnot could never be! . . . It was like we all communicated with each other and possessed ourselves at a more human level than was usually possible out in cold whitey land.[6]

The demise of the Negro leagues, however inevitable, meant an end to "an important black economic and cultural institution," cultural critic Gerald Early wrote, the erasure of something that "encompassed many of the best and worst elements of African-American life." Blacks never fully absorbed the leagues' loss because they never fully understood the "ironically compressed expression of shame and pride, of degradation and achievement that those leagues represented," he wrote.[7]

For O'Neil, the death of the Negro leagues provided yet another irony for black Americans, "the hardest one," because not only did the black business of baseball die, black businesses related to baseball it disappeared, as well. O'Neil wrote that among these casualties were

> the ones that were dependent on black baseball and black entertainment. The Streets Hotel had to close because it couldn't compete with the Muehlebach Hotel [in] downtown [in Kansas City]. The Vincennes in Chicago went out because the ballplayers were staying in the Loop now. Instead of the Woodside [in New York City], they were staying in Times Square. A way of life came to an end along with black baseball. But I guess it couldn't be any other way.[8]

As integration marched on, incrementally and with many setbacks, the black press and its readers left black baseball further and further behind. It was time, according to the black sportswriters, to achieve on an integrated stage and to claim the respect that that achievement merited. One black press writer, Eddie Gant, wrote in a 1940 issue of the *Defender,* as if to predict the story of Jackie Robinson, that the "rise of the Negro athlete to fame in America" was a saga not yet fully told, a story of battling prejudice, Jim Crow, and discrimination "all along the line." The black athlete's "undeniable brilliance and fair play" had won the respect and admiration of sports fans all over the country, he wrote.[9]

Like the Negro leagues, the black press risked making itself irrelevant in fighting for integration into mainstream American life. The paradox of being a protest press dedicated to integrating blacks into American life meant that the more this press succeeded, the less justification there would be for its own inherently temporal existence. Like the Negro leagues, from the founding of the *Freedom's Journal* in 1827, the black press has been designed for a particularly historical "moment" and task. Black writers began finding work at daily papers and, subsequently, those papers began covering the black community. With vastly greater resources and reach, mainstream papers easily attracted the best writers and reporters from the black press and recruited the best new talent coming out of colleges and universities. This cycle mirrored the talent drain that rapidly diluted the Negro leagues. Who could blame black journalists for taking more money, just like the black players before them, or for benefiting from greater resources and wanting to reach vastly larger audiences than those of the black weeklies? As long-time *Courier* writer and executive, P. L. Prattis, wrote in 1947, black journalism students choosing to work for a Negro newspaper had the opportunity of "restricted growth in a restricted, segregated field." The black press in 1947 could offer only a journalism "made necessary by the depressive and enervating effects of segregation."[10]

Black press historian Armistead S. Pride was among the first to point out that black sportswriters, like the baseball players they wrote about, were victims of Jim Crow. Segregation hid their talents from mainstream America, restricted their careers, limited their income-earning potential, shut them out of major and minor league press boxes, and subjected them to slights and insults wherever they went. Yet these writers referred to their own plight on only the rarest of occasions and almost always only when asked directly about Jim Crowism.

As early as June 1949, when still only four major league teams had integrated, the black newspapers confronted their own future, an era that would begin "when and if the causes for which they are 'special pleaders' are corrected," the *Courier* stated.[11] At a conference for black newspapers organized to ask and answer the central question of mission and purpose, the consensus was that the black press needed to turn to "the larger responsibility of impartial and unbiased news reporting," in other words to surrender the very quality that made the black press uniquely the voice of the communities it served. Like the Negro leagues, the black press began to question whether it had legitimacy outside the context of segregation.

For his part, Pride argued at the time that, like black churches, colleges and schools, music and literature, the black press would indeed survive, even flourish, as long as there was a cause for which to fight. "It is extremely unlikely that desegregation will bring Utopia in America," he wrote in the *Pittsburgh Courier* in 1957, a year in which the Detroit Tigers, Philadelphia Phillies, and Boston Red Sox remained all-white.[12] Though professional and major college sports increasingly became the domains of black athletes, they were "the only area[s] where they are right on top," wrote Donald McRae, biographer of Joe Louis and Jesse Owens.[13] Within baseball, however, progress was slow and not always certain. The "desegregation of most clubs advanced with remarkable hesitancy," wrote Jackie Robinson scholar Jules Tygiel.[14] Teams adopted de facto quotas. Racism continued to rule in spring training in the South, where black and white players were housed separately as late as 1963.[15] Because they were so vast and because their member clubs played in southern hamlets and towns that were bastions of Jim Crow customs, the minor leagues, in particular, stubbornly clung to segregation well into the 1960s.

This book is part of a greater effort toward a fuller record of the black experience and of the newspaper's role as a chronicler, reflector, and even shaper of that experience. As such, it is an examination of how the black press viewed itself as a change agent on behalf of its readers. But hopefully it is more than that. Hopefully it exposes a new readership to the contributions to American society of both the black press and the Negro leagues, for segregation always deprives the majority responsible for the separation, as well. Sam Lacy, who died as this book was being written, in May 2003 at age 99, once said that he felt that "whites [too] were being deprived" by not being able to enjoy the talent and play in the Negro leagues. "I could see both were being cheated," he said.[16] Oh, for the ability to time-travel and, therefore, have the opportunity to see Cool Papa Bell run the bases, Josh Gibson belt a homerun, Satchel Paige throw his midnight creeper, or Oscar Charleston chase down flies in centerfield.

Of course, Lacy also wrote, "Oh, we've come a long way. . . . But we've still got a long way to go."[17] In some respects, progress made in years past is being surrendered anew. Studies show that America's schools, to cite one example, are re-segregating, while the country's historically black colleges in many cases struggle even to survive.[18] White flight and white resistance to black equality has negatively affected public education in the twenty-first century by re-segregating schools and communities on a massive scale. The flight of the black middle classes has contributed, as well, as has indifference on the part of government. Just as Negro league baseball suffered in the previous century, predominantly minority schools have scant resources with which to work. And as was the case in professional baseball in the last century, desegregation in schools in this century will not occur serendipitously. Deliberate change and dogged persistence will be necessary.

Exemplars of persistence in the past, black newspapers cannot be counted upon in this century. In part because of past successes in the fight against racial segregation, these newspapers are a shadow of themselves, smaller in reach and influence. Lacy's sense of deprivation on both sides of the racial divide is, unfortunately, as valid as it has ever been.

Like black baseball and historically black colleges, the black press has seen its mission and very identity challenged by diversity.[19] A question for the *New Pittsburgh Courier,* Kansas City *Call, Atlanta World,* and other black newspapers in the twenty-first century, beyond the questions related to survival, is how to remain a distinct forum for African American voices and ideas. It is a question starkly similar to that faced by black baseball a half-century ago.

Notes

NOTES TO THE INTRODUCTION

1. Quoted in Jerry Malloy, ed., *Sol White's History of Colored Base Ball* (Lincoln, Neb.: University of Nebraska Press, 1995), 74.
2. Walter Leavy, "50 years of blacks in baseball," *Ebony* 50, no. 8 (June 1995): 38.
3. Neil Lanctot, *Fair Dealing and Clean Playing: The Hilldale Club and the Development of Black Professional Baseball, 1910–1932* (Jefferson, N.C.: McFarland & Co., 1994), 61.
4. Jules Tygiel, *Extra Bases, Reflections on Jackie Robinson, Race, and Baseball History* (Lincoln: University of Nebraska Press, 2002), 72.
5. Arthur Ashe, *A Hard Road to Glory* (New York: Warner Books, 1988), 87.
6. Donn Rogosin, *Invisible Men: Life in Baseball's Negro Leagues* (New York: Kodansha International, 1995), 22–23. The Booster Club was made up of black merchants, fraternal organizations, deacons, and various community organizations. In return for their support, the Monarchs played benefit games for various organizations, such as the Negro National Business League, the NAACP, and the Red Cross, as well as churches, hospitals, and youth organizations. Several cities featured booster clubs, such as the Hilldale (Philadelphia) Royal Rooters and Baltimore's Frontiers Club. Tygiel described the Monarchs' booster club as "the most lavish of these organizations" (*Extra Bases,* 72). Formed in 1926, Kansas City's boosters sponsored banquets for the players, staged beauty contests at ball games, and organized the big opening day parade each season.
7. Tygiel, *Extra Bases*, 72.
8. The term "Race man" refers to a black man who saw himself as a defender of his race and an advocate for his people and the rightful place he believed African Americans should hold in society. By this definition, W. E. B. Du Bois was perhaps the quintessential "Race man."
9. Rogosin, *Invisible Men*, 34–35.

10. W. E. B. Du Bois, *The Souls of Black Folk* (1903), available online at http://www.bartleby.com/114/.
11. Henry Lewis Suggs, *The Black Press in the Middle West, 1865–1985* (Westport, Conn.: Greenwood Press, 1996), 1.
12. Ibid.
13. Juliet E. K. Walker, "The Promised Land: The Chicago Defender and the Black Press," in Suggs, ed., *The Black Press in the Middle West*, 24.
14. Barnstorming refers to the practice of taking a team on the road and playing whatever competition that could be found. The Harlem Globetrotters continue to use this method in the twenty-first century, albeit with far more organization in terms of scheduling, arranging venues, marketing, and selling tickets than Negro league assemblies could muster. The barnstorming lifestyle of ballplayers was a focus in the 1976 motion picture, *The Bingo Long Traveling All-Stars & Motor Kings*.
15. Gerald Early, "Understanding Integration: Why Blacks and Whites Must Come Together as Americans," *Civilization* 3, no. 5 (1996), 52.

NOTES TO CHAPTER ONE

1. *The Strange Career of Jim Crow* (New York: Oxford University Press, 1957). The origins of the term "Jim Crow" are murky, but in 1832, Thomas D. Rice wrote a song and dance called 'Jim Crow' and by 1838 it had become common parlance. The expression first appears in a dictionary in 1904 (Woodward, 7).
2. Paul Debono, *Indianapolis ABCs: History of a Premier Team in the Negro Baseball Leagues* (Jefferson, N.C.: McFarland Press, 1997), 44.
3. Jerry Malloy, "The Pittsburgh Keystones and the 1887 Colored League, Baseball in Pittsburgh," in *Baseball in Pittsburgh* (Cleveland: Society for American Baseball Research, 1995), 49. Brown also owned the Pittsburgh Keystones, one of the more successful early black teams.
4. Neil Lanctot, *Fair Dealing and Clean Playing: The Hilldale Club and the Development of Black Professional Baseball, 1910–1932* (Jefferson, N.C.: McFarland & Co., 1994), 11.Town ball, like England's lawn game of cricket, is a likely forerunner of baseball. It sometimes is referred to also as the Massachusetts game or the New England game.
5. Harry Silcox, "Efforts to Desegregate Baseball in Philadelphia: The Pythian Baseball Club, 1866–1872," unpublished manuscript, National Baseball Library (undated), 1–8. Archives of the Pythian Baseball Club are housed in the Historical Society of Pennsylvania in Philadelphia.
6. Charles A. Peverelly, *The Book of American Pastimes, Containing a History of the Principal Base-Ball, Cricket, Rowing, and Yachting Clubs of the United States* (New York: The Author, 1866), 337.
7. Ibid.
8. White in Malloy, 8.
9. To get enough players to form the Athletics, Thompson orchestrated the merging of three black teams—Philadelphia's Orians and Keystone Athletics, and the Manhattans of Washington, D.C. (see Lanctot, 12–13).

Notes to Chapter One

10. Spalding, *Baseball* (San Francisco: Halo Books, 1991), 85–6. The book originally was published originally as *America's National Game* in 1911.
11. Ibid., 95.
12. Jerry Malloy, "The Birth of the Cuban Giants: The Origins of Black Professional Baseball," *Nine*, v. 2, no. 2 (Spring 1994), 236.
13. Most famous of McGraw's attempts was disguising black player Charlie Grant as "Chief Tokohoma," a Cherokee Indian, in 1901. White Sox owner Charles Comiskey complained to the Commissioner's office, and McGraw was forced to drop the charade.
14. Personal interview, 9 January 2004, Chapel Hill, N.C.
15. *Colored Baseball and Sports Monthly* (October 1934), 16.
16. Sol White's description of the players as being waiters first and secondarily baseball players differs from Malloy's, who believes they were ballplayers first, then later, after the season's end, given hotel positions.
17. Lanctot, *Fair Dealing and Clean Playing*, 16.
18. John Betts, *America's Sporting Heritage: 1850–1950* (Reading, Mass: Addison-Wesley, 1974), 98.
19. Dan Burley, writing in the *Chicago Defender* in 1936, stated that the first Race team in Chicago was Willie Peters' Union Giants formed in 1870 ("Sports Secret Service Department," 30 May 1936, 13).
20. White, in Malloy, 12.
21. *Sporting Life*, 18 May 1887, no page number available.
22. Leslie Heaphy, "Shadowed Diamonds: The Growth and Decline of the Negro Leagues," Ph.D. dissertation (University of Toledo, 1995), 14. By the end of the nineteenth century, more than sixty all-black teams had organized, most of them in the Northeast.
23. Lanctot, *Fair Dealing and Clean Playing*, 17–18. Common terms in the white press referencing black teams included "coons," "duskies," and "chocolates." Neumann, *The Spiral of Silence: Public Opinion—Our Social Skin* (Chicago: University of Chicago Press, 1993).
24. "The Negro Since Freedom," in C. Vann Woodward's *Comparative Approach to American History* (New York: Oxford University Press, 1997), 166.
25. It is possible that another player, William Edward White, preceded Walker as the first black player in the major leagues. White apparently played one game for the Providence Greys of the National League on June 21, 1879, five years before Walker played for the Blue Stockings, while enrolled as a student at Brown University. It has not yet been confirmed, however, that White indeed was black (see Stefan Fatsis, "If Sleuths Are Right, Jackie Robinson Has New Company," *Wall Street Journal*, 30 January 2004, A1). A native of Milner, Ga., White got a hit in the Greys game, scored a run, and fielded a dozen balls without error.
26. For a wonderfully written, carefully researched biography of Walker, see David W. Zang, *Fleet Walker's Divided Heart, The Life of Baseball's First Black Major Leaguer* (Lincoln: University of Nebraska Press, 1995).
27. Jim Bankes, *The Pittsburgh Crawfords* (Jefferson, N.C.: McFarland Press, 2001), 3. For more on how the color line was drawn in the major leagues, in particular the efforts of bigoted major league players such as Cleveland's Cap

Anson, see Robert Peterson, *Only the Ball Was White: A History of Legendary Black Players and All-Black Professional Teams* (New York: Oxford University Press, 1970), 29–30. Walker played his last season at the professional level in 1889, for the Syracuse Stars of the International League, the league in which Jackie Robinson would play as a Montreal Royal in 1946.
28. For a discussion on black nationalism, see Wilson J. Moses, *The Golden Age of Black Nationalism, 1850–1925* (Hamden, Conn.: Archon Books, 1978).
29. "One Hundred Lynchings," *Cleveland Gazette*, 30 January 1909, 1. According to the *Gazette,* the number of lynchings in 1890 was 127 and in 1892, 235, the highest number for the twenty-four years listed.
30. Letter to the editor, *The Sporting Life,* 14 March 1888, 5.
31. Dean Sullivan, ed., *Early Innings, A Documentary History of Baseball, 1825–1908* (Lincoln: University of Nebraska Press, 1995), 69.
32. Tom Gilbert, *Baseball and the Color Line* (New York: Franklin Watts, 1995), 26.
33. Cited in Malloy, xv.
34. White in Malloy, 74.
35. Lanctot, *Fair Dealing and Clean Playing,* 29.
36. The Cuban Giants' success resulted in many appropriations (and misappropriations) of its name by other teams, including Genuine Cuban Giants, Cuban X-Giants, and Original Cuban Giants.
37. P. L. Prattis, "Racial Segregation and Negro Journalism," *Phylon* 8, no. 4 (Winter 1947): 309.
38. Ibid., 311.
39. Malloy, xxxviii.
40. In May 1917, Dave Wyatt of the *Chicago Defender* noted that the average black professional team was lucky to last three years (in Lanctot, 27).
41. Heaphy, "Shadowed Diamonds," 43.
42. Charles E. Whitehead, *A Man and His Diamonds* (New York: Vantage Press, 1980), 23. See also Brian Carroll, "When to Stop the Cheering: A content analysis of changes in black press coverage of the Negro leagues" in William Simons, ed., *The 14th Annual Symposium on Baseball and American Culture,* (Jefferson, N.C.: McFarland Press, 2001).
43. Bruce Lenthall, "Covering More than the Game: Baseball and Racial Issues in an African-American Newspaper, 1919–1920," in Alvin Hall, ed., *The 15th Cooperstown Symposium on Baseball and American Culture (1990),* ed. Alvin Hall (Jefferson, N.C.: McFarland Press, 2002), 58.
44. Whitehead, *A Man and His Diamonds,* 27.
45. "Frank Leland Laid to Rest," *Chicago Defender,* 21 November 1914, 5; Michael E. Lomax, "Black Entrepreneurship in the National Pastime: The Rise of Semiprofessional Baseball in Black Chicago, 1890–1915," *Journal of Sport History 25,* no. 1 (Spring 1998), 48.
46. Lomax, "Black Entrepreneurship," 49.
47. Ibid., 50. The complex was to be called the Chateau de la Plaisance (Allan Spear, *Black Chicago, The Making of a Negro Ghetto, 1890–1920,* Chicago: University of Chicago Press, 1967, 117).

Notes to Chapter One

48. "Major General R.R. Jackson, Assistant Supt. Armour Station. Financial Secretary Appomattox Club," Chicago *Broad Ax,* 27 December 1902, 6.
49. "Beauregard F. Moseley, Lawyer, Orator, Ex-Journalist and Property Holder," Chicago *Broad Ax,* 29 December 1906, 1.
50. The ad ran throughout 1908 in the *Broad Ax.*
51. "The Freeman to Publish the Standing of National League of Colored Ball Players," *Indianapolis Freeman,* 24 August 1907, 7; "Growing Interest in Proposed League," *Indianapolis Freeman,* 16 November 1907, 6; "To Organize Colored League," *Indianapolis Freeman,* 23 November 1907, 6; "Roberts in Favor of the League," *Indianapolis Freeman,* 7 December 1907, 6; "League Meeting a Successful One," *Indianapolis Freeman,* 28 December 1907, 6; "A Successful Meeting is Sighted," *Indianapolis Freeman,* 25 January 1908, 6; and "League Determined to Open This Season," *Indianapolis Freeman,* 7 March 1908, 6.
52. "Make War on the Leland Giants," *Indianapolis Freeman,* 1 February 1908, 6; "An Understanding about the League," *Indianapolis Freeman,* 15 February 1908, 6.
53. *Indianapolis Freeman,* 4 November 1916, 4. The photo was taken on the eve of the "World's Series" championship between Foster's American Giants and Taylor's ABCs. Before owning the ABCs in Indianapolis, Taylor started the first black team in Washington, D.C. (Dan Burley, "Sports Secret Service Department," *Chicago Defender,* 30 May 1936, 13).
54. "Growing Interest in Proposed League," *Indianapolis Freeman,* 16 November 1907, 6.
55. "Roberts in Favor of the League," *Indianapolis Freeman,* 21 December 1907, 8.
56. "League Determined to Open This Season," *Indianapolis Freeman,* 7 March 1908, 6. Also proposed was a franchise league fee of fifty dollars per team.
57. "League Baseball Fever High," *Indianapolis Freeman,* 21 June 1908, 7.
58. "League Determined to Open This Season," *Indianapolis Freeman,* 7 March 1908, 6.
59. "A Historical Account of a Great Game of Ball," *Indianapolis Freeman* 7 September 1907, 7.
60. *Indianapolis Freeman,* 16 April 1910, 9–13.
61. "Success of the Negro As a Ball Player," *Indianapolis Freeman,* 9. The article was written by "C.D.M.," which presumably is an erroneous reference to Harold D. McGrath, the paper's lead sports columnist that year. He wrote the weekly "In the Field of Sport." There was no *Freeman* writer that year with the initials C.D.M., nor do they belong to any of the league's principal organizers.
62. Foster was joined in his effort by *Defender* writer Major R. R. Jackson and Beauregard Moseley, Leland's erstwhile partners. This campaign followed similar efforts in 1887 and 1889.
63. "Great Interest Srown [sic]," *Indianapolis Freeman,* 16 April 1910, 10.
64. J. M. Batchman, "Base Ball Business Side," *Indianapolis Freeman,* 16 April 1910, 11.

65. Lomax, "Black Entrepreneurship," 57. For more on Chicago's emergence as the center of black baseball, see Lomax's Ph.D. dissertation, "Black Baseball, Black Community, Black Entrepreneurs: The History of the Negro National and Eastern Colored Leagues, 1880–1930" (Ohio State University, 1996).
66. See T. Ella Strother, "The Race-Advocacy Function of the Black Press," *Black American Literature Forum* 12, no. 3 (Autumn 1978): 92–99. Strother included a content analysis of the *Chicago Defender* demonstrating that paper's advocacy and development of what she calls "race conciousness" (92).
67. Arnold R. Hirsch, *Making the Second Ghetto: Race and Housing in Chicago, 1940–1960* (Cambridge, England: Cambridge University Press, 1983), 41.
68. See William Jordan, "'The Damnable Dilemma': African-American Accommodation and Protest during World War I," *The Journal of American History* 81, no. 4 (March 1995): 1562–1583.
69. See Rayford Logan, *The Negro in the United States, a Brief History* (Princeton, N.J.: D. Van Nostrand, 1956).
70. Charlotte G. O'Kelly, "Black Newspapers and the Black Protest Movement: Their Historical Relationship," *Phylon* 43, no. 1 (Spring 1982): 5.
71. August Meier, "Booker T. Washington and the Negro Press With Special Reference to the *Colored American*," *Journal of Negro History* 39 (January 1953): 67–90.
72. O'Kelly, "Black Newspapers," 3.
73. Armistead Scott Pride and Clint C. Wilson, *A History of the Black Press* (Washington, D.C.: Howard University Press, 1997), 147.
74. See Lawrence D. Hogan's excellent history of the ANP, *A Black National News Service: The Associated Negro Press and Claude Barnett, 1919–1945* (Rutherford, N.J.: Fairleigh Dickinson University Press, 1984).
75. Joel Williamson, *The Crucible of Race* (New York: Oxford University Press, 1984), vii.
76. Fourteenth Census (Washington, D.C., 1921), cited in Richard Bak, *Turkey Stearnes and the Detroit Stars* (Detroit: Wayne State University Press, 1994), 119. Describing the bon vivant attitudes of the times, Bak writes that for Americans "stuck at the confluence of postwar disillusionment and incredible technological progress, morals loosened, hemlines were raised. . . . Most people thought of little else but having a good time in what promised to be a new age of permanent prosperity."
77. U.S. Census Reports.
78. Henry La Brie III, *The Black Newspaper in America; a Guide* (Iowa City: Institute for Communication Studies at the University of Iowa, 1970), 112.
79. O'Kelly, "Black Newspapers," 4.
80. Henry Lewis Suggs, *The Black Press in the Middle West, 1865–1985* (Westport, Conn.: Greenwood Press, 1996), 355.
81. E. Franklin Frazier, *The Negro Family in the United States* (New York: Dryden Press, 1939), 510.
82. Martin E. Dann, *The Black Press, 1827–1890: The Quest for National Identity* (New York: Putnam, 1971), 8.

83. Frederick G. Detweiler, *The Negro Press in the United States* (Chicago: University of Chicago Press, 1921), 11.
84. Herman D. Bloch, "The Employment Status of the New York Negro in Retrospect," *The Phylon Quarterly* 20, no. 4 (Winter 1959): 329.
85. For more on the *Defender*'s founding and about Abbott, see Roi Ottley, *The Lonely Warrior: The Life and Times of Robert S. Abbott* (Chicago: H. Regnery Co., 1955).
86. Pride and Wilson, A History of the Black Press, 137.
87. Frederick Lewis Allen, *Only Yesterday: An Informal History of the 1920s* (New York: John Wiley & Sons, 1997), 251.
88. For more on Rice and this era for sportswriting, see Mark Inabinett, "Grantland Rice and His Heroes: The Sportswriter as Mythmaker in the 1920s," *Journalism History* 22, no. 3 (Autumn 1996): 125–127.
89. Pride and Wilson, *A History of the Black Press*, 139.
90. Ibid., 155.
91. For more on the Double V campaign and its part in the larger protest movement regarding treatment of troops abroad and continued segregationist practices at home, see Phillip McGuire, "Desegregation of the Armed Forces: Black Leadership, Protest and World War II," *Journal of Negro History* 68, no. 2 (Spring 1983): 147–158. See also Patrick S. Washburn, *A Question of Sedition: The Federal Government's Investigation of the Black Press During World War II* (New York: Oxford University Press, 1986). The *Courier*'s efforts to end discrimination in the armed services began much earlier, but the Double V was its largest, most coordinated, and most successful campaign.
92. Pride and Wilson, *A History of the Black Press*, 139.
93. See Neil A. Wynn, "The Impact of the Second World War on the American Negro," *Journal of Contemporary History* 6, no. 2 (1971): 46.
94. Journalistic "crusades" were a defining role of even mainstream journalism from 1890 through 1915 or so (Frank Luther Mott, *American Journalism: A History of Newspapers in the United States Through 250 Years* [New York: Macmillan, 1941], 573). Mott described a crusade as "any campaign against an abuse or in promotion of a public benefit which is prosecuted by a newspaper with zeal and enterprise" (573).
95. Howard Bryant writes very eloquently of this backwardness on the part of professional baseball in his chronicle of race conflict in Boston. See *Shut Out* (New York: Routledge, 2002).

NOTES TO CHAPTER TWO

1. For more on the Black Sox, see Eliot Asinof, *Eight Men Out* (New York: Holt, Rinehart & Winston, 1963).
2. The drowning of Eugene Williams on a blisteringly hot July 27 afternoon sparked the worst of these riots. Police made no arrests despite numerous claims from blacks that Williams had been stoned by whites. Over the next several days thirty-eight died and more than 500 more were wounded.

3. In Allan Spear, *Black Chicago, The Making of a Negro Ghetto, 1890–1920* (Chicago: University of Chicago Press, 1967), 221. He cited the 4 August 1919 issue of the *Chicago Tribune*.
4. A definitive account of the "black metropolis" is St. Clair Drake's and Horace Cayton's *Black Metropolis* (New York: Harcourt, Brace & Co., 1945).
5. Spear, *Black Chicago*, 81. According to the author, Abbott started the newspaper with twenty-five cents in capital and a press run of three hundred copies.
6. The "Great Northern Drive" was a phrase coined by the *Defender* in March 1917 to publicize the migration (24 March 1917).
7. Robert Peterson, *Only the Ball Was White: A History of Legendary Black Players and All-Black Professional Teams* (New York: Oxford University Press, 1970), 104.
8. Robert Cottrell, *The Best Pitcher in Baseball: The Life of Rube Foster, Negro League Giant* (New York: New York University Press, 2001), 4.
9. Effa Manley and Leon Herbert Hardwick, *Negro Baseball . . . before Integration* (Chicago: Adams Press, 1976), 6.
10. Foster bested Waddell in an exhibition game in 1904 (Cottrell, *The Best Pitcher in Baseball*,19.)
11. The campaign finally met success in March 1981.
12. "Giants Take Three-Game Series," *Indianapolis Freeman*, 31 August 1907, 7. The ABCs were named for the American Brewing Company (Debono, *Indianapolis ABCs*, 18).
13. Foster and Wyatt played together in Chicago in 1902 and with the Cuban X-Giants in 1903, according to James A. Riley, *The Biographical Encyclopedia of the Negro Baseball Leagues* (New York: Carroll & Graf, 1994), 290.
14. "Booker T. Washington or the Fifteenth Amendment," *Indianapolis Freeman*, 21 September 1907, 7.
15. Jackson, a Republican, was alderman for Chicago's 2nd Ward from 1918–1923 and for the 3rd Ward from 1923–1939.
16. See Jackson's letter to the editor, "No Baseball War in Chicago," *Indianapolis Freeman*, 18 December 1908, 18.
17. *Defender*, 4 October 1911, 11. In the same article, Lewis wrote how important he felt it was that any new league be owned and controlled by "race men." Lewis, who began his career at the Louisville *Courier-Journal*. was the *Defender*'s third managing editor (Fay Young, "Fay Says," *Chicago Defender*, 30 January 1954, 16).
18. Cottrell, *The Best Pitcher in Baseball*, 41, quoting Young's column in the *Defender*.
19. Young became the *Defender*'s sports editor in 1907.
20. Ibid.
21. Rube Foster's "Explanation to the Base Ball Public of the United States," *Indianapolis Freeman*, 7 August 1915, 11. He signed the letter, "Yours for the Good of Colored baseball." Taylor's baseball-playing brothers were Ben Taylor and Candy Jim Taylor.

Notes to Chapter Two

22. "C. I. Taylor Standing Up For His Baseball Integrity," *Indianapolis Freeman*, 14 August 1915, 8.
23. Ibid.
24. Ibid. The letters were dated 5 May and 17 May 1915.
25. "Rube Wants Championship Without Fighting For It," *Indianapolis Freeman*, 11 November 1915, 7.
26. Ibid.
27. Neil Lanctot, *Fair Dealing and Clean Playing: The Hilldale Club and the Development of Black Professional Baseball, 1910–1932* (Jefferson, N.C.: McFarland & Co., 1994), 41. After World War I, white baseball also paid for the baseball writers' travel costs on the road (Stanley Woodward, *Sports Page* [New York: Greenwood Press, 1968], 141).
28. *Philadelphia Tribune*, 13 October 1917, cited in Lanctot, *Fair Dealing and Clean Playing*, 48. The Hilldales fielded perhaps Philadelphia's most consistently successful professional and semi-professional clubs, and the city had them in abundance.
29. Greenlee, who according to his son bailed out the *Courier* at least once financially, owned the Pittsburgh Crawfords (Rob Ruck, *Sandlot Seasons: Sport in Black Pittsburgh,* [Champagne: University of Illinois Press 1993], 135 and 151. Ruck interviewed Charles Greenlee in 1980).
30. Brad Snyder, *Beyond the Shadow of the Senators* (Chicago: Contemporary Books, 2003), 36. The father, Cumberland "Cap" Willis Posey ran the largest black-owned business in Pittsburgh, the Diamond Coke and Coal Company. He served as the first president of the *Courier* and was, with Robert Vann, one of the newspaper's founding incorporators.
31. In Charles E. Whitehead, *A Man and His Diamonds* (New York: Vantage Press, 1980), 51.
32. Ibid.
33. Robert C. Cottrell, *Blackball, the Black Sox, and the Babe: Baseball's Crucial 1920 Season* (Jefferson, N.C.: McFarland, 2002), 65.
34. David Wyatt, "The Annual 'Chestnut' Negro Base Ball League," *Indianapolis Freeman*, 27 January 1917, 7.
35. Ibid.
36. See Wyatt's impassioned treatise on why baseball had to succeed for the black community in the 5 October 1907 issue of the *Freeman*, 6. In the piece, "No Means of Comparison Between Colored and Best White Clubs," Wyatt protests that there is "no way of measuring in a satisfactory manner, the strength of our colored players," since blacks were banned from the major leagues. This theme of benchmarking achievement against white culture was common. And the inability to make such comparisons was unique to baseball. Bicycling, boxing, racing, running, and "foot-ball" were all integrated, according to Wyatt.
37. Wyatt, "The Annual 'Chestnut' Negro Base Ball League," 7.
38. Cottrell, *The Best Pitcher in Baseball*, 34.
39. David Wyatt, "Baseball," *Indianapolis Freeman*, 13 October 1917, 7.
40. Whitehead, *A Man and His Diamonds*, 64.

41. Quote ("plunging into sport") from a 28 June 1919 editorial in the *New York Times*, "The Revival of Sport."
42. John Rickards Betts, *America's Sporting Heritage 1850–1950* (Reading, Mass.: Addison-Wesley, 1974), 181.
43. In Cottrell, *The Best Pitcher in Baseball*, 139.
44. Leslie Heaphy, "Shadowed Diamonds: The Growth and Decline of the Negro Leagues," Ph.D. dissertation (University of Toledo, 1995), 50.
45. There are a few exceptions. The Atlantic City *Daily Press* in New Jersey covered the Bacharachs, including box scores of every home game and many away games (Snyder, *Beyond the Shadow*, 21).
46. Buck O'Neil, with Steve Wulf and David Conrads, *I Had It Made* (New York: Fireside, 1996), 22–23. Dick "King Richard" Lundy played more than twenty years and is considered to have been the best shortstop of the twenties. Lloyd played a quarter-century and is considered by many to have been the greatest Negro leaguer of all time (Riley, *The Biographical Encyclopedia*, 486–496).
47. See Bak, *Turkey Stearnes and the Detroit Stars*, which chronicles the Detroit Stars and professional black baseball in Detroit.
48. *Tribune*, 13 April 1918, cited in Lanctot, *Fair Dealing and Clean Playing*, 74.
49. Betts, *America's Sporting Heritage*, 123.
50. Rube Foster, "Pitfalls of Baseball," *Chicago Defender*, 26 April 1919, 14.
51. Neil Lanctot, *Negro League Baseball* (Lincoln: University of Nebraska Press, 2004), 9.
52. Foster, "Pitfalls of Baseball," *Chicago Defender*, 3 January 1920, 9; 10 January 1920, 9; 17 January 1920, 9; 31 January 1920, 9.
53. Ira Lewis, "Baseball Circuit for Next Season," *Chicago Defender*, 4 October 1919, 10.
54. For more on black magazines at the time, see Charles S. Johnson, "The Rise of the Negro Magazine," *Journal of Negro History* 13, no. 1 (January 1928): 7–21. Competition included *The Crisis*, *The Colored American Review*, *Upreach Magazine*, *Half Century*, and *The Crusader*, among others.
55. C. I. Taylor, "The Future of Colored Baseball," *The Competitor*, February 1920, 76.
56. Ibid.
57. Ibid., 77.
58. Most accounts put the founding at the YMCA on Kansas City's Paseo Street (see "Baseball Magnates Hold Conference," *Chicago Defender*, 14 February 1920, 11; and Thomas C. Palmer, Jr., "Kansas City cultural center pays tribute to the music and the Negro leagues: A sweet celebration of jazz & baseball," *Boston Globe*, 16 May 1999, M1). The *Defender* called the location of the founding meetings the "Community Center," probably referring to The Paseo YMCA ("Baseball Writers and Mgrs. Are Royally Entertained," *Chicago Defender*, 28 February 1920, 11).
59. J. D. Howard was publisher of the *Ledger*; A. D. Williams was the paper's chief sportswriter. The latter Williams would switch to the Kansas City *Call* later in the decade.

Notes to Chapter Two

60. "Baseball Magnates Hold Conference," 11.
61. "Kansas City Selected for Meeting of Baseball Magnates," *Chicago Defender*, 7 February 1920, 11.
62. "Baseball Writers and Mgrs. Are Royally Entertained," 11. In the 5 June 1920 issue of the *Defender*, Gilmore is described as a "lieutenant" to Wilkinson and the Monarchs, implying some degree of editorial control of the *Call*'s sports pages wielded by Wilkinson and his Kansas City team ("Kansas City Notes," *Chicago Defender*, 9).
63. Ibid.
64. Manley and Hardwick, *Negro Baseball*, 6. Manley referred to Wyatt as Dave Wright. A "Dave Wright" is mentioned in no other account of the founding, and Wyatt was the *Freeman's* chief baseball correspondent.
65. "Baseball Magnates Hold Conference," 11. The four writers would later form the core of the National Sportswriter Association, which black press writers organized in 1922 during Negro National League meetings in Chicago that December. The association's first president was the *Defender*'s Fay Young. Also joining was Arthur D. Williams of the *Indianapolis Ledger* (see Debono, *Indianapolis ABCs*, 49).
66. Personal interview with Chuck Stone, former editor of the *Chicago Defender* and Washington *Afro-American*, among other newspapers, 28 August 2002, Chapel Hill, N.C.
67. "Baseball Men Write League Constitution," *Chicago Defender*, 21 February 1920, 9.
68. See Whitehead, *A Man and His Diamonds*, and Cottrell, *The Best Pitcher in Baseball*.
69. "Western Circuit Organized; to Become Effective April 1, 1921," *Chicago Defender*, 21 February 1920, 9.
70. In Mark Ribowsky, *A Complete History of the Negro Leagues, 1884–1955* (Seacaucus, N.J.: Citadel Press, 1995), 104.
71. "Detroit Stars Ready For Next Season," *Chicago Defender*, 14 February 1920, 11.
72. "Sport Editorial," *Chicago Defender*, 12 February 1921, 6. In the column, Young put the Detroit Stars' profits for the 1920 season at $30,000.
73. Bak, *Turkey Stearnes*, 56.
74. According to Lanctot (*Fair Dealing and Clean Playing*, 252), black vice leaders invested in baseball as a money-laundering scheme and to avoid paying income tax. For more on Chicago's numbers runners, see Nathan Thompson, *Kings: The True Story of Chicago's Policy Kings and Numbers Racketeers, An Informal History* (Chicago: Bronzeville Press, 1994).
75. Blount was referred to as owner of the Stars on several occasions by the *Defender* (see "Magnates To Meet Here Last of January," 7 January 1922, 10). The parity plan did not work. Foster's American Giants won the Negro National League championship its first three seasons. The Stars, in contrast, were a second-tier team throughout the league's existence.
76. In Whitehead, *A Man and His Diamonds*, 74.
77. "National Baseball League Formed," *The Competitor*, March 1920, 66.
78. Ibid., 67.

79. Dave Wyatt, "National League of Colored Clubs Prepare for Season's Opening," *The Competitor*, April 1920, 73–74. Wyatt referred to Blount as the Stars' owner.
80. William Harper, *How You Played the Game, The Life of Grantland Rice* (Columbia.: University of Missouri Press, 1999), 18.
81. Charles Fountain, *Sportswriter: The Life and Times of Grantland Rice* (New York: Oxford University Press, 1993), 343.
82. For more on the portrayals of the owners as heroes for the black community of the period, see Brian Carroll, "Early Twentieth Century Heroes: Portrayals in the Sporting Pages of the *Pittsburgh Courier* and *Chicago Defender*," in *Journalism History* 31, no. 4 (Spring 2006), 34–42.
83. Quote from Joseph Farrell, "Classical Genre in Theory and Practice," *New Literary History* 34, 3 (Fall 2003): 399. Pindar's *Olympian* Odes were composed in honor of victories "won" by rulers and chariot owners such as Hieron and Theron (quote from Charles Paul Segal, "God and Man in Pindar's First and Third *Olympian* Odes," *Harvard Studies in Classical Philology* 68 [1964]: 211). Segal puts the competitions in the year 476 B.C. A sample from Pindar's "Olympian 1" ode, written to honor Hieron of Syracuse for a single-horse race in 476 B.C.: "The rich and blessed hearth of Hieron, who wields the scepter of law in Sicily of many flocks, reaping every excellence at its peak, and is glorified by the choicest music, which we men often play around his hospitable table . . . the king of Syracuse who delights in horses. His glory shines in the settlement of fine men" (Pindar, *Olympian Odes*, Olympian 1).
84. "Big League Making Progress," *The Competitor*, April 1920, 69.
85. Ibid.
86. U.S. Census Reports.
87. Heaphy, "Shadowed Diamonds," 51. Two good studies of the exodus from the South are Nicholas Lemann, *The Promised Land: The Great Black Migration and How It Changed America* (New York: Vintage Books, 1992) and Carole Marks, *Farewell, We're Good and Gone: The Great Black Migration (Blacks in the Diaspora)* (Bloomington: Indiana University Press, 1989).
88. Lanctot, *Fair Dealing and Clean Playing*, 28.
89. Carl R. Osthaus, "The Rise and Fall of Jesse Binga, Black Financier," *Journal of Negro History* 58, no. 1 (January 1973): 46. The Binga State Bank sponsored several athletic teams in Chicago's city leagues, including a baseball team. See *Chicago Defender*, 18 March 1922, 10.
90. *Chicago Defender*, 14 February 1920, 16.
91. Advertisement in 7 June 1924 *Chicago Defender*, 13. Foster co-owned the garage with Clifford O. Stark. Schorling was son-in-law to Charles Comiskey, owner of the Chicago White Sox.
92. "League Game Sunday," *Chicago Defender*, 8 May 1920, 9.
93. Manley and Hardwick, *Negro Baseball*, 12.
94. In Cottrell, *The Best Pitcher in Baseball*, 155.
95. "Ten Cities Are Represented at the Meeting; Circuit Is to Join the National League in 1921," *Chicago Defender*, 6 March 1920, 11.

Notes to Chapter Two

96. Dave Wyatt, "Success of the League Is Up To The Fans," *Chicago Defender*, 3 April 1920, 9.
97. "Here and There," *Chicago Defender*, 9 August 1913, 7.
98. *Pittsburgh Courier*, 15 July 1938, 5.
99. "Rough Stuff! Actions on the Baseball Field That Should Be Immediately Stopped!" *Chicago Defender*, 14 August 1920, 6.
100. In another example, the 9 November 1918 *Defender* includes an announcement from Foster imploring fans to behave, part of Foster's broader effort to get the Chicago Cubs to agree to an exhibition game. The announcement ran after Foster banned an unruly fan from American Giants games (Whitehead, *A Man and His Diamonds*, 64).
101. "Annual Meeting of the National Association," *Indianapolis Freeman*, 27 November 1920, 7.
102. Mister Fan, "NL Circuit Will Be Changed at January Meeting," *Chicago Defender*, 26 November 1921, 10.
103. Rube Foster, "Rube Foster Tells What Baseball Needs to Succeed," *Chicago Defender*, 10 December 1921, 10.
104. Rube Foster, "Rube Foster Tells What Baseball Needs to Succeed," *Chicago Defender*, 17 December 1921, 10.
105. Rube Foster, "Rube Foster Tells What Baseball Needs to Succeed," *Chicago Defender*, 24 December 1921, 10.
106. Rube Foster, "Rube Foster Tells What Baseball Needs to Succeed," *Chicago Defender*, 31 December 1921, 10.
107. Ibid.
108. Ibid.
109. Sam Lacy, "Looking 'em Over With The Tribune," *Washington Tribune*, 25 December 1937, 12.
110. "Demand for Umpires of Color is Growing Among the Fans," *Chicago Defender*, 9 October 1920, 10.
111. Ibid.
112. "Hilldale Beats Babe Ruth," *Chicago Defender*, 16 October 1919, 10.
113. According to Ruth biographer Richard Creamer, Ruth was "called 'nigger' so often that many people assumed that he was indeed partly black" (*Babe, The Legend Comes To Life* [New York: Simon & Schuster, 1992], 185). Ruth's extraordinarily large lips, swarthy complexion, and broad, flat nose contributed to the perception, but, as delicious as the possibility is—of the one black player major league baseball could not keep out so thoroughly rewriting the sport's record books—there is not a shred of empirical, biological evidence to support the claim. . . . It is true, however, that Ty Cobb refused to room with Ruth at a Georgia hunting lodge because of Cobb's assumption that Ruth was black (Daniel Okrent, "Background Check: Was Babe Ruth Black?" *Sports Illustrated*, 7 May 2001, 27).
114. Bruce Lenthall, "Covering More than the Game: Baseball and Racial Issues in an African-American Newspaper, 1919–1920," in *The Cooperstown Symposium on Baseball and American Culture (1990)*, ed. Alvin Hall (Jefferson, N.C.: McFarland Press, 2002), 62.

115. The *Whip* was financed by, among others, Jesse Binga and Oscar DePriest. The paper was a reliable ally of organized labor, the working class, and black business, and it was a leader in the Double V and "Don't Buy Where You Can't Work" protests (Juliet E.K. Walker, "The Promised Land: The *Chicago Defender* and the Black Press in Illinois, 1862–1970," in *The Black Press in the Middle West, 1865–1985*, Henry Lewis Suggs, ed. [Westport, Conn.: Greenwood Press, 1996], 32).

NOTES TO CHAPTER THREE

1. Dave Wyatt, "Big Crowd Sees Stars Battle," *Chicago Defender*, 20 May 1920, 9.
2. Ibid.
3. Robert L. Vann, "Football As A Vehicle," *Pittsburgh Courier*, 1 December 1923, 1.
4. "Magnates To Meet Here Last of January," *Chicago Defender*, 7 January 1922, 10. Present at the meeting were Ira F. Lewis of the *Courier*, Elwood Knox of the *Freeman*, and several *Defender* writers. Which "three papers" are meant by the *Defender* statement is not known.
5. "Baseball Men and Scribes Gather For League Meetings," *Chicago Defender*, 28 January 1922, 10.
6. "Sports Writers Organize," *Chicago Defender*, 18 February 1922, 10.
7. The only instance in the *Defender* during the 1922 season, for example, of coverage from the association was a 5 August 1922 story on the Giants versus the ABCs under the byline "National Sport Writers' Association Service." The short story was probably written by Knox.
8. "Christians Are Urged To Pull Together in Church Worship," *Chicago Defender*, 23 September 1922, 1.
9. In a way, Abbott helped create the neediness, as well. The "Great Northern Drive," or Great Migration he so aggressively promoted in the *Defender* produced the population surges and resulting needs for food and shelter. In 1937, for example, the Goodfellows Club filled and distributed 2,600 Christmas baskets to needy families ("2600 Given Baskets By Goodfellows," *Chicago Defender*, 9 January 1937, 1). The club also put on shows and benefits. More than 5,000 attended and another 3,000 were turned away from the Eighth Annual Goodfellows Benefit show in December 1936, which was held at Chicago's Regal Theatre. Performing were Louis Armstrong, Mildred Bailey, and Kay Kyser (James J. Gentry, "Seven Thousand Fans At Defender Show," *Chicago Defender*, 9 January 1937, 3).
10. Charlotte G. O'Kelly, "Black Newspapers and the Black Protest Movement: Their Historical Relationship," *Phylon* 43, no. 1 (Spring 1984), 13.
11. The "Golden Age" description came from Gallico, in *The Golden People* (New York: Doubleday & Company, 1964), 24. For other first-person accounts of this era of sports journalism, see Stanley Walker, *City Editor* (New York: Frederick A. Stokes Co., 1934), and Stanley Woodward, *Sports Page* (New York: Greenwood Press, 1968).

12. Gallico, *Farewell to Sport* (New York: Alfred A. Knopf, 1938), 45, 70.
13. Andrew Rube Foster, "Rube Foster Has A Word To Say To The Baseball Fans," *Chicago Defender*, 5 January 1924, 3, section 2.
14. Foster's co-owners of the Chicago Leland Giants and Chicago American Giants were black. The owner of the park in which Foster's teams played, Schorling Park, was white. The "Bronzeville" name for the South Side of Chicago was immortalized on 22 September 1934, when Abbott teamed up with policy king Ed Jones and James G. Gentry to stage the first "Mayor of Bronzeville" election, which was held at the Eighth Regiment Armory on Giles and 35th streets (Nathan Thompson, *Kings: The True Story of Chicago's Policy Kings and Numbers Racketeers* [Chicago: Bronzeville Press, 1994], 12).
15. "Rube Foster Banqueted By Cleveland Business Men," *Chicago Defender*, 17 February 1923, 10. The *Whip*'s editor was Wilbur Cooper. At the banquet, the Stars' treasurer, J.E. Reed, gave a talk on "baseball from a business standpoint."
16. "Y.W.C.A. Day Sunday, June 24," *Chicago Defender*, 16 June 1923, 9. DePriest, Abbott, and Binga also were all members of the Appomattox Club, an elite club for black Republicans founded in 1900 by Chicago attorney Ed Wright. For Gillespie's claim, Thompson, *Kings*, 185.
17. "Appomattox Club Nominate Officers," *Chicago Defender*, 22 October 1924, 8, section 2; and "Associated Business Club Holds Meeting," *Pittsburgh Courier*, 26 September 1925, 10.
18. For more on Taylor's memberships, see Michael E. Lomax, "Black Baseball, Black Entrepreneurs, Black Community," Ph.D. dissertation (Ohio State University, 1996), 294. For descriptions of Taylor's pool hall and emporium, see "C. I. Taylor And His A.B.C. Base Ball Club," *Indianapolis Freeman*, 23 December 1916, 7.
19. Arthur Williams, "C. I. Taylor, Veteran Manager and Baseball Club Owner, Dead," reprinted in the *Chicago Defender*, 4 March 1922, 10. According to Williams' account, thousands of people "of both races" surged up and down Indiana Avenue in Indianapolis to visit Taylor's home, while a "swelling throng" overwhelmed Bethel for the funeral service.
20. *Pittsburgh Courier*, 6 April 1947, 17.
21. Anderson succeeded as 2nd Ward alderman Major R. R. Jackson, who had succeeded Oscar DePriest. Anderson served 1923–1933.
22. Mister Fan, "American Giants Beat City Champions," *Chicago Defender*, 21 April 1917, 7. It is not known for certain which *Defender* writer used the eponymous Mister Fan byline, or whether it was used by a *Defender* writer at all. It probably was a device used by Fay Young, the paper's sports editor and primary baseball writer, to provide a fan's perspective of the games. The other two local businessmen in Foster's box were George Holt and Harry Basken.
23. Use of the term "mentality" is to suggest, as historian Joel Williamson put it in his seminal book, that the publishers and owners had certain discrete ideas in common, but that those ideas were not necessarily knit into a smoothly finished, comprehensive way of thinking. They did share more

than mere opinions or attitudes, however (*The Crucible of Race: Black-White Relations in the American South Since Emancipation* [New York: Oxford University Press, 1984], 4).
24. Hilldale Successful in Securing Improved Trolley Service," *Philadelphia Tribune*, 29 June 1918, 7.
25. Andrew Rube Foster, "Rube Foster Reviews The World Series And Tells A Little Baseball History," *Chicago Defender*, 15 November 1924, 12. Foster's prominence and influence in the community is reflected in the article's headline. Foster's team, the American Giants, did not even appear in the Colored World Series.
26. Postwar enthusiasm for the sport surprised everyone; national interest in the World Series soared. Baseball had become "a mass consumer product," according to Grantland Rice's biographer, William Harper (*How You Played the Game, The Life of Grantland Rice*, Columbia: University of Missouri Press (1999), 246.
27. Robert L. Vann, "Football As A Vehicle," *Pittsburgh Courier*, 1 December 1923, 1.
28. Dave Wyatt, "Players Developed, Need Trained Officials Now," *Chicago Defender*, 7 January 1922, 10.
29. Ibid.
30. "A Case of Good Judgment," *Chicago Defender*, 12 February 1920, 6 ("example") and "Detroit Stars Start Playing Ball," *Chicago Defender*, 12 April 1924, 10 ("lieutenant" and "best known"). Also in April 1924, in the *Courier*, Blount was described in a headline as "One of Diamond's Most Picturesque Figures" (12 April 1924, 10).
31. "Baseball On A Sane Basis Is Plan Of Magnates," *Chicago Defender*, 13 December 1924, 7; "Tenny Blount Quits Baseball; Mack Park For Rent," *Chicago Defender*, 20 December 1924, 8, section 2; "Players Insist That Blount Is Holding Salary," *Chicago Defender*, 13 December 1924, 6, section 2; "No More Baseball For Me," *Pittsburgh Courier*, 20 December 1924, 12; and "Foster Elected League Head," *Baltimore Afro-American*, 3 January 1925, 5.
32. "Call for National League Issued," *Chicago Defender*, 7 February 1920, 11.
33. "Success of the League Is Up to the Fans," *Chicago Defender*, 3 April 1920, 9.
34. Mister Fan, *Chicago Defender*, 30 January 1923. No headline or page number; only fragments of this edition of the paper survive.
35. "Cleveland Business Man Buys Tate's Baseball Park," *Chicago Defender*, 14 July 1923, 9.
36. "National League News," *Chicago Defender*, 11 March 1922, 10. In this instance, the outlaws were the Lincoln Giants of New York City. The ECL's other teams were the Hilldales, Baltimore Black Sox, Brooklyn Royal Giants, Cuban Stars, and Atlantic City Bacharachs.
37. Indicative of Strong's views, the Bushwicks played home games at Dexter Park while the Royal Giants had no home field and were relegated to securing fields whenever and wherever they could.
38. Lomax, "Black Entrepreneurship," 312.

Notes to Chapter Three

39. "Black Sox Incorporate," *Baltimore Afro-American,* 29 July 1921, 2.
40. Neil Lanctot, *Fair Dealing and Clean Playing: The Hilldale Club and the Development of Black Professional Baseball, 1910–1932* (Jefferson, N.C.: McFarland & Co., 1994), 96.
41. Ira F. Lewis, "New League Not Needed," *The Competitor,* May 1921, 39.
42. Ibid.
43. Lester A. Walton, "Square Deal for Red Caps," *New York Age,* 8 June 1918, 6.
44. "Whitworth To Pitch For Am. Giants Again," *Chicago Defender,* 3 March 1922, 10.
45. Ibid.
46. Ibid., 10; and "League Meet Promises To Be Very Hot," *Chicago Defender,* 18 November 1922, 10. A player's signing by the American Giants was described as "the first gun fired in a war" between the Negro National League and outlaw teams. Just below this article was a bulletin offering readers updated scores of American Giants games at the telephone number Douglas 0697.
47. The first Colored World Series preceded the inaugural Major League Baseball World Series by two months.
48. "Hilldale Played Only 59 League Games During 1923," *Chicago Defender,* 12 January 1924, 2, section 2.
49. Ollie Womack, "Western Man Says 'Let's Have Negro World Series,'" *Pittsburgh Courier,* 16 August 1924, 7.
50. "World Series Between East and West Possible," *Chicago Defender,* 30 August 1924, 11.
51. "Conditions Confronting Negro Baseball—The Cure," *Pittsburgh Courier,* 16 March 1924, 6 (emphases in original). In the unbylined article, the paper claimed to have "done more than the outside public know [sic] in trying to bring about an amicable agreement between the two sections."
52. "World Series Report," *Chicago Defender,* 1 November 1924, 12. The numbers show the players indeed would have made more money barnstorming. Foster argued after the Series, however, that without the league teams they played for, there would not have been any team with which to barnstorm (see Andrew Rube Foster, "Rube Foster Reviews The World Series And Tells A Little Baseball History," *Chicago Defender,* 15 November 1924, 12).
53. "The Sportive Realm," *Pittsburgh Courier,* 6 September 1924, 1, section 3. In addition to being the *Courier*'s principal baseball writer in the 1920s, Wilson was Pennsylvania's deputy state athletic commissioner. In the 1930s he would briefly serve as commissioner of the Negro National League.
54. "Arrangements Complete For Big Series," *Pittsburgh Courier,* 6 September 1924, 1. The story outlined that share-winners were to: "1. Deduct the cost of park from gross receipts. 2. Deduct cost of 18 round trip tickets from Philadelphia to Kansas City and return, berth, room and board," and so on. Profits would be disbursed only after assigning advertising expenses, commissions, and costs for umpires and newspapermen, who would get tickets and provide "necessary help" and promotion.

55. "Two World Series Teams Compared," *Kansas City Call*, 31 October 1924, 6; Charles A. Starks, "Baseball and Race Progress," *Philadelphia Tribune*, 16 October 1924, 8.
56. Frank A. Young, "Kansas City Monarchs Win World Series," *Chicago Defender*, 25 October 1924, 8, section 2. Winters pitched for Hilldale; Rogan for Kansas City. The other official scorer was Lloyd Thompson, former player and secretary for Hilldale, press agent for the ECL, and a free-lance sportswriter and cartoonist for the *Philadelphia Tribune* (Frank Young, "Eastern Nine Enters Series Favorites Over Westerners As Fandom Awaits Outcome," *Chicago Defender*, 3 October 1924, 6, section 2).
57. Ibid. It is an interesting stance by Young because later, in 1926, he would attack Gilmore for arguing that NNL teams should seek publicity from the white papers, implying, at least in Young's view, that the white papers could do the teams more good than the black newspapers. Young defiantly proclaimed that "Without the Race newspapers the league would blow up" ("Gilmore Seeks To Be Head Of National League; Takes Rap At Weekly Newspapers," *Chicago Defender*, 11 September 1926, 8).
58. Quote from a story in the *Philadelphia Tribune*, 25 October 1924, as cited in Lanctot, *Fair Dealing*, 121.
59. "Hilldale Meets Winner Of Kansas City-St. Louis Series; New York Gets 1 Game," *Chicago Defender*, 19 September 1925, 7, section 2; and "World Series Dope," *Chicago Defender*, 26 September 1925, 5, section 2. For more on barnstorming baseball clubs, see Bill Heward and Dimitri V. Gat, *Some Are Called Clowns* (New York: Thomas Y. Crowell Co., 1974).
60. Fay, "Change The Umpires," *Chicago Defender*, 19 August 1922, 10.
61. Tom Johnson, "Baseball: Spectators-Players-Umpires," *Chicago Defender*, 25 August 1923, 12. This story also ran in the *Courier* ("Baseball: Spectators-Players-Umpires," 25 August 1923, 7).
62. Billy Donaldson, "Big League Stories," *Chicago Defender*, 17 November 1923, 12.
63. "White Super Picked By Hilldale Owner," *Baltimore Afro-American*, 28 March 1925, 12. Dallas wrote for the *Philadelphia Public Ledger*.
64. In Lomax, "Black Entrepreneurship," 415.
65. Rollo Wilson, "Eastern Snapshots," *Pittsburgh Courier*, 28 March 1925, 15.
66. Frank A. Young, "Lloyd Goes to Connors," *Chicago Defender*, 4 February 1922, 10. See also "Pitchers Brown And Rile Jump To The Outlaws," *Chicago Defender*, 17 February 1923, 10. Lincoln Giant pitcher Dave Brown was described as leaving "organized ball" to play for "the outlaws," the ECL, while remaining "the property" of the Negro National League.
67. "Foster's Ire Aroused Over Ball Player's Charges," *Chicago Defender*, 24 November 1923, 9.
68. "Fay Says," *Chicago Defender*, 7 January 1927, 11.
69. Mister Fan, "National League Season Opens Saturday, April 28," *Chicago Defender*, 21 April 1923, 10.
70. "National League Season Opens April 28," *Chicago Defender*, 5 April 1924, 11; and "Pitching Staff of Foster to Be Drawn From 10 Men," *Chicago Defender*, 19 January 1924, 10. The fifth season "promises to give fans a

greater season than any previous, with competition more keen than at any time during the history of the league," according to the eponymous Fan.
71. Frank A. Young, "Eleven Thousand See The Monarchs Beaten, 15–13, By The American Giants," *Chicago Defender*, 5 May 1923, 9.
72. *Chicago Defender*, 12 May 1923, 9; and "17,000 See Foster Win," *Chicago Defender*, 2 June 1923, 9. The *Courier* also emphasized crowd sizes, at least when they were large. "18,000 Choke Park When American Giants Win," is one example, appearing in the 16 May 1925 *Courier*, page 12.
73. Rollo Wilson, "Eastern Snapshots," *Pittsburgh Courier*, 20 June 1925, 13.
74. "Why National League Seeks Business Brains to Run Baseball Clubs," *Chicago Defender,* 30 January 1926, 5, section 2. The article includes detailed financials on all NNL teams, showing Chicago making more than twice any other team and in some cases more than four times the revenues of other clubs.
75. "Fay Says," *Chicago Defender*, 23 February 1924, 10. Williams also worked at different times for the ABCs and the Detroit Stars. He was named NNL secretary in May 1926.
76. "East and West Leagues End Session," *Chicago Defender*, 13 December 1924, 7, section 2. The *Courier* described the meetings as "so heated . . . that even newspaper men were barred for the first day" ("Big Leagues Hold Annual Meetings," 12 December 1924, 7). For the *Defender*, Blount had gone from "one of the most popular" league owners to a pariah in less than one season. This article referred to players as "the property of clubs they finished the 1924 season with."
77. "Club Owners In West To Back 'Rube' Foster," *Pittsburgh Courier*, 14 February 1925, 7.
78. Frank Young, "Fay Says," *Chicago Defender*, 24 October 1925, 6, section 2. Less than 4,000 attended the deciding game; as few as 1,500 attended earlier games.
79. "Frank A. Young, "Directors of National League Hold Future of Our Baseball in Their Hands," *Chicago Defender*, 11 September 1926, 9.
80. William E. Clark, "Resentment Felt Over Domination of Eastern and Western Leagues By Rube Foster and Nat Strong," *New York Age,* 23 January 1926, 6; and (quote) Bill Gibson, "Eastern League Needs New Head," *Afro-American*, 14 August 1926, 8.
81. Rollo Wilson, "Sports Shots," *Pittsburgh Courier*, 20 November 1926, 12; Frank A. Young, "World Series Games Just A Joke," *Chicago Defender*, 23 October 1926, 7, section 2.
82. "Fay Says," *Chicago Defender*, 3 November 1928, 6, section 2.
83. Ibid.
84. "Few Faces To Be Seen In American Giants Lineup As Result of Drastic Shake-Up," *Chicago Defender*, 23 August 1930, 10.
85. "Fay Says," *Chicago Defender*, 7 January 1927, 11. Young wrote that, "If the players can't be handled, baseball is doomed."
86. Philip Foner and Ronald Lewis, *The Black Worker: A Documentary History from Colonial Times to the Present*, vol. 6 (Philadelphia: Temple University Press, 1979), 2. Presumably because the Depression had already

inflicted its wrath on poor blacks, who did not yet invest in the stock market in numbers, Black Tuesday in late-October 1929 was not even reported on by the *Defender*.
87. "Fay Says," *Chicago Defender*, 22 October 1927, 6, section 2; and "Fay Says," *Chicago Defender*, 22 January 1927, 8, section 2.
88. Old-Timer, "Chicago May Not Have Ball Club When League Season Gets Under Way," *Chicago Defender*, 5 February 1927, 4, section 2.
89. Bolden initially resisted joining the ECL but ultimately agreed to become a founding member.
90. "Pitchers Brown And Rile Jump To The Outlaws," 10; and "Eastern League Schedule Gives Fans Real Laugh," *Chicago Defender*, 28 April 1923, 10. The source of amusement was the schedule's brevity—just thirty-one games, which compared to 105 games for the NNL. Even this sparse schedule was not followed.
91. Fay Young, "Fay Speaks," *Chicago Defender*, 14 October 1922, 10. Young briefly explained the New York Giants' surprising four-game sweep of the cross-town Yankees.
92. "Am. Giants To Play Tigers 2 Game Series," *Chicago Defender*, 14 October 1922, 10. Foster's Giants were to play the Detroit Tigers, minus Detroit's best player, Ty Cobb, a notorious racist, but saw the set scrubbed by the Cubs and White Sox, which controlled the venue. Chicago's big league teams, which refused to play Foster's Giants, had their own inter-city games planned. The Philadelphia Athletics did play the Bacharach Giants, and the St. Louis Cardinals played the St. Louis Stars. The World Series champion New York Giants beat the Lincoln Giants with part of their team.
93. Donn Rogosin, *Invisible Men: Life in Baseball's Negro Leagues* (New York: Atheneum, 1983), v.
94. "Who'll Be The Next," *Competitor*, October/November 1920, 221.
95. Ibid.
96. Frank A. Young, "The American Giants-Detroit Tigers Games," *Chicago Defender*, 27 October 1923, 12, as one example. "Chicago fans saw something that they have waited a long time to see. Many bet it couldn't be done," Young wrote, celebrating the achievement of getting the two races on the field rather than discussing the fact that the two were forcibly separated in the first place.
97. "Fans Glad To See Buckner Back As White Sox Trainer," *Chicago Defender*, 11 February 1922, 10. Buckner had been released in 1917, perhaps because of the racist views of Sox player Eddie Collins, then re-hired in 1922. The Pittsburgh Pirates (George Asten) and New York Giants, also, employed black trainers.
98. "Bill Buckner in Texas," *Chicago Defender*, 4 March 1922, 10. The twenties were a period of rapid growth for the KKK, which the *Defender* chronicled and protested. Robert S. Abbott wrote a page-one editorial in September 1922 critical of this growth, ending it with the words, "To Hell with the Ku Klux Klan," and his signature (Abbott, "Ku Klux Made Possible By Bigotry and Cowardice of American White Man," *Chicago Defender*, 2 September 1922, 1).

99. Wendell Smith, "Smitty's Sports Spurts," *Pittsburgh Courier*, 5 August 1939, 17. Haley's magic did not work. The Giants suffered through a dismal season. Adding Josh Gibson or Buck Leonard as players would presumably have done far more to help the Giants' fortunes.
100. Lanctot, *Fair Dealing and Clean Playing*, 185.
101. *New York Amsterdam News*, 16 September 1926, cited in Lanctot, *Fair Dealing and Clean Playing*, 185.
102. As Susan Drucker has argued, sports heroes are more about the illusion of heroism than the embodiment of truly heroic values. The ways that playing fields, photography, publicity, and media coverage construct myths of heroes and heroism point to a celebrification process that turns athletes into "pseudo-heroes" (Susan J. Drucker and Robert S. Cathcart, eds., *American Heroes in a Media Age*, Cresskill, N.J.: Hampton Press [1994], vii).

NOTES TO CHAPTER FOUR

1. Attendance estimates vary in the newspapers between 25,000 and 30,000.
2. "65,000 Attend Pageant and East-West Game in Chicago," *Pittsburgh Courier*, 17 September 1934, 1. The 65,000 count combines attendance at a musical pageant in Chicago the night before the game and that for the game itself.
3. "Sez Ches," *Pittsburgh Courier*, 1 September 1934, 5, section 2. The game was the subject of six stories in the issue. The *Defender* made this same argument after the 1936 Classic, when 30,000 attended, and the newspaper encouraged fans again to write Landis to plea for integration ("30,000 Jam Shows We're Game's Asset," *Chicago Defender*, 29 August 1936, 13).
4. Booker T. Washington, "Atlanta Compromise Speech," 18 September 1895.
5. R. R. Wright, Sr., "Bus. Opportunities for American Negro Are Many, Says Major Wright," *Pittsburgh Courier*, 29 June 1935, 7, section 2.
6. Elmer Knox interview with Donn Rogosin, October 1979, quoted in Rogosin, *Invisible Men: Life in Baseball's Negro Leagues* (New York: Atheneum, 1983).
7. Gus Greenlee and Cum Posey, "Posey's Points," *Pittsburgh Courier*, 26 March 1938, 17. These words hint at what the owners envisioned, which was integration through the addition of an all-black team into the major leagues, not integrated teams throughout major league baseball.
8. Sportswriters would make this argument many times throughout the 1930s. F. M. Davis provides the prototype in the *Afro-American*, 18 April 1936, 22, in his column, "Sports Snapshots." Fans had to support the leagues so baseball could produce enough talent of such a caliber "that public demand might force some of them into the big leagues," Davis wrote.
9. Monroe also covered theater and film, and he wrote a weekly city life column. He came to the *Defender* from the *Chicago Whip*, a black weekly with far less circulation than the *Defender*, where he was sports editor. Young briefly joined the *Courier* in 1931, writing his "Fay Says" column from Chicago for two months. In 1934 he moved from the *Defender* to the

Kansas City *Call*, where he became managing editor. He returned to the *Defender* in 1937, again as sports editor. For more on Young's career, see Joel Sternberg, "Frank A. 'Fay' Young," *Dictionary of Literary Biography* 241, "American Sportswriters and Writers on Sport," 1992, 332–341.

10. Chester Washington, "Sez Ches," *Pittsburgh Courier*, 22 July 1933, 5, section 2.
11. For more on Dougherty's career, see Anthony Hill, *Pages from the Harlem Renaissance* (New York: P. Lang, 1996).
12. Chester Washington, "Sez Ches," *Pittsburgh Courier*, 12 August 1933, 4, section 2. In 1933, Comiskey's heir, J. Louis Comiskey, told the *Defender* that the question of race had never come up in the team's recruiting or player signings, explaining that when a player of color can prove he belongs, he will be signed. The *Defender* did not challenge this view ("Comiskey Says 'Color' on Diamond Is Sox Problem," *Chicago Defender*, 4 March 1933, 11).
13. Al Monroe, "It's News To Me," *Chicago Defender*, 31 October 1931, 8. To his credit, Comiskey employed fifty men of color, more than any major league owner could claim in 1931. Among the black employees was trainer Bill Buckner.
14. "P.K. Wrigley Speaks," *Chicago Defender*, 27 October 1934, 8.
15. For more, see Brian Carroll, "Mediocrity Under Pressure: The *Chicago Defender* and the integration of the Chicago Cubs," in *From Tinker to Ernie to Ryno: A Social History of the Chicago Cubs*, Gerald C. Wood and Andy Hazucha, eds. (Jefferson, N.C.: McFarland, in press, anticipated 2007).
16. Al Monroe, "What Say," *Chicago Defender*, 3 September 1932, 8. The Yankees and Babe Ruth swept the Cubs in four games.
17. "Sultan of Swat Talks," *Pittsburgh Courier*, 19 August 1933, 4, section 2.
18. Ibid., "Sez Ches," 4, section 2, which reprinted an article from the Winnipeg *Free Press and Bulletin*.
19. Objectivity, an admittedly contested term, is used here to mean a balance and neutrality or impartiality in reporting. The journalistic term is defined and discussed in Harlan S. Stensaas, "Development of the Objectivity Ethic in U.S. Daily Newspapers," *Journal of Mass Media Ethics* 2, no. 1 (Fall/Winter 1986): 50–60.
20. Dan Burley, "Just A Word," *Chicago Defender*, 3 May 1930, 15, section 2.
21. See Charles Fountain, *Sportswriter: The Life and Times of Grantland Rice* (New York: Oxford University Press, 1993). Rice was a member of what has been called the "Gee Whiz" school of sports journalism, which mythicized the athletes and overlooked their foibles and flaws. The first radio broadcast of major league baseball was 5 August 1921. KDKA in Pittsburgh broadcast a game between the Pirates and the Philadelphia Phillies.
22. Cole renamed Schorling's field Cole Park.
23. In a July 1934 column, Wilson described Young as the man "who helped to make Rube Foster famous" ("Sports Shots," *Pittsburgh Courier*, 28 July 1934, 4, section 2).
24. For misspellings, see "Chicago Still Out as East-West League Meet Closes," *Chicago Defender*, 30 January 1932, 8. For descriptions of the reliance on

Notes to Chapter Four

letters and press releases, see Al Monroe, "What Say," *Chicago Defender*, 5 March 1932, 10.
25. "Sports Shots," *Pittsburgh Courier*, 29 July 1933, 4, section 2.
26. Posey's columns included "Pointed Paragraphs" and "Don't You Remember . . . ." He owned the Grays with Rufus "Sonnyman" Jackson, who was the team's largest shareholder, and two other men. An accomplished athlete in his youth, Posey involved himself in Homestead's community life. In November 1931, for example, Posey was elected to the school board of the Bureau of Education of the borough of Homestead ("Posey Wins As School Board Director," *Pittsburgh Courier*, 7 November 1931, 1).
27. Brad Snyder, *Beyond the Shadow of the Senators* (Chicago: Contemporary Books, 2003), 88.
28. "National Baseball League In 3-Day Meet," *Chicago Defender*, 25 January 1930, 16.
29. "Texas, Oklahoma, Louisiana League Will Open Spring Season on Saturday, April 27," *Chicago Defender*, 2 March 1929, 6, section 2. The league's teams were the Tulsa Oilers, Fort Worth Cats, Wichita Black Spudders, Houston Buffaloes, San Antonio Indians, and an Oklahoma City club.
30. Ibid.
31. "Semipro Ball League Sees A Rosy Future," *Chicago Defender*, 12 February 1938, 25.
32. John L. Clark, "League Secretary Hits Ball Moguls," *Chicago Defender*, 8 July 1933, 11; also published in the *Courier* that same week.
33. "Looking Over The Baseball Horizon," *Pittsburgh Courier*, 21 March 1931, 5, section 2.
34. "Hilldale Club Disbands; 'No Business,' Owner Tells Press," *Chicago Defender*, 30 July 1932, 9.
35. Dan Burley, "Sports Squibs," *Chicago Defender*, 28 February 1931, 10. There is record in the *Courier* of a meeting in January, during which the Negro National debated contraction (Wm. Dizzy Dismukes, "National League May Drop 2 Cities," *Pittsburgh Courier*, 31 January 1931, 4, section 2). Frank Young spoke at the meeting, delivering a speech "spotted with criticism." A 1938 *Defender* article, too, wonders "which city won the 1938 league championship," and it suggests the determination of a champion be put on the agenda of the league's annual meeting that year ("American League Baseball Owners Meet Here Dec. 11," *Chicago Defender*, 10 December 1938, 8).
36. "Vet Baseball Man Dies in San Antonio," *Chicago Defender*, 25 April 1953, 27.
37. "The Chicago Defender Will Sponsor Meet," *Chicago Defender*, 20 August 1932, 11; and "Chicago Defender Holds First Annual Softball Meet," *Chicago Defender*, 10 September 1932, 8. Quote from "Chicago Defender Sponsors Tourney," *Chicago Defender*, 19 August 1933, 8.
38. Al Monroe, "Organize Six-Club League," *Chicago Defender*, 14 January 1933, 10.
39. Ibid.
40. "Giants Park Is Sold To Local Business Men," *Chicago Defender*, 20 February 1932, 1.

41. Quote from Andrew Buni, *Robert L. Vann of the Pittsburgh Courier* (London: University of Pittsburgh Press, 1974), 249. According to the *Courier*, Greenlee Field held 6,000 for baseball and 10,000 for boxing fights. The cost of construction varies depending on the account. The park required seventy-five tons of steel and fourteen train car loads of cement to build ("Greenlee Field Data," *Pittsburgh Courier*, 9 July 1932, 5, section 2).
42. Chester Washington, "Sez Ches," *Pittsburgh Courier*, 7 May 1932, 4, section 2. In June, Washington introduced a new column, "Gleanings from Greenlee Field," a roundup of news and notes about events at the venue.
43. William G. Nunn, "WGN Broadcasts," *Pittsburgh Courier*, 21 May 1932, 4, section 2.
44. Ibid., 4 June 1932, 5, section 2.
45. Rob Ruck, *Sandlot Seasons: Sport in Black Pittsburgh* (Urbana, Ill.: University of Illinois Press, 1987), 135 and 151.
46. Nathan Thompson, *Kings: The True Story of Chicago's Policy Kings and Numbers Racketeers* (Chicago: Bronzeville Press, 1994), 113.
47. "Crawfords To 'Carry On' In This Bus," 27 February 1932, 5, section 2.
48. Jim Bankes, *The Pittsburgh Crawfords* (Jefferson, N.C.: McFarland, 2001), 17, 70.
49. *Pittsburgh Courier*, 7 October 1933, 4, section 2. The only time Greenlee's numbers businesses were mentioned in the *Courier* was in January 1931 when the New York Stock Exchange condemned the vocation ("Fatal Rap By Stock Exchange Leaves 'Number' Kings Silent," 31 January 1931, 1).
50. Thompson, *Kings*, 106.
51. Ibid., 13.
52. Ibid.
53. "Future Of Baseball Is Bright, Says Man Who Invested Most," *Pittsburgh Courier*, 6 June 1936, 4, section 2.
54. Posey, *Pittsburgh Courier*, 10 April 1937, 16; Pompez: Edgar T. Rouzeau, "Pompez May Talk," *Pittsburgh Courier*, 6 November 1937, 1.
55. Thompson, *Kings*, 370.
56. "Jones Brothers Offer U.S. $500,000 Compromise," *Chicago Defender*, 1 June 1940, 1.
57. Juliet E. K. Walker, "The Promised Land: The Chicago Defender and the Black Press," in *The Black Press in the Middle West, 1865–1985*, Henry Lewis Suggs, ed. (Westport, Conn.: Greenwood Press, 1996), 38, quoting St. Clair Drake and Horace Cayton in *Black Metropolis* (Chicago: University of Chicago Press), 403.
58. Buni, *Robert L. Vann of the Pittsburgh Courier*, 257. The year prior, the paper issued shareholders, including Cum Posey, their first common stock dividend in seven years.
59. Ibid., 227. In 1930, the *Defender* had circulation of 110,000, compared to the *Courier*'s 38,760. The *New York Age* claimed 45,000. In 1947, the *Courier* had circulation of 277,000 and the *Afro-American* chain collectively boasted 235,000 weekly circulation (Walker, "The Promised Land," 40).

Notes to Chapter Four

60. John Rickards Betts, *America's Sporting Heritage: 1850–1950* (Reading Mass.: Addison-Wesley, 1974), 253.
61. John Drebinger, "Warns That Baseball's Popularity May Be Put to Acid Test This Season—Asks Enthusiastic, Aggressive, Alert Play—Opposes Fraternizing With Rivals on Field," *New York Times*, 11 April 1933, A24.
62. Ibid.
63. "Sez Ches," *Pittsburgh Courier*, 2 September 1933, 4, section 2.
64. Larry Lester, *Black Baseball's National Showcase, The East-West All-Star Game, 1933–1953* (Lincoln: University of Nebraska Press, 2001), 1.
65. Buck O'Neil, *I Was Right On Time* (New York: Simon & Schuster, 1996), 121. According to Larry Lester, more than a million readers annually took part in the voting, and three million voted in 1940 (*Black Baseball's National Showcase, The East-West All-Star Game, 1933–1953*, 152). The voting was decreasingly democratic over time, however, as the *Courier* and *Defender* writers intervened to make sure their cities' teams were well represented.
66. Thompson, *Kings*, 120.
67. O'Neil, *I Was Right On Time*, 121.
68. Lester, *Black Baseball's National Showcase*, 22.
69. Neil Lanctot, *Negro League Baseball* (Lincoln: University of Nebraska Press), 193.
70. "May Give Prizes for All-Star Game," *Chicago Defender*, 12 August 1933, 10.
71. Ibid.
72. "Foster, West, Whips East," *Chicago Defender*, 16 September 1933, 10. The *Defender*'s attorney, Nathan McGill, threw out the ceremonial first pitch, with longtime city alderman William A. Dawson catching.
73. Quote from "Star Baseball Teams Clash Here Sunday," *Chicago Defender*, 25 August 1934, 1. Attendance figures from Dewey R. Jones, "'O, Sing A New Song' Draws 60,000," *Chicago Defender*, 1 September 1934, 1.
74. Al Monroe, "Speaking of Sports," *Chicago Defender*, 16 September 1933, 10. Monroe noted the lack of major league officials in attendance at Comiskey.
75. Ira F. Lewis, "The Passing Review," *Pittsburgh Courier*, 30 April 1932, 5, section 2.
76. ANP, "Negro Stars Could 'Answer Prayers' Of Big League Club Owners Says Chicago Daily News Expert After Witnessing East-West Game," *Pittsburgh Courier*, 23 September 1933. Lundy became a sportswriter for a Newark newspaper after his playing career (Cum Posey, "Posey's Points," *Pittsburgh Courier*, 10 April 1937, 16).
77. Cum Posey, "Posey's Points," *Pittsburgh Courier*, 10 April 1937, 16.
78. "30,000 Jam Shows We're Game's Asset," *Chicago Defender*, 29 August 1936, 13.
79. "Paige Fans 12 To Shade Jones in Hot Mound Duel," *Pittsburgh Courier*, 15 September 1934, 4, section 2.
80. "Satchell [sic] Paige Is Magnet At E-W Game; Players Of Big League Calibre Perform," *Pittsburgh Courier*, 29 August 1936, 5, section 2.
81. John L. Clark, "E-W Game Seen As Economic Boon," *Pittsburgh Courier*, 18 August 1934, 4, section 2.

82. W. Rollo Wilson, "Sports Shots," *Pittsburgh Courier*, 8 September 1934, 4, section 2.
83. "Business Would Take Race's Stars Into Majors," *Chicago Defender*, 12 September 1936, 13. The comment could also be interpreted as indicating the Sox got all they wanted in negotiations to rent out Comiskey for the Classic. The organizing committee for the Classic in 1936 included Greenlee; William P. Harrison, a white hotel manager (Chicago's Grand Hotel); Horace G. Hall, an owner of the American Giants; and Oscar DePriest, a long-serving politician representing Chicago's South Side.
84. "Daily Scribes Fight Ban on Race Players," *Chicago Defender*, 18 February 1933, 10.
85. Ibid.
86. Ibid.
87. For more on Washington's symposium, see Chris Lamb, "'What's Wrong with Baseball?' The *Pittsburgh Courier* and the Beginning of its Campaign to Integrate the National Pastime," *Western Journal of Black Studies*, 2002. The *Courier* conducted another "symposium" in December 1937, using the Minor League Baseball meetings in Pittsburgh as the venue for surveying executives. The consensus was that black players were "certain to reach the big leagues sooner or later" ("Challenge Hurled At Pittsburgh Pirates On Sepia Players Issue," *Pittsburgh Courier*, 11 December 1937, 17).
88. "Would You Like To See Race Ball Players In The Majors?" *Chicago Defender*, 28 October 1933, 10.
89. "Fans Send Landis Request To Lift Color Bar Off Baseball," *Chicago Defender*, 4 November 1933, 11. Baseball Commissioner Landis offered no official response. Urging readers to write letters became common practice for black sports editors. The *Afro-American* encouraged its readers in 1938, for example, to bombard the Brooklyn Dodgers' new general manager, Larry MacPhail, urging an end to discrimination (Art Carter, "From The Bench," 24 April 1938, 24).
90. "Admits Barrier, But Race Stars Could Make It," *Pittsburgh Courier*, 27 January 1935, 5, section 2.
91. Gene Coughlin, "Daily Scribe Speaks Of Jim Crow In The Majors," *Chicago Defender*, 13 July 1935, 13. Neil McDonald, writing for the *Los Angeles Record*, too, wrote critically of baseball's hypocrisy, and, like Coughlin, referenced Joe Louis as an excellent representative of boxing and Jesse Owens as track's best citizen (McDonald, "Daily Writer Tells What Is Wrong With Baseball," *Chicago Defender*, 3 August 1935, 16).
92. "Speaking of Sports," *Chicago Defender*, 22 June 1935, 16.
93. Rusinack and Lamb, 3.
94. "'A Sickening Red Tinge:' The *Daily Worker*'s Fight Against White Baseball," *Cultural Logic* 3, No. 1 (2001): 2. The *Worker* published hundreds of articles calling for integration and, for a while, was the only newspaper outside the black press writing with any regularity on the issue.
95. The buzz in the dailies was trumpeted in a 1,200-word opus on the 1934 season by John L. Clark, in which he made sure to thank the black press. While dailies had at least noticed the existence of a black baseball world, he wrote,

attention that Clark credited the black press for enabling, the lifeblood of the league remained "the liberal, excellent—and I might say, wonderful—cooperation rendered by the Negro press." A black-owned sport played by blacks for blacks had to have "the endorsement of their own racial publications," he wrote, "and that is what the Negro National League got" ("1934 Season Considered Successful," *Pittsburgh Courier*, 5 January 1935, 4, section 2).

NOTES TO CHAPTER FIVE

1. Undated manuscript, Wendell Smith Papers, National Baseball Hall of Fame Library, Cooperstown, N.Y., MSB 1. According to Smith's wife, Wyonella Smith, Tresh lived on the same block as Wendell Smith, whose family was the only black family in their Detroit neighborhood. The realization that only the color of his skin prevented him from a career in baseball "broke his heart," Wyonella Smith said. "He knew he was good enough" (personal interview, 28 October 2001, Chicago).
2. R. E. Wolseley and Laurence R. Campbell, *Exploring Journalism* (New York: Prentice-Hall, 1946), 208.
3. Charlotte O'Kelly, "Black Newspapers and Black Protest: Their Historical Relationship, 1827–1945," *Phylon* 43, No. 1 (Spring 1982), 9.
4. Jerome Holtzman, audiotapes of interviews of Wendell Smith, conducted in Chicago in February 1971 (provided by Smith's wife, Wyonella Smith, in October 2001). The interviews were conducted to produce the book, *No Cheering in the Pressbox* (New York: Holt, Rinehart and Winston, 1974), a volume of interviews with eighteen sportswriters.
5. W. H. Hollins, "The Negro Press in America: A Content Analysis of Five Newspapers" (unpublished M.A. thesis, University of Minnesota, 1945), 75.
6. See Jules Tygiel, *Extra Bases* (Lincoln: Bison Books, 2002), 24–34, a chapter entitled, "Jackie Robinson's Signing: The Untold Story."
7. Neil Lanctot, *Negro League Baseball, The Rise and Ruin of a Black Institution* (Lincoln, Ne.: University of Nebraska Press), 219. Lacy had written part-time for the paper since 1926.
8. Brad Snyder, *Beyond the Shadow of the Senators* (New York: McGraw Hill, 2003), 77.
9. Ibid.
10. Lee Finkle, *Forum for Protest: The Black Press During World War II* (Rutherford, N. J.: Fairleigh Dickinson University Press, 1975), 52. The *Afro-American* claimed at the time a circulation of 100,000.
11. Samuel Harold Lacy remained the *Afro-American*'s sports editor for more than six decades. He died May 2003 at the age of 99, working and writing for the *Afro-American* until just weeks before his death. In 1948, Lacy became the first black member of the Baseball Writers Association of America. In 1997, he was named winner of the J. G. Taylor Spink Award for meritorious contributions to baseball writing, an award that placed him in the writers and broadcasters wing of the National Baseball Hall of Fame.

12. Homestead was a black district of Pittsburgh, where the Grays played most of their games for most of the club's history. Because the team had difficulty securing a venue in Pittsburgh, the Grays played their home games for several seasons at Griffith Stadium.
13. For descriptions of Lacy's involvement, including first-hand accounts, see Sam Lacy and Moses J. Newson, *Fighting For Fairness, The Life Story of Hall of Fame Sportswriter Sam Lacy* (Centreville, Md.: Tidewater Publishers, 1998), and Peter M. Sheingold, "In Black and White: Sam Lacy's Campaign To Integrate Baseball" (unpublished thesis, Hampshire College, 1992).
14. Jerome Holtzman, audiotapes of interviews of Wendell Smith.
15. Sam Lacy, "Looking 'em Over," *Washington Afro-American*, 1 April 1939, 23.
16. Ibid., 15 April 1939, 21.
17. Jules Tygiel, *Baseball's Great Experiment: Jackie Robinson and His Legacy* (New York: Vintage, 1997), 35.
18. Armistead Scott Pride and Clint C. Wilson, *A History of the Black Press*, Moorland-Spingarn Series (Washington, D.C.: Howard University Press, 1997), 139. In 1947, the *Courier* had circulation of approximately 330,000.
19. "Sez Ches," *Pittsburgh Courier*, 16. Washington relinquished the sports editorship to Smith in 1938 and became assistant business manager and secretary of the Pittsburgh Courier Publishing Co.
20. Branch Rickey wanted Smith to ease Robinson's transition and secure housing in segregated towns (Paul Meyer, "Columnist was 'baseball' star," *Pittsburgh Post-Gazette*, 29 September 1994, D1). Smith earned $50 per week as Robinson's "confidant," or the same salary he made as sports editor for the *Pittsburgh Courier*. One of his many roles was traveling ahead of the team and arranging for housing for Robinson in segregated cities and towns.
21. "Defender Man Made Head of Sport Writers," *Chicago Defender*, 24 August 1940, 20.
22. *Pittsburgh Courier*, 29 January 1938, 17.
23. "Smitty's Sports Spurts," *Pittsburgh Courier*, 14 May 1938, 17.
24. Smith's paradoxical goals are an example of what W. E. B. Du Bois described when he discussed the double-consciousness of black Americans. Attempts at reconciliation, which Smith's strivings can be seen to represent, produce what Du Bois called the "double life" that every American Negro of the twentieth century lived (Du Bois, *The Souls of Black Folk* [1903], available online at http://www.bartleby.com/114/).
25. For more on the notion that a pendulum of race perpetually swings between the extremes of separation and assimilation, see Joel Williamson, *A Rage for Order: Black/White Relations in the American South Since Emancipation* (New York: Oxford University Press, 1986).
26. Cited in David Wiggins, "Wendell Smith, the Pittsburgh *Courier-Journal* and the Campaign to Include Blacks in Organized Baseball, 1933–1945," *Journal of Sport History*, 10, no. 2 (1989): 11.
27. "Smitty's Sports Spurts," *Pittsburgh Courier*, 18 February 1939, no page number available.

Notes to Chapter Five

28. Wendell Smith, "'Negroes Will Never Crash Majors,' Says Bill Terry; Carl Hubbell Lauds Colored Players," *Pittsburgh Courier*, 15 July 1939, 13.
29. *Pittsburgh Courier*, 25 July 1942, no page number available. For more on Smith's commentary during the war effort, see Wiggins, "Wendell Smith, the Pittsburgh *Courier-Journal* and the campaign to include blacks in organized baseball."
30. *Pittsburgh Courier*, July through August 1939. The description quoted comes from the 15 July 1939 issue, page 16, in an article headlined, "Are Negro Ball Players Good Enough To 'Crash' The Majors?"
31. Jerome Holtzman, audiotapes of interviews of Wendell Smith.
32. Durocher quote from Wendell Smith, "'I've Seen A Million!'—Leo Durocher," *Pittsburgh Courier*, 5 August 1939, 16; Wendell Smith, "The Sports Beat," *Pittsburgh Courier*, 16 November 1946, no page number available.
33. Wendell Smith, "'Negroes Will Never Crash Majors,' Says Bill Terry; Carl Hubbell Lauds Colored Players," *Pittsburgh Courier*, 15 July 1939, 1.
34. Ibid., 16.
35. "If The Majors Opened The Doors To Sepia Players, These 2 Stars Could Make The Grade!," *Pittsburgh Courier*, 15 July 1939, 17.
36. Quote from "Buc Chiefs Okay 'Series,'" *Pittsburgh Courier*, 5 August 1939, 17.
37. Chester L. Washington, "Harridge Sees East-West Game; Raps Bill Terry," *Pittsburgh Courier*, 12 August 1939, 1.
38. Jerome Holtzman, "Wendell Smith—a pioneer for black athletes," *The Sporting News*, 22 June 1974, no page number available.
39. Chester L. Washington, "Sez Ches," *Pittsburgh Courier*, 15 July 1939, 16. Washington called Smith "fearless" in buttonholing players and managers for interviews.
40. Richard Crepeau, "The Jake Powell Incident and the Press: A Study in Black and White," Baseball History (Summer 1986): 32–46, quote from p. 32. Crepeau content analyzed ten white newspapers and seven black newspapers.
41. Ibid., 33.
42. Dan M. Daniel, "Powell Slur To Bring Bar Against Impromptu Broadcasts By Players," *The Sporting News*, 4 August 1938, 1.
43. "Jake Powell A Policeman? Not In Dayton," *Chicago Defender*, 6 August 1938, 2. Dayton's police department denied to the *Defender* that Powell was ever a member of its force.
44. "Jake Powell Issues Apology For Radio Slur," *Chicago Defender*, 20 August 1938, 20.
45. Crepeau, "The Jake Powell Incident and the Press," 40.
46. "Smitty's Sports Spurts," *Pittsburgh Courier*, 25 May 1940, 17; and 3 August 1940, 17.
47. Randy Dixon, "The Sports Bugle," *Pittsburgh Courier*, 3 February 1940, 16.
48. Ibid., 17 February 1940, 16.
49. A graduate of Howard University Medical School, Powell was one of the first black physicians in the country to specialize in X-rays. He was a co-founder in 1922 of the Victory Mutual Life Insurance Company, and he

purchased the *Amsterdam News* in 1936 along with business partner P. M. H. Savoy (Lanctot, *Negro Leagues*, 88). It was common throughout the history of the Negro leagues for black writers to hold top positions in the leagues' organizational hierarchies. The same week of the Negro league meetings, UCLA won a basketball game thanks to a last-minute shot from Jackie Robinson ("Jackie Robinson's Last Minute Basket Wins For U.C.L.A. Quintet," *Pittsburgh Courier*, 10 February, 1940, 16).

50. Ibid., 10 May 1941, 16.
51. Ibid. In 1943, Dixon went to Europe to become one of the very few war correspondents in the field for the black press.
52. See Effa Manley, "Negro League Owners Spend $480,000 Yearly," *Chicago Defender*, 19 July 1941, 24.
53. "Terror Reigns in Memphis," *Pittsburgh Courier*, 30 November 1940, 1.
54. Cum Posey, "Posey's Points," *Pittsburgh Courier*, 26 April 1941, 16.
55. "Greenlee To Reorganize Crawfords," *Pittsburgh Courier*, 27 April 1940, 16.
56. Randy Dixon, "The Sports Bugle," *Pittsburgh Courier*, 11 May 1940, 16.
57. Both articles from the *Chicago Defender*, 11 May 1940, 16.
58. "25 Foot Leap By Jackie Is Tops," *Pittsburgh Courier*, 1 June 1940, 17; Randy Dixon, "Effa Manley Sees National League's Doom If Newark Loses Fight For Satchell," *Pittsburgh Courier*, 15 June 1940, 17. The black press spelled Paige's nickname alternately as "Satchell" and "Satchel."
59. "Posey's Points," *Pittsburgh Courier*, 17 February 1940, 17.
60. In Snyder, *Beyond the Shadow of the Senators*, 99.
61. Ibid., 88.
62. "Moguls Agree On Inter-loop Games," *Pittsburgh Courier*, 28 June 1941, 17. For more on the Manleys' hiring of Jerry Kessler, the Eagles' only white employee, see James Overmyer, *Queen of the Negro Leagues: Effa Manley and the Newark Eagles* (Lanham, Md.: Scarecrow Trade, 2001), 112–113. Kessler would later represent the Manleys in their dispute with the Dodgers in 1949 over the signing of Monte Irvin and Dodgers' refusal to offer compensation. The dispute prevented Brooklyn's signing of Irvin, who later was signed by the New York Giants.
63. For more, see Philip J. Lowry, *Green Cathedrals* (Reading, Mass.: Addison-Wesley Publishing, 1992), 128–131. The American Giants had to shift home games in 1933 to Indianapolis when Schorling decided to host dog racing instead of black baseball. The team was able to return for the 1934 season since the state of Illinois refused to legalize dog racing.
64. "Dustin' off the News," *Chicago Defender*, 27 July 1940, 1.
65. Ibid., 16 August 1941, 22.
66. "The Stuff Is Here," *Chicago Defender*, 24 February 1940, 24.
67. For examples, see Morgan S. Jensen, "Record Crowd At Yankee Stadium For 4-Team Card," *Pittsburgh Courier*, 26 July 1941, 16 (the attendance was 27,000); and "10,000 See Satchel Paige Beat Chicago 2 to 1," *Chicago Defender*, 24 May 1941, 24.
68. "Dream Come True," *Pittsburgh Courier*, 2 August 1941, 1. The game generated $49,000 in gate receipts, or one and a half times the revenues of the 1940 Classic.

Notes to Chapter Five

69. "East vs. West 1941," *Chicago Defender*, 26 July 1941, 12–15.
70. "40,000 To See East-West Classic Sunday," *Pittsburgh Courier*, 26 July 1941, 17.
71. "The Sports Bugle," *Pittsburgh Courier*, 6 September 1941, 16.
72. Herman Hill, "Jackie Robinson, Nate Moreland Barred At Camp," *Pittsburgh Courier*, 21 March 1942, 16.
73. Paige beat Dizzy Dean 3–1. Negro league historian John Holway put the winning record of black teams against all-white opponents for 445 games from 1886–1948 at 269–172–4, or a winning percentage of .601 (*Voices from the Great Black Baseball Leagues* [New York: De Capo Press, 1992], xviii-xix.)
74. Fay Young, "Through The Years Past Present Future," *Chicago Defender*, 30 May 1942, 24.
75. "Chicagoans Claim Time Is Ripe Now," *Chicago Defender*, 23 May 1942, 24.
76. For more on how the *Defender* fulfilled this self-help philosophy, see Curtis J. Morris, "The Evolution of the *Chicago Defender*," unpublished M.A. thesis (Indiana University, 1951), and Ralph Nelson Davis, "The Negro Newspaper in Chicago," unpublished M.A. thesis (University of Chicago, 1939).
77. "Ban Against Negro Players In Majors Scored By Unions," *Pittsburgh Courier*, 13 June 1942, 17; "Bishop Sheil Joins Fight Against Major League Color Barrier," *Chicago Defender*, 6 June 1942, 24; and "Smitty's Sports-Spurts," *Pittsburgh Courier*, 13 June 1942, 17.
78. "Catholics Call For Fair Play in Major Leagues," *Pittsburgh Courier*, 15 August 1942, 17.
79. "Union Appeals To Cub Chief," *Pittsburgh Courier*, 16 January 1943, 17; "Mass Meeting Sunday On Negroes In Major Leagues," *Chicago Defender*, 6 February 1943, 25.
80. "Furniture Workers Demand Elimination of Ban Against Negro Players In Majors," *Pittsburgh Courier*, 28 August 1943, 18.
81. Randy Dixon, "Willing To Sign Race Player, Phillies Owner Tells Courier," *Pittsburgh Courier*, 1 August 1942, 17; and "'Would Sign Race Player,' Chicago Magnate Tells Committee At Confab," *Pittsburgh Courier*, 26 December 1942, 16. The Phillies and Cubs integrated within forty-eight hours of each other in September 1953. For more on the integration of the Cubs, see Carroll, "'Mediocrity Under Pressure': The integration of the Chicago Cubs as covered by the *Chicago Defender*," in *From Tinker to Ernie to Ryno: A Social History of the Chicago Cubs* (Jefferson, N.C.: McFarland & Co., in press).
82. For more, see Larry Lester, *Black Baseball's National Showcase: The East-West All-Star Game, 1933–1953* (Lincoln: University of Nebraska Press, 2001), 176–184.
83. Exceptions include Lester's *Black Baseball's National Showcase*, and Kelly Rusinack and Chris Lamb, "Baseball on the Radical Agenda: The *Daily Worker* and *Sunday Worker* Journalistic Campaign to Desegregate Major League Baseball, 1933–1947," in *Jackie Robinson: Race, Sports, and the*

American Dream, Joseph Dorinson and Joram Warmund (eds.) (Armonk, N.Y.: M.E. Sharpe, 1998), 75–85. Also, as Richard Crepeau discovered, the *Daily Worker* was the one white newspaper that called for harsh punishment for Jake Powell, and it was the one paper that noted that Powell had been traded to the Yankees for "the viciously anti-Semitic Ben Chapman," who in the 1940s, as manager of the Phillies, would bait Jackie Robinson with racial slurs and epithets (Richard Crepeau, "The Jake Powell Incident and the Press: A Study in Black and White," Baseball History [Summer 1986]: 41).

84. Lucius C. Harper, "Dustin' off the News," *Chicago Defender,* 25 July 1942, 1, 2.
85. "Through The Years," *Chicago Defender,* 25 July 1942, 24.
86. "Statement By Czar Of Majors Creates Vote Avalanche," *Pittsburgh Courier,* 25 July 1942, 16.
87. Robert S. Abbott, the late publisher of the *Defender,* is credited, for example, for beginning the fight and for boycotting major league baseball his entire life ("Bishop Sheil Joins Fight Against Major League Color Barrier," *Chicago Defender,* 6 June 1942, 24). The same article noted the silence on the issue from Chicago's daily newspapers.
88. "Smitty's Sports-Spurts," *Pittsburgh Courier,* 25 July 1942, 17.
89. "Negro Ball Players Might Get Try-Outs," *Chicago Defender,* 1 August 1942, 25.
90. It is interesting that the players Smith and Nunn chose for the tryouts were based on the Pirates' needs, which included help at shortstop, behind the plate, in the outfield, and in starting pitching.
91. Wendell Smith, "Courier To Name Players For Bucs," *Pittsburgh Courier,* 1 August 1942, 1. The players selected were shortstop Willie Wells and pitcher Leon Day of the Newark Eagles, and outfielder Sam Bankhead and catcher Josh Gibson of the Homestead Grays. The Pirates integrated a dozen years later, in 1954, with the signing of Curt Roberts. It is unlikely a coincidence that all four players trafficked in the Negro National League based in Pittsburgh, a common denominator the *Defender*'s Young protested. Young had been secretary for the Chicago-based Negro American for five seasons ("Through The Years," *Chicago Defender,* 29 August 1942, 24).
92. "Smitty's Sports-Spurts," *Pittsburgh Courier,* 29 August 1942, 17.
93. "Pirates' Chief Scout To Handle Epochal Try-Outs," *Pittsburgh Courier,* 22 August 1942, 1.
94. Ibid.
95. Frank A. Young, "Major Leaguers Fail To Drop Color Bar," *Chicago Defender,* 5 December 1942, 25.
96. Ibid.
97. "Why Do Brooklyn's Dodgers Dodge Race Issue, Asks Writer; Says Sepia Stars Would Make Turnstiles Click," *Pittsburgh Courier,* 2 April 1938, 16.
98. "The Sports Beat," *Pittsburgh Courier,* 23 August 1947, 14.
99. "Through The Years," *Chicago Defender,* 8 August 1942, 25.
100. U.S. Congress, House of Representatives, Judiciary Committee, "Study of Monopoly Power of Organized Baseball," part six; hearing before the

Committee of the Judiciary, 82d Congress, first session, 1951, 484, in Steven A. Riess, *Major Problems in American Sport History* (New York: Houghton Mifflin Company, 1977), 372.
101. "Posey Skeptical About Tryouts For Sepia Stars In Big Leagues," *Pittsburgh Courier*, 22 August 1942, 16.
102. "Posey's Points," *Pittsburgh Courier*, 27 June 1942, 17. See also, "Posey's Points," *Pittsburgh Courier*, 27 March 1943, 18, in which Posey reiterates his position. He wrote that, "it is the duty of club owners . . . to build a league for Negro players and raise that league to such a standard that it will get universal recognition."
103. "Smitty's Sports Spurts," *Pittsburgh Courier*, 3 October 1942, 17. Commissioner in 1935, Morton was an eloquent spokesman for integration. In a column for the NAACP's *Crisis* newspaper, Morton argued that "the Negro . . . should resist segregation in every form . . . Every separate institution . . . undeniably tends to perpetuate our present status" (in Lanctot, *Negro Leagues*, 45).
104. "Dustin' off the News," *Chicago Defender*, 25 July 1942, 1, 2.
105. "Coast Owner Refuses Negro Players Tryout," *Pittsburgh Courier*, 27 March 1943, 18.
106. "Through The Years," *Chicago Defender*, 24 October 1942, 24. Young resigned as secretary to the Negro American shortly after writing this column. He had served for five seasons.

NOTES TO CHAPTER SIX

1. In 2001, the National Baseball Hall of Fame and Museum formed a Negro Leagues Researchers/Authors Group research team led by Larry Hogan, Dick Clark, and Larry Lester to conduct a comprehensive statistical study of the Negro leagues.
2. For more on these trends in mainstream sports coverage, see Tom Clark, *The World of Damon Runyon* (New York: Harper and Row, 1978) and Paul Gallico, *The Golden People* (New York: Doubleday & Co., 1964).
3. Leroy Satchel Paige, as told to Hal Lebovitz, *Pitchin' Man: Satchel Paige's Own Story* (Westport, Conn.: Meckler, 1992), 67–68.
4. For more on Paige's career, both the myths and the verifiable records, see James A. Riley, *The Biographical Encyclopedia of The Negro Baseball Leagues* (New York: Carroll and Graf, 1994), 597–600.
5. "Sez Ches," *Pittsburgh Courier*, 5 July 1941, 17.
6. Eddie Murphy, "Daily Scribe Tells Majors Of Value Of Satchel Paige," *Chicago Defender*, 8 February 1936. Murphy's newspaper was not identified.
7. Lester Rodney, "DiMaggio Calls Negro Greatest Pitcher," *Daily Worker*, 13 September 1937.
8. See Buck O'Neil, *I Was Right On Time* (New York: Fireside, 1996), 107–108. See also William G. Nunn, "Satchell [sic] Paige Is Magnet at E-W Game," *Pittsburgh Courier*, 29 August 1936.
9. Fay Young, "The Stuff Is Here," *Chicago Defender*, 20 September 1941, 25.
10. "Satchel Paige Day At Wrigley Field July 18," *Chicago Defender*, 3 July 1943, 25; "Divorce Papers Darken Satchel's Brilliant Day," *Chicago Defender*, 24

July 1943, 1; and "Satchel Paige Here Dec. 8 With Three Dance Bands," *Chicago Defender*, 28 November 1943, 24. At the dance band event, Paige promised to autograph programs "and anything else people stick in front of him," according to the news item.

11. Brian Carroll, "When to Stop the Cheering: A Content Analysis of Changes in Black Press Coverage of the Negro Leagues," in *The 14th Annual Cooperstown Symposium on Baseball and American Culture*, ed. William Simons (Jefferson City, N.C.: McFarland Press, 2001).
12. Ted Shane, "Chocolate Rube Waddell," *Saturday Evening Post*, 27 July 1940, 20, 79–81.
13. "Dustin off the News," *Chicago Defender*, 27 July 1940, 1.
14. Shane, "Chocolate Rube Waddell," 20, 79–80.
15. O'Neil, *I Was Right On Time*, 107. As O'Neil points out, Paige was the first player enshrined in the National Baseball Hall of Fame purely for his career in the black leagues.
16. "Satchelfoots," *Time*, 3 June 1940, 44; "Satchel Paige, Negro Ballplayer, is one of the best pitchers in the game," *Life*, 2 June 1941, 90–92.
17. Leroy Satchel Paige, *Pitchin' Man*, 16.
18. Ibid., 24 June 1943, 24; and "Dustin' off the News," *Chicago Defender*, 2 October 1943, 1.
19. The worst riots were in Detroit, resulting in ten dead, 200 wounded and 245 arrested (John R. Williams, "Race Riots Sweep Nation," *Chicago Defender*, 26 June 1943, 1).
20. The unwritten rule's existence was verified by Erin Lynch, archivist for the Northern Indiana Center for History, the national repository for the All American Girls Professional Baseball League, in South Bend, Indiana (personal interview conducted 10 January 2003, South Bend). For more on the AAGPBL, which was founded in "patriotic service in building morale," see Sharon Roepke, *Diamond Gals: The Story of the All American Girls Professional Baseball League* (Marcellus, Mich.: AAGPL Cards, 1986), and Susan E. Johnston, *When Women Played Hardball* (Seattle: Seal Press, 1994). Neither Roepke nor Johnston address the color line in any context in their books, nor is the color line mentioned in the film, *A League of Their Own*. The American Negro Girls Softball League and "Uncle Bill's" All Colored Girls Softball Team played in the 1940s, but it is unknown whether or not they were professional enterprises.
21. Roepke, *Diamond Gals*, 5. Branch Rickey also invested.
22. The *Courier* did, however, grant bylines to Josh Gibson, Satchel Paige, and John L. Clark for their versions of events.
23. This trend or method might be returning. See the use of blogs by Dallas Mavericks owner Mark Cuban (http://www.blogmaverick.com) and by Oakland Athletics general manager Billy Beane (http://www.athleticsnation.com/). The blogs allow, as the black newspapers enabled, the writers to speak directly to fans—unedited, unfiltered, and unspun.
24. The Negro National League ruthlessly raided the startup Eastern Seaboard League, for example, in 1937, driving the black league out of business.

Black sportswriters Rollo Wilson, Lloyd Thompson, and Otto Briggs all were involved in the Eastern Seaboard's launch.
25. The movie *Bingo Long Traveling All-Stars and Motor Kings* (1976), for example, depicted Negro leaguers, supplying many Americans with what still are their images or conceptions of what it was like to play in the black leagues. The Indianapolis Clowns were an inspiration for the movie.
26. Larry Lester, *Black Baseball's National Showcase: The East-West All-Star Game, 1933–1953* (Lincoln: University of Nebraska Press, 2001), 207.
27. "Smitty's Sports Spurts," *Pittsburgh Courier*, 16 October 1943, 16.
28. Ibid.
29. Wendell Smith, "Pitchers Star As West Beats East In Thriller," *Pittsburgh Courier*, 7 August 1943, 19; Wendell Smith, "Classic Star Dust," *Pittsburgh Courier*, 7 August 1943, 19.
30. Wendell Smith, "Czar of Negro Baseball Would Get $10,000 A Year," *Pittsburgh Courier*, 23 December 1943, 12. Nunn, managing editor of the *Courier*, made the presentation to the owners, and included in it the need for a commissioner for the league.
31. See Neil Lanctot, *Negro League Baseball, The Rise and Ruin of a Black Institution* (Lincoln, Ne.: University of Nebraska Press), 244–245.
32. Wendell Smith, "Smitty's Sports Spurts," *Pittsburgh Courier*, 11 December 1943, 16.
33. "Major Leagues Hear Plea For Negro Baseball Players," *Chicago Defender*, 4 December 1943, 1.
34. "Ira F. Lewis' Factual Speech to Judge Landis And Major League Owners," *Pittsburgh Courier*, 11 December 1943, 14.
35. "Major Leagues Hear Plea For Negro Baseball Players," *Chicago Defender*, 4 December 1943, 1.
36. Jerome Holtzman, audiotapes of interviews of Wendell Smith.
37. See Peter M. Sheingold, "In Black and White: Sam Lacy's Campaign to Integrate Baseball," M.A. thesis, Hampshire College, 1992, 58.
38. "Smitty's Sports Spurts," *Pittsburgh Courier*, 19 February 1944, 14.
39. Brad Snyder, *Beyond the Shadow of the Senators* (New York: McGraw Hill, 2003), 232.
40. Wendell Smith, "'American League Owners Just Want Fair Deal'—Martin," *Pittsburgh Courier*, 25 December 1943, 14.
41. Smith, "'American League Owners Just Want Fair Deal'—Martin."
42. Wendell Smith, "Smitty's Sports Spurts," 18 December 1943, 14.
43. Ibid.
44. Ibid.
45. Don Deleighbur, "Hints Sports Editors May Reject New Statistical Service of NNL," *Pittsburgh Courier*, 18 March 1944, 12.
46. "Made No Promise To Hire Negro Players—Wrigley," *Chicago Defender*, 25 December 1943, 1, 21.
47. Thomas G. Smith, "Outside the Pale: The Exclusion of Blacks from the National Football League, 1933–1946," *Journal of Sport History* 15, no. 3 (Winter 1988): 255–281.

48. "Smitty's Sports Spurts," *Pittsburgh Courier*, 15 January 1944, 15.
49. "Major Leagues Willing To Acknowledge Inferior Talent," *Pittsburgh Courier*, 27 January 1945, 16. Blacks fought during the war in segregated units, sometimes even under another nation's flag, as was the case for the all-black 389th division, which fought under French command.
50. Wendell Smith, "Czar of Negro Baseball Would Get $10,000 A Year," *Pittsburgh Courier*, 23 December 1944, 12. Nunn all but applied for the job of commissioner himself. The owners reported being "impressed," and the following day they organized a steering committee to study the proposal to hire a commissioner.
51. "Through The Years," *Chicago Defender*, 29 April 1944, 21.
52. "Smitty's Sports Spurts," *Pittsburgh Courier*, 2 December 1944, 12.
53. See Sheingold, "In Black and White," 53.
54. Gunnar Myrdal with Richard Sterner and Arnold Rose, *The American Dilemma: The Negro Problem and Modern Democracy* (New York: Harper & Brothers Publishers, 1944), 61.
55. Finkle, *Forum for Protest*, 53.
56. Jules Tygiel, *Baseball's Great Experiment: Jackie Robinson and His Legacy*, 43. Roberts joined the *Courier* from the *Afro-American* in 1943, covering sports in Washington D.C., including the Grays. A football star at Clark University in Atlanta, Roberts also drew sports cartoons and had, according to one historian, an "encyclopedic knowledge of black baseball" (Snyder, *Beyond the Shadow of the Senators*, 186).
57. "Dodger Boss Sees Two Colored Stars In Drill," *Washington Afro-American*, 15 April 1945, 18.
58. In Lester, *Black Baseball's National Showcase,* quoting Lester Rodney, editor of the *Daily Worker*, 242. Also present for the "tryouts" was the *Courier*'s Jimmy Smith, who reported on them for the Pittsburgh paper ("McDuffie, Thomas First Negroes In Big League Uniforms," *Pittsburgh Courier*, 14 April 1945, 12).
59. Lester, *Black Baseball's National Showcase,* 242.
60. The Fenway Park tryouts are famous today, but at the time they garnered little press attention. As a baseball player, Robinson was not well-known, and Sam Jethroe and Marvin Williams were, as black ball players, invisible to white society.
61. Howard Bryant, *Shut Out: A Story of Race and Baseball in Boston* (New York: Routledge, 2002), 38.
62. Details on the city's licensing of Sunday baseball in "Baseball Ban Holds Up Licenses to Boston Nines," *Pittsburgh Courier*, 24 March 1945, no page number available.
63. Wendell Smith, "Boston Councilman Joins In Crusade," *Pittsburgh Courier*, 14 April 1945, 1. Smith also tried to take Roy Campanella, then a "brilliant outfielder" for the Baltimore Elite Giants, but could not get permission from the Elites.
64. Wendell Smith, "Red Sox Consider Negroes," *Pittsburgh Courier*, 21 April 1945, 1. Whether or not top Sox management was in attendance

is not certain. Smith reported that field manager Joe Cronin and general manager Eddie Collins greeted the players at Fenway Park when they arrived at 10:30 in the morning. Other accounts indicate that no Sox personnel with decision-making authority were present that day. Cronin's views, however, are well known. As president of the American League in 1972, he refused to appear with Robinson when the Dodger great retired from the game.
65. At hearings before Massachusetts's civil rights agencies in the late fifties, it became public that not a single black was employed at Fenway Park in any capacity (in Bryant, *Shut Out*, 25). Green, who put on a Red Sox uniform for the first time on July 21, 1959, as a pinch runner on the road in Chicago, hit .233 in 50 games that season. After the game in the locker room, slumped in his chair, Green cried (53).
66. Bryant, *Shut Out*, 26–27.
67. Jerome Holtzman, audiotapes of interviews of Wendell Smith.
68. Ibid.
69. Chris Lamb and Glen Bleske, "Democracy on the Field," *Journalism History* 24, no. 2 (1998): 53.
70. Jackie Robinson, as told to Wendell Smith, *My Own Story* (New York: Greenburg Publishers, 1948), 27.
71. Jerome Holtzman, audiotapes of interviews of Wendell Smith.
72. Sam Lacy, *Washington Afro-American*, 28 February 1948, 15 (reprinted after integration).
73. "AFRO Leads Movement to Abolish Major League Baseball Discrimination," *Washington Afro-American*, 16 June 1945, 18.
74. Sam Lacy, "Looking 'em Over," *Washington Afro-American*, 11 August 1945, 18.
75. Wendell Smith, "Sepia Shortstop And Dodgers' Boss Meet In Brooklyn," *Pittsburgh Courier*, 1 September 1945, 12.
76. "The Courier Supports Organized Negro Baseball," *Pittsburgh Courier*, 3 November 1945, 12.
77. Jackie Robinson, "'Glad of Opportunity And Will Try to Make Good.' Robinson," *Pittsburgh Courier*, 3 November 1945, 1.
78. "The Courier Supports Organized Negro Baseball," *Pittsburgh Courier*, 3 November 1945, 12.
79. Lamb and Bleske, "Democracy on the Field," 52.
80. Bill L. Weaver, "The Black Press and the Assault on Professional Baseball's 'Color Line,' October 1945-April 1947," *Phylon* XL, no. 4 (1979): 303. Several studies have been conducted on press coverage of Robinson's signing, his first spring training, and on his first season with the Dodgers. The better ones include: Patrick Washburn, "New York Newspapers and Robinson's First Season," *Journalism Quarterly* 58, no. 4 (1981): 640–44; Lamb and Bleske, "Democracy on the Field;" Wiggins, "Wendell Smith, The *Pittsburgh Courier-Journal* and the Campaign to Include Blacks in Organized Baseball"; Chris Lamb and Glen Bleske, "The Road to October 23, 1945: The Press and the Integration of Baseball," *Nine:*

A Journal of Baseball and Social Policy 6 (Fall 1997): 48–68; Chris Lamb, "I Never Want Another Trip Like This One: Jackie Robinson's Trip To Integrate Baseball," *Journal of Sport History* 24 (Summer 1997): 177–191; and Glen Bleske, "No Runs, No Hits, No Blacks: Wendell Smith, the Black Press, and a Strategy for Racial Equality in the Spring of 1946," paper presented to the Association of Education in Journalism and Mass Communication Southeast Colloquium (Stone Mountain, Ga., March 1992).

81. William G. Kelley, "Jackie Robinson and the Press," *Journalism Quarterly* 53 (Spring 1976): 137–139.
82. *Brown v. Board of Education*, 347 US 483 (1954).
83. "The Sports Beat," *Pittsburgh Courier*, 3 November 1945, 12.
84. In the mid-1940s, several black organizations dropped "Negro" or "Colored" from their names, including the Negro Newspaper Publishers Association, the National Negro Bankers Association, the Colored Intercollegiate Athletic Association, the Bureau for Colored Children, and the Home for Aged and Infirm Colored Persons (Lanctot, *Negro Leagues*, 304).

NOTES TO CHAPTER SEVEN

1. W. E. B. Du Bois, *The Souls of Black Folk* (1903), available online at http://www.bartleby.com/114/.
2. Sam Lacy, "Club Owners Turn Deaf Ear to AFRO Warning Their Players Might Be Signed," *Washington Afro-American*, 10 November 1945, 31.
3. See "The Courier Supports Organized Negro Baseball!" *Pittsburgh Courier*, 3 November 1945, 12.
4. "Martin Congratulates Rickey on Signing," *Pittsburgh Courier*, 3 November 1945, 12.
5. Born in Atlanta in 1889, Tom Wilson promoted sandlot teams before starting up the Nashville Standard Giants, later the Nashville Elite Giants of the Southern Negro League. The Giants played in Tom Wilson Park, which also served as home during spring training to the white Southern League Nashville Vols. He also owned concerns in real estate, farming, night clubs, and owned and operated the Paradise Ballroom, which he built on the site of Wilson Park.
6. Wendell Smith, "The Sports Beat," *Pittsburgh Courier*, 3 November 1945, 12.
7. Contents of the letter in James Overmyer, *Queen of the Negro Leagues: Effa Manley and the Newark Eagles* (Lanham, Md.: Scarecrow Trade, 2001), 223.
8. "Baseball Owners Protest Jackie Robinson Signing," *Washington Afro-American*, 17 November 1945, 30.
9. Wendell Smith, "The Sports Beat," *Pittsburgh Courier*, 1 December 1945, 12.
10. Frank A. Young, "Major League Points Way To Democracy," *Chicago Defender*, 27 October 1945, 1, 9; Frank A. Young, "Dixie Sports Scribes Differ On Robinson," *Chicago Defender*, 3 November 1945, 9.

11. "Dixie Sports Scribes Differ On Robinson," *Chicago Defender*, 3 November 1945, 9.
12. Donn Rogosin, "Black Baseball: The Life in the Negro Leagues," Ph.D. dissertation, University of Texas at Austin, 1981, 234. Baseball's reserve clause, which lasted in the major leagues until 1975, held that a player belonged to the team that held his contract.
13. "Meeting Winds Up With Same Officers, Same Old Problems," *Pittsburgh Courier*, 22 December 1945, 16.
14. Ibid.
15. In Brad Snyder, *Beyond the Shadow of the Senators* (New York: McGraw Hill, 2003), 253.
16. William Simons, "Jackie Robinson and the American Zeitgeist," in *Cooperstown Symposium on Baseball and American Culture 1997*, ed. Peter M. Rutkoff (Jefferson, N.C.: McFarland Press, 2000), 83.
17. Jerome Holtzman, audiotapes of interviews of Wendell Smith. For much more on Smith's and Rowe's roles with the Dodgers during Robinson's first spring training, see Chris Lamb, *Blackout, The Untold Story of Jackie Robinson's First Spring Training* (Lincoln: University of Nebraska Press, 2004).
18. Chris Lamb and Glen Bleske, "Democracy on the Field," *Journalism History* 24, no. 2 (1998): 54.
19. Wendell Smith, "The Sports Beat," *Pittsburgh Courier*, 17 November 1946, 10.
20. Ibid.
21. "Commissioner 'Happy' Chandler Tells Negro Baseball To 'Get Your House In Order,'" *Pittsburgh Courier*, 26 January 1946, 16.
22. Wendell Smith, "The Sports Beat," *Pittsburgh Courier*, 3 August 1946, 14; and Frank A. Young, "Robinson Not The First Negro Signed To Play in White Organized Baseball," *Chicago Defender*, 27 October 1945, 9.
23. "Commissioner 'Happy' Chandler Tells Negro Baseball to 'Get Your House In Order,'" *Pittsburgh Courier*, 26 January 1946, 16; and Wendell Smith, "The Sports Beat," *Pittsburgh Courier*, 26 January 1946, 16.
24. Wendell Smith, "The Sports Beat," *Pittsburgh Courier*, 16 February 1946, 12.
25. "The Sports Beat," *Pittsburgh Courier*, 14 June 1947, 15.
26. Wendell Smith, "The Sports Beat," *Pittsburgh Courier*, 3 August 1946, 14.
27. "NAL Head Refutes Chandler," *Pittsburgh Courier*, 2 February 1946, 12.
28. Sam Lacy, "Colored Baseball's Pussyfooting Seen Cause of Chandler's Arrogant Actions," *Washington Afro-American*, 26 January 1946, 27.
29. Wendell Smith, "The Sports Beat," *Pittsburgh Courier*, 4 January 1946, 12.
30. In Snyder, *Beyond the Shadow of the Senators*, 230.
31. Wendell Smith, "Secretary of NNL Scores Martin and Wilson for Laxity," *Pittsburgh Courier*, 5 January 1946, 12; Cum Posey, "The Sports Beat," *Pittsburgh Courier*, 2 February 1946, 12 (Posey was a guest columnist in Smith's place).

32. Ches Washington, "Hundreds View Remains of Famed Baseball Leader," *Pittsburgh Courier*, 6 April 1946, 17. Washington described Posey as "a brilliant athlete, a peerless magnate and an outstanding civic leader." It was in this obituary that Washington disclosed that Posey had been a stockholder of the Pittsburgh Courier Publishing Company.
33. "Smitty's Sports Spurts," *Pittsburgh Courier*, 9 September 1939, 17.
34. Ibid.
35. Ibid.
36. "Dustin' off the News," *Chicago Defender*, 4 March 1939, 1 and 2. Harper's column provides a nice, concise history of the segregation of professional baseball and of the growth of popularity among blacks in baseball subsequent to the Civil War. Lucius Clinton Harper joined the *Defender* in 1916 (Fay Young, "Fay Says," *Chicago Defender*, 30 January 1954, 17).
37. Harper, "Dustin' off the News," 4 March 1939, 1.
38. Jim Reisler, *Black Writers/Black Baseball: An Anthology of Articles from Black Sportswriters Who Covered the Negro Leagues* (Jefferson, N.C.: McFarland Press, 1994), 13.
39. Sam Lacy, *Washington Afro-American*, 12 August 1939, no page number available.
40. Phil Dixon and Patrick J. Hannigan, *The Negro Baseball Leagues, 1867–1955: A Photographic History* (Mattituck, N.Y.: Amereon House, 1992), 307.
41. Joe Bostic, *The People's Voice*, 11 July 1942, no page number available. "Scoreboard" was the name of Bostic's weekly column. Bostic was proved right. After Robinson took his skills to Brooklyn, most Negro league teams began losing money.
42. "Pop Anson's 60-Year Ban," *Pittsburgh Courier*, 6 June 1953, 15.
43. *I Never Had It Made*, (written with Alfred Duckett) (New York: G.P. Putnam's & Sons, 1972), 35. See also Jackie Robinson, "What's Wrong With Negro Baseball," *Ebony* 3, no. 8 (June 1948): 19–25, an article in which Robinson is condescending in his descriptions of life in the black leagues. This article was seen by black team owners as betrayal on the part of Robinson, and they let him know it. Most eloquent of these reactions was Effa Manley's article for *Our World* magazine, "Negro Baseball Isn't Dead" (v. 3, no. 8 [August 1948]: 26–29).
44. *Chicago Defender*, March–October 1945.
45. Fay Young, *Chicago Defender*, 17 August 1946, 1 and 9.
46. News of Black Tuesday and the stock market crash of 1929, for example, appeared nowhere in the *Chicago Defender* or *Pittsburgh Courier* in their issues during October and November of that year. Black stockholders, however few there were, had been ravaged by the Depression long before Black Tuesday.
47. Brian Carroll, "The Black Press and the Integration of Baseball: A content analysis of changes in coverage," *Cooperstown Symposium on Baseball and American Culture* (Jefferson, N.C.: McFarland Press, 2003), 216–231.

48. The unit of analysis was an entire issue of the newspaper, not merely its sports pages.
49. Carroll, "The Black Press and the Integration of Baseball."
50. Ibid.
51. Reisler, *Black Writers/Black Baseball*, 12.
52. Carroll, "The Black Press and the Integration of Baseball."
53. Ric Roberts, "Baseball Men Eye A. and T.," *Pittsburgh Courier*, 17 May 1947, 15; and Ric Roberts, "The Goose and Golden Egg," *Pittsburgh Courier*, 31 May 1947, 15. Like Campanella, pitcher Don Newcombe was signed by the Dodgers in 1946 and assigned to Nashua, New Hampshire, Brooklyn's Single A team.
54. Wendell Smith, "The Sports Beat," *Pittsburgh Courier*, 3 May 1947, 14.
55. Fay Young, "Through the Years," *Chicago Defender*, 8 May 1948, 11.
56. In Lanctot, *Negro League Baseball*, 362.
57. Quoted in Rob Ruck, Sandlot Seasons: Sport in Black Pittsburgh (Urbana, Ill.: University of Illinois Press, 1987), 23.
58. Wendell Smith, "The Sports Beat," *Pittsburgh Courier,* 11 May 1946, 12.
59. In Lanctot, 350.
60. Jack Saunders, "The Sports Broadcast," *Pittsburgh Courier*, 4 September 1948, 10.
61. Lacy became the first black writer member of the BWAA, in late 1948. The association accepted his argument that when combined, the multiple editions of the *Afro-American* newspapers yielded a frequency similar to the dailies. Even with BWAA membership, Lacy was barred from Cincinnati's Crosley Field, however.
62. William G. Nunn, *Pittsburgh Courier*, 27 April 1946, 1.
63. Wendell Smith, "The Sports Beat," *Pittsburgh Courier*, 7 June 1947, 12.
64. Rogosin, "Black Baseball: The Life in the Negro Leagues," 12.
65. Wendell Smith, "The Sports Beat," *Pittsburgh Courier*, 26 July 1947, 14.
66. Robert Peterson, *Only The Ball Was White* (New York: Oxford University Press), 197. Johnny Wright was signed by the Dodgers in 1946 and assigned to Montreal with Robinson, primarily to be Robinson's roommate because Robinson otherwise would have been Montreal's only black player.
67. B. B. Martin, a surgeon, was brother to NAL president and Chicago America Giants owner J. B. Martin and to W. S. Martin.
68. Donn Rogosin, *Invisible Men* (Kodansha: New York, 1995), 19.
69. Sam Maltin, "Royals Attract Million In 1946," *Pittsburgh Courier*, 24 August 1946, 14.
70. Wendell Smith, "The Sports Beat," *Pittsburgh Courier*, 21 December 1946, 12.
71. Ric Roberts, "The Game Goes On . . . ," *Negro Baseball Yearbook*, 1946, 5. Roberts was perhaps most consistently wrong in forecasting Negro league fortunes. In 1950, for example, he predicted that "colored baseball" would make a comeback and that black fans would realize that black big leaguers would "not be up there forever" ("Homestead Grays Still Example," *Pittsburgh Courier*, 22 July 1950, 34).

72. James Overmyer, *Queen of the Negro Leagues* (Lanham, Md.: Scarecrow Trade, 1993), 210.
73. The only two teams to make money in 1947: the Cleveland Buckeyes and the New York Cubans.
74. Jim Bankes, *The Pittsburgh Crawfords* (Jefferson, N.C.: McFarland Press, 2001), 126.
75. Dixon and Hannigan. *The Negro Baseball Leagues*, 297.
76. Wendell Smith, "The Sports Beat," *Pittsburgh Courier*, 14 June 1947, 14.
77. "Fay Says," *Chicago Defender*, 22 May 1948, 12.
78. Fay Young, *Chicago Defender*, 4 October 1947, 1 and 10.
79. "9,000 See Cleveland Beat Cubans, 10–7," *Pittsburgh Courier*, 27 September 1947, 15. Page fifteen was the paper's third and final sports page in the 27 September issue.
80. Neil Lanctot, Fair Dealing and Clean Playing: The Hilldale Club and the Development of Black Professional Baseball, 1910–1932. (Jefferson, N.C.: McFarland & Co., 1994), 191.
81. Frank Young, "Robinson Plays Flawless Ball With Brooklyn Dodgers Club," *Chicago Defender*, 19 April 1947, 1; Frank Young, "Fate of Jackie Robinson in Hands of Fans," *Chicago Defender*, 17 May 1947, 1; Frank Young, "Cleveland Seeks 2nd Negro Player," *Chicago Defender*, 5 July 1947, 1; "St. Louis Browns Sign 2 Negro Players," *Chicago Defender*, 12 July 1947, 1; Frank Young, "Big Leagues Scout 8 Negro Players," *Chicago Defender*, 2 August 1947, 1; and Frank Young, "Toughest Spot in Baseball History," *Chicago Defender*, 30 August 1947, 1.
82. For Jackie Robinson's first regular season game as a Dodger, on 15 April 1947 at Ebbets Field, more than 27,000 fans turned out and, according to historian Jim Bankes, more than half of them were black (*The Pittsburgh Crawfords*, 123). In 1959, more than twelve years after Robinson began playing for the Brooklyn Dodgers, the Boston Red Sox became the last team in big league baseball to suit up a black player. Elijah "Pumpsie" Green took the field in July 1959, but he was gone from professional baseball by season's end. See Robert Behn, "Branch Rickey as Public Manager: Fulfilling the Eight Responsibilities of Public Management," *Journal of Public Administration Research and Theory* 7, no. 1 (January 1997): 1–34. For much more on Elijah Green's odyssey and relatively short major league career, as well as on the context of racial relations in Boston at the time, see Howard Bryant's *Shut Out: A Story of Race and Baseball in Boston* (New York: Routledge, 2002).
83. In Jules Tygiel, *Extra Bases* (Lincoln, Neb.: Bison Books, 2002), 128.
84. Effa Manley and Leon Herbert Hardwick, *Negro Baseball . . . Before Integration* (Chicago: Adams Press, 1976), 94.
85. Tygiel, *Extra Bases*, 91.
86. Amiri Baraka, *The Autobiography of Leroi Jones* (Chicago: Lawrence Hill Books, 1997), 51. Robinson attended UCLA, not USC.
87. Ibid.
88. Richard Goldstein, "Barry Halper, 66; Once Owned Many Historic Baseball Items," *New York Times*, 20 December 2005, A27.

NOTES TO CHAPTER EIGHT

1. "Jackie Robinson and the American Mind: Journalistic Perceptions of the Reintegration of Baseball," *Journal of Sport History* 12, no. 1 (Spring 1985): 39.
2. A search in May 2006 on Amazon.com for "Jackie Robinson" turned up 224 book titles. A Google search on "Jackie Robinson," also in 2006, generated 3.1 million findings.
3. There are dozens of studies on the topic. Among the best are William Simons, "Jackie Robinson and the American Mind"; Pat Washburn, "New York Newspapers and Robinson's First Season," *Journalism Quarterly* 58, No. 4 (1981): 640–44; Bill Weaver, "The Black Press and the Assault on Professional Baseball's 'Color Line,' October 1945-April 1947," *Phylon* XL, No. 4 (1979): 303–17; and Chris Lamb and Glen Bleske, "Democracy on the Field," *Journalism History* 24, no. 2 (1998): 51–59.
4. For a comprehensive account of the court martial and the proceedings of the military tribunal that exonerated him, see Arnold Rampersad, *Jackie Robinson: A Biography* (New York: Alfred A. Knopf, 1997), 102–109. Despite a new Army policy forbidding segregation on its bases, in 1942 a military bus driver ordered Robinson to move to the back of the vehicle during transit between McCloskey Hospital in Temple, Texas, and Camp Hood about an hour away. Robinson refused. Upon arrival at Camp Hood, the driver summoned military police officers, who escorted Robinson to the base's commanding officer. Robinson was charged with two violations of Army regulations, leading to a four-hour trial. In *United States v. 2nd Lieutenant Jack R. Robinson*, he was found "not guilty of all specifications and charges" (Rampersad, 109).
5. See Simons, "Jackie Robinson and the American Zeitgeist," *The 15th Cooperstown Symposium on Baseball and American Culture (1990)*, Alvin Hall and Peter Rutkoff, eds. (Jefferson, N.C.: McFarland Press, 1997), 93. William G. Nunn, for example, wrote in a 19 April 1947 *Pittsburgh Courier* article, "Let's Take It In Stride," that Robinson was a UCLA graduate and a former Army lieutenant (18).
6. Chris Lamb, *Blackout, The Untold Story of Jackie Robinson's First Spring Training* (Omaha, Neb.: University of Nebraska Press, 2004), 88.
7. See Simons, "Jackie Robinson and the American Mind."
8. Wendell Smith, "The Sports Beat," *Pittsburgh Courier*, 1 March 1947, 16; and 8 March 1947, 16.
9. Wendell Smith, "Royals Pilot Praises 'Camp,'" *Pittsburgh Courier*, 8 March 1947, 16. Campanella advanced from Nashua to Montreal, Brooklyn's Triple A farm team, for the 1947 season.
10. Wendell Smith, "The Sports Beat," *Pittsburgh Courier*, 15 March 1947, 16; 22 March 1947, 16; and 29 March 1947, 14.
11. For an extensive account of the potential player rebellion, see Leo Durocher and Ed Linn, *Nice Guys Finish Last* (New York: Simon & Schuster, 1975), 203–206. When he learned of the players' plans, Durocher said he called a team meeting in the middle of the night and announced that any

player having difficulty with his decision could asked to be traded or could simply leave the team. "I don't care if the guy is yellow or black, or if he has stripes like a fuckin' zebra!" Durocher shouted to his team. "I'm the manager of this team, and I say he plays. What's more, I say he can make us all rich" (Rampersad, *Jackie Robinson*, 164). Only Bobby Bragan, a catcher from Alabama, asked to be traded by the team.

12. Wendell Smith, "Dodgers Have Drawn 95,000 Fans in Four Exhibition Contests," *Pittsburgh Courier*, 19 April 1947, 1.
13. Wendell Smith, "Jackie Helps Dodgers Near Record Gate," *Pittsburgh Courier*, 31 May 1947, 15. The headline: "Jackie Helps Dodgers Near Record Gate."
14. Wendell Smith, "Dodgers Have Drawn 95,000 Fans in Four Exhibition Contests," *Pittsburgh Courier*, 19 April 1947, 1. The newspaper's top-line banner headline read, "Robinson Packing 'Em In."
15. Wendell Smith, "Fans Swamp Jackie Public Affairs Out," *Pittsburgh Courier*, 26 April 1947, 1; Wendell Smith, "Jackie Bangs Out Homer, Double; Fields Flawlessly," *Pittsburgh Courier*, 26 April 1947, 15; "Rachel's Dad Didn't Approve of Jackie At First . . . But, now!," *Pittsburgh Courier*, 26 April 1947, 13; and Wendell Smith, "46,572 Pack Wrigley Field; Jackie Gets A Walk, But No Hit," *Pittsburgh Courier*, 24 May 1947, 15.
16. *Pittsburgh Courier*, 26 April 1947, 14.
17. Smith wrote with and for Robinson to produce *Jackie Robinson: Our Own Story* (New York: Greenberg Co., 1948).
18. Jackie Robinson, "Jackie Robinson Says," *Pittsburgh Courier*, 19 April 1947, 18.
19. Jackie Robinson, "Jackie Robinson Says," *Pittsburgh Courier*, 10 May 1947, 14.
20. Jackie Robinson, "Jackie Robinson Says," *Pittsburgh Courier*, 17 May 1947, 14.
21. In Rampersad, *Jackie Robinson, A Biography*, 172–3.
22. Jackie Robinson, "Jackie Robinson Says," *Pittsburgh Courier*, 17 May 1947, 14.
23. Jackie Robinson, "Jackie Robinson Says," *Pittsburgh Courier*, 24 May 1947, 14.
24. Jackie Robinson, "Jackie Robinson Says," *Pittsburgh Courier*, 31 May 1947, 15; Rampersad, *Jackie Robinson*, 174; and Wendell Smith, "Frick's Actions Avert Big Strike," *Pittsburgh Courier*, 17 May 1947, 4.
25. Jackie Robinson, "Jackie Robinson Says," *Pittsburgh Courier*, 17 May 1947, 14; 21 June 1947, 14; 28 June 1947, 14; 19 July 1947, 15; 23 August 1947, 24; and 20 September 1947, 14. In 1919, for example, Cobb was accused of kicking Ada Morris, a black chambermaid, down a flight of stairs in a Detroit hotel after she protested his use of racial slurs. While the incident was suppressed by the daily papers and the Tigers, black sportswriters such as Sol White denounced Cobb, noting that his name "should never pass the lips of colored baseball fans" (cited in the 10 May 1919 *Cleveland Advocate* and the 2 August 1924 *Pittsburgh Courier*, in an article by Rollo Wilson).

Notes to Chapter Eight

26. Wendell Smith, "The Sports Beat," *Pittsburgh Courier*, 12 July 1947, 1.
27. Wendell Smith, "Phillies Warned by Baseball Czar Over Robinson Incident," *Pittsburgh Courier*, 10 May 1947, 1; and Wendell Smith, "Frick's Actions Avert Big Strike," *Pittsburgh Courier*, 17 May 1947, 4.
28. Al Dunmore, "Cleveland Owner Kept His Word," *Pittsburgh Courier*, 12 July 1947, 14.
29. "Family Man," *Ebony* (September 1947): 15.
30. "Robinson's Plan For Day When They Have Own Home," *Ebony* (September 1947): 16.
31. "Through The Years," *Chicago Defender*, 12 July 1947, 9.
32. *Pittsburgh Courier*, 12 July 1947, 1 and 14.
33. *Pittsburgh Courier*, 6 September 1947, 14. See also 20 September 1947, 14, and 4 October 1947, 12.
34. Wendell Smith, "The Sports Beat," *Pittsburgh Courier*, 20 September 1947, 14.
35. W. Rollo Wilson, "Eastern Baseball at Nadir," *Pittsburgh Courier*, 4 October 1947, 14.
36. "Through The Years," *Chicago Defender*, 19 April 1947, 10.
37. "Fate of Jackie Robinson In Hands Of Fans," *Chicago Defender*, 17 May 1948, 1.
38. Fay Young, "Through The Years," *Chicago Defender*, 30 June 1945, 9; 7 July 1945, 9; 14 July 1945, 9; and 5 May 1946, 12.
39. Armistead Scott Pride and Clint C. Wilson, *A History of the Black Press* (Washington, D.C.: Howard University Press, 1997), 137.
40. In Rob Ruck, *Baseball in Pittsburgh* (Cleveland: Society for American Baseball Research, 1993), 23.
41. Fay Young, "Through the Years," *Chicago Defender*, 9 October 1948, 1 and 12.
42. Paul Debono, *Indianapolis ABCs: History of a Premier Team in the Negro Baseball Leagues* (Jefferson, N.C.: McFarland Press, 1997), 121.
43. "Sports Beat," *Pittsburgh Courier*, 4 September 1948, 17.
44. Lillian Scott, "Effa Manley 'Hotter Than Horse Radish,'" *Chicago Defender*, 18 September 1948, 12; and "Fay Says—Don't Blame Negro Press," *Chicago Defender*, 18 September 1948, 12. Ironically, Manley had proclaimed just a month before announcing plans to sell that, "Negro Baseball Isn't Dead," which was the title of her article for *Our World* magazine in August (v. 3, no. 8, 26–29). She was reacting to Robinson's criticisms of black baseball in *Ebony* in July.
45. *Cleveland Call and Post*, 8 July 1950, cited in Robert V. Leffler, Jr., "Boom and Bust: The Elite Giants and Black Baseball in Baltimore, 1936–1951," *Maryland Historical Magazine* 87, no. 2 (Summer 1992): 179.
46. Jesse Owens, "Jessie [sic] Owens Corner," *Chicago Defender*, 25 June 1949, 13.
47. Fay Young, "Through the Years," *Chicago Defender*, 8 May 1948, 11.
48. "The Sports Broadcast," *Pittsburgh Courier*, 4 September 1948, 10.
49. Leffler, "Boom and Bust," 180.
50. Wendell Smith, "Sports Beat," *Pittsburgh Courier*, 14 May 1948, 14.

51. Fay Young, "Fay Says," *Chicago Defender*, 18 September 1948, 12.
52. Wendell Smith, "Sports Beat," *Pittsburgh Courier*, 26 January 1946, 16.
53. Haskell Cole, "Cubans and Sepia Yanks On Way Out," *Pittsburgh Courier*, 18 September 1948, 10.
54. Peterson, *Only the Ball Was White*, 203.
55. "'To Uncover Baseball's 'Stars of Tomorrow,'" *Pittsburgh Courier*, 15 May 1948, 13.
56. "Baseball's Bigwigs Laud New Campaign," *Pittsburgh Courier*, 15 May 1948, 13.
57. "N.C. Coach Joins Big Talent Hunt," *Pittsburgh Courier*, 29 May 1948, 15. Turner played for the New York Royal Giants, Chicago American Giants, Hilldales, and Bacharachs of Atlantic City. When he agreed to scout, he was baseball coach at North Carolina State College in Durham, N.C., which later became North Carolina Central University.
58. The other issue dates in which lead stories invited readers to participate were 22 May (page 15), 29 May, (page 13), and 5 June (page 13).
59. Wendell Smith, "The Sports Beat," *Pittsburgh Courier*, 2 October 1948, 10.
60. "Defender School Will Train Boys For Baseball," *Chicago Defender*, 18 September 1948, 1.
61. Wendell Smith, "Signing of Shortstop Causes an Explosion," *Pittsburgh Courier*, 19 February 1949, 10; and "Blow by Blow Account of Bristling Verbal Battle Over Wilson," *Pittsburgh Courier*, 19 February 1949, 10.
62. Frank Young, "Is Negro Baseball Doomed?," *Chicago Defender*, 23 April 1949, 1.
63. See, as an example, Herman Hill, "Four Clubs Sign Young Negro Stars," *Pittsburgh Courier*, 5 March 1949, 11, on the integration of the Pacific Coast League. The PCL first integrated in 1948 when the San Diego Padres signed John Ritchey. Four more PCL clubs integrated in 1949. See also "Sepia Stars Play In Pensacola Game," *Pittsburgh Courier*, 9 April 1949, 23, for the integration of Pensacola in the Southeastern League.
64. See Chester L. Washington, "Veeck Is Optimistic Over Future Housing Outlook in Jim-Crow Texas Town," *Pittsburgh Courier*, 12 March 1949, 10; "'We'll Stay in Same Hotel,' Players Tell Doby, Paige," *Pittsburgh Courier*, 26 March 1949, 1; and Ches Washington, "Hotel Welcomes Tribe Stars, But They Stay Away," *Pittsburgh Courier*, 26 March 1949, 14, section 2.
65. See Brian Carroll, "Wendell Smith's Last Crusade: The Desegregation of Spring Training," in *The 14th Cooperstown Symposium on Baseball and American Culture*, ed. William Simons (Jefferson, N.C.: McFarland Press, 2002), 123–35. Bill Veeck led this fight to de-segregate spring training within major league baseball, first with the Indians and, in 1961, with the White Sox.
66. Wendell Smith, "The Sports Beat," *Pittsburgh Courier*, 12 February 1949, 10.
67. "Sports Editorial: Negro Colleges Must Develop The Big Leagues Stars of Tomorrow," *Pittsburgh Courier*, 12 February 1949, 11.
68. Wendell Smith, "The Sports Beat," *Pittsburgh Courier*, 26 March 1949, 12, section 2.
69. Wendell Smith, "Sports Beat," *Pittsburgh Courier*, 14 May 1949, 22.

70. "Take 'Em Out to the Baseball Game . . . But . . . !," *Pittsburgh Courier*, 5 June 1949, 1.
71. Wendell Smith, "Baseball Czar Will Throw First Ball," *Pittsburgh Courier*, 13 August 1949, 22.
72. R. S. Simmons, "Baltimore Wins 'Series,'" *Pittsburgh Courier*, 1 October 1949, 22.
73. James Edmund Boyack, "Baseball Moguls Eye Tan Stars at Annual Meeting," *Pittsburgh Courier*, 17 December 1949, 23; Wendell Smith, "The Sports Beat," *Pittsburgh Courier*, 24 December 1949, 22; and Wendell Smith, "The Sports Beat," *Pittsburgh Courier*, 16 December 1950, 24. According to Smith, "practically every team" in the Negro American lost money in 1949.

NOTES TO CHAPTER NINE

1. *Bingo Long Traveling All-Stars & Motor Kings*, videocassette, directed by John Badham (Hollywood, Calif.: Universal Pictures, 1976).
2. The origins of the game of baseball are mysterious and contested, as well, and have been for more than a century. For a recent and reasoned attempt at determining when and where baseball emerged and how it evolved, see David Block's *Baseball Before We Knew It: A Search for the Roots of the Game* (Lincoln, Neb.: Bison Books, 2006).
3. Wendell Smith, "The Sports Beat," *Pittsburgh Courier*, 16 December 1950, 24.
4. Wendell Smith, "Sports Beat," *Pittsburgh Courier*, 18 February 1950, 22.
5. Larry Lester, Black Baseball's National Showcase: The East-West All-Star Game, 1933–1953 (Lincoln: University of Nebraska Press, 2001).
6. Wendell Smith, "All-Star Tilt Fails To Impress Scouts From Big Leagues," *Pittsburgh Courier*, 22 August 1953, 14.
7. William G. Nunn, "East-West Game Needs an Overhauling," *Pittsburgh Courier*, 29 August 1953, 14.
8. See, for example, "Fay Says," *Chicago Defender*, 24 July 1954, 16, on how the East-West Game "became a part of Negro life in Chicago"; and "Fay Says," *Chicago Defender*, 7 August 1954, 16, on the "real league" of 1920.
9. Fay Young, "Rube Foster—A Name That All Baseball Fans Revere," *Chicago Defender*, 7 August 1948, 11; "Foster Presiding Elder's Son, Was Country's Greatest Pitcher," *Chicago Defender*, 14 August 1948, 13; "Chicago Cubs Rally To Tie Score Then Umpire's Decision Helps Beat Foster And Leland Giants," *Chicago Defender*, 28 August 1948, 11; and "Foxy Rube Foster's Order To Dave Malarcher Broke Up 20-Inning Game 26 Years Ago, 1–0," *Chicago Defender*, 4 September 1948, 10. There was no installment in the 21 August issue.
10. "Fay Says," *Chicago Defender*, 5 January 1952, 13.
11. Ibid. Not coincidentally, after losing Mays the Black Barons' owner announced he was putting the team up for sale, saying he had lost money and could not continue to operate the club ("NAL Cuts Back To Six Clubs," *Chicago Defender*, 1 January 1952, 13).

12. Gus Greenlee was "one in a million," a man who "took the big gamble," Smith wrote ("Sports Beat," *Pittsburgh Courier*, 19 July 1951, 14).
13. Wendell Smith, "Sports Beat," *Pittsburgh Courier*, 1 June 1951, 12.
14. Wendell Smith, "Sports Beat," *Pittsburgh Courier*, 17 June 1950, 14; 26 August 1950, 14; 1 June 1951, 12; and (quote) 15 August 1953, 14.
15. Geoffrey C. Ward and Ken Burns, *Baseball: An Illustrated History* (New York: Alfred A. Knopf, 1994), 412–417, quote from 413.
16. "Cavaretta [sic] Job Not Easy One, Russ Reports," *Chicago Defender*, 12 March 1952, 12. A story on the Sox 1952 season, for example, listed all of the double-headers scheduled in Comiskey Park and all of the scheduled Sunday games. A display ad appeared several times in the *Defender* in 1954, for example, listing upcoming Sox games and ticket prices (sixty cents, $1.25, $1.75 and $2.50, including tax). No such publicity for the Cubs appeared in the *Defender* during the early 1950s.
17. "Those Sizzling Sox," *Chicago Defender*, 9 June 1951, 6. The letter was submitted by David Lloyd Crowder of Chicago.
18. "Russ' Corner," *Chicago Defender*, 21 April 1951, 16. Cowans spent six days with the Sox during Spring Training, interviewing Lane, Richards, and the two prospects, Bob Boyd and Sam Hairston. Boyd was promoted in 1953.
19. "The Fabulous White Sox," *Chicago Defender*, 16 June 1951, 6.
20. Ibid. The writer described blacks and whites commingling at Comiskey as "the greatest lesson in interracial cooperation that the city has ever seen. . . . We take delight in saluting the fabulous White Sox."
21. That Minoso is Cuban points to the reality that race in fact was not the issue for major league baseball and, by extension, American society. It was skin color. Light-skinned Cubans had played in the major leagues at least as far back as 1911 (Armando Masans, who played for the Cincinnati Reds). At least some in the Sox organization wanted to integrate as early as 1942. The *Daily Worker* quoted Sox manager Jimmy Dykes in 1942 as saying to Jackie Robinson, "I'd love to have you on my team and so would all the other big league managers. But it's not up to us. Get after Landis" (26 May 1942, 8), quoted in Ronald A. Smith, "The Paul Robeson—Jackie Robinson Saga and a Political Collision," *Journal of Sport History* 6, no. 2 (Summer, 1979).
22. "NAL Cuts Back To Six Clubs," *Chicago Defender*, 1 January 1952, 13. After losing Monte Irvin to the Giants, Effa and Abe Manley sold the Newark Eagles, which were moved to Houston, then to New Orleans—three cities in five seasons.
23. "Six New Stars To Shine In Majors," *Chicago Defender*, 19 April 1952, 1.
24. Russ Cowans, "Russ' Corner," *Chicago Defender*, 19 April 1952, 12. Cowans put attendance of the exhibition at 9,052, a number that included "thousands of Negroes." Lane also was credited for hiring another progressive, Paul Richards, to manage the Sox. When asked in 1953 by a group in Alabama calling itself the Preserve Segregation Committee to help it "preserve our segregation traditions and customs in the South," Richards wired back, "I am very sorry, but that question of racial segregation was settled more than 2,000 years ago on Mount Calvary. . . . Christ Jesus

Notes to Chapter Nine

died for us all" (Bruce Adelson, *Brushing Back Jim Crow* [Charlottesville: University of Virginia Press, 1999], 125). The Committee was trying to prevent the Sox and Cardinals—more specifically the teams' black players—from playing in Birmingham in April 1954.

25. Russ J. Cowans, "Minoso, Roddy Set to 'Go,'" *Chicago Defender*, 12 April 1952, 2.
26. "Pirates Farm Negro to Kitty," *Chicago Defender*, 5 July 1952, 12. The Kitty league covered Kentucky, Illinois, and Tennessee.
27. The Columbus (Ohio) Red Birds removed its color barrier for the 1954 season with the additions of Bill Greason and Brooks Lawrence, pitchers.
28. "Four Florida Teams Playing Negro Players," *Chicago Defender*, 31 May 1952, 12. *The Sporting News* was not known for its coverage of professional baseball's racism.
29. Adelson, *Brushing Back Jim Crow*, 47.
30. Yankee manager Casey Stengel's response to Robinson, after Robinson had been struck out by Yankee hurler Allie Reynolds: "Before that black son of a bitch accuses us of being prejudiced, he should learn how to hit an Indian" (in Peter Golenbock, *Dynasty: The New York Yankees* [Englewood Cliffs, N.J.: Prentice-Hall, 1975], 104).
31. "Yankees Race To Ink Negro," *Chicago Defender*, 6 December 1952, 1.
32. By the time the Red Sox integrated, the Dodgers were in Los Angeles and Robinson was as an executive with the Chock Full O' Nuts coffee company.
33. John P. Rossi, *A Whole New Game: Off the Field Changes in Baseball, 1946–1960* (Jefferson, N.C.: McFarland & Company, 1999), 32.
34. Bill Nunn, Jr., "Busch Says Policies of Cardinals Will Change," *Pittsburgh Courier*, 4 April 1953, 15.
35. A.D. Gaither, "'Reds Have Negro Players on Way Up,'—Paul," *Pittsburgh Courier*, 28 February 1953, 14.
36. Wendell Smith, "Sports Beat," *Pittsburgh Courier*, 4 July 1953, 14; and 21 August 1954, 12. In addition to integrating the Cubs along with Banks, Baker became the first black manager of a minor league team when he was named skipper of Batavia in the NY-Penn League by the Pittsburgh Pirates in 1963.
37. The Rookie of the Year Award winners were Robinson, Don Newcombe, Joe Black, and Junior Gilliam, and these four were the only Brooklyn Dodgers to ever win the award.
38. Coincidentally, Robinson and Cavarretta both had good seasons in 1947. Robinson, of course, hit nearly .300 (.297) and was named Rookie of the Year. A Chicago native, Cavarretta hit .314 as the Cubs' left fielder. He played twenty-two seasons, twenty-one of them for the Cubs, including three as a player-manager (1951–1953), and one for the Sox (1954).
39. Brooklyn finished way out front with 105 wins. Milwaukee was a distant second with ninety-two victories, while the Cubs managed only sixty-five wins under Cavarretta to place second to last. Rickey's press release, distributed on 10 April 1947 said only that the Dodgers had "purchased the contract of Jack Roosevelt Robinson from Montreal" (Dave Anderson, "The Days That Brought the Barrier Down," *New York Times* (30 March 1997).

40. For Rickey black America presented an untapped market. A 14 July 1948 exhibition game between Robinson's Dodgers and Doby's Indians drew 64,877, a figure that included an estimated 26,000 blacks, which means that roughly one of every six blacks in Cleveland attended that game (Larry Moffi and Jonathan Kronstadt, *Crossing the Line: Black Major Leaguers, 1947–1959* [Jefferson, N.C.: McFarland & Company, 1994], 8).
41. League attendance overall dipped to postwar low of 14.4 million, off 6.6 million from 1948's high water mark (John P. Rossi, *A Whole New Game: Off the Field Changes in Baseball, 1946–1960* [Jefferson, N.C.: McFarland & Company, 1999]: 105).
42. Baker was signed by the Cubs in 1950, putting him in the Cubs organization long before Ernie Banks. In subsequent seasons, Baker played for Des Moines of the Western League and Los Angeles of the Pacific Coast League.
43. "Baker Returned to Los Angles," *Chicago Defender*, 28 March 1953, 25. Baker's patience is remarkable. On 4 August 1952, he set a team record with Los Angeles for most consecutive games (394), which underlines how long he had to toil in the minor leagues before being given the chance at the highest level (Burt F. Newton, "Angel Record Set By Baker For Durability," *Chicago Defender*, 30 August 1952, 16).
44. "Fay Says," *Chicago Defender*, 2 July 1953, 28.
45. "Russ' Corner," *Chicago Defender*, 6 August 1953, 38.
46. "Cubs To Bring Gene Baker Up," *Chicago Defender*, 3 September 1954, 16. Baker began the year with the Cubs in spring training in Mesa, Ariz., but was sent down to Los Angeles because "at that time it was stated he needed more experience." The Tigers integrated by signing Claude Agee. Dickey, a pitcher, was assigned by the Cubs to their Cedar Rapids, Iowa, farm team. He was not promoted to the major league club. When Baker and Banks took the field in mid-September for the Cubs, they became the first black "keystone combination" (shortstop-and-second baseman) in major league history.
47. "Old Men On Dodgers Win Praise," *Chicago Defender*, 27 August 1953, 19.
48. "Fay Says," *Chicago Defender*, 8 October 1953, 33. The NAACP also sided with Veeck, citing Baltimore's "rigid pattern of segregation," but to no avail ("Baltimore Blasted By The NAACP," *Chicago Defender*, 1 October 1953, 32).
49. "Rodriguez Loses Third Base Post," *Chicago Defender*, 17 January 1953, 12.
50. "Racial Bias Bars Minny and Others," *Chicago Defender*, 11 April 1953, 1. The next day the Sox, with Minoso on the field, played in Nashville. Minoso's homer beat the all-white Philadelphia Athletics, 4–3.
51. "Sox Rookies," *Chicago Defender*, 3 September 1953, 16.
52. A Monarchs-Clowns game in Detroit in June drew more than 21,000, the third-largest crowd to see a baseball game in Detroit ("21,399 See Kaycees Win Twin Bill," *Chicago Defender*, 2 July 1953, 27).
53. In Kansas City that Sunday in mid-May, Stone, who had been signed for $12,000, struck out and grounded out in three innings of play (Russ Cowans, "Richardson Gives 8 Hits To Loses [sic]," *Chicago Defender*, 28 May

1953, 30). For the season, Stone hit .243 in 74 at-bats and 50 games. Seventeen of her eighteen hits were singles, she knocked in only three runs, and she stole one base ("Monarchs Win Crown In NAL," *Chicago Defender*, 24 September 1953, 28). Monarch manager Buck O'Neil wrote in his autobiography that Kansas City's signing of Stone for the 1954 season was "not because she was the best second baseman around but because she could give us a boost at the gate" (*I Was Right On Time*, 194). Stone was in 1954 the highest-paid Monarch.

54. "Clowns Blazing in Second Half," *Chicago Defender*, 23 July 1953, 26.
55. Aaron and four black teammates in Florida integrated the South Atlantic "Sally" League, a fifty-year-old aggregation of mostly Old South cities. He helped Jacksonville win the pennant and double its home attendance. His .362 average led the league. Aaron also scored 150 runs, knocked in 125, and totaled 206 hits—a monster year (Adelson, *Brushing Back Jim Crow*, 87).
56. Clowns Using Giant, Comic To Win Fans," *Chicago Defender*, 13 December 1952, 13; "Clowns Blazing in Second Half," *Chicago Defender*, 23 July 1953, 26. Hamman was heralded for his "hilarious diamond entertainment," which included "in-throws, pepperball shennanigans [sic] and feats of new magic," feats "guaranteed to make even the most case-hardened fan roar with glee" ("Clowns Blazing in Second Half").
57. For more on the history of the Clowns, see Bill Heward (with Dimitri V. Gat), *Some Are Called Clowns: A Season with the Last of the Great Barnstorming Baseball Teams* (New York: Crowell, 1974). The book is a memoir, however, and not a documented history of the Indianapolis Clowns. The Clowns integrated in reverse in 1968, the first year the team signed a handful of white players, which it would do annually after 1968.
58. "Clowns To Bring Lot Of Comedy," *Chicago Defender*, 26 June 1954, 12.
59. "Smitty's Sports Spurts," *Pittsburgh Courier*, 23 January 1943, 16. In yet another irony, Clowns owner Syd Pollock accused Smith of racism in supporting the Cleveland Buckeyes but criticizing his Clowns.
60. "Bar League Ball Clubs From Playing Clowns," *Chicago Defender*, 3 January 1942, 20.
61. "Smitty's Sports Spurts," *Pittsburgh Courier*, 23 January 1943, 16.
62. Front office and manager jobs for blacks, also, would prove scarce for decades. The Cubs did not hire their first black manager until 1999 (Don Baylor), for the club's 124th season.
63. Donn Rogosin, *Invisible Men: Life in Baseball's Negro Leagues* (Kodansha: New York, 1995), 137. House of David players were in many if not most cases not Jewish. Begun as an amusement for a Midwestern religious cult, the team became a profitable traveling attraction by the mid-1930s.
64. "Posey's Points," *Pittsburgh Courier*, 4 April 1942, 16. Posey called the leagues' vote to allow the Clowns as members "one of the biggest mistakes ever made by a baseball organization" ("Posey Points," *Pittsburgh Courier*, 5 July 1941, 16). Italy attacked Ethiopia in 1935, beginning a six-year war the black press closely followed. The black newspapers expressed great sympathy for Ethiopia, which was one of the few countries in the world at the time with a black leader.

65. "July 27 Set As Date Of East-West Game," *Pittsburgh Courier*, 28 June 1941, 16.
66. "Bar League Ball Clubs From Playing Clowns," *Chicago Defender*, 3 January 1942, 20.
67. "Smitty's Sports-Spurts," *Pittsburgh Courier*, 16 May 1942, 17.
68. The Hippopotamus Clowns wore grass skirts and featured pitcher Bolo Power ("Zulos Play Houston Twin Bill June 25," *Pittsburgh Courier*, 24 June 1944, 12).
69. "Minos [sic] And Boyd Play In Games," *Chicago Defender*, 10 April 1954, 18.
70. Lui Virgil Overbea, "Large Crop of Negroes in Majors," *Chicago Defender*, 16 January 1954, 13.
71. The other minor leagues desegregating in 1954 were the Tri-State League (Tennessee, South Carolina, and North Carolina), Evangeline League (Texas and Louisiana), and Cotton States League, the last of which was in 1952–53 the subject of a series of court cases and public referenda on laws and ordinances enforcing racial segregation. The Birmingham City Council, for example, passed in September 1950 an ordinance that made it "unlawful for a negro and a white person to play together or in company with each other in any games," including baseball (Birmingham Segregation Laws, Section 597). The Southern Association integrated when the Atlanta Crackers played Nat Peeples, who had played for both the Monarchs and Clowns.
72. Russ J. Cowans, *Chicago Defender*, 10 April 1954. Flush from their three consecutive successful seasons, the Sox renovated Comiskey Park for the 1954 season at a cost of a quarter-million dollars.
73. At least a partial explanation for the absence of Wrigley as a subject or source in the *Defender* was Wrigley's low opinion of newspapermen in general (see Paul M. Angle, "Mr. Wrigley's Cubs," *Chicago History* 5, no. 2 [1975]: 105–115).
74. Russ J. Cowans, "Busch Fulfills Promise," *Chicago Defender*, 6 February 1954, 29. The Padres in 1954 were a minor league team in the Pacific Coast League. The glow in coverage of the Cardinals also could be partially explained by Busch's rescue of the team a year prior. The team was almost sold and moved to either Milwaukee or Houston before Busch acquired it and kept it in St. Louis.
75. "Tom Impresses Manager Stanky," *Chicago Defender*, 20 March 1954, 19.
76. Fay Young, "Fay Says," *Chicago Defender*, 17 July 1954, 17.
77. "League Head Sees A Good '54 Season," *Chicago Defender*, 15 May 1954, 28.
78. "Clowns To Bring Lot Of Comedy," *Chicago Defender*, 26 June 1954, 12.
79. Fay Young, "Fay Says," *Chicago Defender*, 7 August 1954, 16.
80. *Pittsburgh Courier*, 4 May 1957. The supplement included advertising by major league teams and by major advertisers, like Seagram, using the *Courier* to reach the black middle class.
81. *Pittsburgh Courier*, 13 February 1954, 14.

82. "Sports Beat," *Pittsburgh Courier*, 5 February 1955, 12. J. B. Martin, for example, was a pharmacist and his brother, B. B. Martin, owner of the Memphis Red Sox, was a surgeon. Few numbers runners remained in baseball.
83. John L. Johnson, "Sport Light," Kansas City *Call*, 23 September 1955, 10. Because of silence on the part of owners, the *Call* could not be sure of even when the last game of the season had been played, or where. The final team standings had not been released by the owners or by the league president, J. B. Martin.

NOTES TO THE EPILOGUE

1. C. Vann Woodward, *The Strange Career of Jim Crow* (New York: Oxford University Press, 1989), viii.
2. Quote from Kelly Rusinack and Chris Lamb, "'A Sickening Red Tinge:' The Daily Worker's Fight Against White Baseball," *Cultural Logic* 3, no. 1 (2001): 3.
3. Buck O'Neil, *I Was Right On Time* (New York: Simon & Schuster, 1996), 196.
4. See, for one example, Wendell Smith, "Sports Beat," *Pittsburgh Courier,* 26 January 1946, 16.
5. In 2003, major league baseball approved its first minority controlling owner, Arturo Moreno. Or did it? Moreno, a Phoenix, Arizona, businessman, told the *New York Times* that he did not consider himself a minority, a Mexican-American. He said, "I think we're all Americans; most of us are immigrants from someplace" (Richard Sandomir, "Disney Cuts Losses in Sale Of Angels to Businessman," 17 April 2003, C15). In 2002, major league baseball hired its first African American club president, Ulice Payne, an attorney tapped by the Milwaukee Brewers.
6. Amiri Baraka, *The Autobiography of Leroi Jones* (Chicago: Lawrence Hill Books, 1997), 46, 48. Emphasis on *music* in original.
7. In Geoffrey C. Ward and Ken Burns, *Baseball: An Illustrated History* (New York: Alfred A. Knopf, 1994), 413.
8. O'Neil, *I Was Right On Time*, 196.
9. Eddie Gant, "I Cover The Eastern Front," *Chicago Defender*, 13 January 1940, 20.
10. P. L. Prattis, "Racial Segregation and Negro Journalism," *Phylon* 8, no. 4 (Winter 1947), 308.
11. "Negro Press Here to Stay," *Pittsburgh Courier*, 25 June 1949, 1. The four teams were the Dodgers, Giants, Indians, and St. Louis Browns.
12. Armistead S. Pride, "Negro Newspapers Will Not Die Soon!" *Pittsburgh Courier,* 23 March 1957, 1.
13. Donald McRae, "A Special Bond Between Champions," *New York Times*, 25 May 2003, A31. McRae's book is *Heroes Without A Country: America's Betrayal Of Joe Louis & Jesse Owens* (New York: Ecco, 2003).
14. Jules Tygiel, *Extra Bases: Reflections on Jackie Robinson, Race, and Baseball History* (Lincoln, Neb.: University of Nebraska Press, 2002), 39.

15. See Brian Carroll, "Wendell Smith's Last Crusade: The Desegregation of Spring Training," *The 14th Cooperstown Symposium on Baseball and American Culture*, William Simons (ed.) (Jefferson, N.C.: McFarland Press, 2002), 123–135.
16. Ron Fimrite, "Sam Lacy: Black Crusader," *Sports Illustrated*, 29 October 1994, 91.
17. Ibid., 94.
18. Greg Winter, "Schools Resegregate, Study Finds," *New York Times*, 21 January 2003, A14.
19. "White Students Outnumber Blacks At Some Of Nation's Historically Black Colleges," *Jet* 97, no. 12 (28 February 2000): 31. In 2000, blacks represented only 12 percent of the student body at West Virginia State College, for example, Wendell Smith's alma mater.

Bibliography

MANUSCRIPT COLLECTIONS

Eleanor Roosevelt Papers. Hyde Park, New York: Eleanor Roosevelt National Historic Site, 2003. Available: http://www.nps.gov/elro/glossary/fepc.htm.
Wendell Smith papers, National Baseball Hall of Fame, Cooperstown, New York.

ORAL HISTORIES

Holtzman, Jerome, audiotapes of interviews with Wendell Smith in Chicago in February 1971 (provided by Smith's wife, Wyonella Smith, in October 2001).
Rust, Art, Jr. *Get That Nigger Off the Field: An Oral History of Black Ballplayers from the Negro Leagues to the Present.* New York: Brooklyn Book Mail Services, 1992.

NEWSPAPERS AND MAGAZINES

Abbott's Monthly
Chicago Broad Ax
Chicago Defender
Cleveland Gazette
Colored Baseball and Sports Monthly
The Competitor
Daily Worker
Ebony
Indianapolis Freeman
Indianapolis Ledger
Jet
Kansas City Call
Life
New York Age
New York Amsterdam News

New York Times
The People's Voice
Philadelphia Tribune
Pittsburgh Courier
Saturday Evening Post
The Sporting Life
The Sporting News
Washington Afro-American/Baltimore Afro-American

OTHER

Washington, Booker T. "Atlanta Compromise Speech." Cotton States and International Exposition in Atlanta. Georgia, 18 September 1895. *The American Social History Project / Center for Media and Learning (Graduate Center, CUNY) and the Center for History and New Media (George Mason University)*. Available: http://historymatters.gmu.edu/.

GOVERNMENT DOCUMENTS

Organized Baseball, Report of the Subcommittee on Study of Monopoly Power of the Committee on the Judiciary, United States House, 82d Congr., 2d Session, Report No. 632 (Washington: Government Printing Office, 1952).

U.S. Census of Population and Housing, 1910. Washington: Government Printing Office. Available: http://www.census.gov/prod/www/abs/decennial/1910.htm.

U.S. Census of Population and Housing, 1920. Washington: Government Printing Office. Available: http://www.census.gov/prod/www/abs/decennial/1920.htm.

BOOKS

Allen, Frederick Lewis. *Only Yesterday: An Informal History of the 1920s.* New York: John Wiley & Sons, 1997.

Ashe, Arthur. *A Hard Road to Glory.* New York: Warner Books, 1988.

Asinof, Eliot. *Eight Men Out.* New York: Holt, Rinehart & Winston, 1963.

Bak, Richard. *Turkey Stearnes and the Detroit Stars: The Negro Leagues in Detroit, 1919–1933.* Great Lakes Books. Detroit, Michigan: Wayne State University Press, 1994.

Banker, Stephen. *Black Diamonds.* Westport, Connecticut: Meckler, 1989.

Bankes, Jim. *The Pittsburgh Crawfords.* Jefferson, North Carolina: McFarland Press, 2001.

Baraka, Amiri. *The Autobiography of Leroi Jones.* Chicago: Lawrence Hill Books, 1997.

Barber, Red. *1947: When All Hell Broke Loose in Baseball.* Garden City, New York: Doubleday & Co., 1982.

Betts, John. *America's Sporting Heritage: 1850–1950.* Reading, Massachusetts: Addison-Wesley, 1974.

Brashler, William. *The Story of Negro League Baseball*. New York: Ticknor & Fields, 1994.
——. *Josh Gibson: A Life in the Negro Leagues*. Chicago, Illinois: Ivan R. Dee, 2000.
Brimmer, Andrew F. "The Negro in the National Economy," in John Davis, ed., *The American Negro Reference Book*. Yonkers, New York: Educational Heritage, 1966.
Brown, Warren Henry. *Social Impact of the Black Press*. New York: Carlton Press, 1994.
Bruce, Janet. *The Kansas City Monarchs: Champions of Black Baseball*. Lawrence, Kansas: University Press of Kansas, 1985.
Bryant, Howard. *Shut Out: A Story of Race and Baseball in Boston*. New York: Routledge, 2002.
Buni, Andrew. *Robert L. Vann of the Pittsburgh Courier*. London: University of Pittsburgh Press, 1974.
Bussel, Alan. "Evolution and Revolution: The Search for New Forms." In *Perspectives of the Black Press: 1974*, edited by Henry G. La Brie III, 141–50. Kennebunkport, Maine.: Mercer House Press, 1974.
Campbell, Georgetta Merritt. *Extant Collections of Early Black Newspapers: A Research Guide to the Black Press, 1880–1915*. Troy, New York: Whitston Publishing Co., 1981.
Chadwick, Bruce. When the Game Was Black and White: The Illustrated History of the Negro Leagues. New York: Abbeville Press, 1992.
Clark, Dick, Larry Lester, and Society for American Baseball Research. Negro Leagues Committee. *The Negro Leagues Book*. Cleveland, Ohio: Society for American Baseball Research, 1994.
Cooper, Michael L. *Playing America's Game: The Story of Negro League Baseball*. New York: Lodestar Books, 1993.
Cottrell, Robert. *The Best Pitcher in Baseball: The Life of Rube Foster, Negro League Giant*. New York: New York University Press, 2001.
——. *Blackball, the Black Sox, and the Babe: Baseball's Crucial 1920 Season*. Jefferson, North Carolina: McFarland Press, 2001.
Craft, David. *The Negro Leagues: 40 Years of Black Professional Baseball in Words and Pictures*. New York: Crescent Books, 1993.
Creamer, Richard. *Babe, The Legend Comes To Life*. New York: Simon & Schuster, 1992.
Creamer, Robert and Ralph Houk. *Season of Glory*. New York: G.P. Putnam's Sons, 1988.
Dann, Martin E. *The Black Press, 1827–1890: The Quest for National Identity*. New York: Putnam, 1971.
Debono, Paul. *The Indianapolis ABCs: History of a Premier Team in the Negro Leagues*. Jefferson, North Carolina: McFarland & Co., 1997.
Detweiler, Frederick G. *The Negro Press in the United States*. Chicago: University of Chicago Press, 1921
Dickson, Paul. *The Dickson Baseball Dictionary*. New York: Avon Books, 1989.
Dixon, Phil, and Patrick J. Hannigan. *The Negro Baseball Leagues, 1867–1955: A Photographic History*. Mattituck, New York: Amereon House, 1992.

Drake, St. Clair and Horace Clayton. *Black Metropolis*. New York: Harcourt, Brace & Co., 1945.
Drucker, Susan J. and Robert S. Cathcart (eds.), *American Heroes in a Media Age*. Cresskill, New Jersey: Hampton Press, 1994.
Du Bois, W. E. B. *The Souls of Black Folk* (1903). Available online at http://www.bartleby.com/114/.
Durocher, Leo and Ed Linn. *Nice Guys Finish Last*. New York: Simon & Schuster, 1975.
Entine, Jon. *Taboo: Why Black Athletes Dominate Sports and Why We Are Afraid to Talk About It*. New York: Public Affairs, 2000.
Fields, Wilmer. *My Life in the Negro Leagues: An Autobiography*. Westport, Connecticut: Meckler, 1992.
Finkle, Lee. *Forum for Protest: The Black Press During World War II*. Rutherford, N.J.: Fairleigh Dickinson University Press, 1975.
Foner, Philip and Ronald Lewis. *The Black Worker: A Documentary History from Colonial Times to the Present*, Vol.6. Philadelphia: Temple University Press, 1979.
Fountain, Charles. *Sportswriter: The Life and Times of Grantland Rice*. New York: Oxford University Press, 1993.
Franklin, John Hope. "The Negro since Freedom," in C. Vann Woodward, ed., *Comparative Approach to American History*. New York: Basic Books, 1968.
Frazier, E. Franklin. *The Negro Family in the United States*. New York: Dryden Press, 1939.
Frommer, Harvey. *Rickey and Robinson: The Men Who Broke Baseball's Color Barrier*. New York: Macmillan, 1982.
Gallico, Paul. *Farewell to Sport*. New York: Alfred A. Knopf, 1938.
———. *The Golden People*. New York: Doubleday & Company, 1964.
Gardner, Robert and Dennis Shortelle. *The Forgotten Players: The Story of Black Baseball in America*. New York: Walker and Co., 1993.
Garland, Phyl. "Staying with the Black Press: Problems and Rewards." In *Perspectives of the Black Press: 1974*, edited by Henry G. La Brie III, 171–80. Kennebunkport, Maine.: Mercer House Press, 1974.
Giamatti, Bartlett. *Take Time for Paradise*. New York: Summit Books, 1989.
Gilbert, Tom. *Baseball and the Color Line (the African-American Experience)*. New York: Franklin Watts, 1995.
Graham, Thelma Thurston. "The Black Press and Pressure Groups." In *Perspectives of the Black Press: 1974*, edited by Henry G. La Brie III, 103–09. Kennebunkport, Maine.: Mercer House Press, 1974.
Harper, William. *How You Played the Game, The Life of Grantland Rice*. Columbia, Missouri: University of Missouri Press, 1999.
Henderson, Alexa Benson, and Janice Sumler-Edmond. *Freedom's Odyssey: African American History Essays from* Phylon. Atlanta, Georgia: Clark Atlanta University Press, 1999.
Heward, Bill and Dimitri Gat. *Some Are Called Clowns: A Season with the Last Great Barnstorming Teams*. New York: Thomas Crowell, 1974.
Hirsch, Arnold R. *Making the second ghetto: Race and housing in Chicago, 1940–1960*. Cambridge, England: Cambridge University Press, 1983.

Hogan, Lawrence D. *A Black National News Service: The Associated Negro Press and Claude Barnett, 1919–1945.* Rutherford, New Jersey: Fairleigh Dickinson Press, 1984.

Holway, John. *Voices from the Great Black Baseball Leagues.* New York: Dodd Mead, 1975.

———. *Rube Foster: The Father of Black Baseball.* Washington, D.C.: Pretty Pages, 1982.

———. *Josh and Satch: The Life and Times of Josh Gibson and Satchel Paige.* New York: Carroll & Graf Publishers, 1991.

———. *Blackball Stars: Negro League Pioneers.* New York: Carroll & Graf Publishers, 1992.

———. *Voices from the Great Black Baseball Leagues.* New York: DaCapo Press, 1992.

Holway, John and Buck Leonard. *Black Diamonds: Life in the Negro Leagues from the Men Who Lived It.* Westport, Connecticut: Meckler, 1989.

Howard, Darrell J. *Sunday Coming: Black Baseball in Virginia.* Jefferson, North Carolina: McFarland, 2002.

Humphrey, Kathryn Long. *Satchel Paige.* New York: Franklin Watts, 1988.

Hutton, Frankie. *The Early Black Press in America, 1827 to 1860.* Westport, Connecticut: Greenwood Press, 1993.

Johnston, Susan E. *When Women Played Hardball.* Seattle: Seal Press, 1994.

Johnston, Thomas A. "A Graduate of the Black Press Looks Back." In *Perspectives of the Black Press: 1974,* edited by Henry G. La Brie III, 183–85. Kennebunkport, Maine: Mercer House Press, 1974.

Kein, Sybil. *Gumbo People.* New Orleans, Louisiana: Margaret Media, 1999.

Kelley, Brent P. *Voices from the Negro Leagues: Conversations with 52 Baseball Standouts of the Period 1924–1960.* Jefferson, North Carolina: McFarland, 1998.

———. *The Negro Leagues Revisited: Conversations with 66 More Baseball Heroes.* Jefferson, North Carolina: McFarland, 2000.

LaBlanc, Michael L. *Hotdogs, Heroes & Hooligans: The Story of Baseball's Major League Teams.* Detroit: Visible Ink Press, 1994.

La Brie III, Henry G. *The Black Newspaper in America, A Guide.* Iowa City, Iowa: Institute for Communication Studies University of Iowa, 1970.

———. *The Black Press: A Bibliography.* Kennebunkport, Maine.: Mercer House Press, 1973.

Lacy, Sam and Moses Newson. *Fighting for Fairness, the Life and Story of Hall of Fame Sportswriter Sam Lacy.* Centreville, Maryland: Tidewater Publishing, 1998.

Lamb, Chris. *Blackout, The Untold Story of Jackie Robinson's First Spring Training.* Omaha, Nebraska: University of Nebraska Press, 2004.

Lanctot, Neil. *Fair Dealing and Clean Playing: The Hilldale Club and the Development of Black Professional Baseball, 1910–1932.* Jefferson, North Carolina: McFarland & Co., 1994.

———. *Negro League Baseball, The Rise and Ruin of a Black Institution.* Lincoln: University of Nebraska Press, 2004.

Lemann, Nicholas. *The Promised Land: The Great Black Migration and How It Changed America.* New York: Vintage Books, 1992.

Leonard, Buck. *Buck Leonard: The Black Lou Gehrig: The Hall of Famer's Story in His Own Words.* New York: Carroll & Graf, 1995.
Lester, Larry. *Black Baseball's National Showcase: The East-West All-Star Game, 1933–1953.* Lincoln, Nebraska: University of Nebraska Press, 2001.
Logan, Rayford. *The Negro in the United States, a Brief History.* Princeton, New Jersey: D. Van Nostrand, 1956.
Macht, Norm. *Satchel Paige.* New York: Chelsea House Publishers, 1991.
Malloy, Jerry, ed. *History of Colored Base Ball.* Lincoln, Nebraska: University of Nebraska Press, 1995.
Mander, Mary S. *Framing Friction: Media and Social Conflict.* Urbana, Illinois: University of Illinois Press, 1999.
Manley, Effa and Leon Herbert Hardwick. *Negro Baseball . . . before Integration.* Chicago: Adams Press, 1976.
Mann, Arthur. *The Jackie Robinson Story.* New York: Grosset and Dunlop, 1950.
Margolies, Jacob. *The Negro Leagues: The Story of Black Baseball.* New York: Franklin Watts, 1993.
Marks, Carole. *Farewell, We're Good and Gone: The Great Black Migration (Blacks in the Diaspora).* Bloomington, Indiana: Indiana University, 1989.
Marks, George P. *The Black Press Views American Imperialism (1898–1900), American Negro, His History and Literature.* New York: Arno Press, 1971.
McKissack, Patricia and Frederick McKissack, Jr. *Black Diamond: The Story of the Negro Baseball Leagues.* New York: Scholastic, 1994.
McNary, Kyle P. *Ted "Double Duty" Radcliffe: 36 Years of Pitching & Catching in Baseball's Negro Leagues.* Minneapolis: McNary Publishing, 1994.
McNeil, William. *Baseball's Other All-Stars: The Greatest Players from the Negro Leagues, the Japanese Leagues, the Mexican League, and the Pre-1960 Winter Leagues in Cuba, Puerto Rico, and the Dominican Republic.* Jefferson, North Carolina: McFarland, 2000.
———. *Cool Papas and Double Duties: The All-Time Greats of the Negro Leagues.* Jefferson, North Carolina: McFarland & Co., 2001.
Moore, Joseph T. *Pride against Prejudice: The Biography of Larry Doby.* New York: Praeger, 1988.
Moses, Wilson J. *The Golden Age of Black Nationalism, 1850–1925.* Hamden, Connecticut: Archon Books, 1978.
Mott, Frank Luther. *American Journalism.* New York: Macmillan Co., 1941.
Myrdal, Gunnar with Richard Sterner and Arnold Rose, *The American Dilemma: The Negro Problem and Modern Democracy.* New York: Harper & Brothers, 1944.
O'Neil, Buck. *I Was Right on Time.* New York: Simon & Schuster, 1996.
O'Neil, Buck with Steve Wulf and David Conrads. *I Had It Made.* New York: Fireside, 1996.
Ottley, Roi. *The Lonely Warrior: The Life and Times of Robert S. Abbott.* Chicago: H. Regnery Co., 1955.
Overmyer, James. *Queen of the Negro Leagues: Effa Manley and the Newark Eagles.* Lanham, Maryland: Scarecrow Trade, 2001.
Paige, Leroy "Satchel." *Pitchin Man: Satchel Paige's Own Story.* Westport, Connecticut: Meckler, 1992.

Paige, Leroy "Satchel" and David Lipman. *Maybe I'll Pitch Forever*. New York: Doubleday, 1962.
Penn, I. Garland. *The Afro-American Press and Its Editors*. Salem, New Hampshire: Ayer, 1891.
Peterson, Robert. *Only the Ball Was White: A History of Legendary Black Players and All-Black Professional Teams*. New York: Oxford University Press, 1970.
Peverelly, Charles A. *The Book of American Pastimes, Containing a History of the Principal Base-Ball, Cricket, Rowing, and Yachting Clubs of the United States*. New York: The Author, 1866.
Pride, Armistead Scott, and Association for Education in Journalism. Ad Hoc Committee on Minority Education. *The Black Press, A Bibliography*. Jefferson City: Missouri, 1968.
Pride, Armistead Scott, and Clint C. Wilson. *A History of the Black Press*. Washington, D.C.: Howard University Press, 1997.
Pluto, Terry and Tony Kubek. *Sixty-One, the Team, the Record, the Men*. New York: Macmillan Publishing Co., 1987.
Pulley, Kevin, and James D. White. *Blackball, the Story of Black Baseball*. St. Louis, Missouri: Blackstone Pub., 1996.
Quigley, Martin Peter. *The Original Colored House of David*. Boston: Houghton Mifflin, 1981.
Rampersad, Arnold. *Jackie Robinson: A Biography*. New York: Alfred A. Knopf, 1997.
Reisler, Jim. *Black Writers/Black Baseball: An Anthology of Articles from Black Sportswriters Who Covered the Negro Leagues*. Jefferson, North Carolina: McFarland Press, 1994.
Rhodes, Jane. *Mary Ann Shadd Cary: The Black Press and Protest in the Nineteenth Century*. Bloomington, Indiana: Indiana University Press, 1998.
Ribowsky, Mark. *A Complete History of the Negro Leagues, 1884–1955*. Seacaucus, New Jersey: Citadel Press, 1995.
Riley, James A. The *Biographical Encyclopedia of The Negro Baseball Leagues*. New York: Carroll and Graf, 1994.
Robinson, Frazier, and Paul Bauer. *Catching Dreams: My Life in the Negro Baseball Leagues*. Syracuse, New York: Syracuse University Press, 1999.
Robinson, Jackie. *Baseball Has Done It*. Philadelphia: Lippincott, 1964.
Robinson, Jackie and Alfred Duckett. *I Never Had It Made*. New York: G.P. Putnam's & Sons, 1972.
Robinson, Jackie, as told to Wendell Smith, *Jackie Robinson: My Own Story*. New York: Greenburg Publishers, 1948.
Robinson, Rachel. *Jackie Robinson: An Intimate Portrait*. New York: Harry N. Abrams, 1996.
Rodney, Lester, "White Dodgers, Black Dodgers." In Joseph Dorinson and Joram Warmund, eds., *Jackie Robinson: Race, Sports, and the American Dream*. Armonk, New York: M.E. Sharpe, 1998: 86–97.
Roepke, Sharon. *Diamond Gals: The Story of the All American Girls Professional Baseball League*. Marcellus, Michigan: AAGPL Cards, 1986.

Rogosin, Donn. *Invisible Men: Life in Baseball's Negro Leagues*. New York: Kodansha International, 1995.
Rose, Arnold. *The Negro in America*. New York: Harper and Row, 1948.
Royster, Jacqueline Jones (ed.), *Southern Horrors and Other Writings. The Anti-Lynching Campaign of Ida B. Wells, 1892–1900*. Boston: Bedford Books, 1997.
Ruck, Rob. *Sandlot Seasons: Sport in Black Pittsburgh*. Urbana, Illinois: University of Illinois Press, 1987.
———. *Baseball in Pittsburgh*. Cleveland: Society for American Baseball Research, 1993.
Rusinack, Kelly, "Baseball on the Radical Agenda: The *Daily Worker* and *Sunday Worker* Journalistic Campaign to Desegregate Major League Baseball, 1933–1947." In Joseph Dorinson and Joram Warmund, eds., *Jackie Robinson: Race, Sports, and the American Dream*.Armonk, New York: M.E. Sharpe, 1998: 75–85.
Senna, Carl. *Black Press and the Struggle for Civil Rights*. New York: Franklin Watts, 1994.
Simon, Scott. *Jackie Robinson and the Integration of Baseball*. Hoboken, New Jersey: John Wiley & Sons, 2002.
Sloan, W. David. *The Media and Religion in American History*. Northport, Alabama: Vision Press, 1999.
Snyder, Brad. *Beyond the Shadow of the Senators*. Chicago: Contemporary Books, 2003.
Spalding. Albert. *Baseball*. San Francisco: Halo Books, 1991.
Spear, Allan. *Black Chicago, The Making of a Negro Ghetto, 1890–1920*. Chicago: University of Chicago Press, 1967.
Suggs, Henry Lewis. *The Black Press in the South, 1865–1979*, Contributions in Afro-American and African Studies, No. 74. Westport, Connecticut: Greenwood Press, 1983.
———. The *Black Press in the Middle West, 1865–1985*, Contributions in Afro-American and African Studies, No. 177. Westport, Connecticut: Greenwood Press, 1996.
Sullivan, Dean (ed.), *Early Innings, A Documentary History of Baseball, 1825–1908*. Lincoln: University of Nebraska Press, 1995.
Sundquist, Eric, ed., *The Oxford W. E. B. DuBois Reader*. New York: Oxford University Press, 1996.
Thompson, Nathan. *Kings: The True Story of Chicago's Policy Kings and Numbers Racketeers, An Informal History*. Chicago: Bronzeville Press, 1994.
Tripp, Bernell. *Origins of the Black Press: New York, 1827–1847*. Northport, Ala.: Vision Press, 1992.
Trouppe, Quincy. *20 Years Too Soon: Prelude to Major-League Integrated Baseball*. St. Louis, Missouri: Missouri Historical Society Press, 1995.
Tygiel, Jules. *The Jackie Robinson Reader*. Oxford, England: Oxford University Press, 1983.
———. *Baseball's Great Experiment: Jackie Robinson and His Legacy*. New York: Vintage, 1997.

———. *Extra Bases: Reflections on Jackie Robinson, Race, and Baseball History.* Lincoln, Nebraska: University of Nebraska Press, 2002.
———. *Pastime: Baseball as History.* New York: Oxford University Press, 2000.
Ullman, Victor. *Martin R. Delany: The Beginnings of Black Nationalism.* Boston: Beacon Press, 1971.
Vogel, Todd. *The Black Press: New Literary and Historical Essays.* New Brunswick, New Jersey: Rutgers University Press, 2001.
Ward, Geoffrey C. and Ken Burns, *Baseball: An Illustrated History.* New York: Alfred A. Knopf, 1994.
Washburn, Patrick Scott. *A Question of Sedition: The Federal Government's Investigation of the Black Press During World War II.* New York: Oxford University Press, 1986.
White, Sol, and Jerry Malloy. *Sol White's History of Colored Base Ball, with Other Documents on the Early Black Game, 1886–1936.* Lincoln: University of Nebraska Press, 1995.
Whitehead, Charles E. *A Man and His Diamonds.* New York: Vantage Press, 1980.
Whitehead, Raymond, and E. Frank Stephenson. *They Called Us Cornfield Boys.* Murfreesboro, North Carolina: Meherrin River Press, 1998.
Wiggins, David K. and George Eisen, eds. *Ethnicity and Sport in North American History and Culture.* Westport, Connecticut: Greenwood Press, 1994.
Wiggins, David K., ed., *Sport in America: From Wicked Amusement to National Obsession.* Champaign, Illinois: Human Kinetics, 1995.
———. *Glory Bound: Black Athletes in a White America.* Syracuse, New York: Syracuse University Press, 1997.
Williams, James D. *The Black Press and the First Amendment, Black Perspectives on the Bicentennial.* New York: National Urban League, 1976.
Williamson, Joel. *A Rage for Order. Black/White Relations in the American South Since Emancipation.* New York: Oxford University Press, 1986.
———. *The Crucible of Race: Black-White Relations in the American South Since Emancipation.* New York: Oxford University Press, 1984.
Wolseley, Roland E. and Laurence R. Campbell. *Exploring Journalism.* New York: Prentice-Hall, 1946.
Wolseley, Roland E. *The Black Press, U.S.A.: A Detailed and Understanding Report on What the Black Press Is and How It Came to Be.* Ames, Iowa: Iowa State University Press, 1971.
Woodward, C. Vann. *The Strange Career of Jim Crow.* New York: Oxford University Press, 1989.
Woodward, Stanley. *Sports Page.* New York: Greenwood Press, 1968.
Zang, David W. *Fleet Walker's Divided Heart: The Life of Baseball's First Black Major Leaguer.* Lincoln, Neb.: University of Nebraska Press, 1995.

JOURNAL ARTICLES

Beck, Peggy. "Working in the Shadows of Rickey and Robinson: Bill Veeck, Larry Doby and the Advancement of Black Players in Baseball." In *The Cooperstown*

Symposium on Baseball and American Culture, 1997. Jefferson, N.C.: McFarland & Co., 2000.

Behn, Robert. "Branch Rickey as Public Manager: Fulfilling the Eight Responsibilities of Public Management." *Journal of Public Administration Research and Theory* 7, no. 1 (1997), 1–34.

Bleske, Glen. "Heavy Hitting Sportswriter Wendell Smith." *Media History Digest* 13, no. 2 (1993): 38–42.

Bloch, Herman D. "The Employment Status of the New York Negro in Retrospect." *The Phylon Quarterly* v. 20, no. 4 (Winter 1959).

Bryan, Carter R. "Negro Journalism in America Before Emancipation." *Journalism Monographs* 12 (September 1969).

Carroll, Brian. "Wendell Smith's Last Crusade: The Desegregation of Spring Training." In *The 14th Cooperstown Symposium on Baseball and American Culture*, edited by William Simons, 123–35. Jefferson, N.C.: McFarland Press, 2002.

———. "The Black Press and the Integration of Baseball: A content analysis of changes in coverage." In the *Cooperstown Symposium on Baseball and American Culture*, 216–231. Jefferson, N.C.: McFarland Press, 2003

———. "When to Stop the Cheering: A content analysis of changes in black press coverage of the Negro leagues." In *The 14th Annual Symposium on Baseball and American Culture*, edited by William Simons. Jefferson, N.C.: McFarland Press, 2001.

———. "Early Twentieth Century Heroes: Portrayals in the Sporting Pages of the *Pittsburgh Courier* and *Chicago Defender*." *Journalism History* 31, No. 4 (Spring 2006).

Crepeau, Richard. "The Jake Powell Incident and the Press: A Study in Black and White." *Baseball History* (Summer 1996): 32–46.

Davis, Jack. "Baseball's Reluctant Challenge: Desegregating Major League Spring Training Sites, 1961–1964." *Journal of Sport History* 19, no. 2 (1992): 144–62.

Early, Gerald. "Understanding Integration: Why Blacks and Whites Must Come Together as Americans." *Civilization* 3, No. 5 (1996): 52.

Farrell, Joseph. "Classical Genre in Theory and Practice." *New Literary History* 34, No. 3 (Fall 2003): 399.

Inabinett, Mark. "Grantland Rice and His Heroes: The Sportswriter as Mythmaker in the 1920s." *Journalism History* 22, no. 3 (Autumn 1996): 125–127.

Johnson, Charles S. "The Rise of the Negro Magazine." *Journal of Negro History* v. 13, no. 1 (January 1928): 7–21.

Jordan, William. "'The Damnable Dilemma': African-American Accommodation and Protest during World War I." *The Journal of American History*, v. 81, no. 4 (March 1995): 1562–1583.

Kelley, William G. "Jackie Robinson and the Press." *Journalism Quarterly*, 53 (Spring 1976): 137–139.

Kimball, Richard Ian. "Beyond the 'Great Experiment': Integrated Baseball Comes to Indianapolis." *Journal of Sport History* 26, no. 1 (1999).

Lamb, Chris. "'What's Wrong with Baseball?'; The Pittsburgh Courier and the

Beginning of its Campaign to Integrate the National Pastime," 2002, *Western Journal of Black Studies*.

———. "L'affaire Jake Powell: The Minority Press Goes to Bat against Segregated Baseball," *Journalism & Mass Communication Quarterly* 76, No. 1 (1999): 21–34.

———. "I Never Want Another Trip Like This One: Jackie Robinson's Trip To Integrate Baseball," *Journal of Sport History* 24, No. 2 (Summer 1997): 177–191.

Lamb, Chris and Glen Bleske. "Democracy on the Field." *Journalism History* 24, no. 2 (1998): 51–59.

———. "The Road to October 23, 1945: The Press and the Integration of Baseball." *Nine: A Journal of Baseball and Social Policy* 6 (Fall 1997): 48–68.

———. "Covering the Integration of Baseball—a Look Back." *Editor & Publisher* 27 (January 1996): 48–50.

Leffler, Jr., Robert V. "Boom and Bust: The Elite Giants and Black Baseball in Baltimore, 1936–1951," *Maryland Historical Magazine* 87, No. 2 (Summer 1992): 171–186.

Lenthall, Bruce. "Covering More than the Game: Baseball and Racial Issues in an African-American Newspaper, 1919–1920." In *The Cooperstown Symposium on Baseball and American Culture (1990)*. Jefferson, N.C.: McFarland Press, 1991.

Lomax, Michael E. "Black Entrepreneurship in the National Pastime: The Rise of Semiprofessional Baseball in Black Chicago, 1890–1915." *Journal of Sport History* 25, No. 1 (1988): 43–64.

Malloy, Jerry. "The Pittsburgh Keystones and the 1887 Colored League, Baseball in Pittsburgh." In *Baseball in Pittsburgh*, 49. Cleveland, Ohio: Society for American Baseball Research, 1995.

———. "The Birth of the Cuban Giants: The Origins of Black Professional Baseball." *Nine* 2, No. 2 (Spring 1994): 236.

Mathewson, Albert Dennis. "Major League Baseball's Monopoly Power and the Negro Leagues." *American Business Law Journal* 35, No. 2 (1998): 291–318.

McGuire, Phillip. "Desegregation of the Armed Forces: Black Leadership, Protest and World War II." *Journal of Negro History* 68, No. 2 (Spring 1983): 147–158.

Meier, August. "Booker T. Washington and the Negro Press With Special Reference to the *Colored American*." *Journal of Negro History* 39 (January 1953): 67–90.

Ogbar, Jeffrey O.G. "The Black Press: Soldiers without Swords." *The Oral History Review* 26, no. 1 (1999).

O'Kelly, Charlotte G. "Black Newspapers and the Black Protest Movement: Their Historical Relationship, 1827–1945." *Phylon* 43, No. 1 (Spring 1982): 1–14.

Osthaus, Carl R. "The Rise and Fall of Jesse Binga, Black Financier." *Journal of Negro History* v. 58, no. 1 (January 1973): 39–60.

Prattis, P.L. "Racial Segregation and Negro Journalism." *Phylon* 8, no. 4 (Winter 1947): 305–314.

Rusinack, Kelly and Chris Lamb. "'A Sickening Red Tinge:' *The Daily Worker*'s Fight Against White Baseball," *Cultural Logic* 3, no. 1 (2001): 1–16.

Sangree, Allen. "Fans and Their Frenzies; the Wholesome Madness of Baseball." *Everybody's Magazine* v.17, no. 3 (September 1907).

Segal, Charles Paul. "God and Man in Pindar's First and Third *Olympian* Odes." *Harvard Studies in Classical Philology*, 68 (1964): 211.

Simons, William. "Jackie Robinson and the American Zeitgeist," In *Cooperstown Symposium on Baseball and American Culture 1997*, edited by Peter M. Rutkoff, 77–105. Jefferson, N.C.: McFarland Press, 2000.

———. "Jackie Robinson and the American Mind: Journalistic Perceptions of the Reintegration of Baseball." *Journal of Sport History* 12, No. 1 (Spring 1985): 39–64.

Smith, Thomas G. "Outside the Pale: The Exclusion of Blacks from the National Football League, 1933–1946." *Journal of Sport History* 15, 3 (Winter 1988): 255–281.

Stensaas, Harlan S. "Development of the Objectivity Ethic in U.S. Daily Newspapers." *Journal of Mass Media Ethics* 2, No. 1 (Fall/Winter 1986): 50–60.

Strother, T. Ella. "The Race-Advocacy Function of the Black Press." *Black American Literature Forum*, v. 12, no. 3 (Autumn 1978): 92–99.

Sullivan, Neil J. "Baseball and Race: The Limits of Competition." *Journal of Negro History* 83, No. 3 (1998).

Washburn, Pat. "New York Newspapers and Robinson's First Season." *Journalism Quarterly* 58, no. 4 (1981): 640–44.

Weaver, Bill L. "The Black Press and the Assault on Professional Baseball's 'Color Line,' October 1945-April 1947." *Phylon* XL, no. 4 (1979): 303–17.

Wiggins, David. "Wendell Smith, the Pittsburgh Courier-Journal and the Campaign to Include Blacks in Organized Baseball, 1933–1945." *Journal of Sport History* 10, No. 2 (1989): 5–29.

Wynn, Neil A. "The Impact of the Second World War on the American Negro." *Journal of Contemporary History*, v. 6, no. 2 (1971): 42–53.

UNPUBLISHED MANUSCRIPTS AND PAPERS

Bona, Marc and Chris Lamb. "October 23, 1945: The Beginning of the Integration of Baseball." Paper presented at the Breaking Baseball's Color Line: Jackie Robinson and Fifty Years of Integration conference, Daytona Beach, Florida, 15–17 March 1996.

Carroll, Brian. "The Black Press & the Negro Leagues: When to stop the cheering?" Paper presented at the Association for Education in Journalism and Mass Communication, Miami, Florida., 5–7 August 2002.

Patterson, Doris R. Corbett and Wayne. "The Social Significance of Sport and Its Implications for Race and Baseball." Paper presented at the 14th Annual Cooperstown Symposium on Baseball and American Culture, Cooperstown, New York, 8 June 2002.

Silcox, Harry. "Efforts to Desegregate Baseball in Philadelphia: The Pythian Baseball Club, 1866–1872," unpublished manuscript, National Baseball Library (undated), 1–8.

UNPUBLISHED THESES AND DISSERTATIONS

Hanson, John H. "An Evaluative Assertion Analysis of the Black Press During the Civil Rights Era, 1954–1968." Ph.D. dissertation, Florida State University, 1997.
Heaphy, Leslie. "Shadowed Diamonds: The Growth and Decline of the Negro Leagues," Ph.D. dissertation, University of Toledo, 1995.
Hollins, W.H. "The Negro Press in America: A Content Analysis of Five Newspapers," M.A. thesis, University of Minnesota, 1945.
Lomax, Michael E. "Black Baseball, Black Community, Black Entrepreneurs: The History of the Negro National and Eastern Colored Leagues, 1880–1930," Ph.D. dissertation, Ohio State University, 1996.
Morris, Curtis J. "The Evolution of the *Chicago Defender*," M.A. thesis, Indiana University, 1951.
Ostenby, Peter Marshall. "Other Games, Other Glory: The Memphis Red Sox and the Trauma of Integration, 1948–1955." M.A. thesis, University of North Carolina, 1989.
Richardson, Allen. "A Retrospective Look at the Negro Leagues and Professional Negro Baseball Players." M.A. thesis, San Jose State University, 1980.
Rogosin, Donn. "Black Baseball: The Life in the Negro Leagues." Ph.D. dissertation, University of Texas at Austin, 1981.
Sheingold, Peter M. "In Black and White: Sam Lacy's Campaign to Integrate Baseball," M.A. thesis, Hampshire College, 1992.
Slusser, James Harold. "The Sports Page in American Life in the Nineteen Twenties," M.A. thesis, University of California, 1952.
Williams, L.D. "An Analysis of American Sportswomen in Two Negro Newspapers: The Pittsburgh Courier and the Chicago Defender, 1932–1948." Ph.D. dissertation, Ohio State University, 1987.

MAGAZINE ARTICLES

Banks, Leo W. "An Oasis for Some Pioneers; Lucille and Chester Willis Put up Black Ballplayers When Tucson's Hotels Wouldn't." *Sports Illustrated* (8 May 1989): 116–17.
Fimrite, Ron. "Sam Lacy: Black Crusader." *Sports Illustrated*. (29 October 1994): 91.
Holtzman, Jerome. "Wendell Smith—a Pioneer for Black Athletes." *The Sporting News* (22 June 1974): 15–16.
Leavy, Walter. "50 Years of Blacks in Baseball." *Ebony* 50, no. 8 (June 1995): 38–41.
Manley, Effa. "Negro Baseball Isn't Dead." *Our World* 3, no. 8 (August 1948): 26–29.
No author, "Family Man." *Ebony* 11, no. 11 (September 1947): 15.
No author, "Robinson's Plan For Day When They Have Own Home." *Ebony* 11, no. 11 (September 1947): 16.
No author, "Satchelfoots." *Time* 35 (June 1940): 44.

No author, "The flaws in the diamonds, celebrating the end of segregated baseball." *The Economist* 342, No. 8000 (8 January 1997): 81–84.

Okrent, Daniel. "Background Check: Was Babe Ruth Black?" *Sports Illustrated* (7 May 2001): 27.

Randolph, Laura. "Bill White: National League President." *Ebony* 47, no. 10 (August 1992): 52–53.

Robinson, Jackie. "What's Wrong With Negro Baseball." *Ebony* 3, no. 8 (June 1948): 19–25.

Shoulder, Ken. "Grand Yankee, Brooklyn-Bred Joe Torre Steers the Yankees to a World Championship, Overcoming Personal Troubles and Personal Trauma." *Cigar Aficionado* (February 1997). Available: http://www.cigaraficionado.com/Cigar/CA_Profiles/People_Profile/0,2540,98,00.html.

NEWSPAPER ARTICLES

Fatsis, Stefan. "If Sleuths Are Right, Jackie Robinson Has New Company." *Wall Street Journal*, 30 January 2004, A1.

Lacy, Sam. "Looking 'em Over With The Tribune." *Washington Tribune*, 25 December 1937, 12.

Meyer, Paul. "Columnist Was 'Baseball' Star." Pittsburgh *Post-Gazette*, 29 September 1994, D1.

Palmer, Thomas C., Jr. "Kansas City Cultural Center Pays Tribute to the Music and the Negro Leagues; a Sweet Celebration of Jazz & Baseball." *Boston Globe*, 16 May 1999, M1.

Sandomir, Richard. "Jackie Robinson: Perspective—the Coverage." *New York Times*, 13 April 1997, C9.

VIDEO RECORDINGS INVOLVING THE NEGRO LEAGUES

"A League of Their Own." Burbank, California: Columbia/TriStar Pictures, 1992. Videocassette.

"Baseball's Forgotten Men." Pittsburgh, Pennsylvania: San Pedro Productions Ltd., 1993. Videocassette.

"The Bingo Long Traveling All-Stars & Motor Kings." Universal City, California: MCA Videocassette, 1983. Videocassette.

"There Was Always Sun Shining Someplace Life in the Negro Baseball Leagues." Westport, Connecticut: Refocus Films, 1984. Videocassette.

"Wylie Avenue Days." Pittsburgh, Pennsylvania: QED Communications, 1991. Videocassette.

"Yearbook." Kansas City, Missouri: The Museum, 1993. Videocassette.

Index

A
Aaron, Henry, 186
Abbot, Robert, 16, 19, 22, 26, 34, 35, 40, 45, 49, 51, 52, 79
Afro-American, 4, 59, 63, 70, 89, 91, 93, 100, 106, 129, 130, 138, 140, 142, 147, 166, 176, 187
All-American Girls Professional Baseball League, 128
Allen, T. W., 19
Alston, Tom, 184
American Association, 12, 66, 179
American Association Park, 40
American League, 12, 96, 155, 165, 180, 182
American Sport Writers Association, 92
Anderson, Louie B., 52
Anderson, Marian, 81
Andrews, William T., 108
Angelos, Peter, 53
Appomattox Club, 40, 51, 52, 62
Argyle Hotel, 8, 176
Armstrong, Louis, 79, 81
Associated Business Club, 51
Associated Negro Press, 20, 84, 146
Associated Press, 96, 106
Atlanta Daily World, 93
Atlanta World, 193

B
Bacharach Giants, 42, 43
Bagby, Bill, 93
Baird, Tom, 142, 144
Baker, Gene, 132, 180, 181, 184
Baker, Josephine, 81
Baltimore Black Sox, 14, 43, 55, 77
Baltimore Elite Giants, 37, 170, 173, 178, 185
Bankhead, Dan, 157, 170
Banks, Ernie, 132, 175, 180–182, 184, 184
Baraka, Amiri, 158, 189
Baseball Writers Association of America, 154
Batchman, J.M., 18
Baylor, Don, 4
Bebop, Spec, 182
Bell, James Thomas "Cool Papa", 69, 192
Benson, George, 79
Benswanger, William E., 96, 106
Betts, John, 10
Binga, Jesse, 26, 51
Binga State Bank, 26, 40, 51
Bingo Long Traveling All-Stars & Motor Kings, 175
Birmingham Black Barons, 63, 64, 129, 168, 171, 177, 185
Black, Joe, 179, 181
Black Metropolis, 154
Black Sox scandal, 25, 32
Bleske, Glen, 138, 139
Blount, John "Tenny", 35, 37, 38, 53, 62, 76, 80, 101
Bolden, Ed, 30, 33, 37, 42, 51–53, 55–57, 59, 60, 64, 100, 101
Bolling, Jesse, 19
Bonno, Gus, 105
Bostic, Joe, 70, 71, 87, 91, 92, 108, 134, 135, 138, 149
Boston Bees, 95
Boston Braves, 136
Boston Chronicle, 137
Boston Globe, 14, 136

263

Boston Guardian, 137
Boston Red Sox, 84, 135–137, 180, 184, 192
Boston Resolutes, 10
Boston Royal Giants, 14
Boudreau, Lou, 153
Boyd, Bob, 182
Briggs Stadium, 102
Bright, John, 13
"Bronzeville", 50
Brooklyn Bushwicks, 55
Brooklyn Dodgers, 1, 4, 12, 75, 90, 92, 94, 95, 107, 108, 131, 135, 137–139, 144, 145, 150, 154–156, 160–163, 165–167, 170, 179, 181, 184, 189, 190
Brooklyn Royal Giants, 13, 43, 55, 56
Broun, Heywood, 23, 50, 85
Brown, Oliver "Butts", 100, 101
Brown v. Board of Education, 23, 139, 167, 180, 184, 188
Brown, Walter S., 8
Brown, Willard, 157
Bryant, Howard, 135
Buckner, Bill, 65
Burbridge, Eddie, 93
Burley, Dan, 73–75, 93, 98, 100, 108
Burlington Buffet, 19
Busch, Jr., August A., 180, 184
Butler, Ran, 16, 17

C

Campanella, Roy, 53, 150, 152, 154, 155, 160, 167, 168, 170, 179, 181
Campion, Raymond, 130
Cannon, Jimmy, 38
Carter, Art, 92, 93, 100
Carter, Ashley B., 76
Catholic Interracial Council, 104
Cavarretta, Phil, 181
Chandler, A.B. "Happy", 134, 143, 145–147, 164, 165, 173
Chapman, Ben, 162–164
Charleston, Oscar, 69, 73, 84, 192
Chicago American, 172
Chicago American Giants, 2, 19, 22, 25, 28, 29, 30–32, 34, 37, 38, 40–43, 50, 52, 54, 61, 63, 64, 70, 73, 77, 79, 101, 107, 127, 146, 152, 167, 178, 185
Chicago Bears, 102, 136
Chicago Bee, 176

Chicago *Broad Ax*, 15, 16, 19, 45
Chicago Crusaders, 79
Chicago Cubs, 4, 28, 32, 72, 102, 104, 129, 132, 152, 164, 167, 176–178, 180–182, 184, 185
Chicago Daily News, 84, 96
Chicago Defender, 4, 15, 16, 19, 22, 23, 25, 26, 28–37, 39–45, 47–54, 56–66, 69, 70, 72–77, 79–86, 91, 93, 97–108, 126–130, 133, 140, 143, 147, 148, 150, 152, 153, 156, 157, 165–169, 171, 173, 176–183, 185, 187, 190
Chicago Defender Goodfellows Club, 49
Chicago Giants, 35
Chicago Joint Council of Packing House Workers, 104
Chicago Leland Giants, 15
Chicago Republic, 15
Chicago's Sunday Church League, 61
Chicago Tribune, 150
Chicago Union Giants, 10, 28
Chicago Whales, 28
Chicago *Whip*, 21, 45
Chicago White Sox, 28, 32, 44, 63, 65, 71, 72, 81, 84, 85, 101, 131, 152, 156, 168, 178, 179, 182, 184
Cincinnati Clowns, 128, 183
Cincinnati Reds (also "Red Stockings"), 8, 84, 180
Civil War, 8
Clark, John L., 71, 74, 75, 84, 85
Class B Florida International, 179
Class D "Kitty" League, 179
Cleveland Buckeyes, 136, 153, 156, 167, 168
Cleveland Call and Post, 93, 130, 168
Cleveland Gazette, 8
Cleveland Giants, 77
Cleveland Hornets, 35, 76
Cleveland Indians, 4, 153, 156, 165, 168, 171, 178, 181, 182, 184
Cleveland Stadium, 168
Cleveland Tate Stars, 50, 54, 55
Cleveland *Whip*, 51
Coastal Plain League, 179
Cobb, Lorenzo, 35, 76
Cobb, Ty, 163
Cochrane, Mickey, 66
Cole, Robert A., 37, 73, 76, 77
Coleman Restaurant, 50
Colored World Series, 56–58, 60, 62–64, 83, 129

Index

Columbia Giants, 15
Columbus Blue Birds, 77
Comiskey Park, 69, 71, 81, 83, 84, 101, 102, 129, 178, 185
Comiskey, Charles, 71, 72, 85, 131
Competitor, 35, 38, 39, 65
Cook, Walter, 10
Cotton Club, 79
Coughlin, Gene, 86
Cowans, Russell J., 93, 178, 179, 181, 184
Crawford Grill, 78, 79, 99
Crepeau, Richard, 96
Cuban Giants, 9–11, 13, 176
Cuban House of David, 183
Cuban X-Giants, 10, 13, 15, 28
Cunningham, Evelyn, 172

D

Daily Worker, 70, 71, 87, 91, 104–107, 130, 135, 140, 188
Dallas Black Giants, 75
Dallas Express, 75
Dallas, William, 59, 60
Daniel, Dan, 96
Dann, Martin E., 21
Davis, Miles, 79
Dayton Marcos, 13, 35
Dean, Dizzy, 103
Dempsey, Jack, 38
DePriest, Oscar, 51
Detroit Contender, 33
Detroit Free Press, 33
Detroit News, 33
Detroit Stars, 33, 38, 40, 47, 53, 60, 62, 64, 80, 101
Detroit Tigers, 89, 181, 184, 192
Detroit Times, 33
Detweiler, Frederick, 21
Dewey, Thomas, 135
Dickey, Bill, 181
DiMaggio, Joe, 126
Dismukes, Dizzy, 61, 74
Dixson, Randy, 92, 98–100, 102
Doby, Larry, 153–157, 164, 166, 168, 170–172, 178, 181
Donaldson, Billy, 59
"Double V" campaign, 23, 24, 103, 104
Dougherty, Romeo, 71
Drew, Johnny, 75
Du Bois, W.E.B., 3, 19, 141, 142, 189
Dunjee, Roscoe, 75
Durocher, Leo, 95, 160

E

Early, Gerald, 5, 177, 190
Easter, Luke, 178
Eastern Colored League, 5, 36, 43, 55, 56, 59, 61, 62, 64, 76, 80
East-West Classic, 69, 71, 81–85, 96, 100, 102–104, 129, 133, 150, 155, 173, 175–177
Ebbets Field, 131, 137, 161, 162
Ebony, 23, 153, 164, 166
Egan, Wish, 89
Elks, 106
Ellington, Duke, 79, 81
Elson, Bob, 96
Equator, 12
Ethiopian Clowns, 183

F

Farrell, Henry L., 84
Fenway Park, 140
Foster, Andrew "Rube", 2, 15–18, 25, 27–32, 34, 35, 37–41, 43, 44, 50–54, 56–59, 62, 70, 73, 77–79, 83, 100, 101, 140, 176, 177
Foster, Willie, 83
Franklin, John Hope, 11
Frazier, Franklin E., 21
Freedom's Journal, 191
Frick, Ford, 164
Frisch, Frankie, 132

G

Gaither, A.D., 180
Gallagher, Jim, 132
Gallico, Paul, 50
Gant, Eddie, 190
Garvey, Marcus, 12
"Gentleman's Agreement", 13, 85, 130
Georgia State League, 184
Gibson, Bill, 106
Gibson, Josh, 60, 95, 96, 136, 140, 192
Gillespie, Dizzy, 79
Gillespie, Frank L., 51
Gilliam, Junior, 185
Gilmore, Q.J., 36, 48, 49, 62, 75
Goode, Mal, 153
"Golden Age of Sports", 50
Gottlieb, Eddie, 34, 37, 179
Govern, S.K., 9
Grabiner, Harry, 85
Grand Hotel, 40, 84, 103

Gray, Pete, 109, 144
Greason, Bill, 180
"Great Migration", 20, 21, 26, 39
Green, Elijah "Pumpsie", 137
Green, Joe, 35
Green, Vernon, 170
Greenlee Field, 77–79
Greenlee, Gus, 30, 37, 70, 74, 76–80, 82, 93, 99, 177
Greenwade, Tom, 180
Griffith, Clark, 44, 91, 130, 131, 143
Griffith Stadium, 91, 92, 131
Grimm, Charlie, 72

H
Haley, Cecil, 66
Hamman, Ed, 182
Harlem Globetrotters, 100, 185
Harper, Lucius C., 101, 105, 108, 109, 126, 127, 148
Harridge, William 96
Harris, Vic, 149
Harris, Woogie, 78
Harrison, William, 103
Havana's Cubans, 47
Hayes, Jr., Tom, 171, 177
Herman Hill, 93
Heydler, John A., 81, 85
Hilldales, 30, 33, 42–45, 52, 57, 75
Hilldale Park, 52
Holman, Joe, 100
Holtzman, Jerome, 95
Homestead Grays, 31, 37, 50, 51, 61, 71, 74, 75, 77, 78, 80, 91, 93, 95, 100, 108, 129, 131, 136, 149, 167, 171, 178
Hooper, George, 54, 55
Hopper, Clay, 160, 163
Hord, Earl, 49
Horne, Lena, 79, 81
Hornsby, Rogers, 143
Hotel Ponce de Leon, 9
Howard, Elston, 180
Howard, Janet, 79
Howard, J.D., 16, 36
Howard University, 62
Howe News Bureau, 132
Hueston, William C., 73, 78

I
Indianapolis ABCs, 17, 25, 27–29, 35, 40, 50, 76–78

Indianapolis Clowns, 128, 167, 178, 179, 182–186
Indianapolis Freeman, 15–19, 27–31, 35–37, 43, 51, 52, 70
Indianapolis Indians, 78
Indianapolis *Ledger*, 4, 16, 30, 36, 62
Indianapolis Recorder, 167
International Association, 12
International League, 144
International Workers Order, 104
Irvin, Monte, 53, 177
Ives-Quinn Anti-Discrimination law, 135

J
Jackson, A.L., 51
Jackson, Major Robert R., 15, 28
Jackson, Richard, 93
Jackson, Rufus "Sonnyman", 37, 76
Jamison, Caesar, 58
Jax Zulo Hippopotamus Clowns of New Orleans, 183
Jessamy, Ken, 93
Jet, 23, 153, 166
Jethroe, Sam, 136
Johnson, Connie, 182
Johnson, Johnny, 157, 186
Johnson, Mamie "Peanut", 185
Johnson, Tom, 59
Jones, Bobby, 38
Jones, Ed, 80
Jones, George, 80
Jones, Lucius, 93
Jones, McKissack, 80
Jordan, William, 19
Julian, Hubert, 97

K
Kansas City *Call*, 20, 36, 48, 56–58, 74, 75, 93, 157, 186, 187, 193
Kansas City *Journal-Post*, 58
Kansas City Monarchs, 2, 34, 35, 43, 49, 57, 61, 64, 75, 90, 103, 127, 131, 136, 141, 142, 144, 154, 167, 176, 180–182, 185
Kansas City *Sun*, 48
Kelley, William G., 139
Kessler, Jerry, 101, 168
King, Jr., Martin Luther, 188
"King Tut", 182
Knox, Elwood C., 16–18, 35, 49, 70
Knox, George L., 18, 52
Kountze, Mabray "Doc", 137

Index

Krsnich, Rocky, 182
Ku Klux Klan, 48, 66

L

Lacy, Sam, 70, 71, 87, 89–94, 100, 105, 129, 130, 138, 142, 143, 145–149, 151, 165, 192, 193
Lamar, E.B., 13
Lamb, Chris, 87, 138, 139
Lanctot, Neil, 2, 11, 13
Landis, Kenesaw Mountain, 84, 86, 91, 104, 105, 108, 129, 130, 133, 134
Lane, Frank, 178, 179
League of Colored Base Ball Players, 8, 10
Lebovitz, Hal, 127
Leland, Frank, 15–17, 28
Leland Giants, 13, 17, 19, 22, 27, 28
Leland Giant Booster Club, 19, 22
Lenthall, Bruce, 45
Leonard, Buck, 95, 96, 167
Lester, Larry, 9, 175, 176
Lewis, Cary B., 15–17, 28, 36–38, 41
Lewis, Ira F., 34, 48, 55, 65, 67, 70, 83, 84, 105, 129, 130
Lewis, Joe, 60
Lewis, John Henry, 79
Lewis, Lloyd, 105
Liberty Life Insurance Co., 51
Life, 127
Lincoln Giants, 10, 43
Lomax, Michael, 15
Long, Jimmy, 96
Los Angeles Angels, 181
Los Angeles *Post Record*, 86
Los Angeles *Sentinel*, 21
Lott, Trent, 97
Louisiana Weekly, 93
Louis, Joe, 7, 80, 81, 97, 125, 192
Louisville Courier Journal, 15
Louisville Giants, 14
Low, Nat, 91, 105, 106, 135
Lundy, Dick, 84

M

Mack Park, 40, 47, 53
MacPhail, Larry, 44, 107, 108, 131, 138
Madison Stars, 14
Malarcher, Dave, 104
Malden Riversides, 14
Maltin, Sam, 155
Manley, Abe, 37, 76, 80, 100, 167
Manley, Effa, 27, 36, 40, 99–101, 132, 157, 165, 167, 170
Mantle, Mickey, 180
Martin, B.B., 155
Martin, J.B., 99, 107, 129, 131, 142, 143, 146, 147, 170, 185
Martin, Louis, 130
Martin, W.S., 99
Matthews, John, 35
Mays, Willie, 177, 185
McDuffie, Terris, 135
McGraw, John, 9
McRae, Donald, 192
Medford Independents, 14
Memphis Red Sox, 99, 155
Michigan Chronicle, 130
Mills, Charles, 35
Milwaukee Braves, 185
Minoso, Orestes "Minnie", 72, 178, 179, 182, 184
Monarch Booster Club, 2
Monroe, Al, 70–74, 77, 80, 83, 86, 92, 98
Monroe Elias Sports Bureau, 132
Montreal Royals, 139, 141, 144, 151, 154, 155, 158–160
Morgan, Connie, 185
Morton, Ferdinand Q., 108
Moseley, Beauregard F., 15
Moseley, Bertha, 15
Muchnick, Isadore, 135–137
Muehlebach Hotel, 190
Muhammad Speaks, 176
Murphy, Eddie, 126
Murphy, Howard, 130
Myrdal, Gunnar, 134

N

Nashville Elite Giants, 37, 77, 78, 142
Nashville Vols, 78
National Association for the Advancement of Colored People, 20, 21, 33, 47, 94, 106, 108, 134, 148
National Association of Baseball Players, 13
National Association of Professional Base Ball Players, 9, 13
National Athletic Commission of the International Workers Order, 104
National Baseball Hall of Fame, 27, 60
National Baseball Writers Association, 92
National Colored League of Professional Baseball Clubs, 16, 17
National Football League, 132

National League, 9, 12, 13, 81, 85, 94, 164, 177, 180
National League of Colored Base Ball Clubs, 15
National Maritime Union, 104
National Sports Writers' Association, 49
Navin Field, 40
Negro American League, 3, 5, 101, 103, 128, 131, 132, 136, 142, 143, 148, 167–171, 173, 176–178, 182, 185, 186
Negro Baseball Yearbook, 155, 157
Negro League Baseball Museum, 1
Negro National League, 1, 3–5, 7, 15, 17, 26–29, 31, 35, 41–43, 45, 47, 48, 54–58, 61, 62, 64, 67, 69, 71, 74–78, 81, 82, 93, 99–101, 128, 132, 140, 142, 144, 147, 148, 157, 169, 177, 183, 185
Negro Newspaper Publishers Association, 23
Negro Publishers Association, 129, 130
Negro Southern League, 5, 35, 41, 61, 74, 76
Negro World, 12
Negro World Series, 155, 156, 167
Newark Eagles, 27, 36, 80, 101, 132, 146, 153–157, 167, 171, 177
Newark Herald News, 100, 101
Newark Stars, 37
Newcombe, Don, 152, 155, 167, 170, 181
New Orleans Eagles, 178, 179
New Pittsburgh Courier, 193
New York *Age*, 14, 55, 56, 63, 176
New York *Amsterdam News*, 4, 21, 33, 55, 66, 71, 84, 93, 97, 98, 100, 108, 130
New York Athletic Club, 10
New York Baseball Writers Association, 85
New York Black Yankees, 37, 171
New York Cubans, 37, 40, 80, 156, 178
New York *Daily Mirror*, 86
New York *Daily News*, 86, 107
New York Giants, 9, 66, 94, 95, 102, 132, 135, 156, 171, 177, 184
New York Gorhams, 10
New York Times, 81, 150
New York *World-Telegram*, 85
New York Yankees, 44, 72, 96, 107, 131, 135, 138, 171, 180, 181, 184, 190
Noelle-Neumann, Elisabeth, 11
Norfolk Journal and Guide, 93
Norfolk Red Stockings, 10
North Carolina A&T, 62
Nugent, Gerry, 86, 104
Nunn, William G., 69, 78, 82, 84, 105, 133, 176, 180

O
O'Connor, Leslie, 86
O'Kelly, Charlotte, 19–21, 90
Oklahoma City's *Black Dispatch*, 75
Olivet Baptist Church, 15, 26
O'Neil, Buck, 33, 82, 127, 188, 190
Oriole Park, 102
Overmyer, James, 155
Owens, Jesse, 7, 60, 81, 125, 136, 168, 192

P
Pacific Coast League, 109, 169
Paige, Satchel, 7, 60, 69, 79, 85, 95, 103, 125, 128, 136, 168, 170, 171, 185, 192
Palmer Hotel, 106
Parker, Dan, 86, 105
Parks, Rosa, 180
Partlow, Roy, 155
Paseo Street YMCA, 35
Patterson, John W., 15
Patterson, William, 103
Paul, Gabe, 180
Pegler, Westbrook, 86
Pelican Park, 179
Penn Relays, 102
Penn Station Red Caps, 56
People's Voice, 70, 87, 91, 108, 134, 149
Perry, Norman, 78
Perry Stadium, 78
Peterson, Robert, 155, 169
Philadelphia Athletics, 27, 66
Philadelphia's Excelsiors, 8
Philadelphia Giants, 13
Philadelphia Independent, 98
Philadelphia Item, 14
Philadelphia Phillies, 86, 104, 144, 162, 184, 192
Philadelphia Stars, 37, 136, 155, 157, 179
Philadelphia Tribune, 10, 30, 33, 57, 59, 60, 100
Pindar, 39
Pittsburgh Courier, 4, 14, 23, 24, 30, 31, 33, 35, 42, 47, 50–53, 57, 61–63, 65, 66, 69–76, 78–84, 87, 89, 90, 92–100, 102–108, 127–129,

Index 271

Woodward, C. Vann, 7, 187
World Series, 25, 34, 57, 72, 165, 169, 173, 179, 180, 182
World Series Arbitration Committee, 129
World War I, 21, 32, 39
World War II, 127, 132, 133, 144, 148, 176
Wright, Edward H., 52
Wright, Johnny, 155
Wright, Sr., Major R.R., 70
Wrigley Field, 72, 103, 126
Wrigley, Phil K., 72, 104, 128, 132, 181, 184, 185
Wyatt, David, 16, 18, 19, 25, 28, 31, 32, 35–38, 41, 49, 52–55, 60

Y
Yankee Stadium, 81, 102, 131
Young, A.S. "Doc", 153
Young, Frank A. "Fay", 28, 30, 37, 42, 49, 51, 54, 58, 59, 62–64, 67, 70, 73, 74, 92, 94, 101, 103, 104, 106, 107 109, 126–129, 132, 143, 144, 147, 151–153, 156, 165–169, 171, 176–178, 181–182, 184, 185
YWCA Day, 51

Z
Zulu Cannibal Giants, 183